INTRODUCTION TO THE
THEORY OF COMPUTATION

INTRODUCTION TO THE
THEORY OF COMPUTATION

MICHAEL SIPSER

Massachusetts Institute of Technology

PWS PUBLISHING COMPANY

I(T)P • *An International Thomson Publishing Company*

Boston • Albany • Bonn • Cincinnati • Detroit • London • Madrid
Melbourne • Mexico City • New York • Pacific Grove • Paris
San Francisco • Singapore • Tokyo • Toronto • Washington

PWS PUBLISHING COMPANY
20 Park Plaza, Boston, MA 02116-4324

I(T)Pᵀᴹ
International Thomson Publishing
The trademark ITP is used under license.

Sponsoring Editor: *David Dietz*
Editorial Assistant: *Susan Garland*
Marketing Manager: *Nathan Wilbur*
Production Manager: *Elise S. Kaiser*
Manufacturing Buyer: *Andrew Christensen*
Interior Designer: *Catherine Hawkes*
Cover Designer: *Diane Levy*
Cover Art: *"The Unknown Leonardo"© EMB*
Prepress: *Pure Imaging*
Text Printer/Binder: *Courier/Westford*
Cover Printer: *Coral Graphic Services, Inc.*

*Library of Congress
Cataloging-in-Publication Data*

Sipser, Michael.
   Introduction to the theory of computation /
Michael Sipser.
     p.   cm.
   Includes bibliographical references and index.
   ISBN 0-534-94728-X
   1. Machine theory.   2. Computational
   complexity.   I. Title
QA267.S56 1996b   96-35322
   511.3 --dc20   CIP

Printed and bound in the United States of America.
96 97 98 99 00 — 10 9 8 7 6 5 4 3 2 1

For more information, contact:
PWS Publishing Company
20 Park Plaza
Boston, MA 02116

International Thomson Publishing Europe
Berkshire House I68-I73
High Holborn
London WC1V 7AA
England

Thomas Nelson Australia
102 Dodds Street
South Melbourne, 3205
Victoria, Australia

Nelson Canada
1120 Birchmont Road
Scarborough, Ontario
Canada M1K 5G4

International Thomson Editores
Campos Eliseos 385, Piso 7
Col. Polanco
11560 Mexico D.F., Mexico

International Thomson Publishing GmbH
Königswinterer Strasse 418
53227 Bonn, Germany

International Thomson Publishing Asia
221 Henderson Road
#05-10 Henderson Building
Singapore 0315

International Thomson Publishing Japan
Hirakawacho Kyowa Building, 31
2-2-1 Hirakawacho
Chiyoda-ku, Tokyo 102
Japan

CONTENTS

PREFACE

TO THE STUDENT

Welcome!

You are about to embark on the study of a fascinating and important subject: the theory of computation. It comprises the fundamental mathematical properties of computer hardware, software, and certain applications thereof. In studying this subject we seek to determine what can and cannot be computed, how quickly, with how much memory, and on which type of computational model. The subject has obvious connections with engineering practice, and, as in many sciences, it also has purely philosophical aspects.

I know that many of you are looking forward to studying this material but some may not be here out of choice. You may want to obtain a degree in computer science or engineering, and a course in theory is required—God knows why. After all, isn't theory arcane, boring, and worst of all, irrelevant?

To see that theory is neither arcane nor boring, but instead quite understandable and even interesting, read on. Theoretical computer science does have many fascinating big ideas, but it also has many small and sometimes dull details that can be tiresome. Learning any new subject is hard work, but it becomes easier and more enjoyable if the subject is properly presented. My primary objective in writing this book is to expose you to the genuinely exciting aspects of computer theory, without getting bogged down in the drudgery. Of course, the only way to determine whether theory interests you is to try learning it.

Theory is relevant to practice. It provides conceptual tools that practitioners use in computer engineering. Designing a new programming language for a specialized application? What you learned about *grammars* in this course comes in handy. Dealing with string searching and pattern matching? Remember *finite automata* and *regular expressions*. Confronted with a problem that seems to require more computer time than you can afford? Think back to what you learned about *NP-completeness*. Various application areas, such as modern cryptographic protocols, rely on theoretical principles that you will learn here.

Theory also is relevant to you because it shows you a new, simpler, and more elegant side of computers, which we normally consider to be complicated machines. The best computer designs and applications are conceived with elegance in mind. A theoretical course can heighten your aesthetic sense and help you build more beautiful systems.

Finally, theory is good for you because studying it expands your mind. Computer technology changes quickly. Specific technical knowledge, though useful today, becomes outdated in just a few years. Consider instead the abilities to think, to express yourself clearly and precisely, to solve problems, and to know when you haven't solved a problem. These abilities have lasting value. Studying theory trains you in these areas.

Practical considerations aside, nearly everyone working with computers is curious about these amazing creations, their capabilities, and their limitations. A whole new branch of mathematics has grown up in the past 30 years to answer certain basic questions. Here's a big one that remains unsolved: If I give you a large number, say, with 500 digits, can you find its factors (the numbers that divide it evenly), in a reasonable amount of time? Even using a supercomputer, no one presently knows how to do that in all cases *within the lifetime of the universe!* The factoring problem is connected to certain secret codes in modern cryptosystems. Find a fast way to factor and fame is yours!

TO THE EDUCATOR

This book is intended as an upper-level undergraduate or introductory graduate text in computer science theory. It contains a mathematical treatment of the subject, designed around theorems and proofs. I have made some effort to accommodate students with little prior experience in proving theorems, though more experienced students will have an easier time.

My primary goal in presenting the material has been to make it clear and interesting. In so doing, I have emphasized intuition and "the big picture" in the subject over some lower level details.

For example, even though I present the method of proof by induction in Chapter 0 along with other mathematical preliminaries, it doesn't play an important role subsequently. Generally I do not present the usual induction proofs of the correctness of various constructions concerning automata. If presented clearly, these constructions convince and do not need further argument. An induction may confuse rather than enlighten because induction itself is a rather sophisticated technique that many find mysterious. Belaboring the obvious with an induction risks teaching students that mathematical proof is a formal manipulation instead of teaching them what is and what is not a cogent argument.

A second example occurs in Parts II and III, where I describe algorithms in prose instead of pseudocode. I don't spend much time programming Turing machines (or any other formal model). Students today come with a programming background and find the Church–Turing thesis to be self-evident. Hence I don't present lengthly simulations of one model by another to establish their equivalence.

Besides giving extra intuition and suppressing some details, I give what might be called a classical presentation of the subject material. Most theorists will find the choice of material, terminology, and order of presentation consistent with that of other widely used textbooks. I have introduced original terminology in only a few places, when I found the standard terminology particularly obscure or confusing. For example I introduce the term *mapping reducibility* instead of *many–one reducibility*.

Practice through solving problems is essential to learning any mathematical subject. In this book, the problems are organized into two main categories called *Exercises* and *Problems*. The Exercises review definitions and concepts. The Problems require some ingenuity. Problems marked with a star are more difficult. I have tried to make both the Exercises and Problems interesting challenges.

THE CURRENT EDITION

Introduction to the Theory of Computation first appeared as a Preliminary Edition in paperback. The current edition differs from the Preliminary Edition in several substantial ways. The final three chapters are new: Chapter 8 on space complexity; Chapter 9 on provable intractability; and Chapter 10 on advanced topics in complexity theory. Chapter 6 was expanded to include several advanced topics in computability theory. Other chapters were improved through the inclusion of additional examples and exercises.

Comments from instructors and students who used the Preliminary Edition were helpful in polishing Chapters 0–7. Of course, the errors they reported have been corrected in this edition.

Chapters 6 and 10 give a survey of several more advanced topics in computability and complexity theories. They are not intended to comprise a cohesive unit in the way that the remaining chapters are. These chapters are included to allow the instructor to select optional topics that may be of interest to the serious student. The topics themselves range widely. Some, such as *Turing reducibility* and *alternation*, are direct extensions of other concepts in the book. Others, such as *decidable logical theories* and *cryptography*, are brief introductions to large fields.

FEEDBACK TO THE AUTHOR

The internet provides new opportunities for interaction between authors and readers. I have received much e-mail offering suggestions, praise, and criticism, and reporting errors for the Preliminary Edition. Please continue to correspond!

I try to respond to each message personally, as time permits. The e-mail address for correspondence related to this book is

`sipserbook@math.mit.edu` .

A web site that contains a list of errata is maintained. Other material may be added to that site to assist instructors and students. Let me know what you would like to see there. The location for that site is

`http://www-math.mit.edu/~sipser/book.html` .

ACKNOWLEDGMENTS

I could not have written this book without the help of many friends, colleagues, and my family.

I wish to thank the teachers who helped shape my scientific viewpoint and educational style. Five of them stand out. My thesis advisor, Manuel Blum, is due a special note for his unique way of inspiring students through clarity of thought, enthusiasm, and caring. He is a model for me and for many others. I am grateful to Richard Karp for introducing me to complexity theory, to John Addison for teaching me logic and assigning those wonderful homework sets, to Juris Hartmanis for introducing me to the theory of computation, and to my father for introducing me to mathematics, computers, and the art of teaching.

This book grew out of notes from a course that I have taught at MIT for the past 15 years. Students in my classes took these notes from my lectures. I hope they will forgive me for not listing them all. My teaching assistants over the years, Avrim Blum, Thang Bui, Andrew Chou, Benny Chor, Stavros Cosmadakis, Aditi Dhagat, Wayne Goddard, Parry Husbands, Dina Kravets, Jakov Kučan, Brian O'Neill, Ioana Popescu, and Alex Russell, helped me to edit and expand these notes and provided some of the homework problems.

Nearly three years ago, Tom Leighton persuaded me to write a textbook on the theory of computation. I had been thinking of doing so for some time, but it took Tom's persuasion to turn theory into practice. I appreciate his generous advice on book writing and on many other things.

I wish to thank Eric Bach, Peter Beebee, Cris Calude, Marek Chrobak, Anna Chefter, Guang-Ien Cheng, Elias Dahlhaus, Michael Fischer, Steve Fisk, Lance Fortnow, Henry J. Friedman, Jack Fu, Seymour Ginsburg, Oded Goldreich, Brian Grossman, David Harel, Micha Hofri, Dung T. Huynh, Neil Jones, H. Chad Lane, Kevin Lin, Michael Loui, Silvio Micali, Tadao Murata, Christos Papadimitriou, Vaughan Pratt, Daniel Rosenband, Brian Scassellati, Ashish Sharma, Nir Shavit, Alexander Shen, Ilya Shlyakhter, Matt Stallman, Perry Susskind, Y. C. Tay, Joseph Traub, Osamu Watanabe, Peter Widmayer, David Williamson, Derick Wood, and Charles Yang for comments, suggestions, and assistance as the writing progressed.

The following people provided additional comments that have improved this book: Isam M. Abdelhameed, Eric Allender, Michelle Atherton, Rolfe Blodgett, Al Briggs, Brian E. Brooks, Jonathan Buss, Jin Yi Cai, Steve Chapel, David Chow,

Michael Ehrlich, Yaakov Eisenberg, Farzan Fallah, Shaun Flisakowski, Hjalmtyr Hafsteinsson, C. R. Hale, Maurice Herlihy, Vegard Holmedahl, Sandy Irani, Kevin Jiang, Rhys Price Jones, James M. Jowdy, David M. Martin Jr., Manrique Mata-Montero, Ryota Matsuura, Thomas Minka, Farooq Mohammed, Tadao Murata, Jason Murray, Hideo Nagahashi, Kazuo Ohta, Constantine Papageorgiou, Joseph Raj, Rick Regan, Rhonda A. Reumann, Michael Rintzler, Arnold L. Rosenberg, Larry Roske, Max Rozenoer, Walter L. Ruzzo, Sanatan Sahgal, Leonard Schulman, Steve Seiden, Joel Seiferas, Ambuj Singh, David J. Stucki, Jayram S. Thathachar, H. Venkateswaran, Tom Whaley, Christopher Van Wyk, Kyle Young, and Kyoung Hwan Yun.

Robert Sloan used an early version of the manuscript for this book in a class that he taught and provided me with invaluable commentary and ideas from his experience with it. Mark Herschberg, Kazuo Ohta, and Latanya Sweeney read over parts of the manuscript and suggested extensive improvements. Shafi Goldwasser helped me with material in Chapter 10.

I received expert technical support from William Baxter at Superscript, who wrote the LaTeX macro package implementing the interior design, and from Larry Nolan at the MIT mathematics department, who keeps everything running.

It has been a pleasure to work with the folks at PWS Publishing in creating the final product. I mention Michael Sugarman, David Dietz, Elise Kaiser, Monique Calello, Susan Garland and Tanja Brull because I have had the most contact with them, but I know that many others have been involved, too. Thanks to Jerry Moore for the copy editing, to Diane Levy for the cover design, and to Catherine Hawkes for the interior design.

I am grateful to the National Science Foundation for support provided under grant CCR-9503322.

My father, Kenneth Sipser, and sister, Laura Sipser, converted the book diagrams into electronic form. My other sister, Karen Fisch, saved us in various computer emergencies, and my mother, Justine Sipser, helped out with motherly advice. I thank them for contributing under difficult circumstances, including insane deadlines and recalcitrant software.

Finally, my love goes to my wife, Ina, and my daughter, Rachel. Thanks for putting up with all of this.

Cambridge, Massachusetts   **Michael Sipser**
October, 1996

0

INTRODUCTION

Let's begin with an overview of those areas in the theory of computation that we present in this course. Then, you'll have a chance to learn and/or review some mathematical concepts that you will need later.

0.1

AUTOMATA, COMPUTABILITY, AND COMPLEXITY

This book focuses on three traditionally central areas of the theory of computation: automata, computability, and complexity. They are linked by the question:

What are the fundamental capabilities and limitations of computers?

This question goes back to the 1930s when mathematical logicians first began to explore the meaning of computation. Technological advances since that time have greatly increased our ability to compute and have brought this question out of the realm of theory into the world of practical concern.

In each of the three areas—automata, computability, and complexity—this question is interpreted differently, and the answers vary according to the interpretation. Following this introductory chapter, we'll explore each area in a separate part of this book. Here, we introduce these parts in reverse order because starting from the end you can better understand the reason for the beginning.

COMPLEXITY THEORY

Computer problems come in different varieties; some are easy and some hard. For example, the sorting problem is an easy one. Say that you need to arrange a list of numbers in ascending order. Even a small computer can sort a million numbers rather quickly. Compare that to a scheduling problem. Say that you must find a schedule of classes for the entire university to satisfy some reasonable constraints, such as that no two classes take place in the same room at the same time. The scheduling problem seems to be much harder than the sorting problem. If you have just a thousand classes, finding the best schedule may require centuries, even with a supercomputer.

What makes some problems computationally hard and others easy?

This is the central question of complexity theory. Remarkably, we don't know the answer to it, though it has been intensively researched for the past 25 years. Later, we explore this fascinating question and some of its ramifications.

In one of the important achievements of complexity theory thus far, researchers have discovered an elegant scheme for classifying problems according to their computational difficulty. It is analogous to the periodic table for classifying elements according to their chemical properties. Using this scheme, we can demonstrate a method for giving evidence that certain problems are computationally hard, even if we are unable to prove that they are so.

You have several options when you confront a problem that appears to be computationally hard. First, by understanding which aspect of the problem is at the root of the difficulty, you may be able to alter it so that the problem is more easily solvable. Second, you may be able to settle for less than a perfect solution to the problem. In certain cases finding solutions that only approximate the perfect one is relatively easy. Third, some problems are hard only in the worst case situation, but easy most of the time. Depending on the application, you may be satisfied with a procedure that occasionally is slow but usually runs quickly. Finally, you may consider alternative types of computation, such as randomized computation, that can speed up certain tasks.

One applied area that has been affected directly by complexity theory is the ancient field of cryptography. In most fields, an easy computational problem is preferable to a hard one because easy ones are cheaper to solve. Cryptography is unusual because it specifically requires computational problems that are hard, rather than easy, because secret codes should be hard to break without the secret key or password. Complexity theory has pointed cryptographers in the direction of computationally hard problems around which they have designed revolutionary new codes.

COMPUTABILITY THEORY

During the first half of the twentieth century, mathematicians such as Kurt Gödel, Alan Turing, and Alonzo Church discovered that certain basic problems cannot be solved by computers. One example of this phenomenon is the problem of determining whether a mathematical statement is true or false. This task is the bread and butter of mathematicians. It seems like a natural for solution by computer because it lies strictly within the realm of mathematics. But no computer algorithm can perform this task.

Among the consequences of this profound result was the development of ideas concerning theoretical models of computers that eventually would help lead to the construction of actual computers.

The theories of computability and complexity are closely related. In complexity theory, the objective is to classify problems as easy ones and hard ones, whereas in computability theory the classification of problems is by those that are solvable and those that are not. Computability theory introduces several of the concepts used in complexity theory.

AUTOMATA THEORY

Automata theory deals with the definitions and properties of mathematical models of computation. These models play a role in several applied areas of computer science. One model, called the *finite automaton*, is used in text processing, compilers, and hardware design. Another model, called the *context-free grammar*, is used in programming languages and artificial intelligence.

Automata theory is an excellent place to begin the study of the theory of computation. The theories of computability and complexity require a precise definition of a *computer*. Automata theory allows practice with formal definitions of computation as it introduces concepts relevant to other nontheoretical areas of computer science.

0.2 ■

MATHEMATICAL NOTIONS AND TERMINOLOGY

As in any mathematical subject, we begin with a discussion of the basic mathematical objects, tools, and notation that we expect to use.

SETS

A *set* is a group of objects represented as a unit. Sets may contain any type of object, including numbers, symbols, and even other sets. The objects in a set are called its *elements* or *members*. Sets may be described formally in several ways. One way is by listing its elements inside braces. Thus the set

$$\{7, 21, 57\}$$

contains the elements 7, 21, and 57. The symbols $\in$ and $\notin$ denote set membership and nonmembership, respectively. We write $7 \in \{7, 21, 57\}$ and $8 \notin \{7, 21, 57\}$. For two sets A and B, we say that A is a *subset* of B, written $A \subseteq B$, if every member of A also is a member of B. We say that A is a ***proper subset*** of B, written $A \subsetneq B$, if A is a subset of B and not equal to B.

The order of describing a set doesn't matter, nor does repetition of its members. We get the same set by writing $\{57, 7, 7, 7, 21\}$. If we do want take the number of occurrences of members into account we call the group a ***multiset*** instead of a set. Thus $\{7\}$ and $\{7, 7\}$ are different as multisets but identical as sets. An ***infinite set*** contains infinitely many elements. We cannot write a list of all the elements of an infinite set, so we sometimes use the "..." notation to mean, "continue the sequence forever." Thus we write the set of ***natural numbers*** $\mathcal{N}$ as

$$\{1, 2, 3, \ldots\}.$$

The set of ***integers*** $\mathcal{Z}$ is written

$$\{\ldots, -2, -1, 0, 1, 2, \ldots\}.$$

The set with 0 members is called the ***empty set*** and is written $\emptyset$.

When we want to describe a set containing elements according to some rule, we write $\{n|$ rule about $n\}$. Thus $\{n| n = m^2$ for some $m \in \mathcal{N}\}$ means the set of perfect squares.

If we have two sets A and B, the ***union*** of A and B, written $A \cup B$, is the set we get by combining all the elements in A and B into a single set. The ***intersection*** of A and B, written $A \cap B$, is the set of elements that are in both A and B. The ***complement*** of A, written $\overline{A}$, is the set of all elements under consideration that are *not* in A.

As is often the case in mathematics, a visual picture helps clarify a concept. For sets, we use a type of picture called a ***Venn diagram***. It represents sets as regions enclosed by circular lines. Let the set START-t be the set of all English words that start with the letter "t." For example, in the following figure the circle represents the set START-t. Several members of this set are represented as points inside the circle.

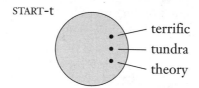

FIGURE **0.1**
Venn diagram for the set of English words starting with "t"

Similarly, we represent the set END-z of English words that end with "z" in the following figure.

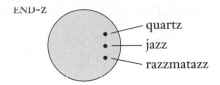

FIGURE   0.2
Venn diagram for the set of English words ending with "z"

To represent both sets in the same Venn diagram we must draw them so that they overlap, indicating that they share some elements, as shown in the following figure. For example, the word *topaz* is in both sets. The figure also contains a circle for the set START-j. It doesn't overlap the circle for START-t because no word lies in both sets.

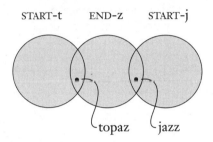

FIGURE   0.3
Overlapping circles indicate common elements

The next two Venn diagrams depict the union and intersection of sets A and B.

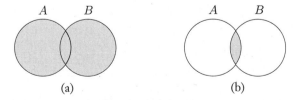

FIGURE   0.4
Diagrams for (a) $A \cup B$ and (b) $A \cap B$

SEQUENCES AND TUPLES

A **sequence** of objects is a list of these objects in some order. We usually designate a sequence by writing the list within parentheses. For example, the sequence 7, 21, 57 would be written

$$(7, 21, 57).$$

In a set the order doesn't matter, but in a sequence it does. Hence $(7, 21, 57)$ is not the same as $(57, 7, 21)$. Repetition is not permitted in a set but is allowed in a sequence, so $(7, 7, 21, 57)$ is different from both of the other sequences, whereas the set $\{7, 21, 57\}$ is identical to the set $\{7, 7, 21, 57\}$.

As with sets, sequences may be finite or infinite. Finite sequences often are called **tuples**. A sequence with k elements is a **k-tuple**. Thus $(7, 21, 57)$ is a 3-tuple. A 2-tuple is also called a **pair**.

Sets and sequences may appear as elements of other sets and sequences. For example, the **power set** of A is the set of all subsets of A. If A is the set $\{0, 1\}$, the power set of A is the set $\{\emptyset, \{0\}, \{1\}, \{0, 1\}\}$. The set of all pairs whose elements are 0s and 1s is $\{(0, 0), (0, 1), (1, 0), (1, 1)\}$

If A and B are two sets, the **Cartesian product** or **cross product** of A and B, written $A \times B$, is the set of all pairs wherein the first element is a member of A and the second element is a member of B.

EXAMPLE   **0.1** ....

If $A = \{1, 2\}$ and $B = \{x, y, z\}$,

$$A \times B = \{(1, x), (1, y), (1, z), (2, x), (2, y), (2, z)\}.$$

■

We can also take the Cartesian product of k sets, $A_1, A_2, \ldots, A_k$, written $A_1 \times A_2 \times \cdots \times A_k$. It is the set consisting of all k-tuples $(a_1, a_2, \ldots, a_k)$ where $a_i \in A_i$.

EXAMPLE   **0.2** ....

If A and B are as in Example 0.1,

$$A \times B \times A = \{(1, x, 1), (1, x, 2), (1, y, 1), (1, y, 2), (1, z, 1), (1, z, 2),$$
$$(2, x, 1), (2, x, 2), (2, y, 1), (2, y, 2), (2, z, 1), (2, z, 2)\}.$$

■

If we have the Cartesian product of a set with itself, we use the shorthand

$$\overbrace{A \times A \times \cdots \times A}^{k} = A^k.$$

The set $\mathcal{N}^2$ equals $\mathcal{N} \times \mathcal{N}$. It consists of all pairs of natural numbers. We also may write it as $\{(i, j)|\, i, j \geq 1\}$.

FUNCTIONS AND RELATIONS

Functions are central to mathematics. A ***function*** is an object that sets up an input–output relationship. A function takes an input and produces an output. In every function, the same input always produces the same output. If f is a function whose output value is b when the input value is a, we write

$$f(a) = b.$$

A function also is called a ***mapping***, and, if $f(a) = b$, we say that f maps a to b.

For example, the absolute value function abs takes a number x as input and returns x if x is positive and $-x$ if x is negative. Thus $abs(2) = abs(\,2) = 2$. Addition is another example of a function, written add. The input to the addition function is a pair of numbers and the output is the sum of those numbers.

The set of possible inputs to the function is called its ***domain***. The outputs of a function come from a set called its ***range***. The notation for saying that f is a function with domain D and range R is

$$f: D \longrightarrow R.$$

In the case of the function abs, if we are working with integers, the domain and the range are $\mathcal{Z}$, so we write $abs: \mathcal{Z} \longrightarrow \mathcal{Z}$. In the case of the addition function for integers, the domain is the set of pairs of integers $\mathcal{Z} \times \mathcal{Z}$ and the range is $\mathcal{Z}$, so we write $add: \mathcal{Z} \times \mathcal{Z} \longrightarrow \mathcal{Z}$. Note that a function may not necessarily use all the elements of the specified range. The function abs never takes on the value -1 even though $-1 \in \mathcal{Z}$. A function that does use all the elements of the range is said to be ***onto*** the range.

We may describe a specific function in several ways. One way is with a procedure for computing an output from a specified input. Another way is with a table that lists all possible inputs and gives the output for each input.

Consider the function $f: \{0, 1, 2, 3, 4\} \longrightarrow \{0, 1, 2, 3, 4\}$.

n	$f(n)$
0	1
1	2
2	3
3	4
4	0

This function adds 1 to its input and then outputs the result modulo 5. A number modulo m is the remainder after division by m. For example, the minute hand on a clock face counts modulo 60. When we do modular arithmetic we define $\mathcal{Z}_m = \{0, 1, 2, \ldots, m - 1\}$. With this notation, the aforementioned function f has the form $f \colon \mathcal{Z}_5 \longrightarrow \mathcal{Z}_5$.

■

EXAMPLE   **0.5** ....

Sometimes a two-dimensional table is used if the domain of the function is the Cartesian product of two sets. Here is another function $g \colon \mathcal{Z}_4 \times \mathcal{Z}_4 \longrightarrow \mathcal{Z}_4$. The entry at the row labeled i and the column labeled j in the table is the value of $g(i, j)$.

g	0	1	2	3
0	0	1	2	3
1	1	2	3	0
2	2	3	0	1
3	3	0	1	2

The function g is the addition function modulo 4.

■

When the domain of a function f is $A_1 \times \cdots \times A_k$ for some sets $A_1, \ldots, A_k$, the input to f is a k-tuple $(a_1, a_2, \ldots, a_k)$ and we call the a_i the **arguments** to f. A function with k arguments is called a **k-ary function** and k is called the **arity** of the function. If k is 1, f has a single argument and f is called a **unary function**. If k is 2, f is a **binary function**. Certain familiar binary functions are written in a special **infix notation**, with the symbol for the function placed between its two arguments, rather than in **prefix notation**, with the symbol preceding. For example, the addition function add usually is written in infix notation with the $+$ symbol between its two arguments as in $a + b$ instead of in prefix notation $add(a, b)$.

A **predicate** or **property** is a function whose range is $\{\text{TRUE}, \text{FALSE}\}$. For example, let $even$ be a property that is TRUE if its input is an even number and FALSE if its input is an odd number. Thus $even(4) = \text{TRUE}$ and $even(5) = \text{FALSE}$.

A property whose domain is a set of k-tuples $A \times \cdots \times A$ is called a **relation**, a **k-ary relation**, or a **k-ary relation on A**. A common case is a 2-ary relation, called a **binary relation**. When writing an expression involving a binary relation, we customarily use infix notation. For example, "less than" is a relation usually written with the infix operation symbol $<$. "Equality," written with the $=$ symbol is another familiar relation. If R is a binary relation, the statement aRb means that $aRb = \text{TRUE}$. Similarly if R is a k-ary relation, the statement $R(a_1, \ldots, a_k)$ means that $R(a_1, \ldots, a_k) = \text{TRUE}$.

EXAMPLE **0.6** ··

In a children's game called Scissors–Paper–Stone, the two players simultaneously select a member of the set {SCISSORS, PAPER, STONE} and indicate their selections with hand signals. If the two selections are the same, the game starts over. If the selections differ, one player wins, according to the relation *beats*.

beats	SCISSORS	PAPER	STONE
SCISSORS	FALSE	TRUE	FALSE
PAPER	FALSE	FALSE	TRUE
STONE	TRUE	FALSE	FALSE

From this table we determine that SCISSORS *beats* PAPER is TRUE and that PAPER *beats* SCISSORS is FALSE.

Sometimes describing predicates with sets instead of functions is more convenient. The predicate $P\colon D \longrightarrow \{\text{TRUE}, \text{FALSE}\}$ may be written (D, S), where $S = \{a \in D \mid P(a) = \text{TRUE}\}$, or simply S if the domain D is obvious from the context. Hence the relation *beats* may be written

$$\{(\text{SCISSORS}, \text{PAPER}), (\text{PAPER}, \text{STONE}), (\text{STONE}, \text{SCISSORS})\}$$

A special type of binary relation, called an ***equivalence relation*** captures the notion of two objects being equal in some feature. A binary relation R is an equivalence relation if R satisfies three conditions:

1. R is ***reflexive*** if for every x, xRx;
2. R is ***symmetric*** if for every x and y, xRy if and only if yRx; and
3. R is ***transitive*** if for every x, y, and z, xRy and yRz implies xRz.

EXAMPLE **0.7** ··

Define an equivalence relation on the natural numbers, written $\equiv_7$. For $i, j \in \mathcal{N}$ say that $i \equiv_7 j$, if $i - j$ is a multiple of 7. This is an equivalence relation because it satisfies the three conditions. First, it is reflexive, as $i - i = 0$, which is a multiple of 7. Second, it is symmetric, as $i - j$ is a multiple of 7 if $j - i$ is a multiple of 7. Third, it is transitive, as whenever $i - j$ is a multiple of 7 and $j - k$ is a multiple of 7, then $i - k = (i - j) + (j - k)$ is the sum of two multiples of 7 and hence a multiple of 7, too.

GRAPHS

An **undirected graph**, or simply a **graph**, is a set of points with lines connecting some of the points. The points are called **nodes** or **vertices**, and the lines are called **edges**, as shown in the following figure.

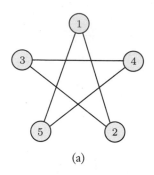
(a)

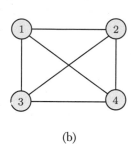
(b)

FIGURE 0.5
Examples of graphs

The number of edges at a particular node is the **degree** of that node. In Figure 0.5(a) all the nodes have degree 2. In Figure 0.5(b) all the nodes have degree 3. No more than one edge is allowed between any two nodes.

In a graph G that contains nodes i and j, the pair (i, j) represents the edge that connects i and j. The order of i and j doesn't matter in an undirected graph, so the pairs (i, j) and (j, i) represent the same edge. Sometimes we describe edges with sets, as in $\{i, j\}$, instead of pairs because the order of the nodes is unimportant. If V is the set of nodes of G and E is the set of edges, we say $G = (V, E)$. We can describe a graph with a diagram or more formally by specifying V and E. For example, a formal description of the graph in Figure 0.5(a) is

$$(\{1, 2, 3, 4, 5\}, \ \{(1, 2), \ (2, 3), \ (3, 4), \ (4, 5), \ (5, 1)\}),$$

and a formal description of the graph in Figure 0.5(b) is

$$(\{1, 2, 3, 4\}, \ \{(1, 2), \ (1, 3), \ (1, 4), \ (2, 3), \ (2, 4), \ (3, 4)\}).$$

Graphs frequently are used to represent data. Nodes might be cities and edges the connecting highways, or nodes might be electrical components and edges the wires between them. Sometimes, for convenience, we label the nodes and/or edges of a graph, which then is called a **labeled graph**. The following figure depicts a graph whose nodes are cities and whose edges are labeled with the dollar cost of the cheapest nonstop air fare for travel between those cities if flying nonstop between them is possible.

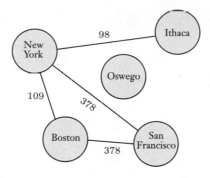

FIGURE   **0.6**
Cheapest nonstop air fares between various cities

We say that graph G is a ***subgraph*** of graph H if the nodes of G are a subset of the nodes of H. As shown in the following figure, the edges of G are the edges of H on the corresponding nodes.

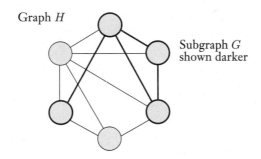

Graph H

Subgraph G
shown darker

FIGURE   **0.7**
Graph G (shown darker) is a subgraph of H

A ***path*** in a graph is a sequence of nodes connected by edges. A ***simple path*** is a path that doesn't repeat any nodes. A graph is ***connected*** if every two nodes has a path between them. A path is a ***cycle*** if it starts and ends in the same node. A ***simple cycle*** is one that doesn't repeat any nodes except for the first and last. A graph is a ***tree*** if it is connected and has no simple cycles, as shown in the following figure. The nodes of degree 1 in a tree are called the ***leaves*** of the tree. Sometimes there is a specially designated node of a tree called the ***root***.

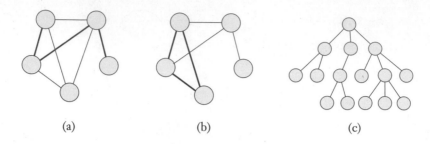

(a)   (b)   (c)

FIGURE   **0.8**
(a) A path in a graph, (b) a cycle in a graph, and (c) a tree

If it has arrows instead of lines, the graph is a ***directed graph***, as shown in the following figure. The number of arrows pointing from a particular node is the ***outdegree*** of that node, and the number of arrows pointing to a particular node is the ***indegree***.

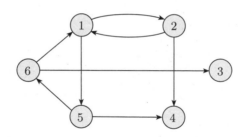

FIGURE   **0.9**
A directed graph

In a directed graph we represent an edge from i to j as a pair (i, j). The formal description of a directed graph G is (V, E) where V is the set of nodes and E is the set of edges. The formal description of the graph in Figure 0.9 is

$$(\{1,2,3,4,5,6\}, \{(1,2), (1,5), (2,1), (2,4), (5,4), (5,6), (6,1), (6,3)\}).$$

A path in which all the arrows point in the same direction as its steps is called a ***directed path***. A directed graph is ***strongly connected*** if a directed path connects every two nodes.

EXAMPLE   **0.8**   ....

The directed graph representing the relation given in Example 0.6 is

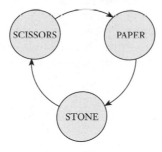

FIGURE   **0.10**
The graph of a relation

Directed graphs are a handy way of depicting binary relations. If R is a binary relation whose domain is $D \times D$, a labeled graph $G = (D, E)$ represents R, where $E = \{(x, y) \mid xRy\}$. Example 0.8 is an illustration.

If V is the set of nodes and E is the set of edges, the notation for a graph G consisting of these nodes and edges is $G = (V, E)$.

STRINGS AND LANGUAGES

Strings of characters are fundamental building blocks in computer science. The alphabet over which the strings are defined may vary with the application. For our purposes, we define an **alphabet** to be any finite set. The members of the alphabet are the **symbols** of the alphabet. We generally use capital Greek letters Σ and Γ to designate alphabets and a typewriter font for symbols from an alphabet. The following are a few examples of alphabets.

$\Sigma_1 = \{0,1\}$

$\Sigma_2 = \{a, b, c, d, e, f, g, h, i, j, k, l, m, n, o, p, q, r, s, t, u, v, w, x, y, z\}$

$\Gamma = \{0, 1, x, y, z\}$

A **string over an alphabet** is a finite sequence of symbols from that alphabet, usually written next to one another and not separated by commas. If $\Sigma_1 = \{0,1\}$, then 01001 is a string over Σ_1. If $\Sigma_2 = \{a, b, c, \dots, z\}$, then abracadabra is a string over Σ_2. If w is a string over Σ, the **length** of w, written $|w|$, is the number of symbols that it contains. The string of length zero is called the **empty string** and is written ε. The empty string plays the role of 0 in a number system. If w has length n, we can write $w = w_1 w_2 \cdots w_n$ where each $w_i \in \Sigma$. The *reverse* of w, written $w^{\mathcal{R}}$, is the string obtained by writing w in the opposite order (i.e., $w_n w_{n-1} \cdots w_1$). String z is a *substring* of w if z appears consecutively within w. For example, cad is a substring of abracadabra.

If we have string x of length m and string y of length n, the *concatenation* of x and y, written xy, is the string obtained by appending y to the end of x, as in $x_1 \cdots x_m y_1 \cdots y_n$. To concatenate a string with itself many times we use the superscript notation

$$\overbrace{xx \cdots x}^{k} = x^k.$$

The *lexicographic ordering* of strings is the same as the familiar dictionary ordering, except that shorter strings precede longer strings. Thus the lexicographic ordering of all strings over the alphabet $\{0,1\}$ is $(\varepsilon, 0, 1, 00, 01, 10, 11, 000, \dots)$.

A *language* is a set of strings.

BOOLEAN LOGIC

Boolean logic is a mathematical system built around the two values TRUE and FALSE. Though originally conceived of as pure mathematics, this system is now considered to be the foundation of digital electronics and computer design. The values TRUE and FALSE are called the *Boolean values* and are often represented by the values 0 and 1. We use Boolean values in situations with two possibilities, such as a wire that may have a high or a low voltage, a proposition that may be true or false, or a question that may be answered yes or no.

We can manipulate Boolean values with specially designed operations, called the *Boolean operations*. The simplest such operation is the *negation* or **NOT** operation, designated with the symbol $\neg$. The negation of a Boolean value is the opposite value. Thus $\neg 0 = 1$ and $\neg 1 = 0$. The *conjunction*, or **AND**, operation is designated with the symbol $\wedge$. The conjunction of two Boolean values is 1 if both of those values are 1. The *disjunction*, or **OR**, operation is designated with the symbol $\vee$. The disjunction of two Boolean values is 1 if either of those values are 1. We summarize this information in the following table:

$0 \wedge 0 = 0$	$0 \vee 0 = 0$	$\neg 0 = 1$
$0 \wedge 1 = 0$	$0 \vee 1 = 1$	$\neg 1 = 0$
$1 \wedge 0 = 0$	$1 \vee 0 = 1$	
$1 \wedge 1 = 1$	$1 \vee 1 = 1$	

We use Boolean operations for combining simple statements into more complex Boolean expressions, just as we use the arithmetic operations $+$ and $\times$ to construct complex arithmetic expressions. For example, if P is the Boolean value representing the truth of the statement "the sun is shining" and Q represents the truth of the statement "today is Monday", we may write $P \wedge Q$ to represent the truth value of the statement "the sun is shining *and* today is Monday" and similarly for $P \vee Q$ with *and* replaced by *or*. The values P and Q are called the **operands** of the operation.

Several other Boolean operations occasionally appear. The **exclusive or**, or **XOR**, operation is designated by the $\oplus$ symbol and is 1 if either but not both of its two operands are 1. The **equality** operation, written with the symbol $\leftrightarrow$, is 1 if both of its operands have the same value. Finally, the **implication** operation is designated by the symbol $\rightarrow$ and is 0 if its first operand is 1 and its second operand is 0; otherwise $\rightarrow$ is 1. We summarize this information in the following table:

$$0 \oplus 0 = 0 \qquad 0 \leftrightarrow 0 = 1 \qquad 0 \rightarrow 0 = 1$$
$$0 \oplus 1 = 1 \qquad 0 \leftrightarrow 1 = 0 \qquad 0 \rightarrow 1 = 1$$
$$1 \oplus 0 = 1 \qquad 1 \leftrightarrow 0 = 0 \qquad 1 \rightarrow 0 = 0$$
$$1 \oplus 1 = 0 \qquad 1 \leftrightarrow 1 = 1 \qquad 1 \rightarrow 1 = 1$$

We can establish various relationships among these operations. In fact, we can express all Boolean operations in terms of the AND and NOT operations, as the following identities show. The two expressions in each row are equivalent. Each row expresses the operation in the left-hand column in terms of operations above it and AND and NOT.

$$
\begin{array}{ll}
P \vee Q & \neg(\neg P \wedge \neg Q) \\
P \rightarrow Q & \neg P \vee Q \\
P \leftrightarrow Q & (P \rightarrow Q) \wedge (Q \rightarrow Q) \\
P \oplus Q & \neg(P \leftrightarrow Q)
\end{array}
$$

The **distributive law** for AND and OR comes in handy in manipulating Boolean expressions. It is similar to the distributive law for addition and multiplication, which states that $a \times (b+c) = (a \times b) + (a \times c)$. The Boolean version comes in the following two forms:

- $P \wedge (Q \vee R)$ equals $(P \wedge Q) \vee (P \wedge R)$, and its dual

- $P \vee (Q \wedge R)$ equals $(P \vee Q) \wedge (P \vee R)$.

Note that the dual of the distributive law for addition and multiplication does not hold in general.

SUMMARY OF MATHEMATICAL TERMS

Alphabet	A finite set of objects called symbols
Argument	An input to a function
Binary relation	A relation whose domain is a set of pairs
Boolean operation	An operation on Boolean values.
Boolean value	The values TRUE or FALSE, often represented by 0 or 1.
Cartesian product	An operation on sets forming a set of all tuples of elements from respective sets
Complement	An operation on a set, forming the set of all elements not present
Concatenation	An operation that sticks strings from one set together with strings from another set.
Conjunction	Boolean AND operation.
Connected graph	A graph with paths connecting every two nodes
Cycle	A path that starts and ends in the same node
Directed graph	A collection of points and arrows connecting some pairs of points
Disjunction	Boolean OR operation.
Domain	The set of possible inputs to a function
Edge	A line in a graph
Element	An object in a set
Empty set	A set with no members
Empty string	The string of length zero
Equivalence relation	A binary relation that is reflexive, symmetric, and transitive
Function	An operation that translates inputs into outputs
Graph	A collection of points and lines connecting some pairs of points
Intersection	An operation on sets forming the set of common elements
k-tuple	A list of k objects
Language	A set of strings
Member	An object in a set
Node	A point in a graph
Pair	A list of two elements, also called a 2-tuple
Path	A sequence of nodes in a graph connected by edges
Predicate	A function whose range is TRUE, FALSE
Property	A predicate
Range	The set from which outputs of a function are drawn
Relation	A predicate, most typically when the domain is a set of k-tuples
Sequence	A list of objects
Set	A group of objects
Simple path	A path without repetition
String	A finite list of symbols from an alphabet
Symbol	A member of an alphabet
Tree	A graph without cycles
Union	An operation on sets combining all elements into a single set
Vertex	A point in a graph

0.3

DEFINITIONS, THEOREMS, AND PROOFS

Theorems and proofs are the heart and soul of mathematics and definitions are its spirit. These three entities are central to every mathematical subject, including ours.

Definitions describe the objects and notions that we use. A definition may be simple, as in the definition of *set* given earlier in this chapter, or complex as in the definition of *security* in a cryptographic system. Precision is essential to any mathematical definition. When defining some object we must make clear what constitutes that object and what does not.

After we have defined various objects and notions, we usually make ***mathematical statements*** about them. Typically a statement expresses that some object has a certain property. The statement may or may not be true, but like a definition, it must be precise. There must not be any ambiguity about its meaning.

A ***proof*** is a convincing logical argument that a statement is true. In mathematics an argument must be airtight, that is, convincing in an absolute sense. That is rather different from the notion of proof that we use in everyday life or in the law. A murder trial demands proof "beyond any reasonable doubt." The weight of evidence may compel the jury to accept the innocence or guilt of the suspect. However, evidence plays no role in a mathematical proof. A mathematician demands proof beyond *any* doubt.

A ***theorem*** is a mathematical statement proved true. Generally we reserve the use of that word for statements of special interest. Occasionally we prove statements that are interesting only because they assist in the proof of another, more significant statement. Such statements are called ***lemmas***. Occasionally a theorem or its proof may allow us to conclude easily that other, related statements are true. These statements are called ***corollaries*** of the theorem.

FINDING PROOFS

The only way to determine the truth or falsity of a mathematical statement is with a mathematical proof. Unfortunately, finding proofs isn't always easy. It can't be reduced to a simple set of rules or processes. During this course, you will be asked to present proofs of various statements. Don't despair at the prospect! Even though no one has a recipe for producing proofs, some helpful general strategies are available.

First, carefully read the statement you want to prove. Do you understand all the notation? Rewrite the statement in your own words. Break it down and consider each part separately.

Sometimes the parts of a multipart statement are not immediately evident. One frequently occurring type of multipart statement has the form "P if and only if Q", often written "P iff Q", where both P and Q are mathematical statements. This notation is shorthand for a two-part statement. The first part is "P only if

Q," which means: If P is true, then Q is true, written $P \Rightarrow Q$. The second is "P if Q," which means: If Q is true, then P is true, written $P \Leftarrow Q$. The first of these parts is the ***forward direction*** of the original statement and the second is the ***reverse direction***. We write "P if and only if Q" as $P \Longleftrightarrow Q$. To prove a statement of this form you must prove each of the two directions. Often, one of these directions is easier to prove than the other.

Another type of multipart statement states that two sets A and B are equal. The first part states that A is a subset of B, and the second part states that B is a subset of A. Thus one common way to prove that $A = B$ is to prove that every member of A also is a member of B and that every member of B also is a member of A.

Next, when you want to prove a statement or part thereof, try to get an intuitive, "gut" feeling of why it should be true. Experimenting with examples is especially helpful. Thus, if the statement says that all objects of a certain type have a particular property, pick a few objects of that type and observe that they actually do have that property. After doing so, try to find an object that fails to have the property, called a ***counterexample***. If the statement actually is true, you will not be able to find a counterexample. Seeing where you run into difficulty when you attempt to find a counterexample can help you understand why the statement is true.

EXAMPLE **0.9** ....

Suppose that you want to prove the statement *for every graph G, the sum of the degrees of all the nodes in G is an even number*.

First, pick a few graphs and observe this statement in action. Here are some examples.

sum = 2+2+2   sum = 2+3+4+3+2
    = 6   = 14

Next, try to find a counterexample, that is, a graph in which the sum is an odd number.

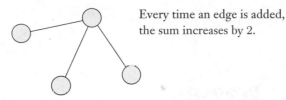

Every time an edge is added,
the sum increases by 2.

Can you now begin to see why the statement is true and how to prove it?

If you are still stuck trying to prove a statement, try something easier. Attempt to prove a special case of the statement. For example, if you are trying to prove that some property is true for every $k > 0$, first try to prove it for $k = 1$. If you succeed, try it for $k = 2$, and so on until you can understand the more general case. If a special case is hard to prove, try a different special case or perhaps a special case of the special case.

Finally, when you believe that you have found the proof, you must write it up properly. A well-written proof is a sequence of statements, wherein each one follows by simple reasoning from previous statements in the sequence. Carefully writing a proof is important, both to enable a reader to understand it and for you to be sure that it is free from errors.

The following are a few tips for producing a proof.

- *Be patient.* Finding proofs takes time. If you don't see how to do it right away, don't worry. Researchers sometimes work for weeks or even years to find a single proof.

- *Come back to it.* Look over the statement you want to prove, think about it a bit, leave it, and then return a few minutes or hours later. Let the unconscious, intuitive part of your mind have a chance to work.

- *Be neat.* When you are building your intuition for the statement you are trying to prove, use simple, clear pictures and/or text. You are trying to develop your insight into the statement, and sloppiness gets in the way of insight. Furthermore, when you are writing a solution for another person to read, neatness will help that person understand it.

- *Be concise.* Brevity helps you express high-level ideas without getting lost in details. Good mathematical notation is useful for expressing ideas concisely. But be sure to include enough of your reasoning when writing up a proof so that the reader can easily understand what you are trying to say.

For practice, let's prove one of DeMorgan's laws.

THEOREM   **0.10** ···

For any two sets A and B, $\overline{A \cup B} = \overline{A} \cap \overline{B}$.

First, is the meaning of this theorem clear? If you don't understand the meaning of the symbols $\cup$ or $\cap$ or the overbar, review the discussion on page 4.

To prove this theorem we must show that the two sets $\overline{A \cup B}$ and $\overline{A} \cap \overline{B}$ are equal. Recall that we may prove that two sets are equal by showing that every member of one set also is a member of the other and vice versa. Before looking at the following proof, consider a few examples and then try to prove it yourself.

PROOF   This theorem states that two sets, $\overline{A \cup B}$ and $\overline{A} \cap \overline{B}$, are equal. We prove this assertion by showing that every element of one also is an element of the other, and vice versa.

Suppose that x is an element of $\overline{A \cup B}$. Then x is not in $A \cup B$ from the definition of the complement of a set. Therefore x is not in A and x is not in B, from the definition of the union of two sets. In other words, x is in $\overline{A}$ and x is in $\overline{B}$. Hence the definition of the intersection of two sets shows that x is in $\overline{A} \cap \overline{B}$.

For the other direction, suppose that x is in $\overline{A} \cap \overline{B}$. Then x is in both $\overline{A}$ and $\overline{B}$. Therefore x is not in A and x is not in B, and thus not in the union of these two sets. Hence x is in the complement of the union of these sets; in other words, x is in $\overline{A \cup B}$ which completes the proof of the theorem.

···

Let's try another one.

THEOREM   **0.11** ···

In any graph G, the sum of the degrees of the nodes of G is an even number.

PROOF   Every edge in G is connected to two nodes. Each edge contributes 1 to each node to which it is connected. Therefore each edge contributes 2 to the sum of the degrees of all the nodes. Hence, if G contains e edges, then the sum of the degrees of all the nodes of G is $2e$, which is an even number.

···

0.4

TYPES OF PROOF

Several types of arguments arise frequently in mathematical proofs. Here, we describe a few that often occur in the theory of computation. Note that a proof may contain more than one type of argument because the proof may contain within it several different subproofs.

PROOF BY CONSTRUCTION

Many theorems state that a particular type of object exists. One way to prove such a theorem is by demonstrating how to construct the object. This technique is a ***proof by construction***.

Let's use a proof by construction to prove the following theorem. We define a graph to be ***k-regular*** if every node in the graph has degree k.

THEOREM   **0.12**

For each even number n greater than 2, there exists a 3-regular graph with n nodes.

PROOF   Let n be an even number greater than 2. Construct a graph $G = (V, E)$ with n nodes as follows. The set of nodes of G is $V = \{0, 1, \ldots, n-1\}$, and the set of edges of G is the set

$$E = \{\, \{i,\, i+1\} \mid \text{ for } 0 \le i \le n-2 \} \cup \{\, \{n-1,\, 0\}\,\}$$
$$\cup \{\, \{i,\, i+n/2\} \mid \text{ for } 0 \le i \le n/2 - 1 \}.$$

Picture the nodes of this graph written consecutively around the circumference of a circle. In that case the edges described in the top line of E go between adjacent pairs around the circle. The edges described in the bottom line of E go between nodes on opposite sides of the circle. This mental picture clearly shows that every node in G has degree 3.

PROOF BY CONTRADICTION

In one common form of argument for proving a theorem, we assume that the theorem is false and then show that this assumption leads to an obviously false consequence, called a contradiction. We use this type of reasoning frequently in everyday life, as in the following example.

EXAMPLE 0.13 ··

Jack sees Jill, who has just come in from outdoors. On observing that she is completely dry, he knows that it is not raining. His "proof" that it is not raining is that, *if it were raining* (the assumption that the statement is false), *Jill would be wet* (the obviously false consequence). Therefore it must not be raining. ■

Next, let's prove by contradiction that the square root of 2 is an irrational number. A number is ***rational*** if it is a fraction m/n where m and n are integers; in other words, a rational number is the *ratio* of integers m and n. For example, $2/3$ obviously is a rational number. A number is ***irrational*** if it is not rational.

THEOREM 0.14 ··

$\sqrt{2}$ is irrational.

PROOF   First, we assume for the purposes of later obtaining a contradiction that $\sqrt{2}$ is rational. Thus

$$\sqrt{2} = \frac{m}{n},$$

where both m and n are integers. If both m and n are divisible by the same integer greater than 1, divide both by that integer. Doing so doesn't change the value of the fraction. Now, both m and n cannot be even numbers.

We multiply both sides of the equation by n and obtain

$$n\sqrt{2} = m.$$

We square both sides and obtain

$$2n^2 = m^2.$$

Because m^2 is 2 times the integer n^2, we know that m^2 is even. Therefore m, too, is even, as the square of an odd number always is odd. So we can write $m = 2k$ for some integer k. Then, substituting $2k$ for m, we get

$$2n^2 = (2k)^2$$
$$= 4k^2.$$

Dividing both sides by 2 we obtain

$$n^2 = 2k^2.$$

But this result shows that n^2 is even and hence that n is even. Thus we have established that both m and n are even. But we had earlier reduced m and n so that they were *not* both even, a contradiction.

PROOF BY INDUCTION

Proof by induction is an advanced method used to show that all elements of an infinite set have a specified property. For example, we may use a proof by induction to show that an arithmetic expression computes a desired quantity for every assignment to its variables or that a program works correctly at all steps or for all inputs.

To illustrate how proof by induction works, let's take the infinite set to be the natural numbers, $\mathcal{N} = \{1, 2, 3, \ldots\}$, and say that the property is called $\mathcal{P}$. Our goal is to prove that $\mathcal{P}(k)$ is true for each natural number k. In other words, we want to prove that $\mathcal{P}(1)$ is true, as well as $\mathcal{P}(2)$, $\mathcal{P}(3)$, $\mathcal{P}(4)$, and so on.

Every proof by induction consists of two parts, the **induction step** and the **basis**. Each part is an individual proof on its own. The induction step proves that for each $i \geq 1$, if $\mathcal{P}(i)$ is true, then so is $\mathcal{P}(i+1)$. The basis proves that $\mathcal{P}(1)$ is true.

When we have proven both of these parts, the desired result follows, namely, that $\mathcal{P}(i)$ is true for each i. Why? First, we know that $\mathcal{P}(1)$ is true because the basis alone proves it. Second, we know that $\mathcal{P}(2)$ is true because the induction step proves that, if $\mathcal{P}(1)$ is true then $\mathcal{P}(2)$ is true, and we already know that $\mathcal{P}(1)$ is true. Third, we know that $\mathcal{P}(3)$ is true because the induction step proves that, if $\mathcal{P}(2)$ is true then $\mathcal{P}(3)$ is true, and we already know that $\mathcal{P}(2)$ is true. This process continues for all natural numbers, showing that $\mathcal{P}(4)$ is true, $\mathcal{P}(5)$ is true, and so on.

Once you understand the preceding paragraph, you can easily understand variations and generalizations of the same idea. For example, the basis doesn't necessarily need to start with 1; it may start with any value b. In that case the induction proof shows that $\mathcal{P}(k)$ is true for every k that is at least b.

In the induction step the assumption that $\mathcal{P}(i)$ is true is called the **induction hypothesis**. Sometimes having the stronger induction hypothesis that $\mathcal{P}(j)$ is true for every $j \leq i$ is useful. The induction proof still works because, when we want to prove that $\mathcal{P}(i+1)$ is true we have already proved that $\mathcal{P}(j)$ is true for every $j \leq i$.

The format for writing down a proof by induction is as follows.

Basis: Prove that $\mathcal{P}(1)$ is true.

$$\vdots$$

Induction step: For each $i \geq 1$, assume that $\mathcal{P}(i)$ is true and use this assumption to show that $\mathcal{P}(i+1)$ is true.

$$\vdots$$

Now, let's prove by induction the correctness of the formula used to calculate the size of monthly payments of home mortgages. When buying a home, many people borrow some of the money needed for the purchase and repay this loan over a certain number of years. Typically, the terms of such repayments stipulate that a fixed amount of money is paid each month to cover the interest, as well as part of the original sum, so that the total is repaid in 30 years. The formula for calculating the size of the monthly payments is shrouded in mystery, but actually is quite simple. It touches many people's lives, so you should find it interesting. We use induction to prove that it works, making it a good illustration of that technique.

First, we set up the names and meanings of several variables. Let P be the *principal*, the amount of the original loan. Let I be the yearly *interest rate* of the loan, where $I = 0.06$ indicates a 6% rate of interest. Let Y be the monthly payment. For convenience we define another variable M from I, for the monthly multiplier. It is the rate at which the loan changes each month because of the interest on it. So $M = 1 + I/12$.

Two things happen each month. First, the amount of the loan tends to increase because of the monthly multiplier. Second, the amount tends to decrease because of the monthly payment. Let P_t be the amount of the loan outstanding after the tth month. Then $P_0 = P$ is the amount of the original loan, $P_1 = MP_0 - Y$ is the amount of the loan after one month, $P_2 = MP_1 - Y$ is the amount of the loan after two months, and so on. Now we are ready to state and prove a theorem by induction on t that gives a formula for the value of P_t.

THEOREM 0.15 ···

For each $t \geq 0$,

$$P_t = PM^t - Y \left(\frac{M^t - 1}{M - 1} \right).$$

PROOF

Basis: Prove that the formula is true for $t = 0$. If $t = 0$, then the formula states that

$$P_0 = PM^0 - Y \left(\frac{M^0 - 1}{M - 1} \right).$$

We can simplify the right-hand side by observing that $M^0 = 1$. Thus we get

$$P_0 = P,$$

which holds because we have defined P_0 to be P. Therefore we have proved that the basis of the induction is true.

Induction step: For each $k \geq 0$ assume that the formula is true for $t = k$ and show that it is true for $t = k + 1$. The induction hypothesis states that

$$P_k = PM^k - Y \left(\frac{M^k - 1}{M - 1} \right).$$

Our objective is to prove that

$$P_{k+1} = PM^{k+1} - Y \left(\frac{M^{k+1} - 1}{M - 1} \right).$$

We do so with the following steps. First, from the definition of P_{k+1} from P_k, we know that

$$P_{k+1} = P_k M - Y.$$

Therefore, using the induction hypothesis to calculate P_k,

$$P_{k+1} = \left[PM^k - Y \left(\frac{M^k - 1}{M - 1} \right) \right] M - Y.$$

Multiplying through by M and rewriting Y yields

$$P_{k+1} = PM^{k+1} - Y \left(\frac{M^{k+1} - M}{M - 1} \right) - Y \left(\frac{M - 1}{M - 1} \right)$$

$$= PM^{k+1} - Y \left(\frac{M^{k+1} - 1}{M - 1} \right).$$

Thus the formula is correct for $t = k + 1$, which proves the theorem.

Problem 0.13 asks you to use this formula to calculate actual mortgage payments.

EXERCISES

0.1 Examine the following formal descriptions of sets so that you understand which members they contain. Write a short informal English description of each set.

    a. $\{1, 3, 5, 7, \ldots\}$.

    b. $\{\ldots, -4, -2, 0, 2, 4, \ldots, \}$.

    c. $\{n \mid n = 2m \text{ for some } m \text{ in } \mathcal{N}\}$.

    d. $\{n \mid n = 2m \text{ for some } m \text{ in } \mathcal{N}, \text{ and } n = 3k \text{ for some } k \text{ in } \mathcal{N}\}$.

    e. $\{w \mid w \text{ is a string of 0s and 1s and } w \text{ equals the reverse of } w\}$.

    f. $\{n \mid n \text{ is an integer and } n = n + 1\}$.

0.2 Write formal descriptions of the following sets.

    a. The set containing the numbers 1, 10, and 100.
    b. The set containing all integers that are greater than 5.
    c. The set containing all natural numbers that are less than 5.
    d. The set containing the string aba.
    e. The set containing the empty string.
    f. The set containing nothing at all.

0.3 Let A be the set $\{x, y, z\}$, and B be the set $\{x, y\}$.

    a. Is A a subset of B?
    b. Is B a subset of A?
    c. What is $A \cup B$?
    d. What is $A \cap B$?
    e. What is $A \times B$?
    f. What is the power set of B?

0.4 If A has a elements and B has b elements, how many elements are in $A \times B$? Explain your answer.

0.5 If C is a set with c elements, how many elements are in the power set of C? Explain your answer.

0.6 Let X be the set $\{1, 2, 3, 4, 5\}$ and Y be the set $\{6, 7, 8, 9, 10\}$. The unary function $f: X \longrightarrow Y$ and the binary function $g: X \times Y \longrightarrow Y$ are described in the following tables.

n	$f(n)$
1	6
2	7
3	6
4	7
5	6

g	6	7	8	9	10
1	10	10	10	10	10
2	7	8	9	10	6
3	7	7	8	8	9
4	9	8	7	6	10
5	6	6	6	6	6

    a. What is the value of $f(2)$?
    b. What are the range and domain of f?
    c. What is the value of $g(2, 10)$?
    d. What are the range and domain of g?
    e. What is the value of $g(4, f(4))$?

0.7 For each part, give a relation that satisfies the condition.

    a. Reflexive and symmetric but not transitive
    b. Reflexive and transitive but not symmetric
    c. Symmetric and transitive but not reflexive

0.8 Consider the undirected graph $G = (V, E)$ where V, the set of nodes, is $\{1, 2, 3, 4\}$ and E, the set of edges, is $\{\{1, 2\}, \{2, 3\}, \{1, 3\}, \{2, 4\}, \{1, 4\}\}$. Draw the graph G. What is the degree of node 1? of node 3? Indicate a path from node 3 to node 4 on your drawing of G.

0.9 Write a formal description of the following graph.

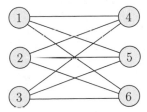

PROBLEMS

0.10 Find the error in the following proof that $1 = 2$.

Consider the equation $a = b$. Multiply both sides by a to obtain $a^2 = ab$. Subtract b^2 from both sides to get $a^2 - b^2 = ab - b^2$. Now factor each side, $(a+b)(a-b) = b(a-b)$, and divide each side by $(a-b)$, to get $a+b = b$. Finally, let a and b equal 1, which shows that $2 = 1$.

0.11 Find the error in the following proof that all horses are the same color.

CLAIM: In any set of h horses, all horses are the same color.

PROOF: By induction on h.

Basis: For $h = 1$. In any set containing just one horse, all horses clearly are the same color.

Induction step: For $k \geq 1$ assume that the claim is true for $h = k$ and prove that it is true for $h = k+1$. Take any set H of $k+1$ horses. We show that all the horses in this set are the same color. Remove one horse from this set to obtain the set H_1 with just k horses. By the induction hypothesis, all the horses in H_1 are the same color. Now replace the removed horse and remove a different one to obtain the set H_2. By the same argument, all the horses in H_2 are the same color. Therefore all the horses in H must be the same color, and the proof is complete.

*0.12** Ramsey's theorem. Let G be a graph. A **clique** in G is a subgraph in which every two nodes are connected by an edge. An **anti-clique**, also called an **independent set**, is a subgraph in which every two nodes are not connected by an edge. Show that every graph with n nodes contains either a clique or an anti-clique with at least $\frac{1}{2} \log_2 n$ nodes.

0.13 Use Theorem 0.15 to derive a formula for calculating the size of the monthly payment for a mortgage in terms of the principal P, interest rate I, and the number of payments t. Assume that, after t payments have been made, the loan amount is reduced to 0. Use the formula to calculate the dollar amount of each monthly payment for a 30-year mortgage with 360 monthly payments on an initial loan amount of $100,000 with an 8% annual interest rate.

PART ONE

AUTOMATA AND LANGUAGES

1

REGULAR LANGUAGES

The theory of computation begins with a question: What is a computer? It is perhaps a silly question, as even my four-year-old daughter knows that this thing I type on is a computer. But these real computers are quite complicated—too much so to allow us to set up a manageable mathematical theory of them directly. Instead we use an idealized computer called a ***computational model***. As with any model in science, a computational model may be accurate in some ways but perhaps not in others. Thus we will use several different computational models, depending on the features we want to focus on. We begin with the simplest model, called the ***finite state machine*** or ***finite automaton***.

1.1

FINITE AUTOMATA

Finite automata are good models for computers with an extremely limited amount of memory. What can a computer do with such a small memory? Many useful things! In fact, we interact with such computers all the time, as they lie at the heart of various electromechanical devices.

As shown in the following figures, the controller for an automatic door is one example of such a device. Often found at supermarket entrances and exits, automatic doors swing open when sensing that a person is approaching. An automatic door has a pad in front to detect the presence of a person about to walk through the doorway. Another pad is located to the rear of the doorway so that the controller can hold the door open long enough for the person to pass all the way through and also so that the door does not strike someone standing behind it as it opens.

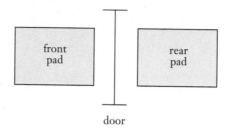

FIGURE   **1.1**
Top view of an automatic door

The controller is in either of two states: "OPEN" or "CLOSED," representing the corresponding condition of the door. As shown in the following figures, there are four possible input conditions: "FRONT" (meaning that a person is standing on the pad in front of the doorway), "REAR" (meaning that a person is standing on the pad to the rear of the doorway), "BOTH" (meaning that people are standing on both pads), and "NEITHER" (meaning that no one is standing on either pad).

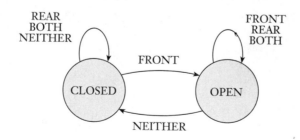

FIGURE   **1.2**
State diagram for automatic door controller

input signal

		NEITHER	FRONT	REAR	BOTH
state	CLOSED	CLOSED	OPEN	CLOSED	CLOSED
	OPEN	CLOSED	OPEN	OPEN	OPEN

FIGURE 1.3
State transition table for automatic door controller

The controller moves from state to state, depending on the input it receives. When in the CLOSED state and receiving input NEITHER or REAR, it remains in the CLOSED state. In addition, if the input BOTH is received, it stays CLOSED because opening the door risks knocking someone over on the rear pad. But if the input FRONT arrives, it moves to the OPEN state. In the OPEN state, if input FRONT, REAR, or BOTH is received, it remains in OPEN. If input NEITHER arrives, it returns to CLOSED.

For example, a controller might start in state CLOSED and receive the following series of input signals: FRONT, REAR, NEITHER, FRONT, BOTH, NEITHER, REAR, NEITHER. It then would go through the series of states: CLOSED (starting), OPEN, OPEN, CLOSED, OPEN, OPEN, CLOSED, CLOSED, CLOSED.

Thinking of an automatic door controller as a finite automaton is useful because that suggests standard ways of representation as in Figures 1.2 and 1.3. This controller is a computer that has just a single bit of memory, capable of recording which of the two states the controller is in. Other common devices have controllers with somewhat larger memories. In an elevator controller a state may represent the floor the elevator is on and the inputs might be the signals received from the buttons. This computer might need several bits to keep track of this information. Controllers for various household appliances such as dishwashers and electronic thermostats, as well as parts of digital watches and calculators, are additional examples of computers with limited memories. The design of such devices requires keeping the methodology and terminology of finite automata in mind.

Finite automata and their probabilistic counterpart *Markov chains* are useful tools when we are attempting to recognize patterns in data. These devices are used in speech processing and in optical character recognition. Markov chains have even been used to model and predict price changes in financial markets.

We will now take a close look at finite automata from a mathematical perspective. We will develop a precise definition of a finite automaton, terminology for describing and manipulating finite automata, and theoretical results that describe their power and limitations. Besides giving us a clearer understanding of what finite automata are and what they can and cannot do, the theoretical development allows us to practice and become more comfortable with mathematical definitions, theorems, and proofs in a relatively simple setting.

In beginning to describe the mathematical theory of finite automata, we do so in the abstract, without reference to any particular application. The following figure depicts a finite automaton called M_1.

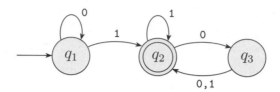

FIGURE   **1.4**
A finite automaton called M_1 that has three states

Figure 1.4 is called the *state diagram* of M_1. It has three *states*, labeled q_1, q_2, and q_3. The *start state*, q_1, is indicated by the arrow pointing at it from nowhere. The *accept state*, q_2, is the one with a double circle. The arrows going from one state to another are called *transitions*.

When this automaton receives an input string such as 1101, it processes that string and produces an output. The output is either *accept* or *reject*. We will consider only this yes/no type of output for now to keep things simple. The processing begins in M_1's start state. The automaton receives the symbols from the input string one by one from left to right. After reading each symbol, M_1 moves from one state to another along the transition that has that symbol as its label. When it reads the last symbol, M_1 produces its output. The output is *accept* if M_1 is now in an accept state and *reject* if it is not.

For example, when we feed the input string 1101 to the machine M_1 in Figure 1.4, the processing proceeds as follows.

1. start in state q_1;

2. read 1, follow transition from q_1 to q_2;

3. read 1, follow transition from q_2 to q_2;

4. read 0, follow transition from q_2 to q_3;

5. read 1, follow transition from q_3 to q_2;

6. *accept* because M_1 is in an accept state q_2 at the end of the input.

Experimenting with this machine on a variety of input strings reveals that it accepts the strings 1, 01, 11, and 0101010101. In fact, M_1 accepts any string that ends with a 1, as it goes to its accept state q_2 whenever it reads the symbol 1. In addition, it accepts strings 100, 0100, 110000, and 0101000000, and any string that ends with an even number of 0s following the last 1. It rejects other strings, such as 0, 10, 101000. Can you describe the language consisting of all strings that M_1 accepts? We will do so shortly.

FORMAL DEFINITION OF A FINITE AUTOMATON

In the preceding section we used state diagrams to introduce finite automata. Now we define finite automata formally. Though state diagrams are easier to grasp intuitively, we need the formal definition, too, for two specific reasons.

First, a formal definition is precise. It resolves any uncertainties about what is allowed in a finite automaton. If you were uncertain about whether finite automata were allowed to have 0 accept states or whether they must have exactly one transition exiting every state for each possible input symbol, you could consult the formal definition and verify that the answer is yes in both cases. Second, a formal definition provides notation. Good notation helps you think and express your thoughts clearly.

The language of a formal definition is somewhat arcane, having some similarity to the language of a legal document. Both need to be precise, and every detail must be spelled out.

A finite automaton has several parts. It has a set of states and rules for going from one state to another, depending on the input symbol. It has an input alphabet that indicates the allowed input symbols. It has a start state and a set of accept states. The formal definition says that a finite automaton is a list of those five objects: set of states, input alphabet, rules for moving, start state, and accept states. In mathematical language a list of five elements is often called a 5-tuple. Hence we define a finite automaton to be a 5-tuple consisting of these five parts.

We use something called a **transition function**, frequently denoted δ, to define the rules for moving. If the finite automaton has an arrow from a state x to a state y labeled with the input symbol 1, that means that, if the automaton is in state x when it reads a 1, it then moves to state y. We can indicate the same thing with the transition function by saying that $\delta(x, 1) = y$. This notation is a kind of mathematical shorthand. Putting it all together we arrive at the formal definition of finite automata.

DEFINITION   **1.1**   ···

A **finite automaton** is a 5-tuple $(Q, \Sigma, \delta, q_0, F)$, where

1. Q is a finite set called the **states**,
2. Σ is a finite set called the **alphabet**,
3. $\delta: Q \times \Sigma \longrightarrow Q$ is the **transition function**,[1]
4. $q_0 \in Q$ is the **start state**, and
5. $F \subseteq Q$ is the **set of accept states**.[2]

The formal definition precisely describes what we mean by a finite automaton. For example, returning to the earlier question of whether 0 accept states is

---

[1] Refer back to page 7 if you are uncertain about the meaning of $\delta: Q \times \Sigma \longrightarrow Q$.
[2] Accept states sometimes are called **final states**.

allowable, you can see that setting F to be the empty set $\emptyset$ yields 0 accept states, which is allowable. Furthermore the transition function δ specifies exactly one next state for each possible combination of a state and an input symbol. That answers our other question affirmatively, showing that exactly one transition arrow exits every state for each possible input symbol.

We can use the notation of the formal definition to describe individual finite automata by specifying each of the five parts listed in Definition 1.1. For example, let's return to the finite automaton M_1 depicted in Figure 1.4.

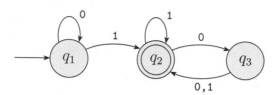

FIGURE 1.5
The finite automaton M_1

We can describe M_1 formally by writing $M_1 = (Q, \Sigma, \delta, q_1, F)$, where

1. $Q = \{q_1, q_2, q_3\}$,
2. $\Sigma = \{0,1\}$,
3. δ is described as

	0	1
q_1	q_1	q_2
q_2	q_3	q_2
q_3	q_2	q_2

4. q_1 is the start state, and
5. $F = \{q_2\}$.

If A is the set of all strings that machine M accepts, we say that A is the **language of machine** M and write $L(M) = A$. We say that M **recognizes** A or that M **accepts** A. Because the term *accept* has different meanings when we refer to machines accepting strings and machines accepting languages, we prefer the term *recognize* for languages in order to avoid confusion.

A machine may accept several strings, but it always recognizes only one language. If the machine accepts no strings, it still recognizes one language, namely, the empty language $\emptyset$.

In our example, let

$$A = \{w|\ w \text{ contains at least one 1 and}$$
$$\text{an even number of 0s follow the last 1}\}.$$

Then $L(M_1) = A$, or equivalently, M_1 recognizes A.

EXAMPLES OF FINITE AUTOMATA

EXAMPLE   **1.2** ···

The following is the state diagram of finite automaton M_2.

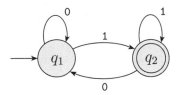

FIGURE   **1.6**

State diagram of the two-state finite automaton M_2

In the formal description $M_2 = (\{q_1, q_2\}, \{0,1\}, \delta, q_1, \{q_2\})$. The transition function δ is

	0	1
q_1	q_1	q_2
q_2	q_1	q_2

Remember that the state diagram of M_2 and the formal description of M_2 contain the same information, only in different form. You can always go from one to the other if necessary.

A good way to begin understanding any machine is to try it on some sample input strings. When you do these "experiments" to see how the machine is working, its method of functioning often becomes apparent. On the sample string 1101 the machine M_2 starts in its start state q_1 and proceeds first to state q_2 after reading the first 1, and then to states q_2, q_1, and q_2 after reading 1, 0, and 1. The string is accepted because the state q_2 is an accept state. But string 110 leaves M_2 in state q_1, so it is rejected. After trying a few more examples, you would see that M_2 accepts all strings that end in a 1. Thus $L(M_2) = \{w|\ w \text{ ends in a 1}\}$.

EXAMPLE   **1.3**   ···

Consider the finite automaton M_3.

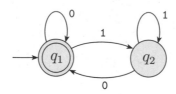

FIGURE   **1.7**
State diagram of the two-state finite automaton M_3

Machine M_3 is similar to M_2 except for the location of the accept state. As usual, the machine accepts all strings that leave it in an accept state when it has finished reading. Note that, because the start state is also an accept state, M_3 accepts the empty string ε. As soon as a machine begins reading the empty string it is at the end, so if the start state is an accept state, ε is accepted. In addition to the empty string, this machine accepts any string ending with a 0. Here,

$$L(M_3) = \{w|\ w \text{ is the empty string } \varepsilon \text{ or ends in a } 0\}.$$

EXAMPLE   **1.4**   ···

The following figure shows a five-state machine M_4

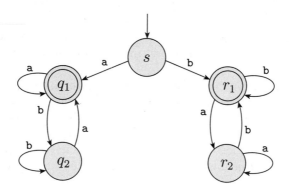

FIGURE   **1.8**
Finite automaton M_4

M_4 has two accept states, q_1 and r_1 and operates over the alphabet $\Sigma = \{a, b\}$. Some experimentation shows that it accepts strings a, b, aa, bb, and bab, but not strings ab, ba, or bbba. This machine begins in state s, and after it reads the first symbol in the input, it either goes left into the q states or right into the r states. In either case it can never return to the start state (in contrast to the previous examples), as it has no way to get from any other state back to s. If the first symbol in the input string is a, then it goes left and accepts when the string ends with an a. Similarly, if the first symbol is a b, the machine goes right, and accepts when the string ends in b. So M_4 accepts all strings that start and end with a, or that start and end with b. In other words, M_4 accepts strings that start and end with the same symbol.

EXAMPLE   **1.5**   ....

The following diagram shows machine M_5, which has a four-symbol input alphabet, $\Sigma = \{\langle\text{RESET}\rangle, 0, 1, 2\}$. We treat $\langle\text{RESET}\rangle$ as a single symbol.

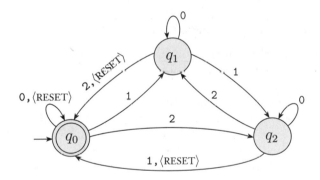

FIGURE   **1.9**
Finite automaton M_5

M_5 keeps a running count of the sum of the numerical input symbols it reads, modulo 3. Every time it receives the $\langle\text{RESET}\rangle$ symbol it resets the count to 0. It accepts if the sum is 0, modulo 3, or in other words, if the sum is a multiple of 3.

EXAMPLE   **1.6**   ....

Describing a finite automaton by state diagram is not possible in some cases. That may occur when the diagram would be too big to draw or if, as in this example, the description depends on some unspecified parameter. In these cases we resort to a formal description to specify the machine.

Consider a generalization of Example 1.5 using the same four symbol alphabet Σ. For each $i \geq 1$ let A_i be language of all strings where the sum of the numbers is a multiple of i, except that the sum is reset to 0 whenever the symbol $\langle \text{RESET} \rangle$ appears. We show that each A_i is regular by giving a finite automaton B_i accepting A_i. We then describe the machine B_i formally as follows: $B_i = (Q_i, \Sigma, \delta_i, q_0, \{q_0\})$, where Q_i is the set of i states $\{q_0, q_1, q_2, \ldots, q_{i-1}\}$, and we design the transition function δ_i so that for each j, if B_i is in q_j, the running sum is j, modulo i. For each q_j let

$$\delta_i(q_j, 0) = q_j,$$
$$\delta_i(q_j, 1) = q_k \text{ where } k = j + 1 \text{ modulo } i,$$
$$\delta_i(q_j, 2) = q_k \text{ where } k = j + 2 \text{ modulo } i, \text{ and}$$
$$\delta_i(q_j, \langle \text{RESET} \rangle) = q_0.$$

FORMAL DEFINITION OF COMPUTATION

So far we have described finite automata informally, using state diagrams, and with a formal definition, as a 5-tuple. The informal description is easier to grasp at first, but the formal definition is useful for making the notion totally precise, resolving any ambiguities that may have occurred in the informal description. Next we do the same for a finite automaton's computation. We already have an informal idea of the way it computes, and we now formalize it mathematically.

Let $M = (Q, \Sigma, \delta, q_0, F)$ be a finite automaton and $w = w_1 w_2 \cdots w_n$ be a string over the alphabet Σ. Then M ***accepts*** w if a sequence of states $r_0, r_1, \ldots, r_n$ exists in Q with the following three conditions:

1. $r_0 = q_0$,
2. $\delta(r_i, w_{i+1}) = r_{i+1}$ for $i = 0, \ldots, n - 1$, and
3. $r_n \in F$.

Condition 1 says that the machine starts in the start state. Condition 2 says that the machine goes from state to state according to the transition function. Condition 3 says that the machine accepts its input if it ends up in an accept state. We say that M ***recognizes language*** A if $A = \{w | M \text{ accepts } w\}$.

DEFINITION   **1.7**   ···

A language is called a ***regular language*** if some finite automaton recognizes it.

EXAMPLE **1.8** ⋯⋯⋯⋯⋯⋯⋯⋯⋯⋯⋯⋯⋯⋯⋯⋯⋯⋯⋯⋯⋯⋯⋯⋯⋯⋯⋯⋯⋯⋯⋯⋯⋯⋯⋯⋯⋯⋯

Take machine M_5 from Example 1.5. Let w be the string

$$10\langle\text{RESET}\rangle22\langle\text{RESET}\rangle012$$

Then M_5 accepts w according to the formal definition of computation because the sequence of states it enters when computing on w is

$$q_0, q_1, q_1, q_0, q_2, q_1, q_0, q_0, q_1, q_0,$$

which satisfies the three conditions. The language of M_5 is

$$L(M_5) = \{w|\ \text{the sum of the symbols in } w \text{ is 0 modulo 3,}$$
$$\text{except that } \langle\text{RESET}\rangle \text{ resets the count to 0}\}.$$

As M_5 recognizes this language, it is a regular language.

DESIGNING FINITE AUTOMATA

Whether it be of automaton or artwork, design is a creative process. As such it cannot be reduced to a simple recipe or formula. However, you might find a particular approach helpful when designing various types of automata. That is, put *yourself* in the place of the machine you are trying to design and then see how you would go about performing the machine's task. Pretending that you are the machine is a psychological trick that helps engage your whole mind in the design process.

Let's design a finite automaton using the "reader as automaton" method just described. Suppose that you are given some language and want to design a finite automaton that recognizes it. Pretending to be the automaton, you receive an input string and must determine whether it is a member of the language the automaton is supposed to recognize. You get to see the symbols in the string one by one. After each symbol you must decide whether the string seen so far is in the language. The reason is that you, like the machine, don't know when the end of the string is coming, so you must always be ready with the answer.

First, in order to make these decisions, you have to figure out what you need to remember about the string as you are reading it. Why not simply remember all you have seen? Bear in mind that you are pretending to be a finite automaton and that this type of machine has only a finite number of states, which means a finite memory. Imagine that the input is extremely long, say, from here to the moon, so that you could not possibly remember the entire thing. You have a finite memory, say, a single sheet of paper, which has a limited storage capacity. Fortunately, for many languages you don't need to remember the entire input. You only need to remember certain crucial information. Exactly which information is crucial depends on the particular language considered.

For example, suppose that the alphabet is $\{0,1\}$ and that the language consists of all strings with an odd number of 1s. You want to construct a finite automaton E_1 to recognize this language. Pretending to be the automaton, you start getting an input string of 0s and 1s symbol by symbol. Do you need to remember the entire string seen so far in order to determine whether the number of 1s is odd? Of course not. Simply remember whether the number of 1s seen so far is even or odd and keep track of this information as you read new symbols. If you read a 1, flip the answer, but if you read a 0, leave the answer as is.

But how does this help you design E_1? Once you have determined the necessary information to remember about the string as it is being read, you represent this information as a finite list of possibilities. In this instance, the possibilities would be

1. even so far, and
2. odd so far.

Then you assign a state to each of the possibilities. These are the states of E_1, as shown in the following figure.

FIGURE **1.10**
The two states q_{even} and q_{odd}

Next, you assign the transitions by seeing how to go from one possibility to another upon reading a symbol. So, if state q_{even} represents the even possibility and state q_{odd} represents the odd possibility, you would set the transitions to flip state on a 1 and stay put on a 0, as shown in the following figure.

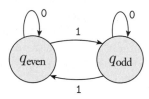

FIGURE **1.11**
Transitions telling how the possibilities rearrange

Next, you set the start state to be the state corresponding to the possibility associated with having seen 0 symbols so far (the empty string ε). In this case the start state corresponds to state q_{even} because 0 is an even number. Last, set the accept states to be those corresponding to possibilities where you want to accept the input string. Set q_{odd} to be an accept state because you want to accept when you have seen an odd number of 1s. These additions are shown in the following figure.

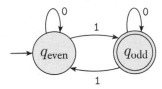

FIGURE **1.12**
Adding the start and accept states

EXAMPLE **1.9** ··

This example shows how to design a finite automaton E_2 to recognize the regular language of all strings that contain the string 001 as a substring. For example, 0010, 1001, 001, and 11111110011111 are all in the language, but 11 and 0000 are not. How would you recognize this language if you were pretending to be E_2? As symbols come in, you would initially skip over all 1s. If you come to a 0, then you note that you may have just seen the first of the three symbols in the pattern 001 you are seeking. If at this point you see a 1, there were too few 0s, so you go back to skipping over 1s. But if you see a 0 at that point, you should remember that you have just seen two symbols of the pattern. Now you simply need to continue scanning until you see a 1. If you find it, remember that you succeeded in finding the pattern and continue reading the input string until you get to the end.

So there are four possibilities: You

1. haven't just seen any symbols of the pattern,

2. have just seen a 0,

3. have just seen 00, or

4. have seen the entire pattern 001.

Assign the states q, q_0, q_{00}, and q_{001} to these possibilities. You can assign the transitions by observing that from q reading a 1 you stay in q, but reading a 0 you move to q_0. In q_0 reading a 1 you return to q, but reading a 0 you move to q_{00}. In q_{00}, reading a 1 you move to q_{001}, but reading a 0 leaves you in q_{00}. Finally, in q_{001} reading a 0 or a 1 leaves you in q_{001}. The start state is q, and the only accept state is q_{001}, as shown in the following figure.

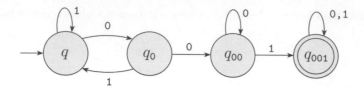

FIGURE **1.13**
Accepts strings containing 001

THE REGULAR OPERATIONS

In the preceding two sections we introduced and defined finite automata and regular languages. We now begin to investigate their properties. Doing so will help develop a toolbox of techniques to use when you design automata to recognize particular languages. The toolbox also will include ways of proving that certain other languages are nonregular (i.e., beyond the capability of finite automata).

In arithmetic, the basic objects are numbers and the tools are operations for manipulating them, such as $+$ and $\times$. In the theory of computation the objects are languages and the tools include operations specifically designed for manipulating them. We define three operations on languages, called the *regular operations*, and use them to study properties of the regular languages.

DEFINITION **1.10** $\cdots\cdots\cdots\cdots\cdots\cdots\cdots\cdots\cdots\cdots\cdots\cdots\cdots\cdots\cdots\cdots\cdots\cdots\cdots\cdots\cdots\cdots\cdots\cdots\cdots\cdots\cdots\cdots$

Let A and B be languages. We define the regular operations *union*, *concatenation*, and *star* as follows.

- **Union**: $A \cup B = \{x \mid x \in A \text{ or } x \in B\}$.

- **Concatenation**: $A \circ B = \{xy \mid x \in A \text{ and } y \in B\}$.

- **Star**: $A^* = \{x_1 x_2 \ldots x_k \mid k \geq 0 \text{ and each } x_i \in A\}$.

You are already familiar with the union operation. It simply takes all the strings in both A and B and lumps them together into one language.

The concatenation operation is a little trickier. It attaches a string from A in front of a string from B in all possible ways to get the strings in the new language.

The star operation is a bit different from the other two because it applies to a single language rather than two. That is, the star operation is a *unary operation* instead of a *binary operation*. It works by attaching any number of strings in A together to get a string in the new language. Because "any number" includes 0 as a possibility, the empty string ε is always a member of A^*, no matter what A is.

EXAMPLE   **1.11**

Let the alphabet Σ be the standard 26 letters $\{a, b, \ldots, z\}$. If $A = \{\texttt{good}, \texttt{bad}\}$ and $B = \{\texttt{boy}, \texttt{girl}\}$, then

$A \cup B = \{\texttt{good}, \texttt{bad}, \texttt{boy}, \texttt{girl}\}$,

$A \circ B = \{\texttt{goodboy}, \texttt{goodgirl}, \texttt{badboy}, \texttt{badgirl}\}$, and

$A^* = \{\varepsilon, \texttt{good}, \texttt{bad}, \texttt{goodgood}, \texttt{goodbad}, \texttt{badgood}, \texttt{badbad},$
$\qquad \texttt{goodgoodgood}, \texttt{goodgoodbad}, \texttt{goodbadgood}, \texttt{goodbadbad}, \ldots \}$.

Let $\mathcal{N} = \{1, 2, 3, \ldots\}$ be the set of natural numbers. When we say that $\mathcal{N}$ is *closed under multiplication* we mean that, for any x and y in $\mathcal{N}$, the product $x \times y$ also is in $\mathcal{N}$. In contrast $\mathcal{N}$ is not closed under division, as 1 and 2 are in $\mathcal{N}$ but $1/2$ is not. Generally speaking, a collection of objects is **closed** under some operation if applying that operation to members of the collection returns an object still in the collection. We show that the collection of regular languages is closed under all three of the regular operations. In Section 1.3 we show that these are useful tools for manipulating regular languages and understanding the power of finite automata. We begin with the union operation.

THEOREM   **1.12**

The class of regular languages is closed under the union operation.

In other words, if A_1 and A_2 are regular languages, so is $A_1 \cup A_2$.

PROOF IDEA   We have regular languages A_1 and A_2 and want to show that $A_1 \cup A_2$ also is regular. Because A_1 and A_2 are regular, we know that some finite automaton M_1 recognizes A_1 and some finite automaton M_2 recognizes A_2. To prove that $A_1 \cup A_2$ is regular we demonstrate a finite automaton, call it M, that recognizes $A_1 \cup A_2$.

This is a proof by construction. We construct M from M_1 and M_2. Machine M must accept its input exactly when either M_1 or M_2 would accept it in order to recognize the union language. It works by *simulating* both M_1 and M_2 and accepting if either of the simulations accept.

How can we make machine M simulate M_1 and M_2? Perhaps it first simulates M_1 on the input and then simulates M_2 on the input. But we must be careful here! Once the symbols of the input are read and used to simulate M_1, we cannot "rewind the input tape" to try the simulation on M_2. We need another approach.

Pretend that you are M. As the input symbols arrive one by one, you simulate both M_1 and M_2 simultaneously. That way only one pass through the input is necessary. But can you keep track of both simulations with finite memory? All you need to remember is the state that each machine would be in if it had read up to this point in the input. Therefore you need to remember a pair of states. How many possible pairs are there? If M_1 has k_1 states and M_2 has k_2 states, the number of pairs of states, one from M_1 and the other from M_2, is the product $k_1 \times k_2$. This product will be the number of states in M, one for each pair. The transitions of M go from pair to pair, updating the current state for both M_1 and M_2. The accept states of M are those pairs wherein either M_1 or M_2 is in an accept state.

PROOF

Let M_1 recognize A_1, where $M_1 = (Q_1, \Sigma, \delta_1, q_1, F_1)$, and
$\qquad M_2$ recognize A_2, where $M_2 = (Q_2, \Sigma, \delta_2, q_2, F_2)$.

Construct M to recognize $A_1 \cup A_2$, where $M = (Q, \Sigma, \delta, q_0, F)$.

1. $Q = \{(r_1, r_2) \mid r_1 \in Q_1 \text{ and } r_2 \in Q_2\}$.
   This set is the ***Cartesian product*** of sets Q_1 and Q_2 and is written $Q_1 \times Q_2$. It is the set of all pairs of states, the first from Q_1 and the second from Q_2.

2. Σ, the alphabet, is the same as in M_1 and M_2. In this theorem and in all subsequent similar theorems, we assume for simplicity that both M_1 and M_2 have the same input alphabet Σ. The theorem remains true if they have different alphabets, Σ_1 and Σ_2. We would then modify the proof to let $\Sigma = \Sigma_1 \cup \Sigma_2$.

3. δ, the transition function, is defined as follows. For each $(r_1, r_2) \in Q$ and each $a \in \Sigma$, let

$$\delta\big((r_1, r_2), a\big) = \big(\delta_1(r_1, a), \delta_2(r_2, a)\big).$$

   Hence δ gets a state of M (which actually is a pair of states from M_1 and M_2), together with an input symbol, and returns M's next state.

4. q_0 is the pair (q_1, q_2).

5. F is the set of pairs in which either member is an accept state of M_1 or M_2. We can write it as

$$F = \{(r_1, r_2) \mid r_1 \in F_1 \text{ or } r_2 \in F_2\}.$$

   This expression is the same as $F = (F_1 \times Q_2) \cup (Q_1 \times F_2)$. (Note that it is *not* the same as $F = F_1 \times F_2$. What would that give us instead?[3])

This concludes the construction of the finite automaton M that recognizes the union of A_1 and A_2. This construction is fairly simple, and thus its correctness is evident from the strategy that is described in the proof idea. More complicated constructions require additional discussion to prove correctness. A formal

---

[3]This expression would define M's accept states to be those for which *both* members of the pair are accept states. In this case M would accept a string only if both M_1 *and* M_2 accept it, so the resulting language would be the *intersection* and not the union. In fact, this result proves that the class of regular languages are closed under intersection.

correctness proof for a construction of this type usually proceeds by induction. For an example of a construction proved correct, see the proof of Theorem 1.28. Most of the constructions that you will encounter in this course are fairly simple and so do not require a formal correctness proof.

We have just shown that the union of two regular languages is regular, thereby proving that the class of regular languages is closed under the union operation. We now turn to the concatenation operation and attempt to show that the class of regular languages is closed under that operation, too.

THEOREM 1.13

The class of regular languages is closed under the concatenation operation.

In other words, if A_1 and A_2 are regular languages then so is $A_1 \circ A_2$.

To prove this theorem let's try something along the lines of the proof of the union case. As before, we can start with finite automata M_1 and M_2 recognizing the regular languages A_1 and A_2. But now, instead of constructing automaton M to accept its input if either M_1 or M_2 accept, it must accept if its input can be broken into two pieces, where M_1 accepts the first piece and M_2 accepts the second piece. The problem is that M doesn't know where to break its input (i.e., where the first part ends and the second begins). To solve this problem we introduce a new technique called nondeterminism.

1.2

NONDETERMINISM

Nondeterminism is a useful concept that has had great impact on the theory of computation. So far in our discussion, every step of a computation follows in a unique way from the preceding step. When the machine is in a given state and reads the next input symbol, we know what the next state will be—it is determined. We call this *determinic* computation. In a *nondeterministic* machine, several choices may exist for the next state at any point.

Nondeterminism is a generalization of determinism, so every deterministic finite automaton is automatically a nondeterministic finite automaton. As the following figure shows, nondeterministic finite automata may have additional features.

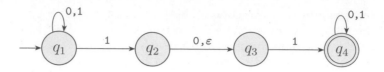

FIGURE   **1.14**
The nondeterministic finite automaton N_1

The difference between a deterministic finite automaton, abbreviated DFA, and a nondeterministic finite automaton, abbreviated NFA, is immediately apparent. First, every state of a DFA always has exactly one exiting transition arrow for each symbol in the alphabet. The nondeterministic automaton shown in Figure 1.14 violates that rule. State q_1 has one exiting arrow for 1, but it has two for 0; q_2 has one arrow for 0, but it has none for 1. In an NFA a state may have zero, one, or many exiting arrows for each alphabet symbol.

Second, in a DFA, labels on the transition arrows are symbols from the alphabet. This NFA has an arrow with the label ε. In general, an NFA may have arrows labeled with members of the alphabet or ε. Zero, one, or many arrows may exit from each state with the label ε.

How does an NFA compute? Suppose that we are running an NFA on an input string and come to a state with multiple ways to proceed. For example, say that we are in state q_1 in NFA N_1 and that the next input symbol is a 0. Without reading any input, the machine splits into multiple copies of itself and follows *all* the possibilities in parallel. Each copy of the machine takes one of the possible ways to proceed and continues as before. If there are subsequent choices, the machine splits again. If the next input symbol doesn't appear on any of the arrows exiting the state occupied by a copy of the machine, that copy of the machine dies, along with the branch of the computation associated with it. Finally, if *any one* of these copies of the machine is in an accept state at the end of the input, the NFA accepts the input string.

If a state with an ε symbol on an exiting arrow is encountered, something similar happens. Without reading any input, the machine splits into multiple copies, one following each of the exiting ε-labeled arrows and one staying at the current state. Then the machine proceeds nondeterministically as before.

Nondeterminism may be viewed as a kind of parallel computation wherein several "processes" can be running concurrently. When the NFA splits to follow several choices, that corresponds to a process "forking" into several children, each proceeding separately. If at least one of these processes accepts then the entire computation accepts.

Another way to think of a nondeterministic computation is as a tree of possibilities. The root of the tree corresponds to the start of the computation. Every branching point in the tree corresponds to a point in the computation at which the machine has multiple choices. The machine accepts if at least one of the computation branches ends in an accept state, as shown in the following figure.

Deterministic
computation

Nondeterministic
computation

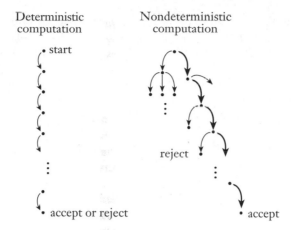

start

reject

accept or reject

accept

FIGURE **1.15**
Deterministic and nondeterministic computations with an accepting
branch

Let's consider some sample runs of the NFA N_1 shown in Figure 1.14. On input
010110 start in the start state q_1 and read the first symbol 0. From q_1 there is only
one place to go on a 0, namely, back to q_1, so remain there.

Next read the second symbol 1. In q_1 on a 1 there are two choices: either stay
in q_1 or move to q_2. Nondeterministically, the machine splits in two to follow
each choice. Keep track of the possibilities by placing a finger on each state where
a machine could be. So you now have fingers on states q_1 and q_2. An ε arrow exits
state q_2 so the machine splits again; keep one finger on q_2, and move the other
to q_3. You now have fingers on q_1, q_2, and q_3.

When the third symbol 0 is read, take each finger in turn. Keep the finger
on q_1 in place, move the finger on q_2 to q_3, and remove the finger that has been
on q_3. That last finger had no 0 arrow to follow and corresponds to a process that
simply "dies." At this point you have fingers on states q_1 and q_3.

When the fourth symbol 1 is read, split the finger on q_1 into fingers on states
q_1 and q_2, then further split the finger on q_2 to follow the ε arrow to q_3, and move
the finger that was on q_3 to q_4. You now have a finger on each of the four states.

When the fifth symbol 1 is read, the fingers on q_1 and q_3 result in fingers on
states q_1, q_2, q_3, and q_4, as you saw with the fourth symbol. The finger on state
q_2 is removed. The finger that was on q_4 stays on q_4. Now you have two fingers
on q_4, so remove one, because you only need to remember that q_4 is a possible
state at this point, not that it is possible for multiple reasons.

When the sixth and final symbol 0 is read, keep the finger on q_1 in place, move
the one on q_2 to q_3, remove the one that was on q_3, and leave the one on q_4 in

place. You are now at the end of the string, and you accept if some finger is on an accept state. You have fingers on states q_1, q_3, and q_4, and as q_4 is an accept state, N_1 accepts this string. The computation of N_1 on input 010110 is depicted in Figure 1.16.

What does N_1 do on input 010? Start with a finger on q_1. After reading the 0 you still have a finger only on q_1, but after the 1 there are fingers on q_1, q_2, and q_3 (don't forget the ε arrow). After the third symbol 0, remove the finger on q_3, move the finger on q_2 to q_3, and split the finger on q_1 into fingers on q_1, q_2, and q_3. At this point you are at the end of the input, and as no finger is on an accept state, N_1 rejects this input.

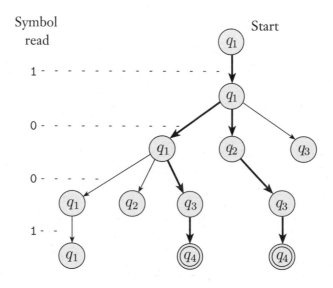

FIGURE 1.16
The computation of N_1 on input 010110 61

By continuing to experiment in this way, you will see that N_1 accepts all strings that contain either 101 or 11 as a substring.

Nondeterministic finite automata are useful in several respects. As we will show, every NFA can be converted into an equivalent DFA, and constructing NFAs is sometimes easier than directly constructing DFAs. An NFA may be much smaller than its deterministic counterpart, or its functioning may be easier to understand. Nondeterminism in finite automata is also a good introduction to nondeterminism in more powerful computational models because finite automata are especially easy to understand. Now we turn to several examples of NFAs.

EXAMPLE **1.14** ···

Let A be the language consisting of all strings over $\{0,1\}$ containing a 1 in the third position from the end (i.e., 000100 is in A but 0011 is not). The following four-state NFA N_2 recognizes A.

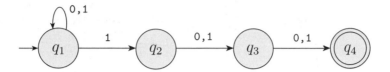

FIGURE **1.17**
The NFA N_2 recognizing A

One good way to view the computation of this NFA is to say that it stays in the start state q_1 until it "guesses" that it is three places from the end. At that point, if the input symbol is a 1, it branches to state q_2 and uses q_3 and q_4 to "check" on whether its guess was correct.

As mentioned, every NFA can be converted into an equivalent DFA, but sometimes that DFA may have many more states. The smallest DFA for A contains eight states. Furthermore, understanding the functioning of the NFA is much easier, as you may see by examining the following figure for the DFA.

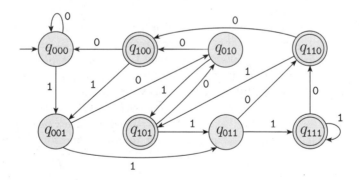

FIGURE **1.18**
A DFA recognizing A

Suppose that we added ε to the labels on the arrows going from q_2 to q_3 and from q_3 to q_4 in machine N_2 in Figure 1.17. In other words, both arrows would then have the label $0, 1, \varepsilon$ instead of just $0, 1$. What language would N_2 recognize with this modification? Try modifying the DFA in Figure 1.18 to recognize that language.

Consider the following NFA N_3 that has an input alphabet $\{0\}$ consisting of a single symbol. An alphabet containing only one symbol is called a ***unary*** alphabet.

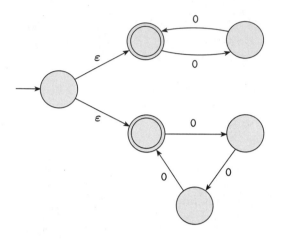

FIGURE   1.19
The NFA N_3

This machine demonstrates the convenience of having ε arrows. It accepts all strings of the form 0^k where k is a multiple of 2 or 3. (Remember that the superscript denotes repetition, not numerical exponentiation.) For example, N_3 accepts the strings ε, 00, 000, 0000, and 000000, but not 0 or 00000.

Think of the machine operating by initially guessing whether to test for a multiple of 2 or a multiple of 3 by branching into either the top loop or the bottom loop and then checking whether its guess was correct. Of course, we could replace this machine by one that doesn't have ε arrows or even any nondeterminism at all, but the machine shown is the easiest one to understand for this language.

■

We give another example of an NFA in the following figure. Practice with it to satisfy yourself that it accepts the strings ε, a, baba, and baa, but that it doesn't accept the strings b, bb, and babba. Later we use this machine to illustrate the procedure for converting NFAs to DFAs.

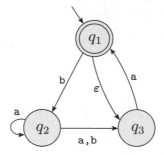

FIGURE   **1.20**
The NFA N_4

FORMAL DEFINITION OF A NONDETERMINISTIC FINITE AUTOMATON

The formal definition of a nondeterministic finite automaton is similar to that of a deterministic finite automaton. Both have states, an input alphabet, a transition function, a start state, and a collection of accept states. However, they differ in one essential way: in the type of transition function. In a DFA the transition function takes a state and an input symbol and produces the next state. In an NFA the transition function takes a state and an input symbol *or the empty string* and produces *the set of possible next states.* In order to write the formal definition, we need to set up some additional notation. For any set Q we write $\mathcal{P}(Q)$ to be the collection of all subsets of Q. Here $\mathcal{P}(Q)$ is called the *power set* of Q. For any alphabet Σ we write Σ_ε to be $\Sigma \cup \{\varepsilon\}$. Now we can easily write the formal description of the type of the transition function in an NFA. It is $\delta\colon Q \times \Sigma_\varepsilon \longrightarrow \mathcal{P}(Q)$, and we are ready to give the formal definition.

DEFINITION   **1.17**

A *nondeterministic finite automaton* is a 5-tuple $(Q, \Sigma, \delta, q_0, F)$, where

1. Q is a finite set of states,
2. Σ is a finite alphabet,
3. $\delta\colon Q \times \Sigma_\varepsilon \longrightarrow \mathcal{P}(Q)$ is the transition function,
4. $q_0 \in Q$ is the start state, and
5. $F \subseteq Q$ is the set of accept states.

EXAMPLE **1.18**

Recall the NFA N_1:

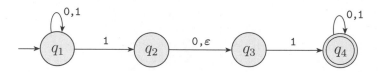

The formal description of N_1 is $(Q, \Sigma, \delta, q_1, F)$, where

1. $Q = \{q_1, q_2, q_3, q_4\}$,

2. $\Sigma = \{0,1\}$,

3. δ is given as

	0	1	ε
q_1	$\{q_1, q_2\}$	$\{q_1\}$	$\emptyset$
q_2	$\{q_3\}$	$\emptyset$	$\{q_3\}$
q_3	$\emptyset$	$\{q_4\}$	$\emptyset$
q_4	$\{q_4\}$	$\{q_4\}$	$\emptyset$

4. q_1 is the start state, and

5. $F = \{q_4\}$.

The formal definition of computation for an NFA also is similar to that for a DFA. Let $N = (Q, \Sigma, \delta, q_0, F)$ be an NFA and w a string over the alphabet Σ. Then we say that N ***accepts*** w if we can write w as $w = y_1 y_2 \cdots y_m$, where each y_i is a member of Σ_ε and a sequence of states $r_0, r_1, \ldots, r_m$ exists in Q with the following three conditions:

1. $r_0 = q_0$,

2. $r_{i+1} \in \delta(r_i, y_{i+1})$, for $i = 0, \ldots, m - 1$, and

3. $r_m \in F$.

Condition 1 says that the machine starts out in the start state. Condition 2 says that state r_{i+1} is one of the allowable next states when N is in state r_i and reading y_{i+1}. Observe that $\delta(r_i, y_{i+1})$ is the *set* of allowable next states and so we say that r_{i+1} is a member of that set. Finally, Condition 3 says that the machine accepts its input if the last state is an accept state.

EQUIVALENCE OF NFAS AND DFAS

Deterministic and nondeterministic finite automata recognize the same class of languages. Such equivalence is both surprising and useful. It is surprising because NFAs appear to have more power than DFAs, so we might expect that NFAs recognize more languages. It is useful because describing an NFA for a given language sometimes is much easier than describing a DFA for that language.

Say that two machines are ***equivalent*** if they recognize the same language.

THEOREM **1.19** ···

Every nondeterministic finite automaton has an equivalent deterministic finite automaton.

···

PROOF IDEA   If a language is recognized by an NFA, then we must show the existence of a DFA that also recognizes it. The idea is to convert the NFA into an equivalent DFA that simulates the NFA.

Recall the "reader as automaton" strategy for designing finite automata. How would you simulate the NFA if you were pretending to be a DFA? What do you need to keep track of as the input string is processed? In the examples of NFAs you kept track of the various branches of the computation by placing a finger on each state that could be active at given points in the input. You updated the fingers by moving, adding, and removing them according to the way the NFA operates. All you needed to keep track of was the set of states with fingers.

If k is the number of states of the NFA, it has 2^k subsets of states. Each subset corresponds to one of the possibilities that DFA must remember, so the DFA simulating the NFA will have 2^k states. Now we need to figure out which will be the start state and accept states of the NFA, and what will be its transition function. We can discuss this more easily after setting up some formal notation.

PROOF   Let $N = (Q, \Sigma, \delta, q_0, F)$ be the NFA recognizing some language A. We construct a DFA M recognizing A. Before doing the full construction, let's first consider the easier case wherein N has no ε arrows. Later we take the ε arrows into account.

Construct $M = (Q', \Sigma, \delta', q_0', F')$.

1. $Q' = \mathcal{P}(Q)$.
   Every state of M is a set of states of N. Recall that $\mathcal{P}(Q)$ is the set of subsets of Q.

2. For $R \in Q'$ and $a \in \Sigma$ let $\delta'(R, a) = \{q \in Q|\ q \in \delta(r, a)$ for some $r \in R\}$.
   If R is a state of M, it is also a set of states of N. When M reads a symbol a in state R, it shows where a takes each state in R. Because each state may go to a set of states, we take the union of all these sets. Another way to write this expression is

   $$\delta'(R, a) = \bigcup_{r \in R} \delta(r, a).\ ^4$$

3. $q_0' = \{q_0\}$.
   M starts in the state corresponding to the collection containing just the start state of N.

4. $F' = \{R \in Q'|\ R$ contains an accept state of $N\}$.
   The machine M accepts if one of the possible states that N could be in at this point is an accept state.

---

[4]The notation $\bigcup_{r \in R} \delta(r, a)$ means: the union of the sets $\delta(r, a)$ for each possible r in R.

Now we need to consider the ε arrows. To do so we set up an extra bit of notation. For any state R of M we define $E(R)$ to be the collection of states that can be reached from R by going only along ε arrows, including the members of R themselves. Formally, for $R \subseteq Q$ let

$$E(R) = \{q \mid q \text{ can be reached from } R \text{ by traveling along 0 or more } \varepsilon \text{ arrows}\}.$$

Then we modify the transition function of M to place additional fingers on all states that can be reached by going along ε arrows after every step. Replacing $\delta(r, a)$ by $E(\delta(r, a))$ achieves this effect. Thus

$$\delta'(R, a) = \{q \in Q \mid q \in E(\delta(r, a)) \text{ for some } r \in R\}.$$

Additionally we need to modify the start state of M to move the fingers initially to all possible states that can be reached from the start state of N along the ε arrows. Changing q_0' to be $E(\{q_0\})$ achieves this effect. We have now completed the construction of the DFA M that simulates the NFA N.

The construction of M obviously works correctly. At every step in the computation of M on an input, it clearly enters a state that corresponds to the subset of states that N could be in at that point. Thus our proof is complete.

If the construction used in the preceding proof were more complex we would need to prove that works as claimed. Usually such proofs proceed by induction on the number of steps of the computation. Most of the constructions that we use in this book are straightforward and so not require such a correctness proof. To see an example of a more complex construction that we do prove correct turn to the proof of Theorem 1.28.

Theorem 1.19 states that every NFA can be converted into an equivalent DFA. Thus nondeterministic finite automata give an alternative way of characterizing the regular languages. We state this fact as a corollary of Theorem 1.19.

COROLLARY **1.20**

A language is regular if and only if some nondeterministic finite automaton recognizes it.

One direction of the "if and only if" states that a language is regular if some NFA recognizes it. Theorem 1.19 shows that any NFA can be converted into an equivalent DFA, so if an NFA recognizes some language, so does some DFA, and hence the language is regular. The other direction states that a language is regular only if some NFA recognizes it. That is, if a language is regular, some NFA must be recognizing it. Obviously, this condition is true because a regular language has a DFA recognizing it and any DFA is also an NFA.

EXAMPLE   **1.21** ···

Let's illustrate the procedure of converting an NFA to a DFA using the machine N_4 that was given in Example 1.16. For clarity, we have relabeled the states of N_4 to be $\{1, 2, 3\}$. Thus in the formal description of $N_4 = (Q, \{a,b\}, \delta, 1, \{1\})$, the set of states Q is $\{1, 2, 3\}$ as shown in the following figure.

To construct a DFA D that is equivalent to N_4, we first determine D's states. N_4 has three states, $\{1, 2, 3\}$, so we construct D with eight states, one for each subset of N_4's states. We label each of D's states with the corresponding subset. Thus D's state set is

$$\{\emptyset, \{1\}, \{2\}, \{3\}, \{1,2\}, \{1,3\}, \{2,3\}, \{1,2,3\}\}.$$

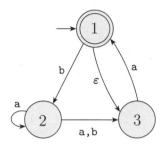

FIGURE   **1.21**
The NFA N_4

Next, we determine the start and accept states of D. The start state is $E(\{1\})$, the set of states that are reachable from 1 by traveling along ε arrows, plus 1 itself. An ε arrow goes from 1 to 3, so $E(\{1\}) = \{1, 3\}$. The new accept states are those containing M's accept state $\{1\}$; thus $\{\{1\}, \{1,2\}, \{1,3\}, \{1,2,3\}\}$.

Finally, we determine D's transition function. Each of D's states goes to one place on input a, and one place on input b. We illustrate the process of determining the placement of D's transition arrows with a few examples.

In D, state $\{2\}$ goes to $\{2,3\}$ on input a, because in N_4, state 2 goes to both 2 and 3 on input a and we can't go farther from 2 or 3 along ε arrows. State $\{2\}$ goes to state $\{3\}$ on input b, because in N_4, state 2 goes only to state 3 on input b and we can't go farther from 3 along ε arrows.

State $\{1\}$ goes to $\emptyset$ on a, because no a arrows exit it. It goes to $\{2\}$ on b.

State $\{3\}$ goes to $\{1,3\}$ on a, because in N_4, state 3 goes to 1 on a and 1 in turn goes to 3 with an ε arrow. State $\{3\}$ on b goes to $\emptyset$.

State $\{1,2\}$ on a goes to $\{2,3\}$ because 1 points at no states with a arrows and 2 points at both 2 and 3 with a arrows and neither point anywhere with ε arrows. State $\{1,2\}$ on b goes to $\{2,3\}$. Continuing in this way we obtain the following diagram for D.

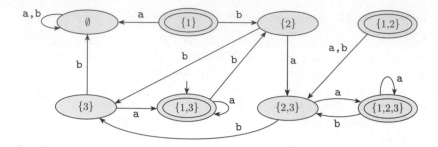

FIGURE **1.22**
A DFA D that is equivalent to the NFA N_4

We may simplify this machine by observing that no arrows point at states $\{1\}$ and $\{1, 2\}$, so they may be removed without affecting the performance of the machine. Doing so yields the following figure.

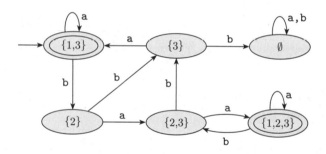

FIGURE **1.23**
DFA D after removing unnecessary states

CLOSURE UNDER THE REGULAR OPERATIONS

Now we return to the closure of the class of regular languages under the regular operations that we began in Section 1.1. Our aim is to prove that the union, concatenation, and star of regular languages are still regular. We abandoned the original attempt to do so when dealing with the concatenation operation was too complicated. The use of nondeterminism makes the proofs much easier.

First, let's consider again closure under union. Earlier we proved closure under union by simulating deterministically both machines simultaneously via a

Cartesian product construction. We now give a new proof to illustrate the technique of nondeterminism. Reviewing the first proof, on page 45, may be worthwhile to see how much easier and more intuitive the new proof is.

THEOREM 1.22 ....

The class of regular languages is closed under the union operation.

....

PROOF IDEA   We have regular languages A_1 and A_2 and want to prove that $A_1 \cup A_2$ is regular. The idea is to take two NFAs, N_1 and N_2 for A_1 and A_2, and combine them into one new NFA, N.

Machine N must accept its input if either N_1 or N_2 accepts this input. The new machine has a new start state that branches to the start states of the old machines with ε arrows. In this way the new machine nondeterministically guesses which of the two machines accepts the input. If one of them accepts the input, N will accept it, too.

We represent this construction in the following figure. On the left we indicate the start and accept states of machines N_1 and N_2 with large circles and some additional states with small circles. On the right we show how to combine N_1 and N_2 into N by adding additional transition arrows.

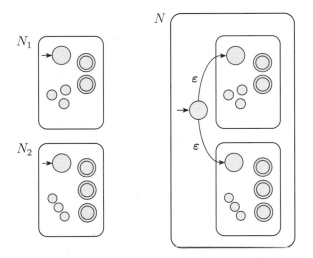

FIGURE 1.24
Construction of an NFA N to recognize $A_1 \cup A_2$

PROOF

Let $N_1 = (Q_1, \Sigma, \delta_1, q_1, F_1)$ recognize A_1, and
   $N_2 = (Q_2, \Sigma, \delta_2, q_2, F_2)$ recognize A_2.

Construct $N = (Q, \Sigma, \delta, q_0, F)$ to recognize $A_1 \cup A_2$.

1. $Q = \{q_0\} \cup Q_1 \cup Q_2$.
   The states of N are all the states of N_1 and N_2, with the addition of a new start state q_0.

2. The state q_0 is the start state of N.

3. The accept states $F = F_1 \cup F_2$.
   The accept states of N are all the accept states of N_1 and N_2. That way N accepts if either N_1 accepts or N_2 accepts.

4. Define δ so that for any $q \in Q$ and any $a \in \Sigma_\varepsilon$,

$$\delta(q, a) = \begin{cases} \delta_1(q, a) & q \in Q_1 \\ \delta_2(q, a) & q \in Q_2 \\ \{q_1, q_2\} & q = q_0 \text{ and } a = \varepsilon \\ \emptyset & q = q_0 \text{ and } a \neq \varepsilon. \end{cases}$$

Now we can prove closure under concatenation. Recall that earlier, without nondeterminism, completing the proof would have been difficult.

THEOREM 1.23

The class of regular languages is closed under the concatenation operation.

PROOF IDEA   We have regular languages A_1 and A_2 and want to prove that $A_1 \circ A_2$ is regular. The idea is to take two NFAs, N_1 and N_2 for A_1 and A_2, and combine them into a new NFA N as we did for the case of union, but this time in a different way, as shown in Figure 1.25.

Assign N's start state to be the start state of N_1. The accept states of N_1 have additional ε arrows that nondeterministically allow branching to N_2 whenever N_1 is in an accept state, signifying that it has found an initial piece of the input that constitutes a string in A_1. The accept states of N are the accept states of N_2 only. Therefore it accepts when the input can be split into two parts, the first accepted by N_1 and the second by N_2. We can think of N as nondeterministically guessing where to make the split.

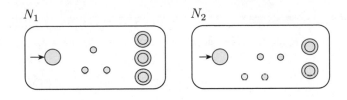

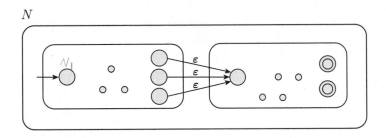

FIGURE   1.25
Construction of N to recognize $A_1 \circ A_2$

PROOF

Let $N_1 = (Q_1, \Sigma, \delta_1, q_1, F_1)$ recognize A_1, and
$\quad N_2 = (Q_2, \Sigma, \delta_2, q_2, F_2)$ recognize A_2.

Construct $N = (Q, \Sigma, \delta, q_1, F_2)$ to recognize $A_1 \circ A_2$.

1. $Q = Q_1 \cup Q_2$.
    The states of N are all the states of N_1 and N_2.

2. The state q_1 is the same as the start state of N_1.

3. The accept states F_2 are the same as the accept states of N_2.

4. Define δ so that for any $q \in Q$ and any $a \in \Sigma_\varepsilon$,

$$
\delta(q, a) = \begin{cases}
\delta_1(q, a) & q \in Q_1 \text{ and } q \notin F_1 \\
\delta_1(q, a) & q \in F_1 \text{ and } a \neq \varepsilon \\
\delta_1(q, a) \cup \{q_2\} & q \subset F_1 \text{ and } a = \varepsilon \\
\delta_2(q, a) & q \in Q_2.
\end{cases}
$$

THEOREM **1.24** ···

The class of regular languages is closed under the star operation.

···

PROOF IDEA   We have a regular language A_1 and want to prove that A_1^* also is regular. We take an NFA N_1 for A_1 and modify it to recognize A_1^*, as shown in the following figure. The resulting NFA N will accept its input whenever it can be broken into several pieces and N_1 accepts each piece.

We can construct N like N_1 with additional ε arrows returning to the start state from the accept state. This way, when processing gets to the end of a piece that N_1 accepts, the machine N has the option of jumping back to the start state to try to read in another piece that N_1 accepts. In addition we must modify N so that it accepts ε, which always is a member of A_1^*. One (slightly bad) idea is simply to add the start state to the set of accept states. This approach certainly adds ε to the recognized language, but it may also add other, undesired strings. Exercise 1.11 asks for an example of the failure of this idea. The way to fix this problem is to add a new start state, which also is an accept state, and which has an ε arrow to the old start state. This solution has the desired effect of adding ε to the language without adding anything else.

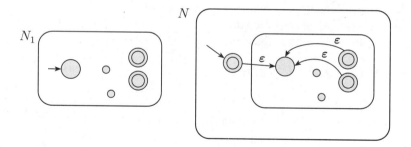

FIGURE **1.26**
Construction of N to recognize A^*

PROOF   Let $N_1 = (Q_1, \Sigma, \delta_1, q_1, F_1)$ recognize A_1.
Construct $N = (Q, \Sigma, \delta, q_0, F)$ to recognize A_1^*.

1. $Q = \{q_0\} \cup Q_1$.
   The states of N are the states of N_1 plus a new start state.
2. The state q_0 is the new start state.
3. $F = \{q_0\} \cup F_1$.
   The accept states are the old accept states plus the new start state.

4. Define δ so that for any $q \in Q$ and any $a \in \Sigma_\varepsilon$,

$$\delta(q,a) = \begin{cases} \delta_1(q,a) & q \in Q_1 \text{ and } q \notin F_1 \\ \delta_1(q,a) & q \in F_1 \text{ and } a \neq \varepsilon \\ \delta_1(q,a) \cup \{q_1\} & q \in F_1 \text{ and } a = \varepsilon \\ \{q_1\} & q = q_0 \text{ and } a = \varepsilon \\ \emptyset & q = q_0 \text{ and } a \neq \varepsilon. \end{cases}$$

1.3

REGULAR EXPRESSIONS

In arithmetic, we can use the operations $+$ and $\times$ to build up expressions such as

$$(5 + 3) \times 4$$

Similarly, we can use the regular operations to build up expressions describing languages, which are called *regular expressions*. An example is:

$$(0 \cup 1)0^*.$$

The value of the arithmetic expression is the number 32. The value of a regular expression is a language. In this case the value is the language consisting of all strings starting with a 0 or a 1 followed by any number of 0s. We get this result by dissecting the expression into its parts. First, the symbols 0 and 1 are shorthand for the sets $\{0\}$ and $\{1\}$. So $(0 \cup 1)$ means $(\{0\} \cup \{1\})$. The value of this part is the language $\{0,1\}$. The part 0^* means $\{0\}^*$, and its value is the language consisting of all strings containing any number of 0s. Second, like the $\times$ symbol in algebra, the concatenation symbol $\circ$ often is implicit in regular expressions. Thus $(0 \cup 1)0^*$ actually is shorthand for $(0 \cup 1) \circ 0^*$. The concatenation attaches the strings from the two parts to obtain the value of the entire expression.

Regular expressions have an important role in computer science applications. In applications involving text, users may want to search for strings that satisfy certain patterns. Regular expressions provide a powerful method for describing such patterns. Utilities such as AWK and GREP in UNIX, modern programming languages such as PERL, and text editors all provide mechanisms for the description of patterns using regular expressions.

EXAMPLE **1.25**

Another example of a regular expression is

$$(0 \cup 1)^*$$

It starts with the language $(0 \cup 1)$ and applies the $*$ operation. The value of this expression is the language consisting of all possible strings of 0s and 1s. If $\Sigma = \{0,1\}$, we can write Σ as shorthand for the regular expression $(0 \cup 1)$. More generally, if Σ is any alphabet, the regular expression Σ describes the language consisting of all strings of length 1 over this alphabet, and Σ^* describes the language consisting of all strings over that alphabet. Similarly $\Sigma^* 1$ is the language that contains all strings that end in a 1. The language $(0\Sigma^*) \cup (\Sigma^* 1)$ consists of all strings that either start with a 0 or end with a 1. ∎

In arithmetic, we say that $\times$ has precedence over $+$ to mean that, when there is a choice, we do the $\times$ operation first. Thus in $2 + 3 \times 4$ the 3×4 is done before the addition. To have the addition done first we must add parentheses to obtain $(2 + 3) \times 4$. In regular expressions, the star operation is done first, followed by concatenation, and finally union, unless parentheses are used to change the usual order.

FORMAL DEFINITION OF A REGULAR EXPRESSION

Say that R is a ***regular expression*** if R is

1. a for some a in the alphabet Σ,
2. ε,
3. $\emptyset$,
4. $(R_1 \cup R_2)$, where R_1 and R_2 are regular expressions,
5. $(R_1 \circ R_2)$, where R_1 and R_2 are regular expressions, or
6. (R_1^*), where R_1 is a regular expression.

In items 1 and 2, the regular expressions a and ε represent the languages $\{a\}$ and $\{\varepsilon\}$, respectively. In item 3, the regular expression $\emptyset$ represents the empty language. In items 4, 5, and 6, the expressions represent the languages obtained by taking the union or concatenation of the languages R_1 and R_2, or the star of the language R_1, respectively.

Don't confuse the regular expressions ε and $\emptyset$. The expression ε represents the language containing a single string, namely, the empty string, whereas $\emptyset$ represents the language that doesn't contain any strings.

Seemingly, we are in danger of defining the notion of regular expression in terms of itself. If true, we would have a ***circular definition***, which would be invalid. However, R_1 and R_2 always are smaller than R. Thus we actually are defining regular expressions in terms of smaller regular expressions and thereby avoiding circularity. A definition of this type is called an ***inductive definition***.

Parentheses in an expression may be omitted. If they are, evaluation is done in the precedence order: star, then concatenation, then union.

When we want to make clear a distinction between a regular expression R and the language that it describes, we write $L(R)$ to be the language of R.

EXAMPLE **1.27** ....

In the following examples we assume that the alphabet Σ is $\{0,1\}$.

1. $0^*10^* = \{w|\ w \text{ has exactly a single 1}\}$.
2. $\Sigma^*1\Sigma^* = \{w|\ w \text{ has at least one 1}\}$.
3. $\Sigma^*001\Sigma^* = \{w|\ w \text{ contains the string 001 as a substring}\}$.
4. $(\Sigma\Sigma)^* = \{w|\ w \text{ is a string of even length}\}$.[5]
5. $(\Sigma\Sigma\Sigma)^* = \{w|\ \text{the length of } w \text{ is a multiple of three}\}$.
6. $01 \cup 10 = \{01, 10\}$.
7. $0\Sigma^*0 \cup 1\Sigma^*1 \cup 0 \cup 1 = \{w|\ w \text{ starts and ends with the same symbol}\}$.
8. $(0 \cup \varepsilon)1^* = 01^* \cup 1^*$.
   The expression $0 \cup \varepsilon$ describes the language $\{0, \varepsilon\}$, so the concatenation operation adds either 0 or ε before every string in 1^*.
9. $(0 \cup \varepsilon)(1 \cup \varepsilon) = \{\varepsilon, 0, 1, 01\}$.
10. $1^*\emptyset = \emptyset$.
    Concatenating the empty set to any set yields the empty set.
11. $\emptyset^* = \{\varepsilon\}$.
    The star operation puts together any number of strings from the language to get a string in the result. If the language is empty, the star operation can put together 0 strings, giving only the empty string.

If we let R be any regular expression, we have the following identities. They are good tests of whether you understand the definition.

$R \cup \emptyset = R$.
Adding the empty language to any other language will not change it.

$R \circ \varepsilon = R$.
Adding the empty string to any string will not change it.

----

[5]The ***length*** of a string is the number of symbols that it contains.

However, exchanging $\emptyset$ and ε in the preceding identities may cause the equalities to fail.

$R \cup \varepsilon$ may not equal R.
For example, if $R = 0$, then $L(R) = \{0\}$ but $L(R \cup \varepsilon) = \{0, \varepsilon\}$.

$R \circ \emptyset$ may not equal R.
For example, if $R = 0$, then $L(R) = \{0\}$ but $L(R \circ \emptyset) = \emptyset$.

Regular expressions are useful tools in the design of compilers for programming languages. Elemental objects in a programming language, called **tokens**, such as the variable names and constants, may be described with regular expressions. For example, a numerical constant that may include a fractional part and/or a sign may be described as a member of the language

$$\{+, -, \varepsilon\} \, (D D^* \cup D D^* . D^* \cup D^* . D D^*),$$

where $D = \{0, 1, 2, 3, 4, 5, 6, 7, 8, 9\}$ is the alphabet of decimal digits. Examples of generated strings are: 72, 3.14159, +7., and -.01 .

Once the syntax of the tokens of the programming language have been described with regular expressions, automatic systems can generate the **lexical analyzer**, the part of a compiler that initially processes the input program.

EQUIVALENCE WITH FINITE AUTOMATA

Regular expressions and finite automata are equivalent in their descriptive power. This fact is rather remarkable, because finite automata and regular expressions superficially appear to be rather different. However, any regular expression can be converted into a finite automaton that recognizes the language it describes, and vice versa. Recall that a regular language is one that is recognized by some finite automaton.

THEOREM 1.28 ....

A language is regular if and only if some regular expression describes it.

This theorem has two directions. We state and prove each direction as a separate lemma.

LEMMA 1.29 ....

If a language is described by a regular expression, then it is regular.

....

PROOF IDEA Say that we have a regular expression R describing some language A. We show how to convert R into an NFA recognizing A. By Corollary 1.20, if an NFA recognizes A then A is regular.

PROOF   Let's convert R into an NFA N. We consider the six cases in the formal definition of regular expressions.

1. $R = a$ for some a in Σ. Then $L(R) = \{a\}$, and the following NFA recognizes $L(R)$.

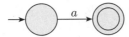

Note that this machine fits the definition of an NFA but not that of a DFA because it has some states with no exiting arrow for each possible input symbol. Of course, we could have presented an equivalent DFA here but an NFA is all we need for now, and it is easier to describe.

Formally, $N = (\{q_1, q_2\}, \Sigma, \delta, q_1, \{q_2\})$, where we describe δ by saying that $\delta(q_1, a) = \{q_2\}$, $\delta(r, b) = \emptyset$ for $r \neq q_1$ or $b \neq a$.

2. $R = \varepsilon$. Then $L(R) = \{\varepsilon\}$, and the following NFA recognizes $L(R)$.

Formally, $N = (\{q_1\}, \Sigma, \delta, q_1, \{q_1\})$, where $\delta(r, b) = \emptyset$ for any r and b.

3. $R = \emptyset$. Then $L(R) = \emptyset$, and the following NFA recognizes $L(R)$.

Formally, $N = (\{q\}, \Sigma, \delta, q, \emptyset)$, where $\delta(r, b) = \emptyset$ for any r and b.

4. $R = R_1 \cup R_2$.
5. $R = R_1 \circ R_2$.
6. $R = R_1^*$.

For the last three cases we use the constructions given in the proofs that the class of regular languages is closed under the regular operations. In other words, we construct the NFA for R from the NFAs for R_1 and R_2 (or just R_1 in case 6) and the appropriate closure construction.

That ends the first part of the proof of Theorem 1.28, giving the forward direction of the if and only if. Before going on to the other direction let's consider some examples whereby we use this procedure to convert a regular expression to an NFA.

EXAMPLE **1.30** ....

We convert the regular expression (ab ∪ a)* to an NFA in a sequence of stages. We build up from the smallest subexpressions to larger subexpressions until we have an NFA for the original expression, as shown in the following diagram. Note that this procedure generally doesn't give the NFA with the fewest states. In this example, the procedure gives an NFA with eight states, but the smallest equivalent NFA has only two states. Can you find it?

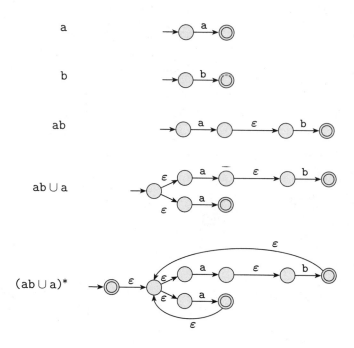

FIGURE **1.27**
Building an NFA from the regular expression (ab ∪ a)*

EXAMPLE   **1.31**

In this second example we convert the regular expression $(a \cup b)^*aba$ to an NFA. A few of the minor steps are not shown.

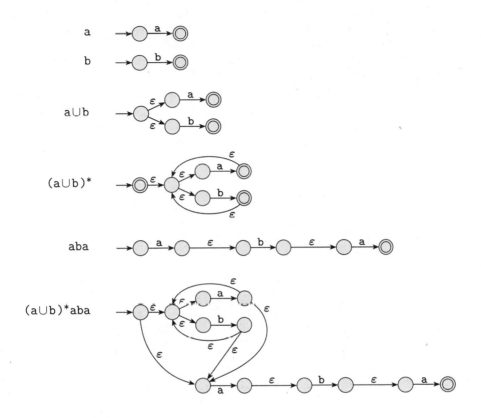

FIGURE   **1.28**
Building an NFA from the regular expression $(0 \cup 1)^*010$

Now let's turn to the other direction of the proof of Theorem 1.28.

If a language is regular, then it is described by a regular expression.

PROOF IDEA   We need to show that, if a language A is regular, a regular expression describes it. Because A is regular, it is accepted by a DFA. We describe a procedure for converting DFAs into equivalent regular expressions.

We break this procedure into two parts, using a new type of finite automaton called a ***generalized nondeterministic finite automaton***, GNFA. First we show how to convert DFAs into GNFAs and then GNFAs into regular expressions.

Generalized nondeterministic finite automata are simply nondeterministic finite automata wherein the transition arrows may have any regular expressions as labels, instead of only members of the alphabet or ε. The GNFA reads blocks of symbols from the input, not necessarily just one symbol at a time as in an ordinary NFA. The GNFA moves along a transition arrow connecting two states by reading a block of symbols from the input, which themselves constitute a string described by the regular expression on that arrow. A GNFA is nondeterministic and so may have several different ways to process the same input string. It accepts its input if its processing can cause the GNFA to be in an accept state at the end of the input. The following figure presents an example of a GNFA.

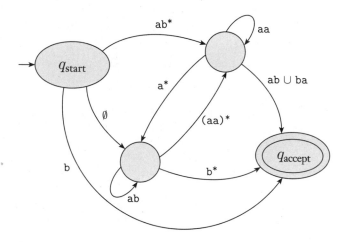

FIGURE **1.29**
A generalized nondeterministic finite automaton

For convenience we require that GNFAs always have a special form that meets the following conditions.

- The start state has transition arrows going to every other state but no arrows coming in from any other state.

- There is only a single accept state, and it has arrows coming in from every other state but no arrows going to any other state. Furthermore, the accept state is not the same as the start state.

- Except for the start and accept states, one arrow goes from every state to every other state and also from each state to itself.

We can easily convert a GNFA into the special form. We simply add a new start state with an ε arrow to the old start state and a new accept state with ε arrows from the old accept states. If any arrows have multiple labels (or if there are multiple arrows going between the same two states in the same direction), we replace each with a single arrow whose label is the union of the previous labels. Finally, we add arrows labeled $\emptyset$ between states that had no arrows. This last step won't change the language recognized because a transition labeled with $\emptyset$ can never be used. From here on we assume that all GNFAs are in the special form.

Now we show how to convert a GNFA into a regular expression. Say that the GNFA has k states. Then, because a GNFA must have a start and an accept state and they must be different from each other, we know that $k \geq 2$. If $k > 2$, we construct an equivalent GNFA form with $k - 1$ states. This step can be repeated on the new GNFA until it is reduced to two states. If $k = 2$, the GNFA has a single arrow that goes from the start state to the accept state. The label of this arrow is the equivalent regular expression. For example, the stages in converting a DFA with three states to an equivalent regular expression are shown in the following figure.

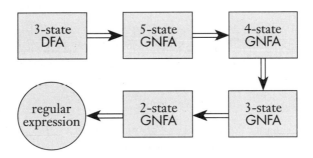

FIGURE   **1.30**
Typical stages in converting a DFA to a regular expression

The crucial step is in constructing an equivalent GNFA with one fewer state when $k > 2$. We do so by selecting a state, ripping it out of the machine, and repairing the remainder so that the same language is still recognized. Any state will do, provided that it is not the start or accept state. We are guaranteed that such a state will exist because $k > 2$. Let's call the removed state q_{rip}.

After removing q_{rip} we repair the machine by altering the regular expressions that label each of the remaining arrows. The new labels compensate for the absence of q_{rip} by adding back the lost computations. The new label going from a state q_i to a state q_j is a regular expression that describes all strings that would take the machine from q_i to q_j either directly or via q_{rip}. We illustrate this approach in the following figure.

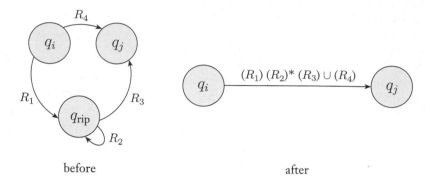

before   after

FIGURE 1.31
Constructing an equivalent GNFA with one fewer state

In the old machine if q_i goes to q_{rip} with an arrow labeled R_1, q_{rip} goes to itself with an arrow labeled R_2, q_{rip} goes to q_j with an arrow labeled R_3, and q_i goes to q_j with an arrow labeled R_4, then in the new machine the arrow from q_i to q_j gets the label

$$(R_1)(R_2)^*(R_3) \cup (R_4).$$

We make this change for each arrow going from any state q_i to any state q_j, including the case where $q_i = q_j$. The new machine recognizes the original language.

PROOF   Let's now carry out this idea formally. First, to facilitate the proof, we formally define the new type of automaton introduced. A GNFA is similar to a nondeterministic finite automaton except for the transition function, which has the form

$$\delta \colon (Q - \{q_{\text{accept}}\}) \times (Q - \{q_{\text{start}}\}) \longrightarrow \mathcal{R}.$$

The symbol $\mathcal{R}$ is the collection of all regular expressions over the alphabet Σ, and q_{start} and q_{accept} are the start and accept states. If $\delta(q_i, q_j) = R$, the arrow from state q_i to state q_j has the regular expression R as its label. The domain of the transition function is $(Q - \{q_{\text{accept}}\}) \times (Q - \{q_{\text{start}}\})$ because an arrow connects every state to every other state, except that no arrows are coming from q_{accept} or going to q_{start}.

DEFINITION   1.33 ....

A *generalized nondeterministic finite automaton*, $(Q, \Sigma, \delta, q_{\text{start}}, q_{\text{accept}})$, is a 5-tuple where

1. Q is the finite set of states,
2. Σ is the input alphabet,
3. $\delta \colon (Q - \{q_{\text{accept}}\}) \times (Q - \{q_{\text{start}}\}) \longrightarrow \mathcal{R}$ is the transition function,
4. q_{start} is the start state, and
5. q_{accept} is the accept state.

A GNFA accepts a string w in Σ^* if $w = w_1 w_2 \cdots w_k$, where each w_i is in Σ^* and a sequence of states $q_0, q_1, \ldots, q_k$ exists such that

1. $q_0 = q_{\text{start}}$ is the start state,
2. $q_k = q_{\text{accept}}$ is the accept state, and
3. for each i, we have $w_i \in L(R_i)$, where $R_i = \delta(q_{i-1}, q_i)$; in other words, R_i is the expression on the arrow from q_{i-1} to q_i.

Returning to the proof of Lemma 1.32, we let M be the DFA for language A. Then we convert M to a GNFA G by adding a new start state and a new accept state and additional transition arrows as necessary. We use the procedure CONVERT(G), which takes a GNFA and returns an equivalent regular expression. This procedure uses *recursion*, which means that it calls itself. An infinite loop is avoided because the procedure calls itself only to process a GNFA that has one fewer state. The case where the GNFA has two states is handled without recursion.

CONVERT(G):

1. Let k be the number of states of G.
2. If $k = 2$, then G must consist of a start state, an accept state, and a single arrow connecting them and labeled with a regular expression R.
   Return the expression R.
3. If $k > 2$, we select any state $q_{\text{rip}} \in Q$ different from q_{start} and q_{accept} and let G' be the GNFA $(Q', \Sigma, \delta', q_{\text{start}}, q_{\text{accept}})$, where

$$Q' = Q - \{q_{\text{rip}}\},$$

   and for any $q_i \in Q' - \{q_{\text{accept}}\}$ and any $q_j \in Q' - \{q_{\text{start}}\}$ let

$$\delta'(q_i, q_j) = (R_1)(R_2)^*(R_3) \cup (R_4),$$

   for $R_1 = \delta(q_i, q_{\text{rip}})$, $R_2 = \delta(q_{\text{rip}}, q_{\text{rip}})$, $R_3 = \delta(q_{\text{rip}}, q_j)$, and $R_4 = \delta(q_i, q_j)$.
4. Compute CONVERT(G') and return this value.

Next we prove that CONVERT returns a correct value.

CLAIM   **1.34**   ···

For any GNFA G, CONVERT(G) is equivalent to G.

We prove this claim by induction on k, the number of states of the GNFA.

Basis: Prove the claim true for $k = 2$ states. If G has only two states, it can have only a single arrow, which goes from the start state to the accept state. The regular expression label on this arrow describes all the strings that allow G to get to the accept state. Hence this expression is equivalent to G.

Induction step: Assume that the claim is true for $k - 1$ states and use this assumption to prove that the claim is true for k states. First we show that G and G' recognize the same language. Suppose that G accepts an input w. Then in an accepting branch of the computation G enters a sequence of states

$$q_{start}, q_1, q_2, q_3, \cdots , q_{accept}.$$

If none of them is the removed state q_{rip}, clearly G' also accepts w. The reason is that each of the new regular expressions labeling the arrows of G' contains the old regular expression as part of a union.

If q_{rip} does appear, removing each run of consecutive q_{rip} states forms an accepting computation for G'. The states q_i and q_j bracketing a run have a new regular expression on the arrow between them that describes all strings taking q_i to q_j via q_{rip} on G. So G' accepts w.

For the other direction, suppose that G' accepts an input w. As each arrow between any two states q_i and q_j in G' describes the collection of strings taking q_i to q_j in G, either directly or via q_{rip}, G must also accept w. Thus G and G' are equivalent.

The induction hypothesis states that when the algorithm calls itself recursively on input G', the result is a regular expression that is equivalent to G' because G' has $k - 1$ states. Hence the regular expression also is equivalent to G, and the algorithm is proved correct.

This concludes the proof of Claim 1.34, Lemma 1.32, and Theorem 1.28.

···

EXAMPLE   **1.35**   ···

In this example we use the preceding algorithm to convert a DFA into a regular expression. We begin with the two-state DFA in Figure 1.32(a).

In (b) we make a four-state GNFA by adding a new start state and a new accept state, called s and a instead of q_{start} and q_{accept} so that we can draw them conveniently. To avoid cluttering up the figure, we do not draw the arrows that are labeled $\emptyset$, even though they are actually present. Note that we replace the label a, b on the self-loop at state 2 on the DFA with the label a∪b at the corresponding point on the GNFA. We do so because the DFA's label represents two transitions, one for a and the other for b, whereas the GNFA may have only a single transition going from 2 to itself.

In (c) we remove state 2, and update the remaining arrow labels. In this case the only label that changes is the one from 1 to a. In (b) it was $\emptyset$, but in (c) it is b(a∪b)*. We obtain this result by following step 3 of the CONVERT procedure. State q_i is state 1, state q_j is a, and q_{rip} is 2, so $R_1 = \text{b}$, $R_2 = \text{a} \cup \text{b}$, $R_3 = \varepsilon$, and $R_4 = \emptyset$. Therefore the new label on the arrow from 1 to a is $(\text{b})(\text{a} \cup \text{b})^*(\varepsilon) \cup \emptyset$. We simplify this regular expression to b(a ∪ b)*.

In (d) we remove state 1 from (c) and follow the same procedure. Because only the start and accept states remain, the label on the arrow joining them is the regular expression that is equivalent to the original DFA.

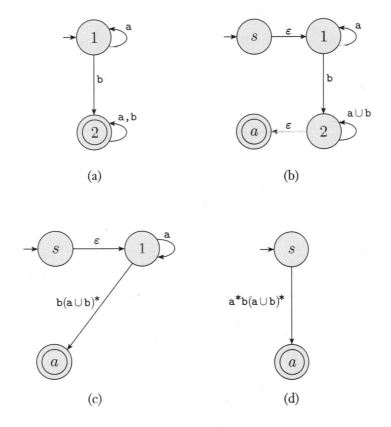

FIGURE **1.32**
Converting a two-state DFA to an equivalent regular expression

EXAMPLE   **1.36**   ···

In this example we begin with a three-state DFA. The steps in the conversion appear in the following figure.

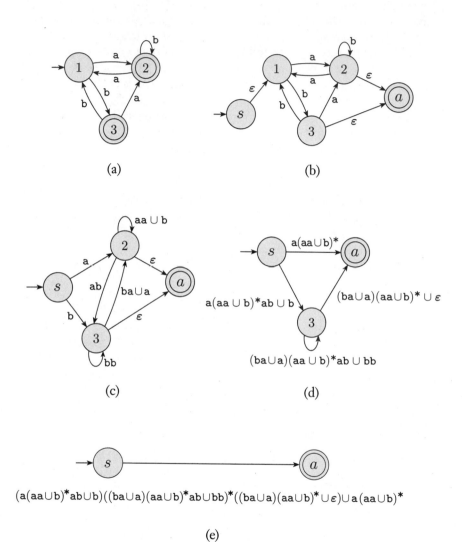

(a)

(b)

(c)

(d)

$(a(aa\cup b)^*ab\cup b)((ba\cup a)(aa\cup b)^*ab\cup bb)^*((ba\cup a)(aa\cup b)^*\cup\varepsilon)\cup a(aa\cup b)^*$

(e)

FIGURE   **1.33**
Converting a three state DFA to an equivalent regular expression

1.4 ■

NONREGULAR LANGUAGES

To understand the power of finite automata you must also understand their limitations. In this section we show how to prove that certain languages cannot be recognized by any finite automaton.

Let's take the language $B = \{0^n1^n|\ n \geq 0\}$. If we attempt to find a DFA that recognizes B, we discover that the machine seems to need to remember how many 0s have been seen so far as it reads the input. Because the number of 0s isn't limited, the machine will have to keep track of an unlimited number of possibilities. But it cannot do so with any finite number of states.

Next, we present a method for proving that languages such as B are not regular. Doesn't the argument already given prove nonregularity, because the number of 0s is unlimited? It does not. Just because the language appears to require unbounded memory doesn't mean that it is necessarily so. It does happen to be true for the language B, but other languages seem to require an unlimited number of possibilities, yet actually are regular. For example, consider two languages over the alphabet $\Sigma = \{0,1\}$:

$C = \{w|\ w$ has an equal number of 0s and 1s$\}$, and

$D = \{w|\ w$ has an equal number of occurrences of 01 and 10 as substrings$\}$.

At first glance an recognizing machine appears to need to count in each case, and therefore neither language appears to be regular. As expected, C is not regular, but surprisingly D is regular![6] Thus our intuition can sometimes lead us astray, which is why we need mathematical proofs for certainty. In this section we show how to prove that certain languages are not regular.

THE PUMPING LEMMA FOR REGULAR LANGUAGES

Our technique for proving nonregularity stems from a theorem about regular languages, traditionally called the ***pumping lemma***. This theorem states that all regular languages have a special property. If we can show that a language does not have this property, we are guaranteed that it is not regular. The property states that all strings in the language can be "pumped" if they are longer than a certain special value, called the ***pumping length***. That means each such string contains a section that can be repeated any number of times with the resulting string remaining in the language.

---

[6]See Problem 1.41.

THEOREM   **1.37**   ....

Pumping lemma   If A is a regular language, then there is a number p (the pumping length) where, if s is any string in A of length at least p, then s may be divided into three pieces, $s = xyz$, satisfying the following conditions:

> **1.** for each $i \geq 0$, $xy^i z \in A$,
>
> **2.** $|y| > 0$, and
>
> **3.** $|xy| \leq p$.

Recall the notation where $|s|$ represents the length of string s, y^i means that i copies of y are concatenated together, and y^0 equals ε.

When s is divided into xyz, either x or z may be ε, but condition 2 says that $y \neq \varepsilon$. Observe that without condition 2 the theorem would be trivially true. Condition 3 states that the pieces x and y together have length at most p. It is an extra technical condition that we occasionally find useful when proving certain languages to be nonregular. See Example 1.39 for an application of condition 3.

....

PROOF IDEA   Let $M = (Q, \Sigma, \delta, q_1, F)$ be a DFA that recognizes A. We assign the pumping length p to be the number of states of M. We show that any string s in A of length at least p may be broken into the three pieces xyz satisfying our three conditions. What if no strings in A are of length at least p? Then our task is even easier because the theorem becomes *vacuously* true: Obviously the three conditions hold for all strings of length at least p if there aren't any such strings.

If s in A has length at least p, consider the sequence of states that M goes through when computing with input s. It starts with q_1 the start state, then goes to, say, q_3, then, say, q_{20}, then q_9, and so on, until it reaches the end of s in state q_{13}. With s in A, we know that M accepts s, so q_{13} is an accept state.

If we let n be the length of s, the sequence of states $q_1, q_3, q_{20}, q_9, \ldots, q_{13}$ has length $n + 1$. Because n is at least p, we know that $n + 1$ is greater than p, the number of states of M. Therefore the sequence must contain a repeated state. This result is an example of the **_pigeonhole principle_**, a fancy name for the rather obvious fact that if p pigeons are placed into fewer than p holes, some hole has to have more than one pigeon in it.

The following figure shows the string s and the sequence of states that M goes through when processing s. State q_9 is the one that repeats.

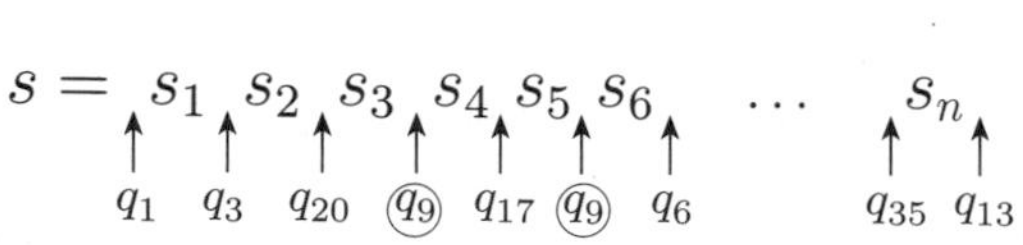

$$s = \underset{q_1}{\uparrow} s_1 \underset{q_3}{\uparrow} s_2 \underset{q_{20}}{\uparrow} s_3 \underset{\textcircled{q_9}}{\uparrow} s_4 \underset{q_{17}}{\uparrow} s_5 \underset{\textcircled{q_9}}{\uparrow} s_6 \underset{q_6}{\uparrow} \quad \cdots \quad \underset{q_{35}}{\uparrow} s_n \underset{q_{13}}{\uparrow}$$

FIGURE   **1.34**
Example showing state q_9 repeating when M reads s

We now divide s into the three pieces x, y, and z. Piece x is the part of s appearing before q_9, piece y is the part between the two appearances of q_9, and piece z is the remaining part of s, coming after the second occurrence of q_9. So x takes M from the state q_1 to q_9, y takes M from q_9 back to q_9 and z takes M from q_9 to the accept state q_{13}, as shown in the following figure.

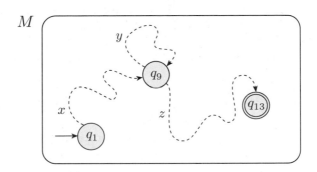

FIGURE   **1.35**
Example showing how the strings x, y, and z affect M

Let's see why this division of s satisfies the three conditions. Suppose that we run M on input $xyyz$. We know that x takes M from q_1 to q_9, and then the first y takes it from q_9 back to q_9, as does the second y, and then z takes it to q_{13}. With q_{13} being an accept state, M accepts input $xyyz$. Similarly, it will accept $xy^i z$ for any $i > 0$. For the case $i = 0$, $xy^i z = xz$, which is accepted for similar reasons. That establishes condition 1.

Checking condition 2, we see that $|y| > 0$, as it was the part of s that occurred between two different occurrences of state q_9.

In order to get condition 3, we make sure that q_9 is the first repetition in the sequence. By the pigeonhole principle, the first $p+1$ states in the sequence must contain a repetition. Therefore $|xy| \leq p$.

PROOF   Let $M = (Q, \Sigma, \delta, q_1, F)$ be a DFA recognizing A and p be the number of states of M.

Let $s = s_1 s_2 \cdots s_n$ be a string in A of length n, where $n \geq p$. Let $r_1, \ldots, r_{n+1}$ be the sequence of states that M enters while processing s, so $r_{i+1} = \delta(r_i, s_i)$ for $1 \leq i \leq n$. This sequence has length $n+1$, which is at least $p+1$. Among the first $p + 1$ elements in the sequence, two must be the same state, by the pigeonhole principle. We call the first of these r_j and the second r_l. Because r_l occurs among the first $p + 1$ places in a sequence starting at r_1, we have $l \leq p + 1$. Now let $x = s_1 \cdots s_{j-1}$, $y = s_j \cdots s_{p-1}$, and $z = s_l \cdots s_n$.

As x takes M from r_1 to r_j, y takes M from r_j to r_j, and z takes M from r_j to r_{n+1}, which is an accept state, M must accept $xy^i z$ for $i \geq 0$. We know that $j \neq p$, so $|y| > 0$; and $l \leq p+1$, so $|xy| \leq p$. Thus we have satisfied all conditions of the pumping lemma.

To use the pumping lemma to prove that a language B is not regular, first assume that B is regular in order to obtain a contradiction. Then use the pumping lemma to guarantee the existence of of a pumping length p such that all strings of length p or greater in B can be pumped. Next, find a string s in B that has length p or greater but that cannot be pumped. Finally, demonstrate that s cannot be pumped by considering all ways of dividing s into x, y, and z (taking condition 3 of the pumping lemma into account if convenient) and, for each such division, finding a value i where $xy^iz \notin B$. This final step often involves grouping the various ways of dividing s into several cases and analyzing them individually. The existence of s contradicts the pumping lemma if B were regular. Hence B cannot be regular.

Finding s sometimes takes a bit of creative thinking. You may need to hunt through several candidates for s before you discover one that works. Try members of B that seem to exhibit the "essence" of B's nonregularity. We further discuss the task of finding s in some of the following examples.

EXAMPLE 1.38

Let B be the language $\{0^n1^n \mid n \geq 0\}$. We use the pumping lemma to prove that B is not regular. The proof is by contradiction.

Assume to the contrary that B is regular. Let p be the pumping length given by the pumping lemma. Choose s to be the string 0^p1^p. Because s is a member of B and s has length more than p, the pumping lemma guarantees that s can be split into three pieces, $s = xyz$, where for any $i \geq 0$ the string xy^iz is in B. We consider three cases to show that this result is impossible.

1. The string y consists only of 0s. In this case the string $xyyz$ has more 0s than 1s and so is not a member of B, violating condition 1 of the pumping lemma. This case is a contradiction.

2. The string y consists only of 1s. This case also gives a contradiction.

3. The string y consists of both 0s and 1s. In this case the string $xyyz$ may have the same number of 0s and 1s, but they will be out of order with some 1s before 0s. Hence it is not a member of B, which is a contradiction.

Thus a contradiction is unavoidable if we make the assumption that B is regular, so B is not regular.

In this example, finding the string s was easy, because any string in B of length p or more would work. In the next two examples some choices for s do not work, so additional care is required.

EXAMPLE 1.39

Let $C = \{w \mid w$ has an equal number of 0s and 1s$\}$. We use the pumping lemma to prove that C is not regular. The proof is by contradiction.

Assume to the contrary that C is regular. Let p be the pumping length given by the pumping lemma. As in Example 1.38, let s be the string $0^p 1^p$. With s being a member of C and having length more than p, the pumping lemma guarantees that s can be split into three pieces, $s = xyz$, where for any $i \geq 0$ the string $xy^i z$ is in C. We would like to show that this outcome is impossible. But wait, it *is* possible! If we let x and z be the empty string and y be the string $0^p 1^p$, then $xy^i z$ always has an equal number of 0s and 1s and hence is in C. So it *seems* that s can be pumped.

Here condition 3 in the pumping lemma is useful. It stipulates that when pumping s it must be divided so that $|xy| \leq p$. That restriction on the way that s may be divided makes it easier to show that the string $s = 0^p 1^p$ we selected cannot be pumped. If $|xy| \leq p$, then y must consist only of 0s, so $xyyz \notin C$. Therefore s cannot be pumped. That gives us the desired contradiction.[7]

Selecting the string s in this example required more care than in Example 1.38. If we had chosen $s = (01)^p$ instead, we would have run into trouble because we need a string that *cannot* be pumped and that string *can* be pumped, even taking condition 3 into account. Can you see how to pump it? One way to do so sets $x = \varepsilon$, $y = 01$, and $z = (01)^{p-1}$. Then $xy^i z \in C$ for every value of i. If you fail on your first attempt to find a string that cannot be pumped, don't despair. Try another one!

An alternative method of proving that C is nonregular follows from our knowledge that B is nonregular. If C were regular, $C \cap 0^* 1^*$ also would be regular. The reasons are that the language $0^* 1^*$ is regular and that the class of regular languages is closed under intersection (proved in the footnote on page 46). But $C \cap 0^* 1^*$ equals B, and we know that B is nonregular from Example 1.38. ∎

EXAMPLE **1.40** ....

Let $F = \{ww | \ w \in \{0,1\}^*\}$. We show that F is nonregular using the pumping lemma.

Assume to the contrary that F is regular. Let p be the pumping length given by the pumping lemma. Let s be the string $0^p 1 0^p 1$. Because s is a member of F and s has length more than p, the pumping lemma guarantees that s can be split into three pieces, $s = xyz$, satisfying the three conditions of the lemma. We show that this outcome is impossible.

Condition 3 is once again crucial, because without it we could pump s if we let x and z be the empty string. With condition 3 the proof follows because y must consist only of 0s, so $xyyz \notin F$.

Observe that we chose $s = 0^p 1 0^p 1$ to be a string that exhibits the "essence" of the nonregularity of F, as opposed to, say, the string $0^p 0^p$. Even though $0^p 0^p$ is a member of F, it fails to demonstrate a contradiction because it can be pumped. ∎

---

[7]We could have used condition 3 in Example 1.38, as well, to simplify its proof.

EXAMPLE **1.41** ....

Here we demonstrate a nonregular unary language. Let $D = \{1^{n^2} | n \geq 0\}$. In other words, D contains all strings of 1s whose length is a perfect square. We use the pumping lemma to prove that D is not regular. The proof is by contradiction.

Assume to the contrary that D is regular. Let p be the pumping length given by the pumping lemma. Let s be the string 1^{p^2}. Because s is a member of D and s has length at least p, the pumping lemma guarantees that s can be split into three pieces, $s = xyz$, where for any $i \geq 0$ the string xy^iz is in D. As in the preceding examples, we show that this outcome is impossible. Doing so in this case requires a little thought about the sequence of perfect squares:

$$0, 1, 4, 9, 16, 25, 36, 49, \ldots$$

Note the growing gap between successive members of this sequence. Large members of this sequence cannot be near each other.

Now consider the two strings xy^iz and $xy^{i+1}z$. These strings differ from each other by a single of repetition of y, and consequently their lengths differ by the length of y. If we choose i very large, the lengths of xy^iz and $xy^{i+1}z$ cannot both be perfect squares because they are too close together. Thus xy^iz and $xy^{i+1}z$ cannot both be in D, a contradiction.

To turn this idea into a proof, we calculate a value of i that gives the contradiction. If $m = n^2$ is a perfect square, the difference between it and the next higher perfect square $(n+1)^2$ is

$$(n+1)^2 - n^2 = n^2 + 2n + 1 - n^2$$
$$= 2n + 1$$
$$= 2\sqrt{m} + 1.$$

The pumping lemma states that both $|xy^iz|$ and $|xy^{i+1}z|$ are perfect squares for any i. But, by letting $|xy^iz|$ be m as above, we see that they both *cannot* be perfect squares if $|y| < 2\sqrt{|xy^iz|} + 1$ because they would be too close together.

Calculating the value for i that leads to a contradiction is now easy. Observe that $|y| \leq |s| = p^2$. Let $i = p^4$; then

$$|y| \leq p^2 = \sqrt{p^4}$$
$$< 2\sqrt{p^4} + 1$$
$$\leq 2\sqrt{|xy^iz|} + 1.$$

EXAMPLE **1.42** ....

Sometimes "pumping down" is useful when we apply the pumping lemma. We use the pumping lemma to show that $E = \{0^i1^j | i > j\}$ is not regular. The proof is by contradiction.

Assume that E is regular. Let p be the pumping length for E given by the pumping lemma. Let $s = 0^{p+1}1^p$. Then s can be split into xyz, satisfying the conditions of the pumping lemma. By condition 3, y consists only of 0s. Let's examine the string $xyyz$ to see whether it can be in E. Adding an extra copy of y increases the number of 0s. But, E contains all strings in 0^*1^* that have more 0s than 1s, so increasing the number of 0s will still give a string in E. No contradiction occurs. We need to try something else.

The pumping lemma states that $xy^iz \in E$ even when $i = 0$, so let's consider the string $xy^0z = xz$. Removing string y decreases the number of 0s in s. Recall that s has just one more 0 than 1. Therefore xz cannot not have more 0s than 1s, so it cannot be a member of E. Thus we obtain a contradiction.

EXERCISES

1.1 The following are the state diagrams of two DFAs, M_1 and M_2. Answer the following questions about these machines.

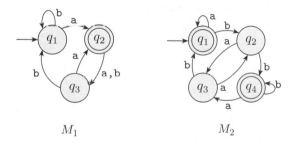

$$M_1 \qquad\qquad\qquad M_2$$

    a. What is the start state of M_1?

    b. What is the set of accept states of M_1?

    c. What is the start state of M_2?

    d. What is the set of accept states of M_2?

    e. What sequence of states does M_1 go through on input aabb?

    f. Does M_1 accept the string aabb?

    g. Does M_2 accept the string ε?

1.2 Give the formal description of the machines M_1 and M_2 pictured in Exercise 1.1.

1.3 The formal description of a DFA M is $(\{q_1, q_2, q_3, q_4, q_5\}, \{u, d\}, \delta, q_3, \{q_3\})$, where δ is given by the following table. Give the state diagram of this machine.

	u	d
q_1	q_1	q_2
q_2	q_1	q_3
q_3	q_2	q_4
q_4	q_3	q_5
q_5	q_4	q_5

1.4 Give state diagrams of DFAs recognizing the following languages. In all cases the alphabet is $\{0,1\}$.

    a. $\{w|\ w$ begins with a 1 and ends with a 0$\}$.

    b. $\{w|\ w$ contains at least three 1s$\}$.

    c. $\{w|\ w$ contains the substring 0101, i.e., $w = x0101y$ for some x and $y\}$.

    d. $\{w|\ w$ has length at least 3 and its third symbol is a 0$\}$.

    e. $\{w|\ w$ starts with 0 and has odd length, or starts with 1 and has even length$\}$.

    f. $\{w|\ w$ doesn't contain the substring 110$\}$.

    g. $\{w|$ the length of w is at most 5$\}$.

    h. $\{w|\ w$ is any string except 11 and 111$\}$.

    i. $\{w|$ every odd position of w is a 1$\}$.

    j. $\{w|\ w$ contains at least two 0s and at most one 1$\}$.

    k. $\{\varepsilon, 0\}$.

    l. $\{w|\ w$ contains an even number of 0s, or exactly two 1s$\}$.

    m. The empty set.

    n. All strings except the empty string.

1.5 Give NFAs with the specified number of states recognizing each the following languages.

    a. The language $\{w|\ w$ ends with 00$\}$ with three states.

    b. The language of Exercise 1.4c with five states.

    c. The language of Exercise 1.4l with six states.

    d. The language $\{0\}$ with two states.

    e. The language $0^*1^*0^*0$ with three states.

    f. The language $\{\varepsilon\}$ with one state.

    g. The language 0^* with one state.

1.6 Use the construction given in the proof of Theorem 1.22 to give the state diagrams of NFAs recognizing the union of the languages described in

    a. Exercises 1.4a and 1.4b.

    b. Exercises 1.4c and 1.4f.

1.7 Use the construction given in the proof of Theorem 1.23 to give the state diagrams of NFAs recognizing the concatenation of the languages described in

    a. Exercises 1.4g and 1.4i.

    b. Exercises 1.4b and 1.4m.

1.8 Use the construction given in the proof of Theorem 1.24 to give the state diagrams of NFAs recognizing the star of the language described in

    a. Exercise 1.4b.

    b. Exercise 1.4j.

    c. Exercise 1.4m.

1.9 Prove that every NFA can be converted to an equivalent one that has a single accept state.

1.10   **a.** Show that, if M is a DFA that recognizes language B, swapping the accept and non-accept states in M yields a new DFA that recognizes the complement of B. Conclude that the class of regular languages is closed under complement.

    b. Show by giving an example that, if M is an NFA that recognizes language C, swapping the accept and non-accept states in M doesn't necessarily yield a new NFA that recognizes the complement of C. Is the class of languages recognized by NFAs closed under complement? Explain your answer.

1.11 Give a counterexample to show that the following construction fails to prove Theorem 1.24, the closure of the class of regular languages under the star operation.[8] Let $N_1 = (Q_1, \Sigma, \delta_1, q_1, F_1)$ recognize A_1. Construct $N = (Q_1, \Sigma, \delta, q_1, F)$ as follows. N is supposed to recognize A_1^*.

    a. The states of N are the states of N_1.

    b. The start state of N is the same as the start state of N_1.

    c. $F = \{q_1\} \cup F_1$.

        The accept states F are the old accept states plus its start state.

    d. Define δ so that for any $q \in Q$ and any $a \in \Sigma_\varepsilon$,

$$\delta(q, a) = \begin{cases} \delta_1(q, a) & q \notin F_1 \text{ or } a \neq \varepsilon \\ \delta_1(q, a) \cup \{q_1\} & q \in F_1 \text{ and } a = \varepsilon. \end{cases}$$

(Suggestion: Convert this formal construction to a picture, as in Figure 1.26.)

1.12 Use the construction given in Theorem 1.19 to convert the following two nondeterministic finite automata to equivalent deterministic finite automata.

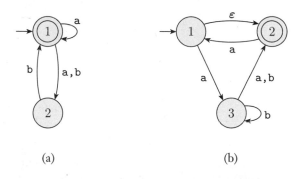

(a)   (b)

---

[8]In other words, you must present a finite automaton, N_1, for which the constructed automaton N does not recognize the star of N_1's language.

1.13 Give regular expressions generating the languages of Exercise 1.4.

1.14 Use the procedure described in Lemma 1.29 to convert the following regular expressions to nondeterministic finite automata.

    a. $(0 \cup 1)^*000(0 \cup 1)^*$

    b. $(((00)^*(11)) \cup 01)^*$

    c. $\emptyset^*$

1.15 For each of the following languages, give two strings that are members and two strings that are *not* members—a total of four strings for each part. Assume the alphabet $\Sigma = \{a,b\}$ in all parts.

    a. a^*b^*.

    b. $a(ba)^*b$.

    c. $a^* \cup b^*$.

    d. $(aaa)^*$.

    e. $\Sigma^*a\Sigma^*b\Sigma^*a\Sigma^*$.

    f. $aba \cup bab$.

    g. $(\varepsilon \cup a)b$.

    h. $(a \cup ba \cup bb)\Sigma^*$.

1.16 Use the procedure described in Lemma 1.32 to convert the following finite automata to regular expressions.

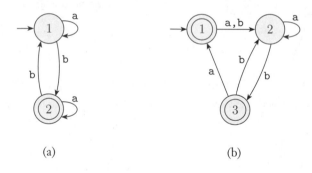

        (a)   (b)

1.17 Use the pumping lemma to show that the following languages are not regular.

    a. $A_1 = \{0^n1^n2^n \mid n \geq 0\}$.

    b. $A_2 = \{ww \mid w \in \{a,b\}^*\}$.

    c. $A_3 = \{a^{2^n} \mid n \geq 0\}$. (Here, a^{2^n} means a string of 2^n a's.)

1.18 Describe the error in the following "proof" that 0^*1^* is not a regular language. (An error must exist because 0^*1^* *is* regular.) The proof is by contradiction. Assume that 0^*1^* is regular. Let p be the pumping length for 0^*1^* given by the pumping lemma. Choose s to be the string 0^p1^p. You know that s is a member of 0^*1^*, but Example 1.38 shows that s cannot be pumped. Thus you have a contradiction. So 0^*1^* is not regular.

1.19 A *finite state transducer* (FST) is a type of deterministic finite automaton whose output is a string and not just *accept* or *reject*. The following are state diagrams of finite state transducers T_1 and T_2.

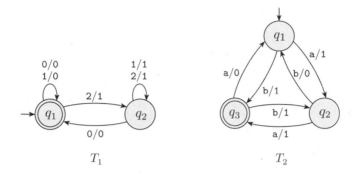

Each transition of an FST is labeled with two symbols, one designating the input symbol for that transition and the other designating the output symbol. The two symbols are written with a slash, /, separating them. In T_1, the transition from q_1 to q_2 has input symbol 2 and output symbol 1. Some transitions may have multiple input–output pairs, such as the transition in T_1 from q_1 to itself. When an FST computes on an input string w, it takes the input symbols $w_1 \cdots w_n$ onc by one and, starting at the start state, follows the transitions by matching the input labels with the sequence of symbols $w_1 \cdots w_n = w$. Every time it goes along a transition, it outputs the corresponding output symbol. For example, on input 2212011, machine T_1 enters the sequence of states $q_1, q_2, q_2, q_2, q_2, q_1, q_1, q_1$ and produces output 1111000. On input abbb, T_2 outputs 1011. Give the sequence of states entered and the output produced in each of the following parts.

    a. T_1 on input 011.
    b. T_1 on input 211.
    c. T_1 on input 0202.
    d. T_2 on input b.
    e. T_2 on input bbab.
    f. T_2 on input bbbbbb.
    g. T_2 on input ε.

1.20 Read the informal definition of the finite state transducer given in Exercise 1.19. Give a formal definition of this model, following the pattern in Definition 1.1 on page 35. Assume that an FST has an input alphabet Σ and an output alphabet Γ but not a set of accept states. Include a formal definition of the computation of an FST. (Hint: An FST is a 5-tuple. It's transition function is of the form $\delta: Q \times \Sigma \longrightarrow Q \times \Gamma$.)

1.21 Using the solution you gave to Exercise 1.20, give a formal description of the machines T_1 and T_2 pictured in Exercise 1.19.

1.22 Read the informal definition of the finite state transducer given in Exercise 1.19. Give the state diagram of an FST with the following behavior. Its input and output alphabets are $\{0,1\}$. Its output string is identical to the input string on the even positions but inverted on the odd positions. For example, on input 0000111 it should output 1010010.

PROBLEMS

1.23 Prove that the following languages are not regular.

   a. $\{0^n 1^m 0^n \mid m, n \geq 0\}$.
   b. The complement of $\{0^n 1^n \mid n \geq 0\}$.
   c. $\{0^m 1^n \mid m \neq n\}$.
   d. $\{w \mid w \in \{0,1\}$ is not a palindrome$\}$.[9]

1.24 For any string $w = w_1 w_2 \cdots w_n$, the **reverse** of w, written $w^{\mathcal{R}}$, is the string w in reverse order, $w_n \cdots w_2 w_1$. For any language A, let $A^{\mathcal{R}} = \{w^{\mathcal{R}} \mid w \in A\}$. Show that if A is regular, so is $A^{\mathcal{R}}$.

1.25 Let

$$\Sigma_3 = \left\{ \begin{bmatrix} 0 \\ 0 \\ 0 \end{bmatrix}, \begin{bmatrix} 0 \\ 0 \\ 1 \end{bmatrix}, \begin{bmatrix} 0 \\ 1 \\ 0 \end{bmatrix}, \cdots, \begin{bmatrix} 1 \\ 1 \\ 1 \end{bmatrix} \right\}.$$

Σ_3 contains all size 3 columns of 0s and 1s. A string of symbols in Σ_3 gives three rows of 0s and 1s. Consider each row to be a binary number and let

$B = \{w \in \Sigma_3^* \mid$ the bottom row of w is the sum of the top two rows$\}$.

For example,

$$\begin{bmatrix} 0 \\ 0 \\ 1 \end{bmatrix} \begin{bmatrix} 1 \\ 0 \\ 0 \end{bmatrix} \begin{bmatrix} 1 \\ 1 \\ 0 \end{bmatrix} \in B, \qquad \text{but} \qquad \begin{bmatrix} 0 \\ 1 \\ 1 \end{bmatrix} \begin{bmatrix} 1 \\ 0 \\ 1 \end{bmatrix} \notin B.$$

Show that B is regular. (Hint: Working with $B^{\mathcal{R}}$ is easier. You may assume the result claimed in Problem 1.24.)

1.26 Let

$$\Sigma_2 = \left\{ \begin{bmatrix} 0 \\ 0 \end{bmatrix}, \begin{bmatrix} 0 \\ 1 \end{bmatrix}, \begin{bmatrix} 1 \\ 0 \end{bmatrix}, \begin{bmatrix} 1 \\ 1 \end{bmatrix} \right\}.$$

Here, Σ_2 contains all columns of 0s and 1s of height two. A string of symbols in Σ_2 gives two rows of 0s and 1s. Consider each row to be a binary number and let

$C = \{w \in \Sigma_2^* \mid$ the bottom row of w is three times the top row$\}$.

For example, $\begin{bmatrix} 0 \\ 0 \end{bmatrix} \begin{bmatrix} 0 \\ 1 \end{bmatrix} \begin{bmatrix} 1 \\ 1 \end{bmatrix} \begin{bmatrix} 0 \\ 0 \end{bmatrix} \in C$, but $\begin{bmatrix} 0 \\ 1 \end{bmatrix} \begin{bmatrix} 0 \\ 1 \end{bmatrix} \begin{bmatrix} 1 \\ 0 \end{bmatrix} \notin C$. Show that C is regular. You may assume the result claimed in Problem 1.24.

1.27 Let Σ_2 be the same as in Problem 1.26. Consider each row to be a binary number and let

$D = \{w \in \Sigma_2^* \mid$ the top row of w is a larger number than is the top bottom$\}$.

For example, $\begin{bmatrix} 0 \\ 0 \end{bmatrix} \begin{bmatrix} 1 \\ 0 \end{bmatrix} \begin{bmatrix} 1 \\ 1 \end{bmatrix} \begin{bmatrix} 0 \\ 0 \end{bmatrix} \in C$, but $\begin{bmatrix} 0 \\ 0 \end{bmatrix} \begin{bmatrix} 0 \\ 1 \end{bmatrix} \begin{bmatrix} 1 \\ 1 \end{bmatrix} \begin{bmatrix} 0 \\ 0 \end{bmatrix} \notin C$. Show that C is regular.

---

[9]A **palindrome** is a string that reads the same forward and backward.

1.28 Let Σ_2 be the same as in Problem 1.26. Consider the top and bottom rows to be strings of 0s and 1s and let

$$E = \{w \in \Sigma_2^* |\text{ the bottom row of } w \text{ is the reverse of the top row of } w\}.$$

Show that E is not regular.

1.29 Let $B_n = \{a^k |\text{ where } k \text{ is a multiple of } n\}$. Show that for each $n \geq 1$, the language B_n is regular.

1.30 Let $C_n = \{x |\ x \text{ is a binary number that is a multiple of } n\}$. Show that for each $n \geq 1$, the language C_n is regular.

1.31 Consider a new kind of finite automaton called an all-paths-NFA. An all-paths-NFA M is a 5-tuple $(Q, \Sigma, \delta, q_0, F)$ that recognizes $x \in \Sigma^*$ if *every* possible computation of M on x ends in a state from F. Note, in contrast, that an ordinary NFA accepts a string if *some* computation ends in an accept state. Prove that all-paths-NFAs recognize the class of regular languages.

1.32 Say that string x is a **prefix** of string y if a string z exists where $xz = y$ and that x is a **proper prefix** of y if in addition $x \neq y$. In each of the following parts we define an operation on a language A. Show that the class of regular languages is closed under that operation.

    a. NOPREFIX$(A) = \{w \in A |\text{ no proper prefix of } w \text{ is a member of } A\}$.

    b. NOEXTEND$(A) = \{w \in A |\ w \text{ is not the proper prefix of any string in } A\}$.

1.33 Read the informal definition of the finite state transducer given in Exercise 1.19. Prove that no FST can output $w^\mathcal{R}$ for every input w if the input and output alphabets are $\{0,1\}$.

1.34 Let x and y be strings and let L be any language. We say that x and y are **distinguishable by L** if some string z exists whereby exactly one of the strings xz and yz are members of L; otherwise, for every string z, $xz \in L$ whenever $yz \in L$ and we say that x and y are **indistinguishable by L**. If x an y are indistinguishable by L we write $x \equiv_L y$. Show that $\equiv_L$ is an equivalence relation.

*1.35 Read Problem 1.34. Let L be a language and let X be a set of strings. Say that X is **pairwise distinguishable by L** if every two distinct strings in X are distinguishable by L. Define the **index of L** to be the maximum number of elements in any set that is pairwise distinguishable by L. The index of L may be finite or infinite.

    a. Show that if L is recognized by a DFA with k states, L has index at most k.

    b. Show that if the index of L is a finite number k, it is recognized by a DFA with k states.

    c. Conclude that L is regular iff it has finite index. Moreover, its index is the size of the smallest DFA recognizing it.

1.36 Let $\Sigma = \{0, 1, +, =\}$ and

$$ADD = \{x=y+z |\ x, y, z \text{ are binary integers, and } x \text{ is the sum of } y \text{ and } z\}.$$

Show that ADD is not regular.

1.37 Show that the language $F = \{w |\ w \text{ is not a palindrome}\}$ satisfies the three conditions of the pumping lemma even though it is not regular. Explain why this fact does not contradict the pumping lemma.

1.38 The pumping lemma says that every regular language has a pumping length p, such that every string in the language can be pumped if it has length p or more. If p is a pumping length for language A, so is any length $p' \geq p$. The **minimum pumping length** for A is the smallest p that is a pumping length for A. For example, if $A = 01^*$, the minimum pumping length is 2. The reason is, the string $s = 0 \in A$ of length 1 cannot be pumped, and any string in A of length 2 or more contains a 1 and hence can be pumped by dividing it so that $x = 0$, $y = 1$, and z is the rest. For each of the following languages, give the minimum pumping length and justify your answer.

    a. 0001^*.

    b. 0^*1^*.

    c. $(01)^*$.

    d. 01.

    e. ε.

1.39 The construction in Theorem 1.28 shows that every GNFA is equivalent to a GNFA with only two states. We can show that an opposite phenomenon occurs for DFAs. Prove that for every $k > 1$ a language $A_k \subseteq \{0,1\}^*$ exists that is recognized by a DFA with k states but not by one with only $k - 1$ states.

***1.40** If A is a set of natural numbers and k is a natural number greater than 1, let

$$B_k(A) = \{w | \ w \text{ is the representation in base } k \text{ of some number in } A\}.$$

Here, we do not allow leading 0s in the representation of a number. For example, $B_2(\{3,5\}) = \{11, 101\}$ and $B_3(\{3,5\}) = \{10, 12\}$. Give an example of a set A for which $B_2(A)$ is regular but $B_3(A)$ is not regular. Prove that your example works.

1.41 Let

$$D = \{w | w \text{ contains an equal number of occurrences of the substrings 01 and 10}\}.$$

Thus $101 \in D$ because 101 contains a single 01 and a single 10, but $1010 \notin D$ because 1010 contains two 10s and one 01. Show that D is a regular language.

***1.42** If A is any language, let $A_{\frac{1}{2}-}$ be the set of all first halves of strings in A so that

$$A_{\frac{1}{2}-} = \{x | \text{ for some } y, \ |x| = |y| \text{ and } xy \in A\}.$$

Show that, if A is regular, then so is $A_{\frac{1}{2}-}$.

***1.43** If A is any language, let $A_{\frac{1}{3}-\frac{1}{3}}$ be the set of all strings in A with their middle thirds removed so that

$$A_{\frac{1}{3}-\frac{1}{3}} = \{xz | \text{ for some } y, \ |x| = |y| = |z| \text{ and } xyz \in A\}.$$

Show that, if A is regular, then $A_{\frac{1}{3}-\frac{1}{3}}$ is not necessarily regular.

***1.44** Give a family of languages E_n, where each E_n can be recognized by an n-state NFA but requires at least c^n states on a DFA for some constant $c > 1$. Prove that your languages have this property.

2

CONTEXT-FREE
LANGUAGES

In Chapter 1 we introduced two different, though equivalent, methods of describing languages: *finite automata* and *regular expressions*. We showed that many languages can be described in this way but that some simple languages, such as $\{0^n 1^n \mid n \geq 0\}$, cannot.

In this chapter we introduce *context-free grammars*, a more powerful method of describing languages. Such grammars can describe certain features that have a recursive structure which makes them useful in a variety of applications.

Context-free grammars were first used in the study of human languages. One way of understanding the relationship of terms such as *noun*, *verb*, and *preposition* and their respective phrases leads to a natural recursion because noun phrases may appear inside verb phrases and vice versa. Context-free grammars can capture important aspects of these relationships.

An important application of context-free grammars occurs in the specification and compilation of programming languages. A grammar for a programming language often appears as a reference for people trying to learn the language syntax. Designers of compilers and interpreters for programming languages often start by obtaining a grammar for the language. Most compilers and interpreters contain a component called a *parser* that extracts the meaning of a program prior to generating the compiled code or performing the interpreted execution. A number of methodologies facilitate the construction of a parser once a context-free grammar is available. Some tools even automatically generate the parser from the grammar.

91

The collection of languages associated with context-free grammars are called the ***context-free languages***. They include all the regular languages and many additional languages. In this chapter, we give a formal definition of context-free grammars and study the properties of context free languages. We also introduce ***pushdown automata***, a class of machines recognizing the context-free languages. Pushdown automata are useful because they allow us to gain additional insight into the power of context-free grammars.

2.1

CONTEXT-FREE GRAMMARS

The following is an example of a context-free grammar, which we'll call G_1.

$$A \rightarrow 0A1$$
$$A \rightarrow B$$
$$B \rightarrow \texttt{\#}$$

A grammar consists of a collection of ***substitution rules***, also called ***productions***. Each rule appears as a line in the grammar and comprises a symbol and a string, separated by an arrow. The symbol is called a ***variable***. The string consists of variables and other symbols called ***terminals***. The variable symbols often are represented by capital letters. The terminals are analogous to the input alphabet and often are represented by lowercase letters, numbers, or special symbols. One variable is designated the ***start variable***. It usually occurs on the left-hand side of the topmost rule. For example, grammar G_1 contains three rules. G_1's variables are A and B, where A is the start variable. Its terminals are 0, 1, and #.

You use a grammar to describe a language by generating each string of that language in the following manner.

1. Write down the start variable. It is the variable on the left-hand side of the top rule, unless specified otherwise.
2. Find a variable that is written down and a rule that starts with that variable. Replace the written down variable with the right-hand side of that rule.
3. Repeat step 2 until no variables remain.

For example, grammar G_1 generates the string 000#111. The sequence of substitutions to obtain a string is called a ***derivation***. A derivation of string 000#111 in grammar G_1 is

$$A \Rightarrow 0A1 \Rightarrow 00A11 \Rightarrow 000A111 \Rightarrow 000B111 \Rightarrow 000\texttt{\#}111$$

You may also represent the same information in a more pictorial way using a ***parse tree***. An example of a parse tree appears in the following figure.

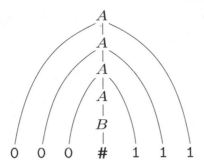

FIGURE **2.1**
Parse tree for 000#111 in grammar G_1

All strings generated in this way constitute the ***language of the grammar***. We write $L(G_1)$ for the language of grammar G_1. Some experimentation with the grammar G_1 shows us that $L(G_1)$ is $\{0^n\#1^n|\, n \geq 0\}$. Any language that can be generated by some context-free grammar is called a ***context-free language*** (CFL). For convenience when presenting a context-free grammar, we abbreviate several rules with the same left-hand variable, such as $A \to 0A1$ and $A \to B$, into a single line $A \to 0A1 \mid B$, using the symbol " | " as an "or."

The following is a second example of a context free grammar called G_2, which describes a fragment of the English language.

$$
\begin{aligned}
\langle\text{SENTENCE}\rangle &\to \langle\text{NOUN-PHRASE}\rangle\langle\text{VERB-PHRASE}\rangle \\
\langle\text{NOUN-PHRASE}\rangle &\to \langle\text{CMPLX-NOUN}\rangle \mid \langle\text{CMPLX-NOUN}\rangle\langle\text{PREP-PHRASE}\rangle \\
\langle\text{VERB-PHRASE}\rangle &\to \langle\text{CMPLX-VERB}\rangle \mid \langle\text{CMPLX-VERB}\rangle\langle\text{PREP-PHRASE}\rangle \\
\langle\text{PREP-PHRASE}\rangle &\to \langle\text{PREP}\rangle\langle\text{CMPLX-NOUN}\rangle \\
\langle\text{CMPLX-NOUN}\rangle &\to \langle\text{ARTICLE}\rangle\langle\text{NOUN}\rangle \\
\langle\text{CMPLX-VERB}\rangle &\to \langle\text{VERB}\rangle \mid \langle\text{VERB}\rangle\langle\text{NOUN-PHRASE}\rangle \\
\langle\text{ARTICLE}\rangle &\to \texttt{a} \mid \texttt{the} \\
\langle\text{NOUN}\rangle &\to \texttt{boy} \mid \texttt{girl} \mid \texttt{flower} \\
\langle\text{VERB}\rangle &\to \texttt{touches} \mid \texttt{likes} \mid \texttt{sees} \\
\langle\text{PREP}\rangle &\to \texttt{with}
\end{aligned}
$$

Grammar g_2 has ten variables (the capitalized grammatical terms written inside brackets); nine terminals (the lower case words); and eighteen rules. Strings in $L(G_2)$ include the following three examples.

```
a boy sees
the boy sees a flower
a girl with a flower likes the boy
```

Each of these strings has a derivation in grammar G_2. The following is a derivation of the first string on this list.

$$\langle \text{SENTENCE} \rangle \Rightarrow \langle \text{NOUN-PHRASE} \rangle \langle \text{VERB-PHRASE} \rangle$$
$$\Rightarrow \langle \text{CMPLX-NOUN} \rangle \langle \text{VERB-PHRASE} \rangle$$
$$\Rightarrow \langle \text{ARTICLE} \rangle \langle \text{NOUN} \rangle \langle \text{VERB-PHRASE} \rangle$$
$$\Rightarrow \text{a } \langle \text{NOUN} \rangle \langle \text{VERB-PHRASE} \rangle$$
$$\Rightarrow \text{a boy } \langle \text{VERB-PHRASE} \rangle$$
$$\Rightarrow \text{a boy } \langle \text{CMPLX-VERB} \rangle$$
$$\Rightarrow \text{a boy } \langle \text{VERB} \rangle$$
$$\Rightarrow \text{a boy sees}$$

FORMAL DEFINITION OF A CONTEXT-FREE GRAMMAR

Let's formalize our notion of a context-free grammar (CFG).

DEFINITION 2.1

A *context-free grammar* is a 4-tuple (V, Σ, R, S), where

1. V is a finite set called the *variables*,
2. Σ is a finite set, disjoint from V, called the *terminals*,
3. R is a finite set of *rules*, with each rule being a variable and a string of variables and terminals, and
4. S is the start symbol.

If u, v, and w are strings of variables and terminals, and $A \to w$ is a rule of the grammar, we say that uAv *yields* uwv, written $uAv \Rightarrow uwv$. Write $u \overset{*}{\Rightarrow} v$ if $u = v$ or if a sequence $u_1, u_2, \ldots, u_k$ exists for $k \geq 0$ and

$$u \Rightarrow u_1 \Rightarrow u_2 \Rightarrow \ldots \Rightarrow u_k \Rightarrow v.$$

The *language of the grammar* is $\{w \in \Sigma^* |\ S \overset{*}{\Rightarrow} w\}$.

In grammar G_1, $V = \{A, B\}$, $\Sigma = \{0, 1, \#\}$, $S = A$, and R is the collection of the three rules appearing on page 92. In grammar G_2,

$$V = \{\langle \text{SENTENCE} \rangle, \langle \text{NOUN-PHRASE} \rangle, \langle \text{VERB-PHRASE} \rangle,$$
$$\langle \text{PREP-PHRASE} \rangle, \langle \text{CMPLX-NOUN} \rangle, \langle \text{CMPLX-VERB} \rangle,$$
$$\langle \text{ARTICLE} \rangle, \langle \text{NOUN} \rangle, \langle \text{VERB} \rangle, \langle \text{PREP} \rangle\},$$

and $\Sigma = \{\text{a}, \text{b}, \text{c}, \ldots, \text{z}, \text{" "}\}$. The symbol " " is the blank symbol, placed invisibly after each word (a, boy, etc.), so the words won't run together.

Often we specify a grammar by writing down only its rules. We can identify the variables as the symbols that appear on the left-hand side of the rules and the terminals as the remaining symbols. By convention, the start variable is the variable on the left-hand side of the first rule.

EXAMPLES OF CONTEXT-FREE GRAMMARS

EXAMPLE **2.2**

Consider grammar $G_3 = (\{S\}, \{a, b\}, R, S)$. The set of rules, R, is

$$S \rightarrow \text{a}S\text{b} \mid SS \mid \varepsilon.$$

This grammar generates strings such as abab, aaabbb, and aababb. You can see more easily what this language is if you think of a as a left parenthesis "(" and b as a right parenthesis ")". Viewed in this way, $L(G_3)$ is the language of all strings of properly nested parentheses.

EXAMPLE **2.3**

Consider grammar $G_4 = (V, \Sigma, R, \langle \text{EXPR} \rangle)$.
V is $\{\langle \text{EXPR} \rangle, \langle \text{TERM} \rangle, \langle \text{FACTOR} \rangle\}$ and Σ is $\{\text{a}, +, \times, (,)\}$. The rules are

$$\langle \text{EXPR} \rangle \rightarrow \langle \text{EXPR} \rangle + \langle \text{TERM} \rangle \mid \langle \text{TERM} \rangle$$
$$\langle \text{TERM} \rangle \rightarrow \langle \text{TERM} \rangle \times \langle \text{FACTOR} \rangle \mid \langle \text{FACTOR} \rangle$$
$$\langle \text{FACTOR} \rangle \rightarrow (\, \langle \text{EXPR} \rangle \,) \mid \text{a}$$

The two strings a+a×a and (a+a)×a can be generated with grammar G_4. The parse trees are shown in the following figure.

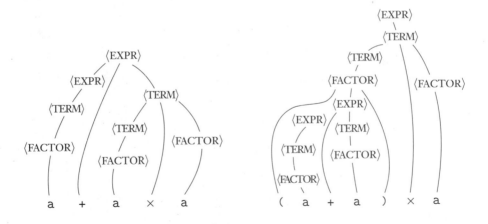

FIGURE **2.2**
Parse trees for the strings a+a×a and (a+a)×a

A compiler translates code written in a programming language into another form, usually one more suitable for execution. To do so the compiler extracts the meaning of the code to be compiled in a process called **parsing**. One representation of this meaning is the parse tree for the code, in the context-free grammar for the programming language. We discuss an algorithm that parses context-free languages later in Theorem 7.14 and in Problem 7.38.

Grammar G_4 describes a fragment of a programming language concerned with arithmetic expressions. Observe how the parse trees in Figure 2.2 "group" the operations. The tree for a+axa groups the x operator and its operands (the second two a's) together as one operand of the + operator. In the tree for (a+a)xa, the grouping is reversed. These groupings fit the standard precedence of multiplication before addition and the use of parentheses to override the standard precedence. Grammar G_4 is designed to capture these precedence relations.

■

DESIGNING CONTEXT-FREE GRAMMARS

As with the design of finite automata, discussed on page 41 in Section 1.1, the design of context-free grammars requires creativity. Indeed, context-free grammars are even trickier to construct than finite automata because we are more accustomed to programming a machine for specific tasks than we are to describing languages with grammars. The following techniques are helpful, singly or in combination, when you're faced with the problem of constructing a CFG.

First, many CFGs are the union of simpler CFGs. If you must construct a CFG for a CFL that you can break into simpler pieces, do so and then construct individual grammars for each piece. These individual grammars can be easily combined into a grammar for the original language by putting all their rules together and then adding the new rule $S \rightarrow S_1 \mid S_2 \mid \cdots \mid S_k$, where the variables S_i are the start variables for the individual grammars. Solving several simpler problems is often easier than solving one complicated problem.

For example, to get a grammar for the language $\{0^n 1^n | n \geq 0\} \cup \{1^n 0^n | n \geq 0\}$, first construct the grammar

$$S_1 \rightarrow 0S_1 1 \mid \varepsilon$$

for the language $\{0^n 1^n | n \geq 0\}$ and the grammar

$$S_2 \rightarrow 1S_2 0 \mid \varepsilon$$

for the language $\{1^n 0^n | n \geq 0\}$ and then add the rule $S \rightarrow S_1 \mid S_2$ to give the grammar

$$
\begin{aligned}
S &\rightarrow S_1 \mid S_2 \\
S_1 &\rightarrow 0S_1 1 \mid \varepsilon \\
S_2 &\rightarrow 1S_2 0 \mid \varepsilon \ .
\end{aligned}
$$

Second, constructing a CFG for a language that happens to be regular is easy if you can first construct a DFA for that language. You can convert any DFA into an equivalent CFG as follows. Make a variable R_i for each state q_i of the DFA. Add the rule $R_i \to aR_j$ to the CFG if $\delta(q_i, a) = q_j$ is a transition in the DFA. Add the rule $R_i \to \varepsilon$ if q_i is an accept state of the DFA. Make R_0 the start variable of the grammar, where q_0 is the start state of the machine. Verify on your own that the resulting CFG generates the same language that the DFA recognizes.

Third, certain context-free languages contain strings with two substrings that are "linked" in the sense that a machine for such a language would need to remember an unbounded amount of information about one of the substrings to verify that it corresponds properly to the other substring. This situation occurs in the language $\{0^n 1^n \mid n \geq 0\}$ because a machine would need to remember the number of 0s in order to verify that it equals the number of 1s. You can construct a CFG to handle this situation by using a rule of the form $R \to uRv$, which generates strings wherein the portion containing the u's corresponds to the portion containing the v's.

Finally, in more complex languages, the strings may contain certain structures that appear recursively as part of other (or the same) structures. That situation occurs in the grammar that generates arithmetic expressions in Example 2.3. Any time the symbol a appears, an entire parenthesized expression might appear recursively instead. To achieve this effect, place the variable symbol generating the structure in the location of the rules corresponding to where that structure may recursively appear.

AMBIGUITY

Sometimes a grammar can generate the same string in several different ways. Such a string will have several different parse trees and thus several different meanings. This result may be undesirable for certain applications, such as programming languages, where a given program should have a unique interpretation.

If a grammar generates the same string in several different ways, we say that the string is derived *ambiguously* in that grammar. If a grammar generates some string ambiguously we say that the grammar is *ambiguous*.

For example, let's consider grammar G_5:

$$\langle \text{EXPR} \rangle \to \langle \text{EXPR} \rangle + \langle \text{EXPR} \rangle \mid \langle \text{EXPR} \rangle \times \langle \text{EXPR} \rangle \mid (\langle \text{EXPR} \rangle) \mid \text{a}$$

This grammar generates the string a+a×a ambiguously. The following figure shows the two different parse trees.

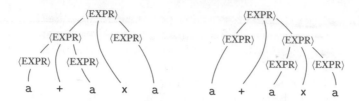

FIGURE **2.3**
The two parse trees for the string a+axa in grammar G_5

This grammar doesn't capture the usual precedence relations and so may group the + before the × or vice versa. In contrast grammar G_4 generates exactly the same language, but every generated string has a unique parse tree. Hence G_4 is unambiguous, whereas G_5 is ambiguous.

Grammar G_2 on page 93 is another example of an ambiguous grammar. The sentence the girl touches the boy with the flower has two different derivations. In Exercise 2.8 you are asked to give the two parse trees and observe their correspondence with the two different ways to read that sentence.

Now we formalize the notion of ambiguity. When we say that a grammar generates a string ambiguously, we mean that the string has two different parse trees, not two different derivations. Two derivations may differ merely in the order in which they replace variables yet not in their overall structure. To concentrate on structure we define a type of derivation that replaces variables in a fixed order. A derivation of a string w in a grammar G is a ***leftmost derivation*** if at every step the leftmost remaining variable is the one replaced. The derivation on page 94 is a leftmost derivation.

DEFINITION **2.4** ··

A string w is derived ***ambiguously*** in context-free grammar G if it has two or more different leftmost derivations. Grammar G is ***ambiguous*** if it generates some string ambiguously.

Sometimes when we have an ambiguous grammar we can find an unambiguous grammar that generates the same language. Some context-free languages, however, can only be generated by ambiguous grammars. Such languages are called ***inherently ambiguous***. Problem 2.24 asks you to prove that the language $\{0^i 1^j 2^k | i = j \text{ or } j = k\}$ is inherently ambiguous.

CHOMSKY NORMAL FORM

When working with context-free grammars, it is often convenient to have them in simplified form. One of the simplest and most useful forms is called the Chomsky normal form. We will find Chomsky normal form useful when we are giving algorithms for working with context-free grammars in Chapters 4 and 7.

DEFINITION **2.5** ··

A context-free grammar is in **Chomsky normal form** if every rule is of the form

$$A \rightarrow BC$$
$$A \rightarrow a$$

where a is any terminal and A, B, and C are any variables—except that B and C may not be the start variable. In addition we permit the rule $S \rightarrow \varepsilon$, where S is the start variable.

THEOREM **2.6** ··

Any context-free language is generated by a context-free grammar in Chomsky normal form.

··

PROOF IDEA We can convert any grammar G into Chomsky normal form. The conversion has several stages wherein rules that violate the conditions are replaced with equivalent ones that are satisfactory. First, we add a new start symbol. Then, we eliminate all ε **rules** of the form $A \rightarrow \varepsilon$. We also eliminate all **unit rules** of the form $A \rightarrow B$. In both cases the grammar is then patched up to be sure that it still generates the same language. Finally, we convert the remaining rules into the proper form.

PROOF First, we add a new start symbol S_0 and the rule $S_0 \rightarrow S$, where S was the original start symbol. This change guarantees that the start symbol doesn't occur on the right-hand side of a rule.

Second, we take care of all ε rules. We remove an ε-rule $A \rightarrow \varepsilon$, where A is not the start variable. Then for each occurrence of an A on the right-hand side of a rule, we add a new rule with that occurrence deleted. In other words, if $R \rightarrow uAv$ is a rule in which u and v are strings of variables and terminals, we add rule $R \rightarrow uv$. We do so for each *occurrence* of an A, so the rule $R \rightarrow uAvAw$ causes us to add $R \rightarrow uvAw$, $R \rightarrow uAvw$, and $R \rightarrow uvw$. If we have the rule $R \rightarrow A$, we add $R \rightarrow \varepsilon$ unless we had previously removed the rule $R \rightarrow \varepsilon$. We repeat these steps until we eliminate all ε rules not involving the start variable.

Third, we handle all unit rules. We remove a unit rule $A \rightarrow B$. Then, whenever a rule $B \rightarrow u$ appears, we add the rule $A \rightarrow u$ unless this was a unit rule previously removed. As before, u is a string of variables and terminals. We repeat these steps until we eliminate all unit rules.

Finally, we convert all remaining rules into the proper form. We replace each rule $A \rightarrow u_1 u_2 \cdots u_k$ where $k \geq 3$ and each u_i is a variable or terminal symbol, with the rules $A \rightarrow u_1 A_1$, $A_1 \rightarrow u_2 A_2$, $A_2 \rightarrow u_3 A_3, \ldots, A_{k-2} \rightarrow u_{k-1} u_k$. The A_i's are new variables. If $k \geq 2$, we replace any terminal u_i in the preceding rule(s) with the new variable U_i and add the rule $U_i \rightarrow u_i$.

··

Let G_6 be the following CFG and convert it to Chomsky normal form by using the conversion procedure just given. The following series of grammars illustrates the steps in the conversion. Rules shown in bold have been just added. Rules shown in gray have just been removed.

1. The original CFG G_6 is shown on the left. The result of applying the first step to make a new start symbol appears on the right.

$$S \to ASA \mid \mathsf{a}B$$
$$A \to B \mid S$$
$$B \to \mathsf{b} \mid \varepsilon$$

$$\boldsymbol{S_0 \to S}$$
$$S \to ASA \mid \mathsf{a}B$$
$$A \to B \mid S$$
$$B \to \mathsf{b} \mid \varepsilon$$

2. Remove ε rules $B \to \varepsilon$, shown on the left, and $A \to \varepsilon$, shown on the right.

$$S_0 \to S$$
$$S \to ASA \mid \mathsf{a}B \mid \boldsymbol{\mathsf{a}}$$
$$A \to B \mid S \mid \boldsymbol{\varepsilon}$$
$$B \to \mathsf{b} \mid \varepsilon$$

$$S_0 \to S$$
$$S \to ASA \mid \mathsf{a}B \mid \mathsf{a} \mid \boldsymbol{SA} \mid \boldsymbol{AS} \mid \boldsymbol{S}$$
$$A \to B \mid S \mid \varepsilon$$
$$B \to \mathsf{b}$$

3a. Remove unit rules $S \to S$, shown on the left, and $S_0 \to S$, shown on the right.

$$S_0 \to S$$
$$S \to ASA \mid \mathsf{a}B \mid \mathsf{a} \mid SA \mid AS \mid S$$
$$A \to B \mid S$$
$$B \to \mathsf{b}$$

$$S_0 \to S \mid \boldsymbol{ASA} \mid \boldsymbol{\mathsf{a}B} \mid \boldsymbol{\mathsf{a}} \mid \boldsymbol{SA} \mid \boldsymbol{AS}$$
$$S \to ASA \mid \mathsf{a}B \mid \mathsf{a} \mid SA \mid AS$$
$$A \to B \mid S$$
$$B \to \mathsf{b}$$

3b. Remove unit rules $A \to B$ and $A \to S$.

$$S_0 \to ASA \mid \mathsf{a}B \mid \mathsf{a} \mid SA \mid AS$$
$$S \to ASA \mid \mathsf{a}B \mid \mathsf{a} \mid SA \mid AS$$
$$A \to B \mid S \mid \boldsymbol{\mathsf{b}}$$
$$B \to \mathsf{b}$$

$$S_0 \to ASA \mid \mathsf{a}B \mid \mathsf{a} \mid SA \mid AS$$
$$S \to ASA \mid \mathsf{a}B \mid \mathsf{a} \mid SA \mid AS$$
$$A \to S \mid \mathsf{b} \mid \boldsymbol{ASA} \mid \boldsymbol{\mathsf{a}B} \mid \boldsymbol{\mathsf{a}} \mid \boldsymbol{SA} \mid \boldsymbol{AS}$$
$$B \to \mathsf{b}$$

4. Convert the remaining rules into the proper form by adding additional variables and rules. The final grammar in Chomsky normal form is equivalent to G_6 and appears as follows. (Actually the procedure given in Theorem 2.6 produces several variables U_i along with several rules $U_i \to \mathsf{a}$. We simplified the resulting grammar by using a single variable U and rule $U \to \mathsf{a}$.)

$$S_0 \rightarrow AA_1 \mid UB \mid \text{a} \mid SA \mid AS$$
$$S \rightarrow AA_1 \mid UB \mid \text{a} \mid SA \mid AS$$
$$A \rightarrow \text{b} \mid AA_1 \mid UB \mid \text{a} \mid SA \mid AS$$
$$A_1 \rightarrow SA$$
$$U \rightarrow \text{a}$$
$$B \rightarrow \text{b}$$

2.2

PUSHDOWN AUTOMATA

In this section we introduce a new type of computational model called ***pushdown automata***. These automata are like nondeterministic finite automata but have an extra component called a ***stack***. The stack provides additional memory beyond the finite amount available in the control. The stack allows pushdown automata to recognize some nonregular languages.

Pushdown automata are equivalent in power to context-free grammars. This equivalence is useful because it gives us two options for proving that a language is context free. We can give either a context-free grammar generating it or a pushdown automaton recognizing it. Certain languages are more easily described in terms of generators, whereas others are more easily described in terms of recognizers.

The following figure is a schematic representation of a finite automaton. The control represents the states and transition function, the tape contains the input string, and the arrow represents the input head, pointing at the next input symbol to be read.

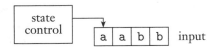

FIGURE 2.4
Schematic of a finite automaton

With the addition of a stack component we obtain a schematic representation of a pushdown automaton, as shown in the following figure.

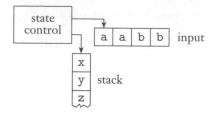

FIGURE   **2.5**
Schematic of a pushdown automaton

A pushdown automaton (PDA), can write symbols on the stack and read them back later. Writing a symbol "pushes down" all the other symbols on the stack. At any time the symbol on the top of the stack can be read and removed. The remaining symbols then move back up. Writing a symbol on the stack is often referred to as *pushing* the symbol, and removing a symbol is referred to as *popping* it. Note that all access to the stack, for both reading and writing, may be done only at the top. In other words a stack is a "last in, first out" storage device. If certain information is written on the stack and additional information is written afterward, the earlier information becomes inaccessible until the later information is removed.

Plates on a cafeteria serving counter illustrate a stack. The stack of plates rests on a spring so that when a new plate is placed on top of the stack, the plates below it move down. The stack on a pushdown automaton is like a stack of plates, with each plate having a symbol written on it.

A stack is valuable because it can hold an unlimited amount of information. Recall that a finite automaton is unable to recognize the language $\{0^n 1^n \mid n \geq 0\}$ because it cannot store very large numbers in its finite memory. A PDA is able to recognize this language because it can use its stack to store the number of 0s it has seen. Thus the unlimited nature of a stack allows the PDA to store numbers of unbounded size. The following informal description shows how the automaton for this language works.

> Read symbols from the input. As each 0 is read, push it onto the stack. As soon as 1s are seen, pop a 0 off the stack for each 1 read. If reading the input is finished exactly when the stack becomes empty of 0s, accept the input. If the stack becomes empty while 1s remain or if the 1s are finished while the stack still contains 0s or if any 0s appear in the input following 1s, reject the input.

As mentioned earlier, pushdown automata may be nondeterministic. This feature is crucial because, in contrast with the finite automata situation, nondeterminism adds power to the capability that pushdown automata would have if they were allowed only to be deterministic. Some languages, such as $\{0^n 1^n \mid n \geq 0\}$, do not require nondeterminism, but others do. We give a language requiring nondeterminism in Example 2.11.

FORMAL DEFINITION OF A PUSHDOWN AUTOMATON

The formal definition of a pushdown automaton is similar to that of a finite automaton, except for the stack. The stack is a device containing symbols drawn from some alphabet. The machine may use different alphabets for its input and its stack, so now we specify both an input alphabet Σ and a stack alphabet Γ.

At the heart of any formal definition of an automaton is the transition function, for that describes its behavior. Recall that $\Sigma_\varepsilon = \Sigma \cup \{\varepsilon\}$ and $\Gamma_\varepsilon = \Gamma \cup \{\varepsilon\}$. The domain of the transition function is $Q \times \Sigma_\varepsilon \times \Gamma_\varepsilon$. Thus the current state, next input symbol read, and top symbol of the stack determine the next move of a pushdown automaton. Either symbol may be ε causing the machine to move without reading a symbol from the input or without reading a symbol from the stack.

For the range of the transition function we need to consider what to allow the automaton to do when it is in a particular situation. It may enter some new state and possibly write a symbol on the top of the stack. The function δ can indicate this action by returning a member of Q together with a member of Γ_ε, that is, a member of $Q \times \Gamma_\varepsilon$. Because we allow nondeterminism in this model, a situation may have several legal next moves. The transition function incorporates nondeterminism in the usual way, by returning a set of members of $Q \times \Gamma_\varepsilon$, that is, a member of $\mathcal{P}(Q \times \Gamma_\varepsilon)$. Putting it all together, our transition function δ takes the form $\delta\colon Q \times \Sigma_\varepsilon \times \Gamma_\varepsilon \longrightarrow \mathcal{P}(Q \times \Gamma_\varepsilon)$.

DEFINITION   **2.8** ....

A **_pushdown automaton_** is a 6-tuple $(Q, \Sigma, \Gamma, \delta, q_0, F)$, where Q, Σ, Γ, and F are all finite sets, and

1. Q is the set of states,
2. Σ is the input alphabet,
3. Γ is the stack alphabet,
4. $\delta\colon Q \times \Sigma_\varepsilon \times \Gamma_\varepsilon \longrightarrow \mathcal{P}(Q \times \Gamma_\varepsilon)$ is the transition function,
5. $q_0 \in Q$ is the start state, and
6. $F \subseteq Q$ is the set of accept states.

A pushdown automaton $M = (Q, \Sigma, \Gamma, \delta, q_0, F)$ computes as follows. It accepts input w if w can be written as $w = w_1 w_2 \cdots w_m$, where each $w_i \in \Sigma_\varepsilon$ and sequences of states $r_0, r_1, \ldots, r_m \in Q$ and strings $s_0, s_1, \ldots, s_m \in \Gamma^*$ exist that satisfy the next three conditions. The strings s_i represent the sequence of stack contents that M has on the accepting branch of the computation.

1. $r_0 = q_0$ and $s_0 = \varepsilon$. This condition signifies that M starts out properly, in the start state and with an empty stack.
2. For $i = 0, \ldots, m-1$, we have $(r_{i+1}, b) \in \delta(r_i, w_{i+1}, a)$, where $s_i = at$ and $s_{i+1} = bt$ for some $a, b \in \Gamma_\varepsilon$ and $t \in \Gamma^*$. This condition states that M moves properly according to the state, stack, and next input symbol.
3. $r_m \in F$. This condition states that an accept state occurs at the input end.

EXAMPLES OF PUSHDOWN AUTOMATA

EXAMPLE **2.9** ....

The following is the formal description of the PDA from page 102 that recognizes the language $\{0^n1^n \mid n \geq 0\}$. Let M_1 be $(Q, \Sigma, \Gamma, \delta, q_1, F)$, where

$Q = \{q_1, q_2, q_3, q_4\}$,

$\Sigma = \{0,1\}$,

$\Gamma = \{0, \$\}$,

$F = \{q_1, q_4\}$, and

δ is given by the following table, wherein blank entries signify $\emptyset$.

Input:	0			1			ε		
Stack:	0	\$	ε	0	\$	ε	0	\$	ε
q_1									$\{(q_2, \$)\}$
q_2			$\{(q_2, 0)\}$	$\{(q_3, \varepsilon)\}$					
q_3				$\{(q_3, \varepsilon)\}$				$\{(q_4, \varepsilon)\}$	
q_4									

We can also use a state diagram to describe a PDA, as shown in the following three figures. Such diagrams are similar to the state diagrams used to describe finite automata, modified to show how the PDA uses its stack when going from state to state. We write "$a, b \rightarrow c$" to signify that when the machine is reading an a from the input it may replace the symbol b on the top of the stack with a c. Any of a, b, and c may be ε. If a is ε, the machine may make this transition without reading any symbol from the input. If b is ε, the machine may make this transition without reading and popping any symbol from the stack. If c is ε, the machine does not write any symbol on the stack when going along this transition.

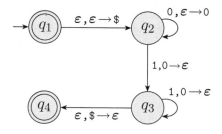

FIGURE **2.6**
State diagram for the PDA M_1 that recognizes $\{0^n1^n \mid n \geq 0\}$

The formal definition of a PDA contains no explicit mechanism to allow the PDA to test for an empty stack. This PDA is able to get the same effect by initially placing a special symbol $ on the stack. Then if it ever sees the $ again, it knows that the stack effectively is empty. Subsequently, when we refer to testing for an empty stack in an informal description of a PDA, we implement the procedure in the same way.

Similarly, PDAs cannot test explicitly for having reached the end of the input string. This PDA is able to achieve that effect because the accept state takes effect only when the machine is at the end of the input. Thus from now on, we assume that PDAs can test for the end of the input, and we know that we can implement it in the same manner.

EXAMPLE **2.10**

This example illustrates a pushdown automaton that recognizes the language

$$\{a^i b^j c^k \mid i, j, k \geq 0 \text{ and } i = j \text{ or } i = k\}.$$

Informally the PDA for this language works by first reading and pushing the a's. When the a's are done the machine has all of them on the stack so that it can match them with either the b's or the c's. This maneuver is a bit tricky because the machine doesn't know in advance whether to match the a's with the b's or the c's. Nondeterminism comes in handy here.

Using its nondeterminism, the PDA can guess whether to match the a's with the b's or with the c's, as shown in the following figure. Think of the machine as having two branches of its nondeterminism, one for each possible guess. If either of them match, that branch accepts and the entire machine accepts. In fact we could show, though we do not do so, that nondeterminism is *essential* for recognizing this language with a PDA.

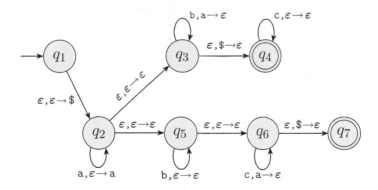

FIGURE **2.7**
State diagram for PDA M_2 that recognizes
$\{a^i b^j c^k \mid i, j, k \geq 0 \text{ and } i = j \text{ or } i = k\}$

EXAMPLE **2.11** ···

In this example we give a PDA M_3 recognizing the language $\{ww^{\mathcal{R}} | w \in \{0,1\}^*\}$. Recall that $w^{\mathcal{R}}$ means w written backwards. The informal description of the PDA follows.

> Begin by pushing the symbols that are read onto the stack. At each point nondeterministically guess that the middle of the string has been reached and then change into popping off the stack for each symbol read, checking to see that they are the same. If they were always the same symbol and the stack empties at the same time as the input is finished, accept; otherwise reject.

The following is the diagram of this machine.

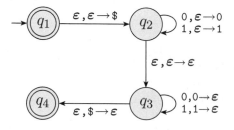

FIGURE **2.8**
State diagram for the PDA M_3 that recognizes $\{ww^{\mathcal{R}} | w \in \{0,1\}^*\}$

EQUIVALENCE WITH CONTEXT-FREE GRAMMARS

In this section we show that context-free grammars and pushdown automata are equivalent in power. Both are capable of describing the class of context-free languages. We show how to convert any context-free grammar into a pushdown automaton that recognizes the same language and vice versa. Recalling that we defined a context-free language to be any language that can be described with a context-free grammar, our objective is the following theorem.

THEOREM **2.12** ···

A language is context free if and only if some pushdown automaton recognizes it.

As usual for "if and only if" theorems, we have two directions to prove. In this theorem, both directions are interesting. First, we do the easier forward direction.

....

If a language is context free, then some pushdown automaton recognizes it.

....

PROOF IDEA Let A be a CFL. From the definition we know that A has a CFG, G, generating it. We show how to convert G into an equivalent PDA, which we call P.

The PDA P that we now describe will work by accepting its input w, if G generates that input, by determining whether there is a derivation for w. Recall that a derivation is simply the sequence of substitutions made as a grammar generates a string. Each step of the derivation yields an ***intermediate string*** of variables and terminals. We design P to determine whether some series of substitutions using the rules of G can lead from the start variable to w.

One of the difficulties in testing whether there is a derivation for w is in figuring out which substitutions to make. The PDA's nondeterminism allows it to guess the sequence of correct substitutions. At each step of the derivation one of the rules for a particular variable is selected nondeterministically and used to substitute for that variable.

The PDA P begins by writing the start variable on its stack. It goes through a series of intermediate strings, making one substitution after another. Eventually it may arrive at a string that contains only terminal symbols, meaning that it has derived a string using the grammar. Then P accepts if this string is identical to the string it has received as input.

Implementing this strategy on a PDA requires one additional idea. We need to see how the PDA stores the intermediate strings as it goes from one to another. Simply using the stack for storing each intermediate string is tempting. However, that doesn't quite work because the PDA needs to find the variables in the intermediate string and make substitutions. The PDA can access only the top symbol on the stack and that may be a terminal symbol instead of a variable. The way around this problem is to keep only *part* of the intermediate string on the stack: the symbols starting with the first variable in the intermediate string. Any terminal symbols appearing before the first variable are matched immediately with symbols in the input string. The following figure shows the PDA P.

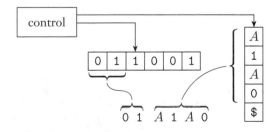

FIGURE 2.9
P representing the intermediate string $01A1A0$

The following is an informal description of P.

1. Place the marker symbol $\$$ and the start variable on the stack.

2. Repeat the following steps forever.

    a. If the top of stack is a variable symbol A, nondeterministically select one of the rules for A and substitute A by the string on the right-hand side of the rule.

    b. If the top of stack is a terminal symbol a, read the next symbol from the input and compare it to a. If they match, repeat. If they do not match, reject on this branch of the nondeterminism.

    c. If the top of stack is the symbol $\$$, enter the accept state. Doing so accepts the input if it has all been read.

PROOF   We now give the formal details of the construction of the pushdown automaton $P = (Q, \Sigma, \Gamma, \delta, q_1, F)$. To make the construction clearer we use shorthand notation for the transition function. This notation provides a way to write an entire string on the stack in one step of the machine. We can simulate this action by introducing additional states to write the string one symbol at a time, as implemented in the following formal construction.

Let q and r be states of the PDA, and let a be in Σ_ε and s be in Γ_ε. Say that we want the PDA to go from q to r when it reads a and pops s. Furthermore we want it to push the entire string $u = u_1 \cdots u_l$ on the stack at the same time. We can implement this action by introducing new states $q_1, \ldots, q_{l-1}$ and setting the transition function

$$\delta(q, a, s) \text{ to contain } (q_1, u_l),$$
$$\delta(q_1, \varepsilon, \varepsilon) = \{(q_2, u_{l-1})\},$$
$$\delta(q_2, \varepsilon, \varepsilon) = \{(q_3, u_{l-2})\},$$
$$\vdots$$
$$\delta(q_{l-1}, \varepsilon, \varepsilon) = \{(r, u_1)\}.$$

We use the notation $(r, u) \in \delta(q, a, s)$ to mean that when q is the state of the automaton, a is the next input symbol, and s is the symbol on the top of the stack, the PDA may read the a and pop the s, then push the string u onto the stack and go on to the state r. The following figure shows this implementation pictorially.

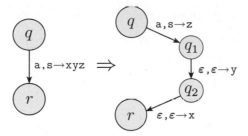

FIGURE 2.10
Implementing the shorthand $\delta(q, a, s) = (r, xyz)$

The states of P are $Q = \{q_{start}, q_{loop}, q_{accept}\} \cup E$, where E is the set of states we need for implementing the shorthand just described. The start state is q_{start}. The only accept state is q_{accept}.

The transition function is defined as follows. We begin by initializing the stack to contain the symbols \$ and S, implementing step 1 in the informal description: $\delta(q_{start}, \varepsilon, \varepsilon) = \{(q_{loop}, S\$)\}$. Then we put in transitions for the main loop of step 2.

First, we handle case (a) wherein the top of the stack contains a variable. Let $\delta(q_{loop}, \varepsilon, A) = \{(q_{loop}, w) |$ where $A \to w$ is a rule in $R\}$.

Second, we handle case (b) wherein the top of the stack contains a terminal. Let $\delta(q_{loop}, a, a) = \{(q_{loop}, \varepsilon)\}$.

Finally, we handle case (c) wherein the empty stack marker \$ is on the top of the stack. Let $\delta(q_{loop}, \varepsilon, \$) = \{(q_{accept}, \varepsilon)\}$.

The state diagram is shown in the following figure.

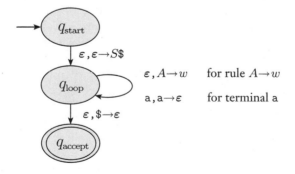

FIGURE 2.11
State diagram of P

EXAMPLE 2.14 ....

We use the procedure developed in Lemma 2.13 to construct a PDA P_1 from the following CFG G.

$$S \to aTb \mid b$$
$$T \to Ta \mid \varepsilon$$

The transition function is shown in the following diagram.

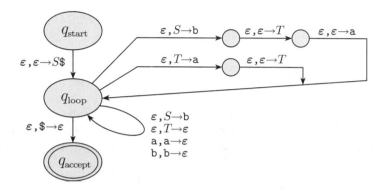

FIGURE 2.12
State diagram of P_1

Now we prove the reverse direction of Theorem 2.12. For the forward direction we gave a procedure for converting a CFG into a PDA. The main idea was to design the automaton so that it simulates the grammar. Now we want to give a procedure for going the other way: converting a PDA into a CFG. We design the grammar to simulate the automaton. This task is a bit tricky because "programming" an automaton is easier than "programming" a grammar.

LEMMA 2.15 ....

If a pushdown automaton recognizes some language, then it is context free.

....

PROOF IDEA We have a PDA P, and we want to make a CFG G that generates all the strings that P accepts. In other words, G should generate a string if that string causes the PDA to go from its start state to an accept state.

To achieve this outcome we design a grammar that does somewhat more. For each pair of states p and q in P the grammar will have a variable A_{pq}. This variable generates all the strings that can take P from p with an empty stack to q with an empty stack. Observe that such strings can also take P from p to q, regardless of the stack contents at p, leaving the stack at q in the same condition as it was at p.

First, we simplify our task by modifying P slightly to give it the following three features.

1. It has a single accept state, q_{accept}.
2. It empties its stack before accepting.
3. Each transition either pushes a symbol onto the stack (a *push* move) or pops one off the stack (a *pop* move), but does not do both at the same time.

Giving P features 1 and 2 is easy. To give it feature 3, we replace each transition that simultaneously pops and pushes with a two transition sequence that goes through a new state, and we replace each transition that neither pops nor pushes with a two transition sequence that pushes then pops an arbitrary stack symbol.

To design G so that A_{pq} generates all strings that take P from p to q, starting and ending with an empty stack, we must understand how P operates on these strings. For any such string x, P's first move on x must be a push, because every move is either a push or a pop and P can't pop an empty stack. Similarly the last move on x must be a pop, because the stack ends up empty.

Two possibilities occur during P's computation on x. Either the symbol popped at the end is the symbol that was pushed at the beginning, or not. If so, the stack is empty only at the beginning and end of P's computation on x. If not, the initially pushed symbol must get popped at some point before the end of x and thus the stack becomes empty at this point. We simulate the former possibility with the rule $A_{pq} \rightarrow aA_{rs}b$ where a is the input symbol read at the first move, b is the symbol read at the last move, r is the state following p, and s the state preceding q. We simulate the latter possibility with the rule $A_{pq} \rightarrow A_{pr}A_{rq}$, where r is the state when the stack becomes empty.

PROOF   Say that $P = (Q, \Sigma, \Gamma, \delta, q_0, \{q_{\text{accept}}\})$ and construct G. The variables of G are $\{A_{pq}|\, p, q \in Q\}$. The start variable is $A_{q_0, q_{\text{accept}}}$. Now we describe G's rules.

- For each $p, q, r, s \in Q$, $t \in \Gamma$, and $a, b \in \Sigma_\varepsilon$, if $\delta(p, a, \varepsilon)$ contains (r, t) and $\delta(s, b, t)$ contains (q, ε) put the rule $A_{pq} \rightarrow aA_{rs}b$ in G.

- For each $p, q, r \in Q$ put the rule $A_{pq} \rightarrow A_{pr}A_{rq}$ in G.

- Finally, for each $p \in Q$ put the rule $A_{pp} \rightarrow \varepsilon$ in G.

You may gain some intuition for this construction from the following figures.

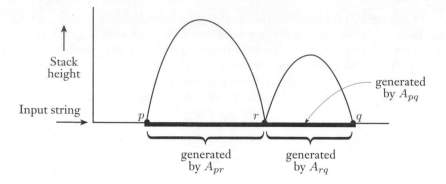

FIGURE **2.13**
PDA computation corresponding to the rule $A_{pq} \rightarrow A_{pr}A_{rq}$

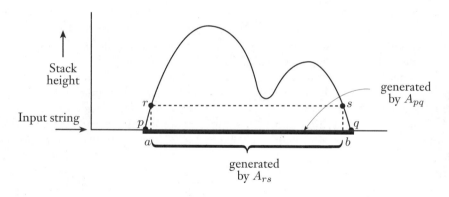

FIGURE **2.14**
PDA computation corresponding to the rule $A_{pq} \rightarrow aA_{rs}b$

Now we prove that this construction works by demonstrating that A_{pq} generates x if and only if (iff) x can bring P from p with empty stack to q with empty stack. We consider each direction of the iff as a separate claim.

CLAIM **2.16** ....

If A_{pq} generates x, then x can bring P from p with empty stack to q with empty stack.

We prove this claim by induction on the number of steps in the derivation of x from A_{pq}.

Basis: The derivation has 1 step.

A derivation with a single step must use a rule whose right-hand side contains no variables. The only rules in G where no variables occur on the right-hand side are $A_{pp} \rightarrow \varepsilon$. Clearly, input ε takes P from p with empty stack to p with empty stack so the basis is proved.

Induction step: Assume true for derivations of length at most k, where $k \geq 1$, and prove true for derivations of length $k + 1$.

Suppose that $A_{pq} \stackrel{*}{\Rightarrow} x$ with $k + 1$ steps. The first step in this derivation is either $A_{pq} \Rightarrow aA_{rs}b$ or $A_{pq} \Rightarrow A_{pr}A_{rq}$. We handle these two cases separately.

In the first case, consider the portion y of x that A_{rs} generates, so $x = ayb$. Because $A_{rs} \stackrel{*}{\Rightarrow} y$ with k steps, the induction hypothesis tells us that P can go from r on empty stack to s on empty stack. Because $A_{pq} \rightarrow aA_{rs}b$ is a rule of G, $\delta(p, a, \varepsilon)$ contains (r, t) and $\delta(s, b, t)$ contains (q, ε). Hence, if P starts at p with an empty stack, after reading a it can go to state r and push t on the stack. Then reading string y can bring it to s and leave t on the stack. Then after reading b it can go to state q and pop t off the stack. Therefore x can bring it from p with empty stack to q with empty stack.

In the second case, consider the portions y and z of x that A_{pr} and A_{rq} respectively generate, so $x = yz$. Because $A_{pr} \stackrel{*}{\Rightarrow} y$ in at most k steps and $A_{rq} \stackrel{*}{\Rightarrow} z$ in at most k steps, the induction hypothesis tells us that y can bring P from p to r, and z can bring P from r to q, with empty stacks at the beginning and end. Hence x can bring it from p with empty stack to q with empty stack. This completes the induction step.

CLAIM   **2.17** ···

If x can bring P from p with empty stack to q with empty stack, A_{pq} generates x.

We prove this claim by induction on the number of steps in the computation of P that goes from p to q with empty stacks on input x.

Basis: The computation has 0 steps.

If a computation has 0 steps, it starts and ends at the same state, say, p. So we must show that $A_{pp} \stackrel{*}{\Rightarrow} x$. In 0 steps, P only has time to read the empty string, so $x = \varepsilon$. By construction, G has the rule $A_{pp} \rightarrow \varepsilon$, so the basis is proved.

Induction step: Assume true for computations of length at most k, where $k \geq 0$, and prove true for computations of length $k + 1$.

Suppose that P has a computation wherein x brings p to q with empty stacks in $k + 1$ steps. Either the stack is empty only at the beginning and end of this computation, or it becomes empty elsewhere, too.

In the first case, the symbol that is pushed at the first move must be the same as the symbol that is popped at the last move. Call this symbol t. Let a be the input read in the first move, b be the input read in the last move, r be the state after the first move, and s be the state before the last move. Then $\delta(p, a, \varepsilon)$ contains (r, t) and $\delta(s, b, t)$ contains (q, ε), and so rule $A_{pq} \rightarrow aA_{rs}b$ is in G.

Let y be the portion of x without a and b, so $x = ayb$. Input y can bring P from r to s without touching the symbol t that is on the stack and so P can go from r with an empty stack to s with an empty stack on input y. We have removed the first and last steps of the $k + 1$ steps in the original computation on x so the computation on y has $(k + 1) - 2 = k - 1$ steps. Thus the induction hypothesis tells us that $A_{rs} \overset{*}{\Rightarrow} y$. Hence $A_{pq} \overset{*}{\Rightarrow} x$.

In the second case, let r be a state where the stack becomes empty other than at the beginning or end of the computation on x. Then the portions of the computation from p to r and from r to q each contain at most k steps. Say that y is the input read during the first portion and z is the input read during the second portion. The induction hypothesis tells us that $A_{pr} \overset{*}{\Rightarrow} y$ and $A_{rq} \overset{*}{\Rightarrow} z$. Because rule $A_{pq} \rightarrow A_{pr} A_{rq}$ is in G, $A_{pq} \overset{*}{\Rightarrow} x$, and the proof is complete.

That completes the proof of Lemma 2.15 and of Theorem 2.12.

We have just proved that pushdown automata recognize the class of context-free languages. This proof allows us to establish a relationship between the regular languages and the context-free languages. Because every regular language is recognized by a finite automaton and every finite automaton is automatically a pushdown automaton that simply ignores its stack, we now know that every regular language is also a context-free language.

COROLLARY **2.18**

Every regular language is context free.

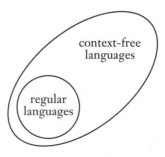

FIGURE **2.15**
Relationship of the regular and context-free languages

2.3 ▪▪▪

NON-CONTEXT-FREE LANGUAGES

In this section we present a technique for proving that certain languages are not context free. Recall that in Section 1.4 we introduced the pumping lemma for showing that certain languages are not regular. Here we present a similar pumping lemma for context-free languages. It states that every context-free language has a special value called the **pumping length** such that all longer strings in the language can be "pumped." This time the meaning of *pumped* is a bit more complex. It means that the string can be divided into five parts so that the second and the fourth parts may be repeated together any number of times and the resulting string still remains in the language.

THE PUMPING LEMMA FOR CONTEXT-FREE LANGUAGES

THEOREM **2.19** ···

Pumping lemma for context-free languages If A is a context-free language, then there is a number p (the pumping length) where, if s is any string in A of length at least p, then s may be divided into five pieces $s = uvxyz$ satisfying the conditions:

1. For each $i \geq 0$, $uv^i xy^i z \in A$,
2. $|vy| > 0$, and
3. $|vxy| \leq p$.

When s is being divided into $uvxyz$, condition 2 says that both v and y may not be the empty string. Otherwise the theorem would be trivially true. Condition 3 states that the pieces v, x, and y together have length at most p. This technical condition sometimes is useful in proving that certain languages are not context free.

···

PROOF IDEA Let A be a CFL and let G be a CFG that generates it. We must show that any sufficiently long string s in A can be pumped and remain in A. The idea behind this approach is simple.

Let s be a very long string in A. (We make clear later what we mean by "very long.") Because s is in A, it is derivable from G and so has a parse tree. The parse tree for s must be very tall because s is very long. That is, the parse tree must contain some long path from the start variable at the root of the tree to one of the terminal symbols at a leaf. On this long path some variable symbol R must repeat because of the pigeonhole principle. As the following figure shows, this repetition allows us to replace the subtree under the second occurrence of R with the subtree under the first occurrence of R and still get a legal parse tree.

Therefore we may cut s into five pieces $uvxyz$ as the figure indicates, and we may repeat the second and fourth pieces and obtain a string still in the language. In other words, uv^ixy^iz is in A for any $i \geq 0$.

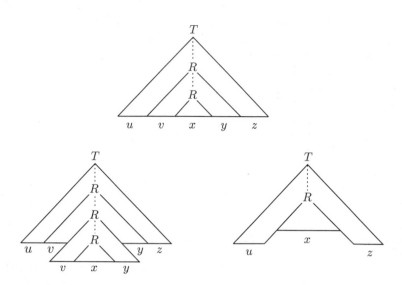

FIGURE **2.16**
Surgery on parse trees

Let's now turn to the details to obtain all three conditions of the pumping lemma. We also show how to calculate the pumping length p.

PROOF   Let G be a CFG for CFL A. Let b be the maximum number of symbols in the right-hand side of a rule. We may assume that $b \geq 2$. In any parse tree using this grammar we know that a node can have no more than b children. In other words at most b leaves are 1 step from the start variable; at most b^2 leaves are at most 2 steps from the start variable; and at most b^h leaves are at most h steps from the start variable. So, if the height of the parse tree is at most h, the length of the string generated is at most b^h.

Let $|V|$ be the number of variables in G. We set p to be $b^{|V|+2}$. Because $b \geq 2$, we know that $p > b^{|V|+1}$, so a parse tree for any string in A of length at least p requires height at least $|V| + 2$.

Suppose that s is a string in A of length at least p. We now show how to pump s. Let τ be a parse tree for s. If s has several parse trees, we choose τ to be a parse tree that has the smallest number of nodes. As $|s| \geq p$, we know that τ has height at least $|V| + 2$, so the longest path in τ has length at least $|V| + 2$. This path must have at least $|V| + 1$ variables because only the leaf is a terminal. With G having only $|V|$ variables, some variable R appears more than once on the path. For convenience later, we select R to be a variable that repeats among the lowest $|V| + 1$ variables on this path.

We divide s into $uvxyz$ according to Figure 2.16. Each occurrence of R has a subtree under it, generating a part of the string s. The upper occurrence of R has a larger subtree and generates vxy, whereas the lower occurrence generates just x with a smaller subtree. Both of these subtrees are generated by the same variable, so we may substitute one for the other and still obtain a valid parse tree. Replacing the smaller by the larger repeatedly gives parse trees for the strings $uv^i xy^i z$ at each $i > 1$. Replacing the larger by the smaller generates the string uxz. That establishes condition 1 of the lemma. We now turn to conditions 2 and 3.

To get condition 2 we must be sure that both v and y are not ε. If they were, the parse tree obtained by substituting the smaller subtree for the larger would have fewer nodes than τ does and would still generate s. This result isn't possible because we had already chosen τ to be a parse tree for s with the smallest number of nodes. That is the reason for selecting τ in this way.

In order to get condition 3 we need to be sure that vxy has length at most p. In the parse tree for s the upper occurrence of R generates vxy. We chose R so that both occurrences fall within the bottom $|V|+1$ variables on the path, and we chose τ to be the longest path in the parse tree, so the subtree where R generates vxy is at most $|V| + 2$ high. A tree of this height can generate a string of length at most $b^{|V|+2} = p$.

....

For some tips on using the pumping lemma to prove that languages are not context free, review page 80 where we discuss the related problem of proving nonregularity with the pumping lemma for regular languages.

EXAMPLE **2.20** ....

Use the pumping lemma to show that the language $B = \{\text{a}^n\text{b}^n\text{c}^n |\, n \geq 0\}$ is not context free.

We assume that B is a CFL and obtain a contradiction. Let p be the pumping length for B that is guaranteed to exist by the pumping lemma. Select the string $s = \text{a}^p\text{b}^p\text{c}^p$. Clearly s is a member of B and of length at least p. The pumping lemma states that s can be pumped, but we show that it cannot. In other words, we show that no matter have we divide s into $uvxyz$, one of the three conditions of the lemma is violated.

First, condition 2 stipulates that either v or y is nonempty. Then we consider one of two cases, depending on whether substrings v and y contain more than one type of alphabet symbol.

1. When both v and y contain only one type of alphabet symbol, v does not contain both a's and b's or both b's and c's, and the same holds for y. In this case the string uv^2xy^2z cannot contain equal numbers of a's, b's, and c's. Therefore it cannot be a member of B. That violates condition 1 of the lemma and is thus a contradiction.

2. When either v or y contain more than one type of symbol uv^2xy^2z may

contain equal numbers of the three alphabet symbols but won't contain them in the correct order. Hence it cannot be a member of B and a contradiction occurs.

One of these cases must occur. Because both cases result in a contradiction, a contradiction is unavoidable. So the assumption that B is a CFL must be false. Thus we have proved that B is not a CFL.   ∎

EXAMPLE 2.21 ....

Let $C = \{\texttt{a}^i\texttt{b}^j\texttt{c}^k \,|\, 0 \leq i \leq j \leq k\}$. We use the pumping lemma to show that C is not a CFL. This language is similar to language B in Example 2.20, but proving that it is not context free is a bit more complicated.

   Assume that C is a CFL and obtain a contradiction. Let p be the pumping length given by the pumping lemma. We use the string $s = \texttt{a}^p\texttt{b}^p\texttt{c}^p$ that we used earlier, but this time we must "pump down" as well as "pump up." Let $s = uvxyz$ and again consider the two cases that occurred in Example 2.20.

1. When both v and y contain only one type of alphabet symbol, v does not contain both a's and b's or both b's and c's, and the same holds for y. Note that the reasoning used previously in case 1 no longer applies. The reason is that C contains strings with unequal numbers of a's, b's, and c's as long as the numbers are not decreasing. We must analyze the situation more carefully to show that s cannot be pumped. Observe that because v and y contain only one type of alphabet symbol, one of the symbols a, b, or c doesn't appear in x or y. We further subdivide this case into three subcases according to which symbol does not appear.

   a. The a's do not appear. Then we try pumping down to obtain the string $uv^0xy^0z = uxz$. That contains the same number of a's as s does, but it contains fewer b's or fewer c's. Therefore it is not a member of C, and a contradiction occurs.

   b. The b's do not appear. Then either a's or c's must appear in v or y because both can't be the empty string. If a's appear, the string uv^2xy^2z contains more a's than b's, so it is not in C. If c's appear, the string uv^0xy^0z contains more b's than c's, so it is not in C. Either way a contradiction occurs.

   c. The c's do not appear. Then the string uv^2xy^2z contains more a's or more b's than c's, so it is not in C, and a contradiction occurs.

2. When either v or y contain more than one type of symbol, uv^2xy^2z will not contain the symbols in the correct order. Hence it cannot be a member of B, and a contradiction occurs.

Thus we have shown that s cannot be pumped in violation of the pumping lemma and that C is not context free.   ∎

EXAMPLE **2.22** ....

Let $D = \{ww | w \in \{0,1\}^*\}$. Use the pumping lemma to show that D is not a CFL. Assume that D is a CFL and obtain a contradiction. Let p be the pumping length given by the pumping lemma.

This time choosing string s is less obvious. One possibility is the string 0^p10^p1. It is a member of D and has length greater than p, so it appears to be a good candidate. But this string *can* be pumped by dividing it as follows, so it is not adequate for our purposes.

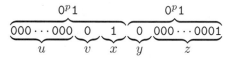

Let's try another candidate for s. Intuitively, the string $0^p1^p0^p1^p$ seems to capture more of the "essence" of the language D than the previous candidate did. In fact, we can show that this string does work, as follows.

We show that the string $s = 0^p1^p0^p1^p$ cannot be pumped. This time we use condition 3 of the pumping lemma to restrict the way that s can be divided. It says that we can pump s by dividing $s = uvxyz$, where $|vxy| \leq p$.

First, we show that the substring vxy must straddle the midpoint of s. Otherwise, if the substring occurs only in the first half of s, pumping s up to uv^2xy^2z moves a 1 into the first position of the second half, and so it cannot be of the form ww. Similarly, if vxy occurs in the second half of s, pumping s up to uv^2xy^2z moves a 0 into the last position of the first half, and so it cannot be of the form ww.

But if the substring vxy straddles the midpoint of s, when we try to pump s down to uxz it has the form $0^p1^i0^j1^p$, where i and j cannot both be p. This string is not of the form ww. Thus s cannot be pumped, and D is not a CFL.

EXERCISES

2.1 Recall the CFG G_4 that we gave in Example 2.3. For convenience, let's rename its variables with single letters as follows.

$$E \rightarrow E + T \mid T$$
$$T \rightarrow T \times F \mid F$$
$$F \rightarrow (E) \mid \text{a}$$

Give parse trees and derivations for each string.

    a. a

    b. a+a

    c. a+a+a

    d. ((a))

2.2   **a.** Use the languages $A = \{a^m b^n c^n | m, n \geq 0\}$ and $B = \{a^n b^n c^m | m, n \geq 0\}$ together with Example 2.21 to show that the class of context-free languages is not closed under intersection.

b. Use part (a) and DeMorgan's law (Theorem 0.10) to show that the class of context-free languages is not closed under complementation.

2.3 Answer each part for the following context-free grammar G:

$$R \rightarrow XRX \mid S$$
$$S \rightarrow aTb \mid bTa$$
$$T \rightarrow XTX \mid X \mid \varepsilon$$
$$X \rightarrow a \mid b$$

a. What are the variables and terminals of G? Which is the start variable?

b. Give three examples of strings in $L(G)$.

c. Give tree examples of strings *not* in $L(G)$.

d. True or False: $T \Rightarrow aba$.

e. True or False: $T \overset{*}{\Rightarrow} aba$.

f. True or False: $T \Rightarrow T$.

g. True or False: $T \overset{*}{\Rightarrow} T$.

h. True or False: $XXX \overset{*}{\Rightarrow} aba$.

i. True or False: $X \overset{*}{\Rightarrow} aba$.

j. True or False: $T \overset{*}{\Rightarrow} XX$.

k. True or False: $T \overset{*}{\Rightarrow} XXX$.

l. True or False: $S \overset{*}{\Rightarrow} \varepsilon$.

m. Give a description in English of $L(G)$.

2.4 Give context-free grammars that generate the following languages. In all parts the alphabet Σ is $\{0,1\}$.

a. $\{w | \ w$ contains at least three 1s$\}$

b. $\{w | \ w$ starts and ends with the same symbol$\}$

c. $\{w | $ the length of w is odd$\}$

d. $\{w | $ the length of w is odd and its middle symbol is a 0$\}$

e. $\{w | \ w$ contains more 1s than 0s$\}$

f. $\{w | \ w = w^R,$ that is, w is a palindrome$\}$

g. The empty set

2.5 Give informal descriptions and state diagrams of pushdown automata for the languages in Exercise 2.4.

2.6 Give context-free grammars generating the following languages.

a. The set of strings over the alphabet $\{a,b\}$ with twice as many a's as b's.

b. The complement of the language $\{a^n b^n | \ n \geq 0\}$.

c. $\{w \# x | \ w^R$ is a substring of x for $w, x \in \{0,1\}^*\}$.

d. $\{x_1 \# x_2 \# \cdots \# x_k | \ k \geq 1,$ each $x_i \in \{a, b\}^*,$ and for some i and j, $x_i = x_j^R\}$.

2.7 Give informal English descriptions of PDAs for the languages in Exercise 2.6.

2.8 Show that the string `the girl touches the boy with the flower` has two different derivations in grammar G_2 on page 93. Describe in English the two different meanings of this sentence.

2.9 Give a context-free grammar that generates the language

$$A = \{\mathsf{a}^i\mathsf{b}^j\mathsf{c}^k \mid i, j, k \geq 0 \text{ and either } i = j \text{ or } j = k\}.$$

Is your grammar ambiguous? Why or why not?

2.10 Give an informal description of a pushdown automaton that recognizes the language A in Exercise 2.9.

2.11 Convert the CFG G_4 given in Exercise 2.1 to an equivalent PDA using the procedure given in Theorem 2.12.

2.12 Convert the CFG G given in Exercise 2.3 to an equivalent PDA using the procedure given in Theorem 2.12.

2.13 Let $G = (V, \Sigma, R, S)$ be the following grammar. $V = \{S, T, U\}$; $\Sigma = \{0, \#\}$; and R is the set of rules:

$$S \rightarrow TT \mid U$$
$$T \rightarrow 0T \mid T0 \mid \#$$
$$U \rightarrow 0U00 \mid \#$$

    a. Describe $L(G)$ in English.

    b. Prove that $L(G)$ is not regular.

2.14 Convert the following CFG into an equivalent CFG in Chomsky normal form, using the procedure given in Theorem 2.6.

$$A \rightarrow BAB \mid B \mid \varepsilon$$
$$B \rightarrow 00 \mid \varepsilon$$

PROBLEMS

2.15 Show that the class of context-free languages is closed under the regular operations, union, concatenation, and star.

2.16 Use the result of Problem 2.15 to give another proof that every regular language is context free, by showing how to convert a regular expression directly to an equivalent context-free grammar.

2.17   **a.** Let C be a context-free language and R be a regular language. Prove that the language $C \cap R$ is context free.

    b. Use part (a) to show that the language $A = \{w \mid w \in \{\mathsf{a}, \mathsf{b}, \mathsf{c}\}^* \text{ and contains equal numbers of a's, b's, and c's}\}$ is not a CFL.

2.18 Use the pumping lemma to show that the following languages are not context free.

    a. $\{0^n1^n0^n1^n \mid n \geq 0\}$

    b. $\{0^n\#0^{2n}\#0^{3n} \mid n \geq 0\}$

    c. $\{w\#x \mid w \text{ is a substring of } x, \text{ where } w, x \in \{\mathsf{a}, \mathsf{b}\}^*\}$.

    d. $\{x_1\#x_2\# \cdots \#x_k \mid k \geq 2, \text{ each } x_i \in \{\mathsf{a}, \mathsf{b}\}^*, \text{ and for some } i \neq j, x_i = x_j\}$.

2.19 Show that, if G is a CFG in Chomsky normal form, then for any string $w \in L(G)$ of length $n \geq 1$, exactly $2n - 1$ steps are required for any derivation of w.

2.20 Let G be a CFG in Chomsky normal form that contains b variables. Show that, if G generates some string using a derivation with more than b steps, $L(G)$ is infinite.

***2.21** Let $G = (V, \Sigma, R, \langle\text{STMT}\rangle)$ be the following grammar.

$$
\begin{aligned}
\langle\text{STMT}\rangle &\rightarrow \langle\text{ASSIGN}\rangle \mid \langle\text{IF-THEN}\rangle \mid \langle\text{IF-THEN-ELSE}\rangle \mid \langle\text{BEGIN-END}\rangle \\
\langle\text{IF-THEN}\rangle &\rightarrow \texttt{if condition then } \langle\text{STMT}\rangle \\
\langle\text{IF-THEN-ELSE}\rangle &\rightarrow \texttt{if condition then } \langle\text{STMT}\rangle \texttt{ else } \langle\text{STMT}\rangle \\
\langle\text{BEGIN-END}\rangle &\rightarrow \texttt{begin } \langle\text{STMT-LIST}\rangle \texttt{ end} \\
\langle\text{STMT-LIST}\rangle &\rightarrow \langle\text{STMT-LIST}\rangle\langle\text{STMT}\rangle \mid \langle\text{STMT}\rangle \\
\langle\text{ASSIGN}\rangle &\rightarrow \texttt{a:=1}
\end{aligned}
$$

$\Sigma = \{\texttt{if}, \texttt{condition}, \texttt{then}, \texttt{else}, \texttt{begin}, \texttt{end}, \texttt{a:=1}\}$.

$V = \{\langle\text{STMT}\rangle, \langle\text{IF-THEN}\rangle, \langle\text{IF-THEN-ELSE}\rangle, \langle\text{BEGIN-END}\rangle, \langle\text{STMT-LIST}\rangle,$
$\quad\langle\text{ASSIGN}\rangle\}$

G is a natural-looking grammar for a fragment of a programming language, but G is ambiguous.

    a. Show that G is ambiguous.

    b. Give a new unambiguous grammar for the same language.

/2.22 Consider the language $B = L(G)$, where G is the grammar given in Exercise 2.13. The pumping lemma for context-free languages, Theorem 2.19, states the existence of a pumping length p for B. What is the minimum value of p that works in the pumping lemma? Justify your answer.

/2.23 Give an example of a language that is not context free but that does satisfy the three conditions of the pumping lemma. Prove that your example works. (See the analogous fact for regular languages in Problem 1.37.)

***2.24** Show that the language A in Exercise 2.9 is inherently ambiguous.

***2.25** Let CFG G be

$$
\begin{aligned}
S &\rightarrow \texttt{a}S\texttt{b} \mid \texttt{b}Y \mid Y\texttt{a} \\
Y &\rightarrow \texttt{b}Y \mid \texttt{a}Y \mid \varepsilon
\end{aligned}
$$

Give a simple description of $L(G)$ in English. Use that description to give a CFG for $\overline{L(G)}$, the complement of $L(G)$.

/*2.26 Let $C = \{x\texttt{\#}y \mid x, y \in \{0,1\}^* \text{ and } x \neq y\}$. Show that C is a context-free language.

***2.27** Let $D = \{xy \mid x, y \in \{0,1\}^* \text{ and } |x| = |y| \text{ but } x \neq y\}$. Show that D is a context-free language.

***2.28** Prove the following stronger form of the pumping lemma, wherein we require *both* pieces v and y to be nonempty when the string s is broken up.

If A is a context-free language, then there is a number k where, if s is any string in A of length at least k, then s may be divided into five pieces, $s = uvxyz$, satisfying the conditions:

    a. For each $i \geq 0$, $uv^i xy^i z \in A$,

    b. $v \neq \varepsilon$ and $y \neq \varepsilon$, and

    c. $|vxy| \leq k$.

PART TWO
COMPUTABILITY THEORY

3

THE CHURCH-TURING THESIS

So far in our development of the theory of computation we have presented several models of computing devices. Finite automata are good models for devices that have a small amount of memory. Pushdown automata are good models for devices that have an unlimited memory that is usable only in the last in, first out manner of a stack. We have shown that some very simple tasks are beyond the capabilities of these models. Hence they are too restricted to serve as models of general purpose computers.

3.1

TURING MACHINES

We turn now to a much more powerful model, first proposed by Alan Turing in 1936, called the *Turing machine*. Similar to a finite automaton but with an unlimited and unrestricted memory, a Turing machine is a much more accurate model of a general purpose computer. A Turing machine can do everything that a real computer can do. Nonetheless, even a Turing machine cannot solve certain problems. In a very real sense, these problems are beyond the theoretical limits of computation.

The Turing machine model uses an infinite tape as its unlimited memory. It has a tape head that can read and write symbols and move around on the tape.

125

Initially the tape contains only the input string and is blank everywhere else. If the machine needs to store information, it may write this information on the tape. To read the information that it has written, the machine can move its head back over it. The machine continues computing until it decides to produce an output. The outputs *accept* and *reject* are obtained by entering designated accepting and rejecting states. If it doesn't enter an accepting or a rejecting state, it will go on forever, never halting.

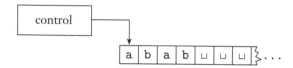

FIGURE **3.1**
Schematic of a Turing machine

The following list summarizes the differences between finite automata and Turing machines.

1. A Turing machine can both write on the tape and read from it.

2. The read–write head can move both to the left and to the right.

3. The tape is infinite.

4. The special states for rejecting and accepting take immediate effect.

Let's consider a Turing machine M_1 for testing membership in the language $B = \{w\#w \mid w \in \{0,1\}^*\}$. That is, we want to design M_1 to accept if its input is a member of B. To understand M_1 better, put yourself in its place by imagining that you are standing on a mile-long input consisting of millions of characters. Your goal is to determine whether the input is a member of B, that is, whether the input comprises two identical strings separated by a # symbol. The input is too long for you to remember it all, but you are allowed to move back and forth over the input and make marks on it. Of course, the obvious strategy is to zig-zag to the corresponding places on the two sides of the # and determine whether they match. Use marks to keep track of which places correspond.

We design M_1 to work in the same way. It makes multiple passes over the input string with the read–write head. On each pass it matches one of the characters on each side of the # symbol. To keep track of which symbols have been checked already, M_1 crosses off each symbol as it is examined. If it crosses off all the symbols, that means that everything matched successfully, and M_1 goes into an accept state. If it discovers a mismatch, it enters a reject state. In summary, M_1's algorithm is as follows.

$M_1 = $ "On input string w:

1. Scan the input to be sure that it contains a single # symbol. If not, *reject*.

2. Zig-zag across the tape to corresponding positions on either side of the # symbol to check on whether these positions contain the same symbol. If they do not, *reject*. Cross off symbols as they are checked to keep track of which symbols correspond.

3. When all symbols to the left of the # have been crossed off, check for any remaining symbols to the right of the #. If any symbols remain, *reject*; otherwise *accept*."

The following figure contains several snapshots of M_1's tape while it is computing in stages 2 and 3 when started on input 011000#011000.

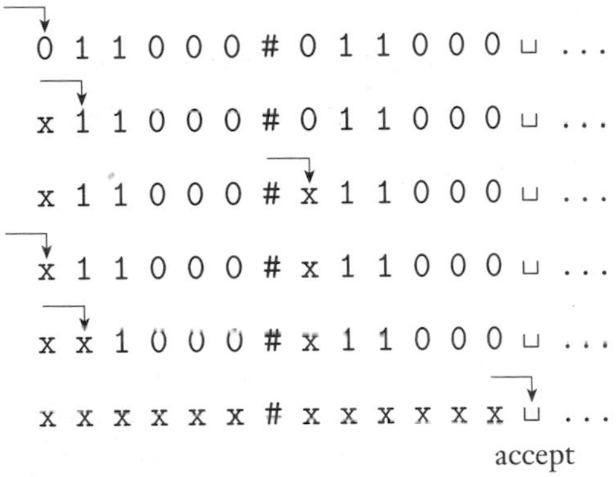

```
  ↓
  0 1 1 0 0 0 # 0 1 1 0 0 0 ⊔ . . .

    ↓
  x 1 1 0 0 0 # 0 1 1 0 0 0 ⊔ . . .

                ↓
  x 1 1 0 0 0 # x 1 1 0 0 0 ⊔ . . .

  ↓
  x 1 1 0 0 0 # x 1 1 0 0 0 ⊔ . . .

    ↓
  x x 1 0 0 0 # x 1 1 0 0 0 ⊔ . . .

                            ↓
  x x x x x x # x x x x x x ⊔ . . .
                              accept
```

FIGURE **3.2**
Snapshots of Turing machine M_1 computing on input 011000#011000

This description of Turing machine M_1 sketches the way it functions but does not give all its details. We can describe Turing machines in complete detail by giving formal descriptions analogous to those introduced for finite and pushdown automata. The formal description specifies each of the parts of the formal definition of the Turing machine model to be presented shortly. In actuality we almost never give formal descriptions of Turing machines because they tend to be very big.

FORMAL DEFINITION OF A TURING MACHINE

The heart of the definition of a Turing machine is the transition function δ because it tells us how the machine gets from one step to the next. For a Turing machine, δ takes the form: $Q \times \Gamma \longrightarrow Q \times \Gamma \times \{L, R\}$. That is, when the machine is in a certain state q and the head is over a tape square containing a symbol a, and if $\delta(q, a) = (r, b, L)$, the machine writes the symbol b replacing the a, and goes to state r. The third component is either L or R and indicates whether the head moves to the left or right after writing. In this case the L indicates a move to the left.

DEFINITION   3.1 ....

A *Turing machine* is a 7-tuple, $(Q, \Sigma, \Gamma, \delta, q_0, q_{\text{accept}}, q_{\text{reject}})$, where Q, Σ, Γ are all finite sets and

1. Q is the set of states,

2. Σ is the input alphabet not containing the special *blank* symbol $\sqcup$,

3. Γ is the tape alphabet, where $\{\sqcup\} \in \Gamma$ and $\Sigma \subseteq \Gamma$,

4. $\delta: Q \times \Gamma \longrightarrow Q \times \Gamma \times \{\text{L}, \text{R}\}$ is the transition function,

5. $q_0 \in Q$ is the start state,

6. $q_{\text{accept}} \in Q$ is the accept state, and

7. $q_{\text{reject}} \in Q$ is the reject state, where $q_{\text{reject}} \neq q_{\text{accept}}$.

A Turing machine $M = (Q, \Sigma, \Gamma, \delta, q_0, q_{\text{accept}}, q_{\text{reject}})$ computes as follows. Initially M receives its input $w = w_1 w_2 \ldots w_n \in \Sigma^*$ on the leftmost n squares of the tape, and the rest of the tape is blank (i.e., filled with blank symbols). The head starts on the leftmost square of the tape. Note that Σ does not contain the blank symbol, so the first blank appearing on the tape marks the end of the input. Once M starts, the computation proceeds according to the rules described by the transition function. If M ever tries to move its head to the left off the left-hand end of the tape, the head stays in the same place for that move, even though the transition function indicates L. The computation continues until it enters either the accept or reject states at which point it halts. If neither occurs, M goes on forever.

As a Turing machine computes, changes occur in the current state, the current tape contents, and the current head location. A setting of these three items is called a *configuration* of the Turing machine. Configurations often are represented in a special way. For a state q and two strings u and v over the tape alphabet Γ we write $u\,q\,v$ for the configuration where the current state is q, the current tape contents is uv, and the current head location is the first symbol of v. The tape contains only blanks following the last symbol of v. For example, $1011q_701111$ represents the configuration when the tape is 101101111, the current state is q_7, and the head is currently on the second 0. The following figure depicts a Turing machine with that configuration.

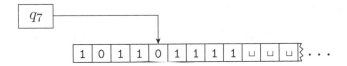

FIGURE **3.3**
A Turing machine with configuration $1011q_701111$

Here we formalize our intuitive understanding of the way that a Turing machine computes. Say that configuration C_1 *yields* configuration C_2 if the Turing machine can legally go from C_1 to C_2 in a single step. We define this notion formally as follows.

Suppose that we have a and b in Γ, as well as u and v in Γ^* and states q_i and q_j. In that case $ua\, q_i\, bv$ and $u\, q_j\, acv$ are two configurations. Say that

$$ua\, q_i\, bv \quad \text{yields} \quad u\, q_j\, acv$$

if in the transition function $\delta(q_i, b) = (q_j, c, \mathrm{L})$. That handles the case where the Turing machine moves leftward. For a rightward move, say that

$$ua\, q_i\, bv \quad \text{yields} \quad uac\, q_j\, v$$

if $\delta(q_i, b) = (q_j, c, \mathrm{R})$.

Special cases occur when the head is at one of the ends of the configuration. For the left-hand end, the configuration $q_i\, bv$ yields $q_j\, cv$ if the transition is left moving (because we prevent the machine from going off the left-hand end of the tape), and it yields $c\, q_j v$ for the right moving transition. For the right-hand end, the configuration $ua\, q_i$ is equivalent to $ua\, q_i\, \sqcup$ because we assume that blanks follow the part of the tape represented in the configuration. Thus we can handle this case as before, with the head no longer at the right-hand end.

The *start configuration* of M on input w is the configuration $q_0\, w$, which indicates that the machine is in the start state q_0 with its head at the leftmost position on the tape. In an *accepting configuration* the state of the configuration is q_{accept}. In a *rejecting configuration* the state of the configuration is q_{reject}. Accepting and rejecting configurations are *halting configurations* and accordingly do not yield further configurations. A Turing machine M *accepts* input w if a sequence of configurations $C_1, C_2, \dots, C_k$ exists where

1. C_1 is the start configuration of M on input w,

2. each C_i yields C_{i+1}, and

3. C_k is an accepting configuration.

The collection of strings that M accepts is *the language of M*, denoted $L(M)$.

DEFINITION **3.2** ....

Call a language *Turing-recognizable* if some Turing machine recognizes it.[1]

When we start a TM on an input, three outcomes are possible. The machine may *accept*, *reject*, or *loop*. By *loop* we mean that the machine simply does not halt. It is not necessarily repeating the same steps in the same way forever as the connotation of looping may suggest. Looping may entail any simple or complex behavior that never leads to a halting state.

A Turing machine M can fail to accept an input by entering the q_{reject} state and rejecting, or by looping. Sometimes distinguishing a machine that is looping from one that is merely taking a long time is difficult. For this reason we prefer Turing machines that halt on all inputs; such machines never loop. These machines are called *deciders* because they always make a decision to accept or reject. A decider that recognizes some language also is said to *decide* that language.

DEFINITION **3.3** ....

Call a language *Turing-decidable* or simply *decidable* if some Turing machine decides it.[2]

Every decidable language is Turing-recognizable but certain Turing-recognizable languages are not decidable. We now give some examples of decidable languages. We present examples of languages that are Turing-recognizable but not decidable after we develop a technique for proving undecidability in Chapter 4.

EXAMPLES OF TURING MACHINES

As we did for finite and pushdown automata, we can give a formal description of a particular Turing machine by specifying each of its seven parts. However, going to that level of detail for Turing machines can be cumbersome for all but the tiniest machines. Accordingly, we won't spend much time giving such descriptions. Mostly we will give only higher level descriptions because they are precise enough for our purposes and are much easier to understand. Nevertheless, it is important to remember that every higher level description is actually just shorthand for its formal counterpart. With patience and care we could describe any of the Turing machines in this book in complete formal detail.

To help you make the connection between the formal descriptions and the higher level descriptions, we give state diagrams in the next two examples. You may skip over them if you already feel comfortable with this connection.

---

[1]It is called a *recursively enumerable* language in some other textbooks.
[2]It is called a *recursive* language in some other textbooks.

EXAMPLE **3.4** ···

Here we describe a TM M_2 that recognizes the language consisting of all strings of 0s whose length is a power of 2. It decides the language $A = \{0^{2^n} \mid n \geq 0\}$.

$M_2 =$ "On input string w:

1. Sweep left to right across the tape, crossing off every other 0.
2. If in stage 1 the tape contained a single 0, *accept*.
3. If in stage 1 the tape contained more than a single 0 and the number of 0s was odd, *reject*.
4. Return the head to the left-hand end of the tape.
5. Go to stage 1."

Each iteration of stage 1 cuts the number of 0s in half. As the machine sweeps across the tape in stage 1, it keeps track of whether the number of 0s seen is even or odd. If that number is odd and greater than 1, the original number of 0s in the input could not have been a power of 2. Therefore the machine rejects in this instance. However, if the number of 0s seen is 1, the original number must have been a power of 2. So in this case the machine accepts.

Now we give the formal description of $M_2 = (Q, \Sigma, \Gamma, \delta, q_1, q_{\text{accept}}, q_{\text{reject}})$.

- $Q = (q_1, q_2, q_3, q_4, q_5, q_{\text{accept}}, q_{\text{reject}})$,

- $\Sigma = \{0\}$, and

- $\Gamma = \{0, \text{x}, \sqcup\}$.

- We describe δ with a state diagram (see Figure 3.4).

- The start, accept, and reject states are q_1, q_{accept}, and q_{reject}.

In the state diagram in Figure 3.4 the label $0 \rightarrow \sqcup, \text{R}$ appears on the transition from q_1 to q_2. It signifies that, when in state q_1 with the head reading 0, the machine goes to state q_2, writes $\sqcup$, and moves the head to the right. In other words, $\delta(q_1, 0) = (q_2, \sqcup, \text{R})$. For clarity we use the shorthand $0 \rightarrow \text{R}$ in the transition from q_3 to q_4, as meaning that the machine moves to the right when reading 0 in state q_4 but doesn't alter the tape, so $\delta(q_3, 0) = (q_4, 0, \text{R})$.

This machine begins by writing a blank symbol over the leftmost 0 on the tape so that it can find the left-hand end of the tape in stage 4. Whereas we would normally use a more suggestive symbol such as # for the left-hand end delimiter, we use a blank here to keep the tape alphabet, and hence the state diagram, small. Example 3.6 gives another method of finding the left-hand end of the tape.

We give a sample run of this machine on input 0000. The starting configuration is $q_1 0000$. The sequence of configurations the machine enters appears following Figure 3.4. Read down the columns and left to right.

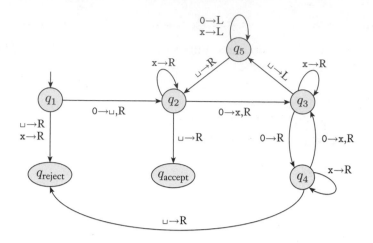

FIGURE **3.4**
State diagram for Turing machine M_2

A sample run of M_2 on input 0000:

$q_1 0000$	$\sqcup q_5 \text{x0x} \sqcup$	$\sqcup \text{x} q_5 \text{xx} \sqcup$
$\sqcup q_2 000$	$q_5 \sqcup \text{x0x} \sqcup$	$\sqcup q_5 \text{xxx} \sqcup$
$\sqcup \text{x} q_3 00$	$\sqcup q_2 \text{x0x} \sqcup$	$q_5 \sqcup \text{xxx} \sqcup$
$\sqcup \text{x0} q_4 0$	$\sqcup \text{x} q_2 \text{0x} \sqcup$	$\sqcup q_2 \text{xxx} \sqcup$
$\sqcup \text{x0x} q_3 \sqcup$	$\sqcup \text{xx} q_3 \text{x} \sqcup$	$\sqcup \text{x} q_2 \text{xx} \sqcup$
$\sqcup \text{x0} q_5 \text{x} \sqcup$	$\sqcup \text{xxx} q_3 \sqcup$	$\sqcup \text{xx} q_2 \text{x} \sqcup$
$\sqcup \text{x} q_5 \text{0x} \sqcup$	$\sqcup \text{xx} q_5 \text{x} \sqcup$	$\sqcup \text{xxx} q_2 \sqcup$
		$\sqcup \text{xxx} \sqcup q_{\text{accept}}$

EXAMPLE **3.5**

The following is a formal description of $M_1 = (Q, \Sigma, \Gamma, \delta, q_1, q_{\text{accept}}, q_{\text{reject}})$, the Turing machine that we informally described on page 127 for deciding the language $B = \{w\#w|\ w \in \{0,1\}^*\}$.

- $Q = (q_1, \dots, q_{14}, q_{\text{accept}}, q_{\text{reject}})$,

- $\Sigma = \{0,1,\#\}$, and $\Gamma = \{0,1,\#,\sqcup\}$.

- We describe δ with a state diagram (see Figure 3.5).

- The start, accept, and reject states are q_1, q_{accept}, and q_{reject}.

In Figure 3.5 depicting the state diagram of TM M_1, you will find the label $0,1 \rightarrow R$ on the transition going from q_3 to itself. That label means that the machine stays in q_3 and moves to the right when it reads a 0 or a 1 in state q_3. It doesn't change the symbol on the tape.

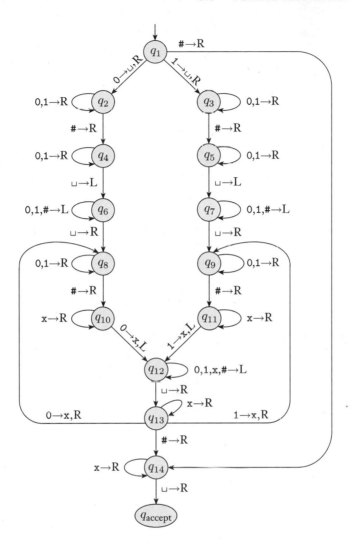

FIGURE 3.5
State diagram for Turing machine M_1

As in Example 3.4, the machine starts by writing a blank symbol to delimit the left-hand edge of the tape. This time it may overwrite a 0 or a 1 when doing so, and it remembers the overwritten symbol by using the finite control.

Stage 1 is implemented by states q_1 through q_7, and stages 2 and 3 by the remaining states. To simplify the figure, we don't show the reject state or the transitions going to the reject state. Those transitions occur implicitly whenever a state lacks an outgoing transition for a particular symbol. Thus, because in state q_5 no outgoing arrow with a # is present, if a # occurs under the head when the machine is in state q_5, it goes to state q_{reject}.

Here, a Turing machine M_3 is doing some elementary arithmetic. It decides the language $C = \{a^i b^j c^k | \ i \times j = k \text{ and } i, j, k \geq 1\}$.

$M_3 = $ "On input string w:

1. Scan the input from left to right to be sure that it is a member of $a^*b^*c^*$ and *reject* if it isn't.
2. Return the head to the left-hand end of the tape.
3. Cross off an a and scan to the right until a b occurs. Shuttle between the b's and the c's, crossing off one of each until all b's are gone.
4. Restore the crossed off b's and repeat stage 3 if there is another a to cross off. If all a's are crossed off, check on whether all c's also are crossed off. If yes, *accept*; otherwise, *reject*."

Let's examine the four stages of M_3 more closely. In stage 1 the machine operates like a finite automaton. No writing is necessary as the head moves from left to right, keeping track using its states of whether the input is in the proper form.

Stage 2 looks equally simple but contains a subtlety. How can the Turing machine find the left-hand end of the input tape? Finding the right-hand end of the input is easy because it is terminated with a blank symbol. But the left-hand end has no terminator initially. One technique that allows the machine to find the left-hand end of the tape is for it to mark the leftmost symbol in some way when the machine starts with its head on that symbol. Then the machine may scan left until it finds the mark when it wants to reset its head to the left-hand end. Example 3.4 illustrated this technique, using a blank symbol to mark the left-hand tape symbol.

A trickier method of finding the left-hand end of the tape takes advantage of the way that we defined the Turing machine model. Recall that, if the machine tries to move its head beyond the left-hand end of the tape, it stays in the same place. We can use this feature to make a left-hand end detector. To detect whether the head is sitting on the left-hand end the machine can write a special symbol over the current position, while recording the symbol that it replaced in the control. Then it can attempt to move the head to the left. If it is still over the special symbol, the leftward move didn't succeed, and thus the head must have been at the left-hand end. If instead it is over a different symbol, some symbols remained to the left of that position on the tape. Before going farther, the machine must be sure to restore the changed symbol to the original.

Stages 3 and 4 have straightforward implementations using several states each.

EXAMPLE **3.7** ....

Here, a Turing machine M_4 is solving what is called the *element distinctness problem*. It is given a list of strings over $\{0,1\}$ separated by #s and its job is to accept if all the strings are different. The language is

$$E = \{\#x_1\#x_2\# \cdots \#x_l|\ \text{each } x_i \in \{0,1\}^* \text{ and } x_i \neq x_j \text{ for each } i \neq j\}.$$

Machine M_4 works by comparing x_1 with x_2 through x_l, then by comparing x_2 with x_3 through x_l, and so on. An informal description of the TM M_4 deciding this language follows.

$M_4 =$ "On input w:

1. Place a mark on top of the leftmost tape symbol. If that symbol was not a #, *reject*.
2. Scan right to the next # and place a second mark on top of it. If no # is encountered before a blank symbol, only x_1 was present, so *accept*.
3. By zig-zagging, compare the two strings to the right of the marked #s. If they are equal, *reject*.
4. Move the rightmost of the two marks to the next # symbol to the right. If no # symbol is encountered before a blank symbol, move the leftmost mark to the next # to its right and the rightmost mark to the # after that. This time, if no # is available for the rightmost mark, all the strings have been compared, so *accept*.
5. Go to Stage 3."

This machine illustrates the technique of marking tape symbols. In stage 2, the machine places a mark above a symbol, # in this case. In the actual implementation, the machine has two different symbols, # and $\overset{\bullet}{\#}$, in its tape alphabet. Saying that the machine places a mark above a # means that the machine writes the symbol $\overset{\bullet}{\#}$ at that location. Removing the mark means that the machine writes the symbol without the dot. In general we may want to place marks over various symbols on the tape. To do so we merely include versions of all these tape symbols with dots in the tape alphabet. ■

We may conclude from the preceding examples that the described languages A, B, C, and E are decidable. All decidable languages are Turing-recognizable, so these languages are also Turing-recognizable. Demonstrating a language that is Turing-recognizable but not decidable is more difficult, which we do in Chapter 4.

3.2 ▪▪▪▪▪▪▪▪▪▪▪▪▪▪▪▪▪▪▪▪▪▪▪▪▪▪▪▪▪▪▪▪▪▪▪▪▪▪▪

VARIANTS OF TURING MACHINES

Alternative definitions of Turing machines abound, including versions with multiple tapes or with nondeterminism. They are called *variants* of the Turing machine model. The original model and its reasonable variants all have the same power—they recognize the same class of languages. In this section we describe some of these variants and the proofs of equivalence in power. We call this invariance to certain changes in the definition *robustness*. Both finite automata and pushdown automata are somewhat robust models, but Turing machines have an astonishing degree of robustness.

To illustrate the robustness of the Turing machine model let's vary the type of transition function permitted. In our definition, the transition function forces the head to move to the left or right after each step; the head may not simply stay put. Suppose that we had allowed the Turing machine the ability to stay put. The transition function would then have the form $\delta\colon Q \times \Gamma \longrightarrow Q \times \Gamma \times \{L, R, S\}$. Might this feature allow Turing machines to recognize additional languages, thus adding to the power of the model? Of course not, because we can convert any TM with the "stay put" feature to one that does not have it. We do so by replacing each stay put transition with two transitions, one that moves to the right and the second back to the left.

This small example contains the key to showing the equivalence of Turing machine variants. To show that two models are equivalent we simply need to show that we can simulate one by the other.

MULTITAPE TURING MACHINES

A *multitape Turing machine* is like an ordinary Turing machine with several tapes. Each tape has its own head for reading and writing. Initially the input appears on tape 1, and the others start out blank. The transition function is changed to allow for reading, writing, and moving the heads on all the tapes simultaneously. Formally, it is

$$\delta\colon Q \times \Gamma^k \longrightarrow Q \times \Gamma^k \times \{L, R\}^k,$$

where k is the number of tapes. The expression

$$\delta(q_i, a_1, \ldots, a_k) = (q_j, b_1, \ldots, b_k, L, R, \ldots, L)$$

means that, if the machine is in state q_i and heads 1 through k are reading symbols a_1 through a_k, the machine goes to state q_j, writes symbols b_1 through b_k, and moves each head to the left or right as specified.

Multitape Turing machines appear to be more powerful than ordinary Turing machines, but we can show they are equivalent in power. Recall that two machines are equivalent if they recognize the same language.

THEOREM **3.8**

Every multitape Turing has an equivalent single tape Turing machine.

PROOF   We show how to convert a multitape TM M to an equivalent single tape TM S. The key idea is to show how to simulate M with S.

Say that M has k tapes. Then S simulates the effect of k tapes by storing their information on its single tape. It uses the new symbol # as a delimiter to separate the contents of the different tapes. In addition to the contents of these tapes, S must keep track of the locations of the heads. It does so by writing a tape symbol with a dot above it to mark the place where the head on that tape would be. Think of these as "virtual" tapes and heads. As before, the "dotted" tape symbols are simply new symbols that have been added to the tape alphabet. The following figure illustrates how one tape can be used to represent three tapes.

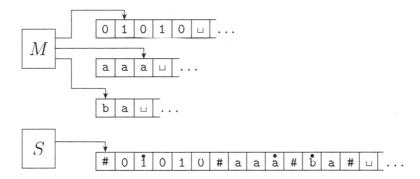

FIGURE 3.6
Representing three tapes with one

$S =$ "On input $w = w_1 \cdots w_n$:

1. First S puts its tape into the format that represents all k tapes of M. The formatted tape contains

$$\#\dot{w_1}w_2 \cdots w_n \ \#\dot{\sqcup}\#\dot{\sqcup}\# \cdots \#$$

2. To simulate a single move, S scans its tape from the first #, which marks the left-hand end, to the $(k + 1)$st #, which marks the right-hand end, in order to determine the symbols under the virtual heads. Then S makes a second pass to update the tapes according to the way that M's transition function dictates.

3. If at any point S moves one of the virtual heads to the right onto a #, this action signifies that M has moved the corresponding head onto the previously unread blank portion of that tape. So S writes a blank symbol on this tape cell and shifts the tape contents, from this cell until the rightmost #, one unit to the right. Then it continues the simulation as before."

COROLLARY **3.9** ··

A language is Turing-recognizable if and only if some multitape Turing machine recognizes it.

PROOF A Turing-recognizable language is recognized by an ordinary (single-tape) Turing machine, which is a special case of a multitape Turing machine. That proves one direction of this corollary. The other direction follows from Theorem 3.8.

NONDETERMINISTIC TURING MACHINES

A nondeterministic Turing machine is defined in the expected way. At any point in a computation the machine may proceed according to several possibilities. The transition function for a nondeterministic Turing machine has the form

$$\delta \colon Q \times \Gamma \longrightarrow \mathcal{P}(Q \times \Gamma \times \{L, R\}).$$

The computation of a nondeterministic Turing machine is a tree whose branches correspond to different possibilities for the machine. If some branch of the computation leads to the accept state, the machine accepts its input. If you feel the need to review nondeterminism, turn to Section 1.2 on page 47. Now we show that nondeterminism does not affect the power of the Turing machine model.

THEOREM **3.10** ··

Every nondeterministic Turing machine has an equivalent deterministic Turing machine.

··

PROOF IDEA We show that we can simulate any nondeterministic TM N with a deterministic TM D. The idea behind the simulation is to have D try all possible branches of N's nondeterministic computation. If D ever finds the accept state on one of these branches, D accepts. Otherwise, D's simulation will not terminate.

We view N's computation on an input w as a tree. Each branch of the tree represents one of the branches of the nondeterminism. Each node of the tree is a configuration of N. The root of the tree is the start configuration. The TM D searches this tree for an accepting configuration. Conducting this search carefully is crucial lest D fail to visit the entire tree. A tempting, though bad, idea is to have D explore the tree by using depth first search. The depth first search strategy goes all the way down one branch before backing up to explore other branches. If D were to explore the tree in this manner, D could go forever down one infinite branch and miss an accepting configuration on some other branch. Hence we design D to explore the tree by using breadth first search instead. This strategy explores all branches to the same depth before going on to explore any branch to the next depth. This method guarantees that D will visit every node in the tree until it encounters an accepting configuration.

PROOF   The simulating deterministic TM D has three tapes. By Theorem 3.8 this arrangement is equivalent to having a single tape. The machine D uses its three tapes in a particular way, as illustrated in the following figure. Tape 1 always contains the input string and is never altered. Tape 2 maintains a copy of N's tape on some branch of its nondeterministic computation. Tape 3 keeps track of D's location in N's nondeterministic computation tree.

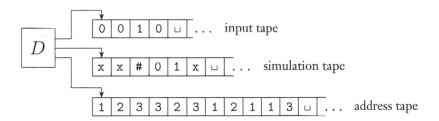

FIGURE   **3.7**
Deterministic TM D simulating nondeterministic TM N

Let's first consider the data representation on tape 3. Every node in the tree can have at most b children, where b is the size of the largest set of possible choices given by N's transition function. To every node in the tree we assign an address that is a string over the alphabet $\Sigma_b = \{1, 2, \ldots, b\}$. We assign the address 231 to the node we arrive at by starting at the root, going to its 2nd child, going to that node's 3rd child, and finally going to that node's 1st child. Each symbol in the string tells us which choice to make next when simulating a step in one branch in N's nondeterministic computation. Sometimes a symbol may not correspond to any choice if too few choices are available for a configuration. In that case the address is invalid and doesn't correspond to any node. Tape 3 contains a string over Σ_b. It represents the branch of N's computation from the root to the node addressed by that string, unless the address is invalid. The empty string is the address of the root of the tree. Now we are ready to describe D.

1. Initially tape 1 contains the input w, and tapes 2 and 3 are empty.
2. Copy tape 1 to tape 2.
3. Use tape 2 to simulate N with input w on one branch of its nondeterministic computation. Before each step of N consult the next symbol on tape 3 to determine which choice to make among those allowed by N's transition function. If no more symbols remain on tape 3 or if this nondeterministic choice is invalid, abort this branch by going to stage 4. Also go to stage 4 if a rejecting configuration is encountered. If an accepting configuration is encountered, *accept* the input.
4. Replace the string on tape 3 with the lexicographically next string. Simulate the next branch of N's computation by going to stage 2.

COROLLARY **3.11** ....

A language is Turing-recognizable if and only if some nondeterministic Turing machine recognizes it.

PROOF Any deterministic TM is automatically a nondeterministic TM and so one direction of this theorem follows immediately. The other direction follows from Theorem 3.10.

....

We can modify the proof of Theorem 3.10 so that if N always halts on all branches of its computation, D will always halt. We call a nondeterministic Turing machine a **decider** if all branches halt on all inputs. Exercise 3.3 asks you to modify the proof in this way to obtain the following corollary to Theorem 3.10.

COROLLARY **3.12** ....

A language is decidable if and only some nondeterministic Turing machine decides it.

ENUMERATORS

As we mentioned in an earlier footnote, some people use the term *recursively enumerable* language for Turing-recognizable language. That term originates from a type of Turing machine variant called an enumerator. Loosely defined, an enumerator is a Turing machine with an attached printer. The Turing machine can use that printer as an output device to print strings. Every time the Turing machine wants to add a string to the list, it sends the string to the printer. Exercise 3.4 asks you to give a formal definition an enumerator. The following figure depicts a schematic of this model.

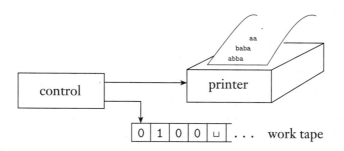

FIGURE **3.8**
Schematic of an enumerator

An enumerator starts with a blank input tape. If the enumerator doesn't halt, it may print an infinite list of strings. The language enumerated by E is the collection of all the strings that it eventually prints out. Moreover, E may generate the strings of the language in any order, possibly with repetitions. Now we are ready to develop the connection between enumerators and Turing-recognizable languages.

THEOREM 3.13 ···

A language is Turing-recognizable if and only if some enumerator enumerates it.

PROOF   First we show that if we have an enumerator E that enumerates a language A, a TM M recognizes A. The TM M works in the following way.

$M = $ "On input w:

  1. Run E. Every time that E outputs a string, compare it with w.
  2. If w ever appears in the output of E, *accept*."

Clearly, M accepts those strings that appear on E's list.

Now we do the other direction. If TM M recognizes a language A, we can construct the following enumerator E for A. Say that $s_1, s_2, s_3, \ldots$ is a list of all possible strings in Σ^*.

$E = $ "Ignore the input.

  1. Repeat the following for $i = 1, 2, 3, \ldots$
  2.   Run M for i steps on each input, $s_1, s_2, \ldots, s_i$.
  3.   If any computations accept, print out the corresponding s_j."

If M accepts a particular string s, eventually it will appear on the list generated by E. In fact, it will appear on the list infinitely many times because M runs from the beginning on each string for each repetition of step 1. This procedure gives the effect of running M in parallel on all possible input strings.

··

EQUIVALENCE WITH OTHER MODELS

So far we have presented several variants of the Turing machine model and have shown them to be equivalent in power. Many other models of general purpose computation have been proposed. Some of these models are very much like Turing machines, while others are quite different. All share the essential feature of Turing machines, namely, unrestricted access to unlimited memory, distinguishing them from weaker models such as finite automata and pushdown automata. Remarkably, *all* models with that feature turn out to be equivalent in power, so long as they satisfy certain reasonable requirements.[3]

---

[3]For example, one requirement is the ability to perform only a finite amount of work in a single step.

To understand this phenomenon consider the analogous situation for programming languages. Many, such as Pascal and LISP, look quite different from one another in style and structure. Can some algorithm be programmed in one of them and not the others? Of course not—we can compile LISP into Pascal and Pascal into LISP, which means that the two languages describe *exactly* the same class of algorithms. So do all other reasonable programming languages. The widespread equivalence of computational models holds for precisely the same reason. Any two computational models that satisfy certain reasonable requirements can simulate one another and hence are equivalent in power.

This equivalence phenomenon has an important philosophical corollary. Even though there are many different computational models, the class of algorithms that they describe is unique. Whereas each individual computational model has a certain arbitrariness to its definition, the underlying class of algorithms that it describes is natural because it is the same class that other models describe. This phenomenon also has had profound implications for mathematics, as we show in the next section.

3.3

THE DEFINITION OF ALGORITHM

Informally speaking, an *algorithm* is a collection of simple instructions for carrying out some task. Commonplace in everyday life, algorithms sometimes are called *procedures* or *recipes*. Algorithms also play an important role in mathematics. Ancient mathematical literature contains descriptions of algorithms for a variety of tasks, such as finding prime numbers and greatest common divisors. In contemporary mathematics algorithms abound.

Even though algorithms have had a long history in mathematics, the notion of algorithm itself was not defined precisely until the twentieth century. Before that, mathematicians had an intuitive notion of what algorithms were and relied upon that notion when using and describing them. But that intuitive notion was insufficient for gaining a deeper understanding of algorithms. The following story relates how the precise definition of algorithm was crucial to one important mathematical problem.

HILBERT'S PROBLEMS

In 1900, mathematician David Hilbert delivered a now-famous address at the International Congress of Mathematicians in Paris. In his lecture, he identified twenty-three mathematical problems and posed them as a challenge for the coming century. The tenth problem on his list concerned algorithms.

Before describing that problem, let's briefly discuss polynomials. A *polynomial* is a sum of terms, where each *term* is a product of certain variables and a constant called a *coefficient*. For example,

$$6 \cdot x \cdot x \cdot x \cdot y \cdot z \cdot z = 6x^3yz^2$$

is a term with coefficient 6, and

$$6x^3yz^2 + 3xy^2 - x^3 - 10$$

is a polynomial with four terms over the variables x, y, and z. A *root* of a polynomial is an assignment of values to its variables so that the value of the polynomial is 0. This polynomial has a root at $x = 5$, $y = 3$, and $z = 0$. This root is an *integral root* because all the variables are assigned integer values. Some polynomials have an integral root and some do not.

Hilbert's tenth problem was to devise an algorithm that tests whether a polynomial has an integral root. He did not use the term *algorithm* but rather "a process according to which it can be determined by a finite number of operations."[4] Interestingly, in the way he phrased this problem, Hilbert explicitly asked that an algorithm be "devised." Thus he apparently assumed that such an algorithm must exist—someone need only find it.

As we now know, no algorithm exists for this task; it is algorithmically unsolvable. For mathematicians of that period to come to this conclusion with their intuitive concept of algorithm would have been virtually impossible. The intuitive concept may have been adequate for giving algorithms for certain tasks, but it was useless for showing that no algorithm exists for a particular task. Proving that an algorithm does not exist requires having a clear definition of algorithm. Progress on the tenth problem had to wait for that definition.

The definition came in the 1936 papers of Alonzo Church and Alan Turing. Church used a notational system called the λ-calculus to define algorithms. Turing did it with his "machines." These two definitions were shown to be equivalent. This connection between the informal notion of algorithm and the precise definition has come to be called the *Church–Turing thesis*.

The Church–Turing thesis provides the definition of algorithm necessary to resolve Hilbert's tenth problem. In 1970, Yuri Matijasevič, building on work of Martin Davis, Hilary Putnam, and Julia Robinson, showed that no algorithm exists for testing whether a polynomial has integral roots. In Chapter 4 we develop the techniques that form the basis for proving that this and other problems are algorithmically unsolvable.

Intuitive notion of algorithms	equals	*Turing machine algorithms*

FIGURE **3.9**
The Church–Turing Thesis

---

[4]Translated from the original German.

Let's phrase Hilbert's tenth problem in our terminology. Doing so helps to introduce some themes that we explore in Chapters 4 and 5. Let

$$D = \{p | \ p \text{ is a polynomial with an integral root}\}.$$

Hilbert's tenth problem asks in essence whether the set D is decidable. The answer is negative. In contrast we can show that D is Turing-recognizable. Before doing so, let's consider a simpler problem. It is an analog of Hilbert's tenth problem for polynomials that have only a single variable, such as $4x^3 - 2x^2 + x - 7$. Let

$$D_1 = \{p | \ p \text{ is a polynomial over } x \text{ with an integral root}\}.$$

Here is a Turing machine M_1 that recognizes D_1:

$M_1 =$ "The input is a polynomial p over the variable x.

1. Evaluate p with x set successively to the values 0, 1, -1, 2, -2, 3, -3, ... If at any point the polynomial evaluates to 0, *accept*."

If p has an integral root, M_1 eventually will find it and accept. If p does not have an integral root, M_1 will run forever. For the multivariable case, we can present a similar Turing machine M that recognizes D. Here, M goes through all possible settings of its variables to integral values.

Both M_1 and M are recognizers but not deciders. We can convert M_1 to be a decider for D_1 because we can calculate bounds within which the roots of a single variable polynomial must lie and restrict the search to these bounds. In Problem 3.18 you are asked to show that the roots of such a polynomial must lie between the values

$$\pm k \frac{c_{\max}}{c_1},$$

where k is the number of terms in the polynomial, $c_{\max}$ is the coefficient with largest absolute value, and c_1 is the coefficient of the highest order term. If a root is not found within these bounds, the machine *rejects*. Matijasevič's theorem shows that calculating such bounds for multivariable polynomials is impossible.

TERMINOLOGY FOR DESCRIBING TURING MACHINES

We have come to a turning point in the study of the theory of computation. We continue to speak of Turing machines, but our real focus from now on is on algorithms. That is, the Turing machine merely serves as a precise model for the definition of algorithm. We will skip over the extensive theory of Turing machines themselves and not spend much time on the low-level programming of Turing machines. We only need to be comfortable enough with Turing machines to believe they capture all algorithms.

With that in mind, let's standardize the way we describe Turing machine algorithms. Initially, we ask: What is the right level of detail to give when describing such algorithms? Students commonly ask this question, especially when preparing solutions to exercises and problems. Let's entertain three possibilities. The first is the *formal description* that spells out in full the Turing machine's states, transition function, and so on. It is the lowest, most detailed, level of description. The second is a higher level of description, called the *implementation description*, in which we use English prose to describe the way that the Turing machine moves its head and the way that it stores data on its tape. At this level we do not give details of states or transition function. Third is the *high-level description*, wherein we use English prose to describe an algorithm, ignoring the implementation model. At this level we do not need to mention how the machine manages its tape or head.

In this chapter we have given formal and implementation-level descriptions of various examples of Turing machines. Practice with lower level Turing machine descriptions helps you understand Turing machines and gain confidence in using them. Once you feel confident, high-level descriptions are sufficient.

We now set up a format and notation for describing Turing machines. The input to a Turing machine is always a string. If we want to provide an object other than a string as input, we must first represent that object as a string. Strings can easily represent polynomials, graphs, grammars, automata, and any combination of those objects. A Turing machine may be programmed to decode the representation so that it can be interpreted in the way we intend. Our notation for the encoding of an object O into its representation as a string is $\langle O \rangle$. If we have several objects $O_1, O_2, \ldots, O_k$, we denote their encoding into a single string by $\langle O_1, O_2, \ldots, O_k \rangle$. The encoding itself can be done in many reasonable ways. It does not matter which one we pick, because a Turing machine can always translate one such encoding into another.

In our format, we describe Turing machine algorithms with an indented segment of text within quotes. We break the algorithm into stages, each usually involving many individual steps of the Turing machine's computation. We indicate the block structure of the algorithm with further indentation. The first line of the algorithm describes the input to the machine. If the input description is simply w, the input is taken to be a string. If the input description is the encoding of an object as in $\langle A \rangle$, the Turing machine first implicitly tests whether the input properly encodes an object of the desired form and rejects it if it doesn't.

EXAMPLE 3.14   ....

Let A be the language consisting of all strings representing undirected graphs that are connected. Recall that a graph is **connected** if every node can be reached from every other node by traveling along the edges of the graph. We write

$$A = \{ \langle G \rangle |\ G \text{ is a connected undirected graph}\}.$$

The following is a high-level description of a TM M that decides A.

M = "On input $\langle G \rangle$, the encoding of a graph G:

1. Select the first node of G and mark it.
2. Repeat the following stage until no new nodes are marked.
3. For each node in G, mark it if it is attached by an edge to a node that is already marked.
4. Scan all the nodes of G to determine whether they all are marked. If they are, *accept*; otherwise *reject*."

For additional practice, let's examine some implementation-level details of Turing machine M. Usually we won't give this level of detail in the future and you won't need to do so either, unless specifically requested in an exercise. First, we must understand how $\langle G \rangle$ encodes the graph G as a string. Consider an encoding that is a list of the nodes of G followed by a list of the edges of G. Each node is a decimal number, and each edge is the pair of decimal numbers that represent the nodes at the two endpoints of the edge. The following figure depicts this graph and its encoding.

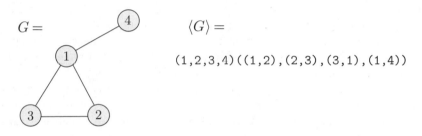

FIGURE **3.10**
A graph G and its encoding $\langle G \rangle$

When M receives the input $\langle G \rangle$, it first checks to determine that the input is the proper encoding of some graph. To do so, M scans the tape to be sure that there are two lists and that they are in the proper form. The first list should be a list of distinct decimal numbers, and the second should be a list of pairs of decimal numbers. Then M checks several things. First, the node list should contain no repetitions, and second, every node appearing on the edge list should also appear on the node list. For the first, we can use the procedure given in Example 3.7 for TM M_4 that checks element distinctness. A similar method works for the second check. If w passes these checks, it is the encoding of some graph G. This verification completes the input check, and M goes on to stage 1.

For stage 1, M marks the first node with a dot on the leftmost digit.

For stage 2, M scans the list of nodes to find an undotted node n_1 and flags it by marking it differently, say, by underlining the first symbol. Then M scans the list again to find a dotted node n_2 and underlines it, too.

Now M scans the list of edges. For each edge, M tests whether the two underlined nodes n_1 and n_2 are the ones appearing in that edge. If they are, M dots n_1, removes the underlines, and goes on from the beginning of stage 2. If they aren't, M checks the next edge on the list. If there are no more edges, $\{n_1, n_2\}$ is not an edge of G. Then M moves the underline on n_2 to the next dotted node and now calls this node n_2. It repeats the steps in this paragraph to check, as before, whether the new pair $\{n_1, n_2\}$ is an edge. If there are no more dotted nodes, n_1 is not attached to any dotted nodes. Then M sets the underlines so that n_1 is the next undotted node and n_2 is the first dotted node and repeats the steps in this paragraph. If there are no more undotted nodes, M has not been able to find any new nodes to dot, so it moves on to stage 4.

For stage 4, M scans the list of nodes to determine whether all are dotted. If they are, it enters the accept state; otherwise it enters the reject state. This completes the description of TM M.

EXERCISES

3.1 This exercise concerns TM M_2 whose description and state diagram appear in Example 3.4. In each of the parts, give the sequence of configurations that M_2 enters when started on the indicated input string.

    a. 0.

    b. 00.

    c. 000.

    d. 000000.

3.2 This exercise concerns TM M_1 whose description and state diagram appear in Example 3.5. In each of the parts, give the sequence of configurations that M_1 enters when started on the indicated input string.

    a. 11.

    b. 1#1.

    c. 1##1.

    d. 10#11.

    e. 10#10.

3.3 Modify the proof of Theorem 3.10 on page 138 to obtain Corollary 3.12 showing that a language is decidable iff some nondeterministic TM decides it. (You may assume the following theorem about trees. If every node in a tree has finitely many children and every branch of the tree has finitely many nodes, the tree itself has finitely many nodes.)

3.4 Give a formal definition of an enumerator. Consider it to be a type of two-tape Turing machine that uses its second tape as the printer. Include a definition of the enumerated language.

3.5 Examine the formal definition of a Turing machine to answer the following questions, and explain your reasoning.

    a. Can a Turing machine ever write the blank symbol $\sqcup$ on its tape?

    b. Can the tape alphabet Γ be the same as the input alphabet Σ?

    c. Can a Turing machine's head *ever* be in the same location in two successive steps?

    d. Can a Turing machine contain just a single state?

3.6 In Theorem 3.13 we showed that a language is Turing-recognizable iff some enumerator enumerates it. Why didn't we use the following simpler algorithm for the forward direction of the proof? As before, $s_1, s_2, \ldots$ is a list of all strings in Σ^*.

$E = $ "Ignore the input.
    1. Repeat the following for $i = 1, 2, 3, \ldots$
    2.   Run M on s_i.
    3.   If it accepts, print out s_i."

3.7 Explain why the following is not a description of a legitimate Turing machine.

$M_{\text{bad}} = $ "The input is a polynomial over variables $x_1, \ldots, x_k$.
    1.   Try all possible settings of $x_1, \ldots, x_k$ to integer values.
    2.   Evaluate p on all of these settings.
    3.   If any of these settings evaluates to 0, *accept*; otherwise, *reject*."

3.8 Give implementation-level descriptions of Turing machines that decide the following languages over the alphabet $\{0,1\}$:

    a. $\{w|\ w$ contains an equal number of 0s and 1s$\}$.

    b. $\{w|\ w$ contains twice as many 0s as 1s$\}$.

    c. $\{w|\ w$ does not contain twice as many 0s as 1s$\}$.

PROBLEMS

3.9 Let a k-PDA be a pushdown automaton that has k stacks. Thus a 0-PDA is an NFA and a 1-PDA is a conventional PDA. You already know that 1-PDAs are more powerful (recognize a larger class of languages) than 0-PDAs.

    a. Show that 2-PDAs are more powerful than 1-PDAs.

    b. Show that 3-PDAs are not more powerful than 2-PDAs.
       (Hint: Simulate a Turing machine tape with two stacks.)

3.10 Say that a ***write-once Turing machine*** is a single-tape TM that can alter each tape square at most once (including the input portion of the tape). Show that this variant Turing machine model is equivalent to the ordinary Turing machine model. (Hint: As a first step consider the case whereby the Turing machine may alter each tape square at most twice. Use lots of tape.)

3.11 A ***Turing machine with doubly infinite tape*** is similar to an ordinary Turing machine except that its tape is infinite to the left as well as to the right. The tape is initially filled with blanks except for the portion that contains the input. Computation is defined as usual except that the head never encounters an end to the tape as it moves leftward. Show that this type of Turing machine recognizes the class of Turing-recognizable languages.

3.12 A *Turing machine with left reset* is similar to an ordinary except that the transition function has the form

$$\delta \colon Q \times \Gamma \longrightarrow Q \times \Gamma \times \{\text{R}, \text{RESET}\}.$$

If $\delta(q, a) = (r, b, \text{RESET})$, when the machine is in state q reading an a, the machine's head jumps to the left-hand end of the tape after it writes b in the tape and enters state r. Note that these machines do not have the usual ability to move the head one symbol left. Show that Turing machines with left reset recognize the class of Turing-recognizable languages.

3.13 A *Turing machine with stay put instead of left* is similar to an ordinary except that the transition function has the form

$$\delta \colon Q \times \Gamma \longrightarrow Q \times \Gamma \times \{\text{R}, \text{S}\}.$$

At each point the machine can move its head right or let it stay in the same position. Show that this Turing machine variant is *not* equivalent the usual version. What class of languages do these machines recognize?

3.14 Show that the collection of decidable languages is closed under the operations of

    a. union.

    b. concatenation.

    c. star.

    d. complementation.

    e. intersection.

3.15 Show that the collection of Turing-recognizable languages is closed under the operations of

    a. union.

    b. concatenation.

    c. star.

    d. intersection.

*★***3.16** Show that a language is decidable iff some enumerator enumerates the language in lexicographic order.

*★***3.17** Show that single-tape TMs that cannot write on the portion of the tape containing the input string can only recognize regular languages.

3.18 Let $c_1 x^n + c_2 x^{n-1} + \cdots + c_n x + c_{n+1}$ be a polynomial with a root at $x = x_0$. Let $c_{\max}$ be the largest absolute value of a c_i. Show that

$$|x_0| < (n+1) \frac{c_{\max}}{|c_1|}.$$

3.19 Let A be the language containing only the single string s, where

$$s = \begin{cases} 0 & \text{if God does not exist} \\ 1 & \text{if God does exist.} \end{cases}$$

Is A decidable? Why or why not? (Note that the answer doesn't depend on your religious convictions.)

4

DECIDABILITY

In Chapter 3 we introduced the Turing machine as a model of a general purpose computer and defined the notion of algorithm in terms of Turing machines by means of the Church–Turing thesis.

In this chapter we begin to investigate the power of algorithms to solve problems. We demonstrate certain problems that can be solved algorithmically and others that cannot. Our objective is to explore the limits of algorithmic solvability. You are probably familiar with solvability by algorithms because much of computer science is devoted to solving problems. The unsolvability of certain problems may come as a surprise.

Why should you study unsolvability? After all, showing that a problem is unsolvable doesn't appear to be of any use if you have to solve it. You need to study this phenomenon for two reasons. First, knowing when a problem is algorithmically unsolvable *is* useful because then you realize that the problem must be simplified or altered before you can find an algorithmic solution. Like any tool, computers have capabilities and limitations that must be appreciated if they are to be used well. The second reason is cultural. Even if you deal with problems that clearly are solvable, a glimpse of the unsolvable can stimulate your imagination and help you gain an important perspective on computation.

4.1

DECIDABLE LANGUAGES

In this section we give some examples of languages that are decidable by algorithms. For example, we present an algorithm that tests whether a string is a member of a context-free language. This problem is related to the problem of recognizing and compiling programs in a programming language. Seeing algorithms solving various problems concerning automata is helpful, because later you will encounter other problems concerning automata that cannot be solved by algorithms.

DECIDABLE PROBLEMS CONCERNING REGULAR LANGUAGES

We begin with certain computational problems concerning finite automata. We give algorithms for testing whether a finite automaton accepts a string, whether the language of a finite automaton is empty, and whether two finite automata are equivalent.

For convenience we use languages to represent various computational problems because we have already set up terminology for dealing with languages. For example, the ***acceptance problem*** for DFAs of testing whether a particular finite automaton accepts a given string can be expressed as a language, A_{DFA}. This language contains the encodings of all DFAs together with strings that the DFAs accept. Let

$$A_{\mathsf{DFA}} = \{\langle B, w\rangle |\ B \text{ is a DFA that accepts input string } w\}.$$

The problem of testing whether a DFA B accepts an input w is the same as the problem of testing whether $\langle B, w\rangle$ is a member of the language A_{DFA}. Similarly, we can formulate other computational problems in terms of testing membership in a language. Showing that the language is decidable is the same as showing that the computational problem is decidable.

In the following theorem we show that A_{DFA} is decidable. Hence this theorem shows that the problem of testing whether a given finite automaton accepts a given string is decidable.

THEOREM **4.1** ....

A_{DFA} is a decidable language.

....

PROOF IDEA   The proof idea is very simple. We only need to present a TM M that decides A_{DFA}.

$M =$ "On input $\langle B, w \rangle$, where B is a DFA and w is a string:

1. Simulate B on input w.
2. If the simulation ends in an accept state, *accept*. If it ends in a nonaccepting state, *reject*."

PROOF   We mention just a few implementation details of this proof. For those of you familiar with writing programs in any standard programming language, imagine how you would write a program to carry out the simulation.

First, let's examine the input $\langle B, w \rangle$. It is a representation of a DFA B together with a string w. One reasonable representation of B is simply a list of its five components, Q, Σ, δ, q_0, and F. When M receives its input, M first checks on whether it properly represents a DFA B and a string w. If not, M rejects.

Then M carries out the simulation in a direct way. It keeps track of B's current state and B's current position in the input w by writing this information down on its tape. Initially, B's current state is q_0 and B's current input position is the leftmost symbol of w. The states and position are updated according to the specified transition function δ. When M finishes processing the last symbol of w, M accepts the input if B is in an accepting state; M rejects the input if B is in a nonaccepting state.

We can prove a similar theorem for nondeterministic finite automata. Let

$$A_{\mathsf{NFA}} = \{\langle B, w \rangle | \ B \text{ is an NFA that accepts input string } w\}.$$

THEOREM **4.2**

A_{NFA} is a decidable language.

PROOF   We present a TM N that decides A_{NFA}. We could design N to operate like M, simulating an NFA instead of a DFA. Instead, we'll do it differently to illustrate a new idea: have N use M as a subroutine. Because M is designed to work with DFAs, N first converts the NFA it receives as input to a DFA before passing it to M.

$N =$ "On input $\langle B, w \rangle$ where B is an NFA, and w is a string:

1. Convert NFA B to an equivalent DFA C using the procedure for this conversion given in Theorem 1.19.
2. Run TM M from Theorem 4.1 on input $\langle C, w \rangle$.
3. If M accepts, *accept*; otherwise *reject*."

Running TM M in stage 2 means incorporating M into the design of N as in a subprocedure.

Similarly, we can test whether a regular expression generates a given string. Let $A_{\mathsf{REX}} = \{\langle R, w\rangle|\ R$ is a regular expression that generates string $w\}$.

THEOREM **4.3** ··

A_{REX} is a decidable language.

PROOF   The following TM P decides A_{REX}.

$P = $ "On input $\langle R, w\rangle$ where R is a regular expression and w is a string:

1. Convert regular expression R to an equivalent DFA A by using the procedure for this conversion given in Theorem 1.28.
2. Run TM M on input $\langle A, w\rangle$.
3. If M accepts, *accept*; if M rejects, *reject*."

Theorems 4.1 and 4.2 illustrate that for decidability purposes, presenting the Turing machine with a DFA, NFA, or regular expression are all equivalent because the machine is able to convert one form of encoding to another.

Now we turn to a different kind of problem concerning finite automata: *emptiness testing* for the language of a finite automaton. In the preceding theorems we had to test whether a finite automaton accepts a particular string. In the next proof we must test whether a finite automaton accepts any strings at all. Let

$$E_{\mathsf{DFA}} = \{\langle A\rangle|\ A \text{ is a DFA and } L(A) = \emptyset\}.$$

THEOREM **4.4** ··

E_{DFA} is a decidable language.

PROOF   A DFA accepts some string if and only if reaching an accept state from the start state by traveling along the arrows of the DFA is possible. To test this condition we can design a TM T that uses a marking algorithm similar to that used in Example 3.14.

$T = $ "On input $\langle A\rangle$ where A is a DFA:

1. Mark the start state of A.
2. Repeat until no new states get marked:
3.   Mark any state that has a transition coming into it from any state that is already marked.
4. If no accept state is marked, *accept*; otherwise *reject*."

The next theorem states that testing whether two DFAs recognize the same language is decidable. Let

$$EQ_{\mathsf{DFA}} = \{\langle A, B\rangle | \ A \text{ and } B \text{ are DFAs and } L(A) = L(B)\}.$$

THEOREM **4.5** ···

EQ_{DFA} is a decidable language.

PROOF   To prove this theorem we use Theorem 4.4. We construct a new DFA C from A and B, where C accepts only those strings that are accepted by either A or B but not by both. Thus, if A and B recognize the same language, C will accept nothing. The language of C is

$$L(C) = \left(L(A) \cap \overline{L(B)}\right) \cup \left(\overline{L(A)} \cap L(B)\right).$$

This expression is sometimes called the ***symmetric difference*** of $L(A)$ and $L(B)$ and is illustrated in the following figure. Here $\overline{L(A)}$ is the complement of $L(A)$. The symmetric difference is useful here because $L(C) = \emptyset$ if and only if $L(A) = L(B)$. We can construct C from A and B with the constructions for proving the class of regular languages closed under complementation, union, and intersection. These constructions are algorithms that can be carried out by Turing machines. Once we have constructed C we can use Theorem 4.4 to test whether $L(C)$ is empty. If it is empty, $L(A)$ and $L(B)$ must be equal.

$F =$ "On input $\langle A, B\rangle$, where A and B are DFAs:

1. Construct DFA C as described.
2. Run TM T from Theorem 4.4 on input $\langle C\rangle$.
3. If T accepts, *accept*. If T rejects, *reject*."

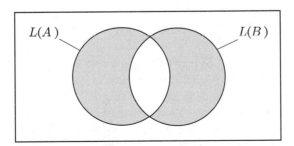

FIGURE **4.1**
The symmetric difference of $L(A)$ and $L(B)$

DECIDABLE PROBLEMS CONCERNING CONTEXT-FREE LANGUAGES

Here, we describe algorithms to test whether a CFG generates a particular string and to test whether the language of a CFG is empty. Let

$$A_{CFG} = \{\langle G, w \rangle | \ G \text{ is a CFG that generates string } w\}.$$

THEOREM **4.6** ··

A_{CFG} is a decidable language.

PROOF IDEA   For CFG G and string w we want to test whether G generates w. One idea is to use G to go through all derivations to determine whether any is a derivation of w. This idea doesn't work, as infinitely many derivations may have to be tried. If G does not generate w, this algorithm would never halt. This idea gives a Turing machine that is an recognizer, but not a decider, for A_{CFG}.

To make this Turing machine into a decider we need to ensure that the algorithm tries only finitely many derivations. In Problem 2.19 on page 121 we showed that, if G were in Chomsky normal form, any derivation of w has $2n - 1$ steps, where n is the length of w. In that case checking only derivations with $2n - 1$ steps to determine whether G generates w would be sufficient. Only finitely many such derivations exist. We can convert G to Chomsky normal form by using the procedure given in Section 2.1.

PROOF   The TM S for A_{CFG} follows.

$S = $ "On input $\langle G, w \rangle$, where G is a CFG and w is a string:
1. Convert G to an equivalent grammar in Chomsky normal form.
2. List all derivations with $2n - 1$ steps, where n is the length of w.
3. If any of these derivations generate w, *accept*; if not, *reject*."

The problem of testing whether a CFL generates a particular string is related to the problem of compiling programming languages. The algorithm in TM S is very inefficient and would never be used in practice, but it is easy to describe and we aren't concerned with efficiency here. In Part Three of this book we address issues concerning the running time and memory use of algorithms. In the proof of Theorem 7.14, we describe a more efficient algorithm for recognizing context-free languages

Recall that we have given procedures for converting back and forth between CFLs and PDAs in Theorem 2.12. Hence everything we say about the decidability of problems concerning CFLs applies equally well to PDAs.

Let's turn now to the emptiness testing problem for the language of a CFG. As we did for DFAs, we can show that the problem of testing whether a CFG generates any strings at all is decidable. Let

$$E_{\mathsf{CFG}} = \{\langle G \rangle \mid G \text{ is a CFG and } L(G) - \emptyset\}.$$

THEOREM **4.7** ....

E_{CFG} is a decidable language.

....

PROOF IDEA   To find an algorithm for this problem we might attempt to use TM S from Theorem 4.6. It states that we can test whether a CFG generates some particular string w. To determine whether $L(G) = \emptyset$ the algorithm might try going through all possible w's, one by one. But there are infinitely many w's to try, so this method could end up running forever. We need to take a different approach.

In order to test whether the language of a grammar is empty, we need to test whether the start variable can generate a string of terminals. The algorithm does so by solving a more general problem. It determines *for each variable* whether that variable is capable of generating a string of terminals. When the algorithm has determined that a variable can generate some string of terminals, the algorithm keeps track of this information by placing a mark on that variable.

First, the algorithm marks all the terminal symbols in the grammar. Then, it scans all the rules of the grammar. If it ever finds a rule that permits some variable to be replaced by some string of symbols all of which are already marked, the algorithm knows that this variable can be marked, too. The algorithm continues in this way until it cannot mark any additional variables. The TM R implements this algorithm.

PROOF

$R = $ "On input $\langle G \rangle$, where G is a CFG:

1. Mark all terminal symbols in G.
2. Repeat until no new variables get marked:
3.   Mark any variable A where G has a rule $A \to U_1 U_2 \cdots U_k$ and each symbol $U_1, \ldots, U_k$ has already been marked.
4. If the start symbol is not marked, *accept*; otherwise *reject*."

Next we consider the problem of testing whether two context-free grammars generate the same language. Let

$$EQ_{\mathsf{CFG}} = \{\langle G, H\rangle |\ G \text{ and } H \text{ are CFLs and } L(G) = L(H)\}.$$

Theorem 4.5 gave an algorithm that decides the analogous language EQ_{DFA} for finite automata. We used the decision procedure for E_{DFA} to prove that EQ_{DFA} is decidable. Because E_{CFG} also is decidable, you might think that we can use a similar strategy to prove that EQ_{CFG} is decidable. But something goes wrong with this idea! The class of context-free languages is *not* closed under complementation or intersection as you proved in Exercise 2.2. In fact, EQ_{CFG} is not decidable, and you will see the technique for proving so in Chapter 5.

Now we show that every context-free language is decidable by a Turing machine.

THEOREM 4.8 ....

Every context-free language is decidable.

PROOF IDEA   Let A be a CFL. Our objective is to show that A is decidable. One (bad) idea is to convert a PDA for A directly into a TM. That isn't hard to do because simulating a stack with the TM's more versatile tape is easy. The PDA for A may be nondeterministic, but that seems okay because we can convert it into a nondeterministic TM and we know that any nondeterministic TM can be converted into an equivalent deterministic TM. Yet, there is a difficulty. Some branches of the PDA's computation may go on forever, reading and writing the stack without coming to a halt. The simulating TM then would also have some nonhalting branches in its computation, and so the TM would not be a decider. A different idea is necessary. Instead, we prove this theorem with the TM S that we designed in Theorem 4.6 to decide A_{CFG}.

PROOF   Let G be a CFG for A and design a TM M_G that decides A. We build a copy of G into M_G. It works as follows.

$M_G = $ "On input w:
  1. Run TM S on input $\langle G, w\rangle$
  2. If this machine accepts, *accept*; if it rejects, *reject*."

Theorem 4.8 provides the final link in the relationship among the four main classes of languages that we have described so far in this course: regular, context free, decidable, and Turing-recognizable. The following figure depicts this relationship.

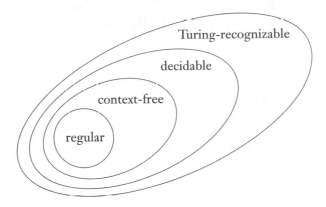

FIGURE 4.2
The relationship among classes of languages

4.2 ▪

THE HALTING PROBLEM

In this section we prove one of the most philosophically important theorems of the theory of computation: there is a specific problem that is algorithmically unsolvable. Computers appear to be so powerful that you may believe that all problems will eventually yield to them. The theorem presented here demonstrates that computers are limited in a very fundamental way.

What sort of problems are unsolvable by computer? Are they esoteric, dwelling only in the minds of theoreticians? No! Even some ordinary problems that people want to solve turn out to be computationally unsolvable.

In one type of unsolvable problem, you are given a computer program and a precise specification of what that program is supposed to do (e.g., sort a list of numbers). You need to verify that the program performs as specified (i.e., that it is correct). Because both the program and the specification are mathematically precise objects, you hope to automate the process of verification by feeding these objects into a suitably programmed computer. However, you will be disappointed. The general problem of software verification is not solvable by computer.

In this section and Chapter 5 you will encounter several computationally unsolvable problems. Our objectives are to help you develop a feel for the types of problems that are unsolvable and to learn techniques for proving unsolvability.

Now we turn to our first theorem that establishes the undecidability of a specific language: the problem of testing whether a Turing machine accepts a given input string. We call it A_{TM} by analogy with A_{DFA} and A_{CFG}. But, whereas A_{DFA} and A_{CFG} were decidable, A_{TM} is not. Let

$$A_{\mathsf{TM}} = \{\langle M, w\rangle \mid M \text{ is a TM and } M \text{ accepts } w\}.$$

THEOREM   **4.9** ···

A_{TM} is undecidable.

Before we get to the proof, let's first observe that A_{TM} is Turing-recognizable. Thus Theorem 4.9 shows that recognizers *are* more powerful than deciders. Requiring a TM to halt on all inputs restricts the kinds of languages that it can recognize. The following Turing machine U recognizes A_{TM}.

$U = $ "On input $\langle M, w \rangle$, where M is a TM and w is a string:
1. Simulate M on input w.
2. If M ever enters its accept state, *accept*; if M ever enters its reject state, *reject*."

Note that this machine loops on input $\langle M, w \rangle$ if M loops on w, which is why this machine does not decide A_{TM}. If the algorithm had some way to determine that M was not halting on w, it could *reject*. Hence A_{TM} is sometimes called the **halting problem**. As we demonstrate, an algorithm has no way to make this determination.

The Turing machine U is interesting in its own right. It is an example of the *universal Turing machine* first proposed by Turing. This machine is called universal because it is capable of simulating any other Turing machine from the description of that machine. The universal Turing machine played an important early role in stimulating the development of stored-program computers.

THE DIAGONALIZATION METHOD

The proof of the undecidability of the halting problem uses a technique called *diagonalization*, discovered by mathematician Georg Cantor in 1873. Cantor was concerned with the problem of measuring the sizes of infinite sets. If we have two infinite sets, how can we tell whether one is larger than the other or whether they are of the same size? For finite sets, of course, answering these questions is easy. We simply count the elements in a finite set, and the resulting number is its size. But, if we try to count the elements of an infinite set, we will never finish! So we can't use the counting method to determine the relative sizes of infinite sets.

For example, take the set of even integers and the set of all strings over $\{0,1\}$. Both sets are infinite and thus larger than any finite set, but is one of the two larger than the other? How can we compare their relative size?

Cantor proposed a rather nice solution to this problem. He observed that two finite sets have the same size if the elements of one set can be paired with the elements of the other set. This method compares the sizes without resorting to counting. We can extend this idea to infinite sets. Let's see what it means more precisely.

DEFINITION   **4.10**

Assume that we have two sets A and B and a function f from A to B. Say that f is **one-to-one** if it never maps two different elements to the same place, that is, if $f(a) \neq f(b)$ whenever $a \neq b$. Say that f is **onto** if it hits every element of B, that is, if for every $b \in B$ there is an $a \in A$ such that $f(a) = b$. Say that A and B are the **same size** if there is a one to one, onto function $f : A \longrightarrow B$. A function that is both one-to-one and onto is called a **correspondence**. In a correspondence every element of A maps to a unique element of B and each element of B has a unique element of A mapping to it. A correspondence is simply a way of pairing the elements of A with the elements of B.

EXAMPLE   **4.11**

Let $\mathcal{N}$ be the set of natural numbers $\{1, 2, 3, \dots\}$ and let $\mathcal{E}$ be the set of even natural numbers $\{2, 4, 6, \dots\}$. Using Cantor's definition of size we can see that $\mathcal{N}$ and $\mathcal{E}$ have the same size. The correspondence f mapping $\mathcal{N}$ to $\mathcal{E}$ is simply $f(n) = 2n$. We can visualize f more easily with the help of a table.

n	$f(n)$
1	2
2	4
3	6
$\vdots$	$\vdots$

Of course, this example seems bizarre. Intuitively, $\mathcal{E}$ is smaller than $\mathcal{N}$ because $\mathcal{E}$ is a proper subset of $\mathcal{N}$. But pairing each member of $\mathcal{N}$ with its own member of $\mathcal{E}$ is possible, so we declare these two sets to be the same size. ■

DEFINITION   **4.12**

A set A is **countable** if either it is finite or it has the same size as $\mathcal{N}$.

EXAMPLE   **4.13**

Now we turn to an even stranger example. If we let $\mathcal{Q}$ be the set of positive rational numbers, that is, $\mathcal{Q} = \{\frac{m}{n} \mid m, n \in \mathcal{N}\}$, $\mathcal{Q}$ seems to be much larger than $\mathcal{N}$. Yet these two sets are the same size. We demonstrate this conclusion by giving a correspondence with $\mathcal{N}$ to show that $\mathcal{Q}$ is countable. One easy way to give a correspondence with $\mathcal{N}$ is to list all the elements of $\mathcal{Q}$. Then we pair the first element on the list with the number 1 from $\mathcal{N}$, the second element on the list with the number 2 from $\mathcal{N}$, and so on. We must check to be sure that every member of $\mathcal{Q}$ appears only once on the list.

To get this list we make an infinite matrix containing all the positive rational numbers, as shown in the following figure. The ith row contains all numbers with numerator i and the jth column has all numbers with denominator j. So the number $\frac{i}{j}$ occurs in the ith row and jth column.

Now we turn this matrix into a list. One (bad) way to attempt it would be to begin the list with all the elements in the first row. That isn't a good approach because the first row is infinite, so the list would never get to the second row. Instead we list the elements on the diagonals, starting from the corner, which are superimposed on the diagram. The first diagonal contains the single element $\frac{1}{1}$, and the second diagonal contains the two elements $\frac{2}{1}$ and $\frac{1}{2}$. So the first three elements on the list are $\frac{1}{1}$, $\frac{2}{1}$, and $\frac{1}{2}$. In the third diagonal a complication arises. It contains $\frac{3}{1}$, $\frac{2}{2}$, and $\frac{1}{3}$. If we simply added these to the list, we would repeat $\frac{1}{1} = \frac{2}{2}$. We avoid doing so by skipping an element when it would cause a repetition. So we add only the two new elements $\frac{3}{1}$ and $\frac{1}{3}$. Continuing in this way we obtain a list all the elements of $\mathcal{Q}$.

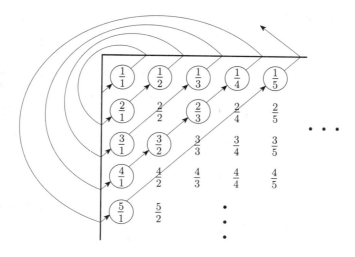

FIGURE **4.3**
A correspondence of $\mathcal{N}$ and $\mathcal{Q}$

After seeing the correspondence of $\mathcal{N}$ and $\mathcal{Q}$, you might think that any two infinite sets can be shown to have the same size. After all, you need only demonstrate a correspondence, and this example shows that surprising correspondences do exist. However, for some infinite sets no correspondence with $\mathcal{N}$ exists. These sets are simply too big. Such sets are called ***uncountable***.

The set of real numbers is an example of an uncountable set. A ***real number*** is one that has a decimal representation. The numbers $\pi = 3.1415926\ldots$ and $\sqrt{2} = 1.4142135\ldots$ are examples of real numbers. Let $\mathcal{R}$ be the set of real numbers. Cantor proved that $\mathcal{R}$ is uncountable. In doing so he introduced the diagonalization method.

THEOREM **4.14**   ....

$\mathcal{R}$ is uncountable.

PROOF   In order to show that $\mathcal{R}$ is uncountable, we show that no correspondence exists between $\mathcal{N}$ and $\mathcal{R}$. The proof is by contradiction. Suppose that a correspondence f existed between $\mathcal{N}$ and $\mathcal{R}$. Our job is to show that f fails to work as it should. For it to be a correspondence, f must pair all the members of $\mathcal{N}$ with all the members of $\mathcal{R}$. But we will find an x in $\mathcal{R}$ that is not paired with anything in $\mathcal{N}$, which will be our contradiction.

The way we find this x is by actually constructing it. We choose each digit of x to make x different from one of the real numbers that is paired with an element of $\mathcal{N}$. In the end we are sure that x is different from any real number that is paired.

We can illustrate this idea by giving an example. Suppose that the correspondence f exists. Let $f(1) = 3.14159\ldots$, $f(2) = 55.55555\ldots$, $f(3) = \ldots$, and so on, just to make up some values for f. Then f pairs the number 1 with $3.14159\ldots$, the number 2 with $55.55555\ldots$, and so on. The following table shows a few values of a hypothetical correspondence f between $\mathcal{N}$ and $\mathcal{R}$.

n	$f(n)$
1	3.14159...
2	55.55555...
3	0.12345...
4	0.50000...
⋮	⋮

We construct the desired x by giving its decimal representation. It is a number between 0 and 1, so all its significant digits are fractional digits following the decimal point. Our objective is to ensure that $x \neq f(n)$ for any n. To ensure that $x \neq f(1)$ we let the first digit of x be anything different from the first fractional digit 1 of $f(1) = 3.\underline{1}4159\ldots$. Arbitrarily, we let it be 4. To ensure that $x \neq f(2)$ we let the second digit of x be anything different from the second fractional digit 5 of $f(2) = 55.5\underline{5}5555\ldots$. Arbitrarily, we let it be 6. The third fractional digit of $f(3) = 0.12\underline{3}45\ldots$ is 3, so we let x be anything different, say, 4. Continuing in this way down the diagonal of the table for f, we obtain all the digits of x, as shown in the following table. We know that x is not $f(n)$ for any n because it differs from $f(n)$ in the nth fractional digit. (A slight problem arises because certain numbers, such as $0.1999\ldots$ and $0.2000\ldots$, are equal even though their decimal representations are different. We avoid this problem by never selecting the digits 0 or 9 when we construct x.)

n	$f(n)$	
1	3.$\underline{1}$4159...	
2	55.5$\underline{5}$5555...	
3	0.12$\underline{3}$45...	$x = 0.4641\ldots$
4	0.500$\underline{0}$0...	
⋮	⋮	

The preceding theorem has an important application to the theory of computation. It shows that some languages are not decidable or even Turing-recognizable, for the reason that there are uncountably many languages yet only countably many Turing machines. Because each Turing machine can recognize a single language and there are more languages than Turing machines, some languages are not recognized by any Turing machine. Such languages are not Turing-recognizable, as we state in the following corollary.

COROLLARY **4.15** ....

Some languages are not Turing-recognizable.

PROOF   To show that the set of all Turing machines is countable we first observe that the set of all strings Σ^* is countable, for any alphabet Σ. With only finitely many strings of each length, we may form a list of Σ^* by writing down all strings of length 0, length 1, length 2, and so on.

The set of all Turing machines is countable because each Turing machine M has an encoding into a string $\langle M \rangle$. If we simply omit those strings that are not legal encodings of Turing machines, we can obtain a list of all Turing machines.

To show that the set of all languages is uncountable we first observe that the set of all infinite binary sequences is uncountable. An *infinite binary sequence* is an unending sequence of 0s and 1s. Let $\mathcal{B}$ be the set of all infinite binary sequences. We can show that $\mathcal{B}$ is uncountable by using a proof by diagonalization similar to the one we used in Theorem 4.14 to show that $\mathcal{R}$ is uncountable.

Let $\mathcal{L}$ be the set of all languages over alphabet Σ. We show that $\mathcal{L}$ is uncountable by giving a correspondence with $\mathcal{B}$, thus showing that the two sets are the same size. Let $\Sigma^* = \{s_1, s_2, s_3, \dots\}$. Each language $A \in \mathcal{L}$ has a unique sequence in $\mathcal{B}$. The ith bit of that sequence is a 1 if $s_i \in A$ and is a 0 if $s_i \notin A$, which is called the ***characteristic sequence*** of A. For example, if A were the language of all strings starting with a 0 over the alphabet $\{0,1\}$, its characteristic sequence χ_A would be

$$
\begin{array}{lcccccccccccc}
\Sigma^* = \{ & \varepsilon, & 0, & 1, & 00, & 01, & 10, & 11, & 000, & 001, & \cdots & \} \ ; \\
A = \{ & & 0, & & 00, & 01, & & & 000, & 001, & \cdots & \} \ ; \\
\chi_A = & 0 & 1 & 0 & 1 & 1 & 0 & 0 & 1 & 1 & \cdots & .
\end{array}
$$

The function $f \colon \mathcal{L} \longrightarrow \mathcal{B}$, where $f(A)$ equals the characteristic sequence of A, is one-to-one and onto and hence a correspondence. Therefore, as $\mathcal{B}$ is uncountable, $\mathcal{L}$ is uncountable as well.

Thus we have shown that the set of all languages cannot be put into a correspondence with the set of all Turing machines. We conclude that some languages are not recognized by any Turing machine.

....

THE HALTING PROBLEM IS UNDECIDABLE

Now we are ready to prove Theorem 4.9, the undecidability of the language

$$A_{\mathsf{TM}} = \{\langle M, w\rangle|\ M \text{ is a TM and } M \text{ accepts } w\}.$$

PROOF   We assume that A_{TM} is decidable and obtain a contradiction. Suppose that H is a decider for A_{TM}. On input $\langle M, w\rangle$, where M is a TM and w is a string, H halts and accepts if M accepts w. Furthermore, H halts and rejects if M fails to accept w. In other words, we assume that H is a TM, where

$$H(\langle M, w\rangle) = \begin{cases} accept & \text{if } M \text{ accepts } w \\ reject & \text{if } M \text{ does not accept } w. \end{cases}$$

Now we construct a new Turing machine D with H as a subroutine. This new TM calls H to determine what M does when the input to M is its own description $\langle M\rangle$. Once D has determined this information, it does the opposite. That is, it rejects if M accepts and accepts if M does not accept. The following is a description of D.

$D =$ "On input $\langle M\rangle$, where M is a TM:
  1. Run H on input $\langle M, \langle M\rangle\rangle$.
  2. Output the opposite of what H outputs; that is, if H accepts, *reject* and if H rejects, *accept*."

Don't be confused by the idea of running a machine on its own description! That is similar to running a program with itself as input, something that does occasionally occur in practice. For example, a compiler is a program that translates other programs. A compiler for the language Pascal may itself be written in Pascal, so running that program on itself would make sense. In summary,

$$D(\langle M\rangle) = \begin{cases} accept & \text{if } M \text{ does not accept } \langle M\rangle \\ reject & \text{if } M \text{ accepts } \langle M\rangle. \end{cases}$$

What happens when we run D with its own description $\langle D\rangle$ as input? In that case we get

$$D(\langle D\rangle) = \begin{cases} accept & \text{if } D \text{ does not accept } \langle D\rangle \\ reject & \text{if } D \text{ accepts } \langle D\rangle. \end{cases}$$

No matter what D does, it is forced to do the opposite, which is obviously a contradiction. Thus neither TM D nor TM H can exist.

Let's review the steps of this proof. Assume that a TM H decides A_{TM}. Then use H to build a TM D that when given input $\langle M\rangle$ accepts exactly when M does not accept input $\langle M\rangle$. Finally, run D on itself. The machines take the following actions, with the last line being the contradiction.

- H accepts $\langle M, w \rangle$ exactly when M accepts w.

- D rejects $\langle M \rangle$ exactly when M accepts $\langle M \rangle$.

- D rejects $\langle D \rangle$ exactly when D accepts $\langle D \rangle$.

Where is the diagonalization in the proof of Theorem 4.9? It becomes apparent when you examine tables of behavior for TMs H and D. In these tables we list all TMs down the rows, $M_1, M_2, \ldots$ and all their descriptions across the columns, $\langle M_1 \rangle, \langle M_2 \rangle, \ldots$ The entries tell whether the machine in a given row accepts the input in a given column. The entry is *accept* if the machine accepts the input but is blank if it rejects or loops on that input. We made up the entries in the following figure to illustrate the idea.

	$\langle M_1 \rangle$	$\langle M_2 \rangle$	$\langle M_3 \rangle$	$\langle M_4 \rangle$	$\cdots$
M_1	accept		accept		
M_2	accept	accept	accept	accept	
M_3					$\cdots$
M_4	accept	accept			
$\vdots$		$\vdots$			

FIGURE **4.4**
Entry i, j is *accept* if M_i accepts $\langle M_j \rangle$

In the following figure the entries are the results of running H on inputs corresponding to Figure 4.4. So if M_3 does not accept input $\langle M_2 \rangle$, the entry for row M_3 and column $\langle M_2 \rangle$ is *reject* because H rejects input $\langle M_3, \langle M_2 \rangle \rangle$.

	$\langle M_1 \rangle$	$\langle M_2 \rangle$	$\langle M_3 \rangle$	$\langle M_4 \rangle$	$\cdots$
M_1	accept	reject	accept	reject	
M_2	accept	accept	accept	accept	$\cdots$
M_3	reject	reject	reject	reject	
M_4	accept	accept	reject	reject	
$\vdots$		$\vdots$			

FIGURE **4.5**
Entry i, j is the value of H on input $\langle M_i, \langle M_j \rangle \rangle$

In the following figure, we added D to Figure 4.5. By our assumption, H is a TM and so is D. Therefore it must occur on the list $M_1, M_2, \ldots$ of all TMs. Note that D computes the opposite of the diagonal entries. The contradiction occurs at the point of the question mark where the entry must be the opposite of itself.

	$\langle M_1 \rangle$	$\langle M_2 \rangle$	$\langle M_3 \rangle$	$\langle M_4 \rangle$	$\cdots$	$\langle D \rangle$	$\cdots$
M_1	*accept*	*reject*	*accept*	*reject*		*accept*	
M_2	*accept*	*accept*	*accept*	*accept*	$\cdots$	*accept*	$\cdots$
M_3	*reject*	*reject*	*reject*	*reject*		*reject*	
M_4	*accept*	*accept*	*reject*	*reject*		*accept*	
$\vdots$			$\vdots$		$\ddots$		
D	*reject*	*reject*	*accept*	*accept*		?	
$\vdots$			$\vdots$				$\ddots$

FIGURE **4.6**
If D is in the figure, a contradiction occurs at "?"

A TURING-UNRECOGNIZABLE LANGUAGE

In the preceding section we demonstrated a language, namely, A_{TM}, that is undecidable. Now we demonstrate a language that isn't even Turing-recognizable. Note that A_{TM} will not suffice for this purpose because we showed that A_{TM} is Turing-recognizable on page 160. The following theorem shows that, if both a language and its complement are Turing-recognizable, the language is decidable. Hence, for any undecidable language, either it or its complement is not Turing-recognizable. Recall that the complement of a language is the language consisting of all strings that are not in the language. We say that a language is *co-Turing-recognizable* if it is the complement of a Turing-recognizable language.

THEOREM **4.16** ··

A language is decidable if and only if it is both Turing-recognizable and co-Turing-recognizable.

In other words, a language is decidable if and only if both it and its complement are Turing-recognizable.

PROOF   We have two directions to prove. First, if A is decidable, we can easily see that both A and its complement $\overline{A}$ are Turing-recognizable. Any decidable language is Turing-recognizable, and the complement of a decidable language also is decidable.

For the other direction, if both A and $\overline{A}$ are Turing-recognizable, we let M_1 be the recognizer for A and M_2 be the recognizer for $\overline{A}$. The following Turing machine M is a decider for A.

M = "On input w:

    1. Run both M_1 and M_2 on input w in parallel.

    2. If M_1 accepts, *accept*; if M_2 accepts, *reject*."

Running the two machines in parallel means that M has two tapes, one for simulating M_1 and the other for simulating M_2. In this case M takes turns simulating one step of each machine, which continues until one of them halts.

    Now we show that M decides A. Every string w is either in A or $\overline{A}$. Therefore either M_1 or M_2 must accept w. Because M halts whenever M_1 or M_2 accepts, M always halts and so it is a decider. Furthermore, it accepts all strings in A and rejects all strings not in A. So M is a decider for A, and thus A is decidable.

....

COROLLARY **4.17** ....

$\overline{A_{\mathsf{TM}}}$ is not Turing-recognizable.

PROOF   We know that A_{TM} is Turing-recognizable. If $\overline{A_{\mathsf{TM}}}$ also were Turing-recognizable, A_{TM} would be decidable. Theorem 4.9 tells us that A_{TM} is not decidable, so $\overline{A_{\mathsf{TM}}}$ must not be Turing-recognizable.

....

■ ■

EXERCISES

4.1 Answer all parts for the following DFA M and give reasons for your answers.

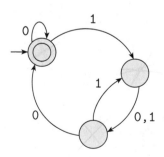

    a. Is $\langle M, 0100 \rangle \in A_{\mathsf{DFA}}$?

    b. Is $\langle M, 011 \rangle \in A_{\mathsf{DFA}}$?

    c. Is $\langle M \rangle \in A_{\mathsf{DFA}}$?

    d. Is $\langle M, 0100 \rangle \in A_{\text{REX}}$?

    e. Is $\langle M \rangle \in E_{\text{DFA}}$?

    f. Is $\langle M, M \rangle \in EQ_{\text{DFA}}$?

4.2 Consider the problem of testing whether a DFA and a regular expression are equivalent. Express this problem as a language and show that it is decidable.

4.3 Let $ALL_{\text{DFA}} = \{\langle A \rangle | \ A \text{ is a DFA that recognizes } \Sigma^*\}$. Show that ALL_{DFA} is decidable.

4.4 Let $A\varepsilon_{\text{CFG}} = \{\langle G \rangle | \ G \text{ is a CFG that generates } \varepsilon\}$. Show that $A\varepsilon_{\text{CFG}}$ is decidable.

4.5 Let $INFINITE_{\text{DFA}} = \{\langle A \rangle | \ L(A) \text{ is an infinite language}\}$. Show that $INFINITE_{\text{DFA}}$ is decidable.

4.6 Let X be the set $\{1, 2, 3, 4, 5\}$ and Y be the set $\{6, 7, 8, 9, 10\}$. We describe the functions $f\colon X \longrightarrow Y$ and $g\colon X \longrightarrow Y$ in the following tables.

n	$f(n)$
1	6
2	7
3	6
4	7
5	6

n	$g(n)$
1	10
2	9
3	8
4	7
5	6

    a. Is f one-to-one? Is g? If not, state why.

    b. Is f onto? Is g? If not, state why.

    c. Is f a correspondence? Is g? If not, state why.

4.7 Let $\mathcal{B}$ be the set of all infinite sequences over $\{0,1\}$. Show that $\mathcal{B}$ is uncountable, using a proof by diagonalization.

4.8 Let $T = \{(i, j, k) | \ i, j, k \in \mathcal{N}\}$. Show that T is countable.

4.9 Review the way that we define sets to be the same size in Definition 4.10 on page 161. Show that "is the same size" is an equivalence relation.

PROBLEMS

4.10 Let

$$A = \{\langle M \rangle | \ M \text{ is a DFA which doesn't accept}$$
$$\text{any string containing an odd number of 1s}\}.$$

Show that A is decidable.

4.11 Let $A = \{\langle R, S \rangle | \ R \text{ and } S \text{ are regular expressions and } L(R) \subseteq L(S)\}$. Show that A is decidable.

4.12 Show that the problem of testing whether a CFG generates some string in 1^* is decidable. In other words, show that $\{\langle G \rangle | \ G \text{ is a CFG over } \{0,1\}^* \text{ and } 1^* \cap L(G) \neq \emptyset\}$ is a decidable language.

*4.13 Show that the problem of testing whether a CFG generates all strings in 1^* is decidable. In other words, show that $\{\langle G \rangle | \ G \text{ is a CFG over } \{0,1\}^* \text{ and } 1^* \subseteq L(G)\}$ is a decidable language.

4.14 Let $A = \{\langle R \rangle |\ R$ is a regular expression describing a language containing at least one string w that has 111 as a substring (i.e., $w = x111y$ for some x and y)$\}$. Show that A is decidable.

*4.15 Let

$$E = \{\langle M \rangle |\ M \text{ is a DFA that accepts}$$
$$\text{some string of the form } ww^R \text{ for } w \in \{0,1\}^*\}.$$

Show that E is decidable.

4.16 Prove that EQ_{DFA} is decidable by testing the two DFAs on all strings up to a certain size. Calculate a size that works.

4.17 Let C be a language. Prove that C is Turing-recognizable iff a decidable language D exists such that $C = \{x|\ \exists y\ (\langle x, y \rangle \in D)\}$.

4.18 Let A and B be two disjoint languages. Say that language C *separates* A and B if $A \subseteq C$ and $B \subseteq \overline{C}$. Show that any two disjoint co-Turing-recognizable languages are separable by some decidable language.

4.19 Let $S = \{\langle M \rangle |\ M$ is a DFA that accepts w^R whenever it accepts $w\}$. Show that S is decidable.

4.20 A *useless state* in a pushdown automaton is never entered on any input string. Consider the problem of testing whether a pushdown automaton has any useless states. Formulate this problem as a language and show that it is decidable.

4.21 Let A be a Turing-recognizable language consisting of descriptions of Turing machines, $\{\langle M_1 \rangle, \langle M_2 \rangle, \ldots\}$, where every M_i is a decider. Prove that some decidable language D is not decided by any decider M_i whose description appears in A. (Hint: You may find it helpful to consider an enumerator for A.)

*4.22 Let B be a Turing-recognizable language consisting of descriptions of Turing machines, $\{\langle M_1 \rangle, \langle M_2 \rangle, \ldots\}$. Show that there is a decidable language C consisting of Turing machines such that every machine described in B has an equivalent one in C and vice versa.

5

REDUCIBILITY

In Chapter 4 we established the Turing machine as our model of a general purpose computer. We presented several examples of problems that are solvable on a Turing machine and gave one example of a problem, A_{TM}, that is computationally unsolvable. In this chapter we examine several additional unsolvable problems. In doing so we introduce the primary method for proving that problems are computationally unsolvable. It is called *reducibility*.

A *reduction* is a way of converting one problem into another problem in such a way that a solution to the second problem can be used to solve the first problem. Such reducibilities come up often in everyday life, even if we don't usually refer to them this way.

For example, suppose that you want to find your way around a new city. You know that this would be easy if you had a map. Thus you can reduce the problem of finding your way around the city to the problem of obtaining a map of the city.

Reducibility always involves two problems, which we call A and B. If A reduces to B, we can use a solution to B to solve A. So in our example, A is the problem of finding your way around the city and B is the problem of obtaining a map. Note that reducibility says nothing about solving A or B alone, but only about the solvability of A in the presence of a solution to B.

The following are further examples of reducibilities. The problem of traveling from Boston to Paris reduces to the problem of buying a plane ticket between the two cities. That problem in turn reduces to the problem of earning the money for the ticket. And that problem reduces to the problem of finding a job.

Reducibility also occurs in mathematical problems. For example, the problem of measuring the area of a rectangle reduces to the problem of measuring its height and width. The problem of solving a system of linear equations reduces to the problem of inverting a matrix.

Reducibility plays an important role in classifying problems by decidability and later in complexity theory as well. When A is reducible to B, solving A cannot be harder than solving B because a solution to B gives a solution to A. In terms of computability theory, if A is reducible to B and B is decidable, A also is decidable. Equivalently, if A is undecidable and reducible to B, B is undecidable. This last version is key to proving that various problems are undecidable.

In short, our method for proving that a problem is undecidable will be: Show that some other problem already known to be undecidable reduces to it.

5.1

UNDECIDABLE PROBLEMS FROM LANGUAGE THEORY

We have already established the undecidability of A_{TM}, the problem of determining whether a Turing machine accepts a given input. Let's consider a related problem, $HALT_{\mathsf{TM}}$, the problem of determining whether a Turing machine halts (by accepting or rejecting) on a given input.[1] We use the undecidability of A_{TM} to prove the undecidability of $HALT_{\mathsf{TM}}$ by reducing A_{TM} to $HALT_{\mathsf{TM}}$. Let

$$HALT_{\mathsf{TM}} = \{\langle M, w\rangle|\ M \text{ is a TM and } M \text{ halts on input } w\}.$$

THEOREM 5.1 ···

$HALT_{\mathsf{TM}}$ is undecidable.

···

PROOF IDEA This proof is by contradiction. We assume that $HALT_{\mathsf{TM}}$ is decidable and use that assumption to show that A_{TM} is decidable, contradicting Theorem 4.9. The key idea is to show that A_{TM} is reducible to $HALT_{\mathsf{TM}}$.

Let's assume that we have a TM R that decides $HALT_{\mathsf{TM}}$. Then we use R to construct S, a TM that decides A_{TM}. To get a feel for the way to construct S, pretend that you are S. Your task is to decide A_{TM}. You are given an input of the

---

[1]In Section 4.2, we used the term *halting problem* for the language A_{TM} even though $HALT_{\mathsf{TM}}$ is the real halting problem. From here on we distinguish between the two by calling A_{TM} the *acceptance problem*.

form $\langle M, w \rangle$. You must output *accept* if M accepts w, and you must output *reject* if M loops or rejects on w. Try simulating M on w. If it accepts or rejects, do the same. But you may not be able to determine whether M is looping, and in that case your simulation will not terminate. That's bad, because you are a decider and thus never permitted to loop. So this idea, by itself, does not work.

Instead, use the assumption that we have TM R that decides $HALT_{\mathsf{TM}}$. With R, you can test whether whether M halts on w. If R indicates that M doesn't halt on w, reject because $\langle M, w \rangle$ isn't in A_{TM}. However, if R indicates that M does halt on w, you can do the simulation without any danger of looping.

Thus, if TM R exists, we can decide A_{TM}, but we know that A_{TM} is undecidable. By virtue of this contradiction we can conclude that R does not exist. Therefore $HALT_{\mathsf{TM}}$ is undecidable.

PROOF   Let's assume for the purposes of obtaining a contradiction that TM R decides $HALT_{\mathsf{TM}}$. We construct TM S to decide A_{TM}, with S operating as follows.

S — "On input $\langle M, w \rangle$, an encoding of a TM M and a string w:
1. Run TM R on input $\langle M, w \rangle$.
2. If R rejects, *reject*.
3. If R accepts, simulate M on w until it halts.
4. If M has accepted, *accept*; if M has rejected, *reject*."

Clearly, if R decides $HALT_{\mathsf{TM}}$, then S decides A_{TM}. Because A_{TM} is undecidable, $HALT_{\mathsf{TM}}$ also must be undecidable.

Theorem 5.1 illustrates our strategy for proving that a problem is undecidable. This strategy is common to most proofs of undecidability, except for the undecidability of A_{TM} itself, which is proved directly via the diagonalization method.

We now present several other theorems and their proofs as further examples of the reducibility method for proving undecidability. Let

$$E_{\mathsf{TM}} = \{\langle M \rangle \mid M \text{ is a TM and } L(M) = \emptyset\}.$$

THEOREM   5.2   ....

E_{TM} is undecidable.

....

PROOF IDEA   We follow the pattern adopted in Theorem 5.1. We assume for the purposes of obtaining a contradiction that E_{TM} is decidable and then show that A_{TM} is decidable—a contradiction. Let R be a TM that decides E_{TM}. We use R to construct TM S that decides A_{TM}. How will S work when it receives input $\langle M, w \rangle$?

One idea is for S to run R on input $\langle M \rangle$ and see whether it accepts. If it does, we know that $L(M)$ is empty and therefore that M does not accept w. But, if R rejects $\langle M \rangle$, all we know is that $L(M)$ is not empty and therefore that M accepts some string, but we still do not know whether M accepts the particular string w. So we need to use a different idea.

Instead of running R on $\langle M \rangle$ we run R on a modification of $\langle M \rangle$. We modify $\langle M \rangle$ to guarantee that M rejects all strings except w, but on input w it works as usual. Then we use R to test whether the modified machine recognizes the empty language. The only string the machine can now accept is w, so its language will be nonempty if and only if it accepts w. If R accepts when it is fed a description of the modified machine, we know that the modified machine doesn't accept anything and that M doesn't accept w.

PROOF Let's write the modified machine described in the proof idea using our standard notation. We call it M_1.

$M_1 =$ "On input x:

1. If $x \neq w$, *reject*.
2. If $x = w$, run M on input w and *accept* if M does."

This machine has the string w as part of its description. It conducts the test of whether $x = w$ in the obvious way, by scanning the input and comparing it character by character with w to determine whether they are the same.

Putting all this together, we assume that TM R decides E_{TM} and construct TM S that decides A_{TM} as follows.

$S =$ "On input $\langle M, w \rangle$, an encoding of a TM M and a string w.

1. Use the description of M and construct the TM M_1 just described.
2. Run R on input $\langle M_1 \rangle$.
3. If R accepts, *reject*; if R rejects, *accept*."

Note that S must actually be able to compute a description of M_1 from a description of M and w. It is able to do so because it needs only add extra states to M that perform the $x = w$ test.

If R were a decider for E_{TM}, S would be a decider for A_{TM}. A decider for A_{TM} cannot exist, so we know that E_{TM} must be undecidable.

....

Another interesting computational problem regarding Turing machines concerns testing whether a given Turing machine recognizes a language that also can be recognized by a simpler computational model. For example we let $REGULAR_{\mathsf{TM}}$ be the problem of testing whether a given Turing machine has an equivalent finite automaton. This problem is the same as testing whether the Turing machine recognizes a regular language. Let

$$REGULAR_{\mathsf{TM}} = \{\langle M \rangle |\ M \text{ is a TM and } L(M) \text{ is a regular language}\}.$$

THEOREM **5.3** ⋯⋯⋯⋯⋯⋯⋯⋯⋯⋯⋯⋯⋯⋯⋯⋯⋯⋯⋯⋯⋯⋯⋯⋯⋯⋯⋯⋯⋯⋯

$REGULAR_{\mathsf{TM}}$ is undecidable.

⋯⋯⋯

PROOF IDEA   As usual for undecidability theorems, this proof is by reduction from A_{TM}. We assume that $REGULAR_{\mathsf{TM}}$ is decidable by a TM R and use this assumption to construct a TM S that decides A_{TM}. Less obvious now is how to use R's ability to assist S in its task. Nonetheless we can do so.

The idea is for S to take its input $\langle M, w \rangle$ and modify M so that the resulting TM recognizes a regular language if and only if M accepts w. We call the modified machine M_2. We design M_2 to recognize the nonregular language $\{0^n 1^n | n \geq 0\}$ if M does not accept w and the regular language Σ^* if M accepts w. We must specify how S can construct such an M_2 from M and w. Here, M_2 works by automatically accepting all strings in $\{0^n 1^n | n \geq 0\}$. In addition, if M accepts w, M_2 accepts all other strings.

PROOF   We let R be a TM that decides $REGULAR_{\mathsf{TM}}$ and construct TM S to decide A_{TM}. Then S works in the following manner.

$S =$ "On input $\langle M, w \rangle$, where M is a TM and w is a string:
1. Construct the following TM M_2.
    $M_2 -$ "On input x:
        1. If x has the form $0^n 1^n$, *accept*.
        2. If x does not have this form, run M on input w and *accept* if M accepts w."
2. Run R on input $\langle M_2 \rangle$.
3. If R accepts, *accept*; if R rejects, *reject*."

⋯⋯⋯

Similarly, the problems of testing whether the language of a Turing machine is a context-free language, a decidable language, or even a finite language, can be shown to be undecidable with similar proofs. In fact, a general result, called Rice's theorem, states that testing *any property* of the languages recognized by Turing machines is undecidable. We give Rice's theorem in Problem 5.22.

So far, our strategy for proving languages undecidable involves a reduction from A_{TM}. Sometimes reducing from some other undecidable language, such as E_{TM}, is more convenient when we are showing that certain languages are undecidable. The following theorem shows that testing the equivalence of two Turing machines is an undecidable problem. We could prove it by a reduction from A_{TM}, but we use this opportunity to give an example of an undecidability proof by reduction from E_{TM}. Let

$$EQ_{\mathsf{TM}} = \{\langle M_1, M_2 \rangle | \ M_1 \text{ and } M_2 \text{ are TMs and } L(M_1) = L(M_2)\}.$$

THEOREM 5.4

EQ_{TM} is undecidable.

PROOF IDEA   Show that, if EQ_{TM} were decidable, E_{TM} also would be decidable, by giving a reduction from E_{TM} to EQ_{TM}. The idea is simple. E_{TM} is the problem of testing whether the language of a TM is empty. EQ_{TM} is the problem of testing whether the languages of two TMs are the same. If one of these languages happens to be $\emptyset$, we end up with the problem of testing whether the language of the other machine is empty, that is, the E_{TM} problem. So in a sense, the E_{TM} problem is a special case of the EQ_{TM} problem wherein one of the machines is fixed to recognize the empty language. This idea makes giving the reduction easy.

PROOF   We let TM R decide EQ_{TM} and construct TM S to decide E_{TM} as follows.

$S = $ "On input $\langle M \rangle$, where M is a TM:
1. Run R on input $\langle M, M_1 \rangle$, where M_1 is a TM that rejects all inputs.
2. If R accepts, *accept*; if R rejects, *reject*."

If R decides EQ_{TM}, S decides E_{TM}. But E_{TM} is undecidable by Theorem 5.2, so EQ_{TM} also must be undecidable.

REDUCTIONS VIA COMPUTATION HISTORIES

The computation history method is an important technique for proving that A_{TM} is reducible to certain languages. This method is often useful when the problem to be shown undecidable involves testing for the existence of something. For example, this method is used to show the undecidability of Hilbert's tenth problem, testing for the existence of integral roots in a polynomial.

The computation history for a Turing machine on an input is simply the sequence of configurations that the machine goes through as it processes the input. It is a complete record of the computation of this machine.

DEFINITION 5.5

Let M be a Turing machine and w an input string. An ***accepting computation history*** for M on w is a sequence of configurations, $C_1, C_2, \ldots, C_l$, where C_1 is the start configuration of M on w, C_l is an accepting configuration of M, and each C_i legally follows from C_{i-1} according to the rules of M. A ***rejecting computation history*** for M on w is defined similarly, except that C_l is a rejecting configuration.

Computation histories are finite sequences. If M doesn't halt on w, no accepting or rejecting computation history exists for M on w. Deterministic machines have at most one computation history on any given input. Nondeterministic machines may have many computation histories on a single input, corresponding to the various computation branches. For now, we continue to focus on deterministic machines. Our first undecidability proof using the computation history method concerns a type of machine called a linear bounded automaton.

DEFINITION 5.6 ....

A *linear bounded automaton* is a restricted type of Turing machine wherein the tape head isn't permitted to move off the portion of the tape containing the input. If the machine tries to move its head off either end of the input, the head stays where it is, in the same way that the head will not move off the left-hand end of an ordinary Turing machine's tape.

A linear bounded automaton is a Turing machine with a limited amount of memory, as shown schematically in the following figure. It can only solve problems requiring memory that can fit within the tape used for the input. Using a tape alphabet larger than the input alphabet allows the available memory to be increased up to a constant factor. Hence we say that for an input of length n, the amount of memory available is linear in n—thus the name of this model.

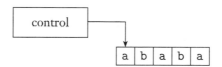

FIGURE 5.1
Schematic of a linear bounded automaton

Despite their memory constraint, linear bounded automata are quite powerful. For example, the deciders for A_{DFA}, A_{CFG}, E_{DFA}, and E_{CFG} all are LBAs. Every CFL can be decided by an LBA. In fact, coming up with a decidable language that can't be decided by an LBA takes some work. We develop the techniques to do so in Chapter 9.

Here, A_{LBA} is the problem of testing whether an LBA accepts its input. Even though A_{LBA} is the same as the undecidable problem A_{TM} where the Turing machine is restricted to be an LBA, we can show that A_{LBA} is decidable. Let

$$A_{\mathsf{LBA}} = \{\langle M, w\rangle|\ M \text{ is an LBA that accepts string } w\}.$$

Before proving the decidability of A_{LBA}, we find the following lemma useful. It says that an LBA can have only a limited number of configurations when a string of length n is the input.

LEMMA **5.7** ....

Let M be an LBA with q states and g symbols in the tape alphabet. There are exactly qng^n distinct configurations of M for a tape of length n.

PROOF   Recall that a configuration of M is like a snapshot in the middle of its computation. A configuration consists of the state of the control, position of the head, and contents of the tape. Here, M has q states. The length of its tape is n, so the head can be in one of n positions, and g^n possible strings of tape symbols appear on the tape. The product of these three quantities is the total number of different configurations of M with a tape of length n.

....

THEOREM **5.8** ....

A_{LBA} is decidable.

....

PROOF IDEA   In order to decide whether LBA M accepts input w, we simulate M on w. During the course of the simulation, if M halts and accepts or rejects, we accept or reject accordingly. The difficulty occurs if M loops on w. We need to be able to detect looping so that we can halt and reject.

The idea for detecting when M is looping is that, as M computes on w, it goes from configuration to configuration. If M ever repeats a configuration it would go on to repeat this configuration over and over again and thus be in a loop. Because M is an LBA, the amount of tape available to it is limited. By Lemma 5.7, M can be in only a limited number of configurations on this amount of tape. Therefore only a limited amount of time is available to M before it will enter some configuration that it has previously entered. Detecting that M is looping is possible by simulating M for the number of steps given by Lemma 5.7. If M has not halted by then, it must be looping.

PROOF   The algorithm that decides A_{LBA} is as follows.

$L =$ "On input $\langle M, w \rangle$, where M is an LBA and w is a string:
  1. Simulate M on w for qng^n steps or until it halts.
  2. If M has halted, *accept* if it has accepted and *reject* if it has rejected. If it has not halted, *reject*."

If M on w has not halted within qng^n steps, it must be repeating a configuration according to Lemma 5.7 and therefore looping. That is why our algorithm rejects in this instance.

....

Theorem 5.8 shows that LBAs and TMs differ in one essential way: For LBAs the acceptance problem is decidable, but for TMs it isn't. However, certain other problems involving LBAs remain undecidable. One is the emptiness problem $E_{\mathsf{LBA}} = \{\langle M\rangle|\ M$ is an LBA where $L(M) = \emptyset\}$. To prove that E_{LBA} is undecidable, we give a reduction that uses the computation history method.

THEOREM 5.9 ···

E_{LBA} is undecidable.

···

PROOF IDEA   This proof is by reduction from A_{TM}. We show that, if E_{LBA} were decidable, A_{TM} would also be. Suppose that E_{LBA} is decidable. How can we use this supposition to decide A_{TM}?

For a TM M and an input w we can determine whether M accepts w by constructing a certain LBA B and then testing whether $L(B)$ is empty. The language that B recognizes comprises all accepting computation histories for M on w. If M accepts w, this language contains one string and so is nonempty. If M does not accept w, this language is empty. If we can determine whether B's language is empty, clearly we can determine whether M accepts w.

Now we describe how to construct B from M and w. Note that we need to show more than the mere existence of B. We have to show how a Turing machine can obtain a description of B given descriptions of M and w.

We construct B to accept its input x if x is an accepting computation history for M on w. Recall that an accepting computation history is the sequence of configurations, $C_1, C_2, \ldots, C_l$ that M goes through as it accepts some string w. For the purposes of this proof we assume that the accepting computation history is presented as a single string, with the configurations separated from each other by the # symbol, as shown in the following figure.

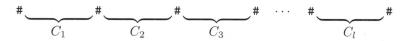

FIGURE 5.2
A possible input to B

The LBA B works as follows. When it receives an input x, B is supposed to accept if x is an accepting computation for M on w. First, B breaks up x according to the delimiters into strings $C_1, C_2, \ldots, C_l$. Then, B checks whether the C_i satisfy the three conditions of a computation history.

1. C_1 is the start configuration for M on w.
2. Each C_{i+1} legally follows from C_i.
3. C_l is an accepting configuration for M.

The start configuration C_1 for M on w is the string $q_0 w_1 w_2 \cdots w_n$, where q_0 is the start state for M on w. Here, B has this string directly built in, so it is able to check the first condition. An accepting configuration is one that contains the q_{accept} state, so B can check the third condition by scanning C_l for q_{accept}. The second condition is the hardest to check. For each pair of adjacent configurations, B checks on whether C_{i+1} legally follows from C_i. This step involves verifying that C_i and C_{i+1} are identical except for the positions under and adjacent to the head in C_i. These positions must be updated according to the transition function of M. Then, B verifies that the updating was done properly by zig-zagging between corresponding positions of C_i and C_{i+1}. To keep track of the current positions while zig-zagging, B marks the current position with dots on the tape. Finally, if conditions 1, 2, and 3 are satisfied, B accepts its input.

Note that the LBA B is *not* constructed for the purposes of actually running it on some input—a common confusion. We construct B only for the purpose of feeding a description of B into the decider for E_{LBA} that we have assumed to exist. Once this decider returns its answer we can invert it to obtain the answer to whether M accepts w. Thus we can decide A_{TM}, a contradiction.

PROOF   Now we are ready to state the reduction of A_{TM} to E_{LBA}. Suppose that TM R decides E_{LBA}. Construct TM S that decides A_{TM} as follows.

$S =$ "On input $\langle M, w \rangle$, where M is a TM and w is a string:
1. Construct LBA B from M and w as described in the proof idea.
2. Run R on input $\langle B \rangle$.
3. If R rejects, *accept*; if R accepts, *reject*."

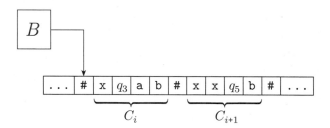

FIGURE 5.3
LBA B checking a TM computation history

If R accepts $\langle B \rangle$, then $L(B) = \emptyset$. Thus M has no accepting computation history on w and M doesn't accept w. Consequently S rejects $\langle M, w \rangle$. Similarly, if R rejects $\langle B \rangle$, the language of B is nonempty. The only string that B can accept is an accepting computation history for M on w. Thus M must accept w. Consequently, S accepts $\langle M, w \rangle$. Figure 5.3 shows such a check of a TM computation history.

....

We can also use the technique of reduction via computation histories to establish the undecidability of certain problems related to context-free grammars and pushdown automata. Recall that in Theorem 4.7 we presented an algorithm to decide whether a context-free grammar generates any strings, that is, whether $L(G) = \emptyset$. Now we show that a related problem is undecidable. It is the problem of testing whether a context-free grammar generates all possible strings. Proving that this problem is undecidable is the main step in showing that the equivalence problem for context-free grammars is undecidable. Let

$$ALL_{CFG} = \{\langle G \rangle|\ G \text{ is a CFG and } L(G) = \Sigma^*\}.$$

THEOREM 5.10 ....

ALL_{CFG} is undecidable.

PROOF This proof is by contradiction. To get the contradiction we assume that ALL_{CFG} is decidable and use this assumption to show that A_{TM} is decidable. This proof is similar to that of Theorem 5.9 but with a small extra twist: It is a reduction from A_{TM} via computation histories, but we have to modify the representation of the computation histories slightly for a technical reason that we explain later.

We now describe how to use a decision procedure for ALL_{CFG} to decide A_{TM}. For a TM M and an input w we construct a CFG G that generates all strings if and only if M does not accept w. So, if M does accept w, G does *not* generate some particular string. This string is—guess what—the accepting computation history for M on w. That is, G is designed to generate all strings that are *not* accepting computation histories for M on w.

To make the CFG G generate all strings that fail to be an accepting computation history for M on w, we utilize the following strategy. A string may fail to be an accepting computation history for several reasons. An accepting computation history for M on w appears as $\#C_1\#C_2\#\cdots\#C_l\#$, where C_i is the configuration of M on the ith step of the computation on w. Then, G generates all strings that

1. *do not* start with C_1,
2. *do not* end with an accepting configuration, or
3. where some C_i *does not* properly yield C_{i+1} under the rules of M.

If M does not accept w, no accepting computation history exists, so *all* strings fail in one way or another. Therefore G would generate all strings, as desired.

Now we get down to the actual construction of G. Instead of constructing G, we construct a PDA D. We know that we can use the construction given in Theorem 2.12 on page 106 to convert D to a CFG. We do so because, for our purposes, designing a PDA is easier than designing a CFG. In this instance, D will start by nondeterministically branching to guess which of the preceding three conditions to check. One branch checks on whether the beginning of the input string is C_1 and accepts if it isn't. Another branch checks on whether the input string ends with a configuration containing the accept state, q_{accept}, and accepts if it isn't.

The third branch is supposed to accept if some C_i does not properly yield C_{i+1}. It works by scanning over the input until it nondeterministically decides that it has come to C_i. Next, it pushes C_i onto the stack until it comes to the end as marked by the # symbol. Then, D pops the stack to compare with C_{i+1}. They are supposed to match except around the head position where the difference is dictated by the transition function of M. Finally, D accepts if it is a mismatch or an improper update.

The problem with this idea is that, when D pops C_i off the stack, it is in reverse order and not suitable for comparison with C_{i+1}. At this point the twist in the proof appears: We write the accepting computation history differently. Every other configuration appears in reverse order. The odd positions remain written in the forward order, but the even positions are written backward. Thus an accepting computation history would appear as shown in the following figure.

FIGURE 5.4
Every other configuration written in reverse order

In this modified form the PDA is able to push a configuration so that when it is popped the order is suitable for comparison with the next one. We design D to accept any string that is not an accepting computation history in the modified form.

In Exercise 5.1 you can use Theorem 5.10 to show that EQ_{CFG} is undecidable.

5.2 ■

A SIMPLE UNDECIDABLE PROBLEM

In this section we show that the phenomenon of undecidability is not confined to problems concerning automata. We give an example of an undecidable problem concerning simple manipulations of strings. It is called the ***Post correspondence problem***, or ***PCP***.

We can describe this problem easily as a type of puzzle. We begin with a collection of dominos, each containing two strings, one on each side. An individual domino looks like

$$\left[\frac{a}{ab}\right]$$

and a collection of dominos looks like

$$\left\{\left[\frac{b}{ca}\right], \left[\frac{a}{ab}\right], \left[\frac{ca}{a}\right], \left[\frac{abc}{c}\right]\right\}$$

The task is to make a list of these dominos (repetitions permitted) so that the string we get by reading off the symbols on the top is the same as the string of symbols on the bottom. This list is called a ***match***. For example, the following list is a match for this puzzle.

$$\left[\frac{a}{ab}\right]\left[\frac{b}{ca}\right]\left[\frac{ca}{a}\right]\left[\frac{a}{ab}\right]\left[\frac{abc}{c}\right].$$

Reading off the top string we get abcaaabc, which is the same as reading off the bottom. We can also depict this match by deforming the dominos so that the corresponding symbols from top and bottom line up.

For some collections of dominos finding a match may not be possible. For example, the collection

$$\left\{\left[\frac{abc}{ab}\right], \left[\frac{ca}{a}\right], \left[\frac{acc}{ba}\right]\right\}$$

cannot contain a match because every top string is longer than the corresponding bottom string.

The Post correspondence problem is to determine whether a collection of dominos has a match. This problem is unsolvable by algorithms.

Before getting to the formal statement of this theorem and its proof, let's state the problem precisely and then express it as a language. An instance of the PCP is a collection P of dominos:

$$P = \left\{ \left[\frac{t_1}{b_1}\right], \left[\frac{t_2}{b_2}\right], \ \cdots \ , \left[\frac{t_k}{b_k}\right] \right\},$$

and a match is a sequence $i_1, i_2, \dots, i_l$, where $t_{i_1} t_{i_2} \cdots t_{i_l} = b_{i_1} b_{i_2} \cdots b_{i_l}$. The problem is to determine whether P has a match. Let

$$PCP = \{\langle P\rangle|\ P \text{ is an instance of the Post correspondence problem}$$
$$\text{with a match}\}.$$

THEOREM **5.11** ....

PCP is undecidable

....

PROOF IDEA   Conceptually this proof is simple, though it has many technical details. The main technique is reduction from A_{TM} via accepting computation histories. We show that from any TM M and input w we can construct an instance P where a match is an accepting computation history for M on w. If we could determine whether the instance has a match, we would be able to determine whether M accepts w.

How can we construct P so that a match is an accepting computation history for M on w? We choose the dominos in P so that making a match forces a simulation of M to occur. In the match, each domino links a position or positions in one configuration with the corresponding one(s) in the next configuration.

Before getting to the construction we handle two small technical points. (Don't worry about them too much on your initial reading through this construction.) First, for convenience in constructing P, we assume that M on w never attempts to move its head off the left-hand end of the tape. That requires first altering M to prevent this behavior. Second, we modify the PCP to require that a match starts with the first domino,

$$\left[\frac{t_1}{b_1}\right].$$

Later we show how to eliminate this requirement. We call this problem the modified Post correspondence problem, MPCP. Let

$$MPCP = \{\langle P\rangle|\ P \text{ is an instance of the Post correspondence problem}$$
$$\text{with a match that starts with the first domino}\}.$$

Now let's move into the details of the proof and design P to simulate M on w.

PROOF   We let TM R decide the PCP and construct S deciding A_{TM}. Let

$$M = (Q, \Sigma, \Gamma, \delta, q_0, q_{\text{accept}}, q_{\text{reject}}),$$

where Q, Σ, Γ, and δ, are the state set, input alphabet, tape alphabet, and transition function of M, respectively.

In this case S constructs an instance of the PCP P that has a match if and only if M accepts w. To do that S first constructs an instance P' of the MPCP. We describe the construction in seven parts, each of which accomplishes a particular aspect of simulating M on w. To explain what we are doing we interleave the construction with an example of the construction in action.

Part 1.   The construction begins in the following manner.

$$\text{Put } \left[\frac{\#}{\#q_0 w_1 w_2 \cdots w_n \#}\right] \text{ into } P' \text{ as the first domino } \left[\frac{t_1}{b_1}\right].$$

Because P' is an instance of the MPCP the match must begin with this domino. Thus the bottom string begins correctly with $C_1 = q_0 w_1 w_2 \cdots w_n$, the first configuration in the accepting computation history for M on w, as shown in the following figure.

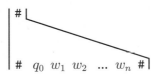

FIGURE   **5.5**
Beginning of the MPCP match

In this depiction of the partial match achieved so far, the bottom string consists of $\#q_0 w_1 w_2 \cdots w_n \#$ and the top string consists only of $\#$. To get a match we need to extend the top string to match the bottom string. We provide additional dominos to allow this extension. The additional dominos cause M's next configuration to appear at the extension of the bottom string by forcing a single-step simulation of M.

In parts 2, 3, and 4, we add to P' dominos that perform the main part of the simulation. Part 2 handles head motions to the right, part 3 handles head motions to the left, and part 4 handles the tape cells not adjacent to the head.

Part 2.   For every $a, b \in \Gamma$ and every $q, r \in Q$,

$$\text{if } \delta(q, a) = (r, b, \text{R}), \text{ put } \left[\frac{qa}{br}\right] \text{ into } P'.$$

Part 3.   For every $a, b, c \in \Gamma$ and every $q, r \in Q$,

$$\text{if } \delta(q, a) = (r, b, \text{L}), \text{ put } \left[\frac{cqa}{rcb}\right] \text{ into } P'.$$

Part 4. For every $a \in \Gamma$,

$$\text{put } \begin{bmatrix} a \\ \overline{} \\ a \end{bmatrix} \text{ into } P'.$$

Now we make up a hypothetical example to illustrate what we have built so far. Let $\Gamma = \{0, 1, 2, \sqcup\}$. Say that w is the string 0100 and that the start state of M is q_0. In state q_0, upon reading a 0, say that the transition function dictates that M enters state q_7, writes a 2 on the tape, and moves its head to the right. In other words, $\delta(q_0, 0) = (q_7, 2, \mathrm{R})$.

Part 1 places the domino

$$\begin{bmatrix} \# \\ \overline{\#q_0 0100} \end{bmatrix} = \begin{bmatrix} t_1 \\ b_1 \end{bmatrix}$$

in P', and the match begins:

In addition, part 2 places the domino

$$\begin{bmatrix} q_0 0 \\ \overline{2q_7} \end{bmatrix}$$

as $\delta(q_0, 0) = (q_7, 2, \mathrm{R})$ and part 4 places the dominos

$$\begin{bmatrix} 0 \\ 0 \end{bmatrix}, \begin{bmatrix} 1 \\ 1 \end{bmatrix}, \begin{bmatrix} 2 \\ 2 \end{bmatrix}, \text{ and } \begin{bmatrix} \sqcup \\ \sqcup \end{bmatrix}$$

in P', as 0, 1, 2, and $\sqcup$ are the members of Γ. That, together with part 5, allows us to extend the match as follows.

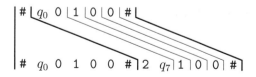

Thus the dominos of parts 2, 3, and 4 let us extend the match by adding the second configuration after the first one. We want this process to continue, adding the third configuration, then the fourth, and so on. For it to happen we need to add one more domino for copying the # symbol.

Part 5.

$$\text{Put} \begin{bmatrix} \# \\ \hline \# \end{bmatrix} \text{ and } \begin{bmatrix} \# \\ \hline \text{\textvisiblespace}\# \end{bmatrix} \text{ into } P'.$$

The first of these dominos allows us to copy the # symbol that marks the separation of the configurations. In addition to that, the second domino allows us to add a blank symbol ⊔ at the end of the configuration to simulate the infinitely many blanks to the right that are suppressed when we write the configuration.

Continuing with the example, let's say that in state q_7, upon reading a 1, M goes to state q_5, writes a 0, and moves the head to the right. That is, $\delta(q_7, 1) = (q_5, 0, \mathrm{R})$. Then we have the domino

$$\begin{bmatrix} q_7 1 \\ \hline 0 q_5 \end{bmatrix} \text{ in } P'.$$

So the latest partial match extends to

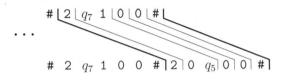

Then, suppose that in state q_5, upon reading a 0, M goes to state q_9, writes a 2, and moves its head to the left. So $\delta(q_5, 0) = (q_9, 2, \mathrm{L})$. Then we have the dominos

$$\begin{bmatrix} 0 q_5 0 \\ \hline q_9 0 2 \end{bmatrix}, \begin{bmatrix} 1 q_5 0 \\ \hline q_9 1 2 \end{bmatrix}, \begin{bmatrix} 2 q_5 0 \\ \hline q_9 2 2 \end{bmatrix}, \text{ and } \begin{bmatrix} \text{\textvisiblespace} q_5 0 \\ \hline q_9 \text{\textvisiblespace} 2 \end{bmatrix}.$$

The first one is relevant because the symbol to the left of the head is a 0. The preceding partial match extends to

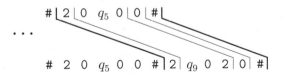

Note that, as we construct a match, we are forced to simulate M on input w. This process continues until M reaches a halting state. If an accept state occurs, we want to let the top of the partial match "catch up" with the bottom so that the match is complete. We can arrange for that to happen by adding additional dominos.

Part 6. For every $a \in \Gamma$,

$$\text{put } \left[\frac{a\, q_{\text{accept}}}{q_{\text{accept}}} \right] \text{ and } \left[\frac{q_{\text{accept}}\, a}{q_{\text{accept}}} \right] \text{ into } P'.$$

This step has the effect of adding "pseudo-steps" of the Turing machine after it has halted, where the head "eats" adjacent symbols until none are left. Continuing with the previous example, if the partial match up to the point when the machine halts in an accept state is

The dominos we have just added allow the match to continue:

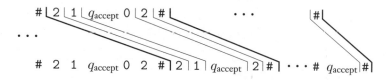

Part 7. Finally we add the domino

and complete the match:

That concludes the construction of P'. Recall that P' is an instance of the MPCP whereby the match simulates the computation of M on w. To finish the proof, recall that the MPCP differs from the PCP in that the match is required to start with the first domino in the list. If we view P' as an instance of the PCP instead of the MPCP, it obviously has a match, regardless of whether M halts on w. Can you find it? (Hint: It is very short.)

We now show how to convert P' to P, an instance of the PCP which still simulates M on w. We do so with a somewhat technical trick. The idea is to build the requirement of starting with the first domino directly into the problem so that stating the explicit requirement becomes unnecessary. We need to introduce some notation for this purpose.

Let $u = u_1 u_2 \cdots u_n$ be any string of length n. Define $\star u$, $u \star$, and $\star u \star$ to be the three strings

$$
\begin{aligned}
\star u &= *u_1 * u_2 * u_3 * \quad \cdots \quad * u_n \\
u\star &= u_1 * u_2 * u_3 * \quad \cdots \quad * u_n * \\
\star u\star &= *u_1 * u_2 * u_3 * \quad \cdots \quad * u_n *.
\end{aligned}
$$

Here, $\star u$ adds the symbol $*$ before every character u, $u \star$ adds one after each character u, and $\star u \star$ adds one both before and after each character u.

To convert P' to P, an instance of the PCP, we do the following. If P' were the collection

$$
\left\{ \left[\frac{t_1}{b_1} \right], \ \left[\frac{t_2}{b_2} \right], \ \left[\frac{t_3}{b_3} \right], \ \cdots, \ \left[\frac{t_k}{b_k} \right] \right\},
$$

we let P be the collection

$$
\left\{ \left[\frac{\star t_1}{\star b_1 \star} \right], \ \left[\frac{\star t_1}{b_1 \star} \right], \ \left[\frac{\star t_2}{b_2 \star} \right], \ \left[\frac{\star t_3}{b_3 \star} \right], \ \cdots, \ \left[\frac{\star t_k}{b_k \star} \right], \ \left[\frac{* \diamond}{\diamond} \right] \right\}.
$$

Considering P as an instance of the PCP, we see that the only domino that could possibly start a match is the the first one,

$$
\left[\frac{\star l_1}{\star b_1 \star} \right],
$$

because it is the only one where both the top and the bottom start with the same symbol, namely $*$. Besides forcing the match to start with the first domino, the presence of the $*$s doesn't affect possible matches because they simply interleave with the original symbols. The original symbols now occur in the even positions of the match. The domino

$$
\left[\frac{* \diamond}{\diamond} \right]
$$

is there to allow the top to add the extra $*$ at the end of the match.

5.3

MAPPING REDUCIBILITY

We have shown how to use the reducibility technique to prove that various problems are undecidable. In this section we formalize the notion of reducibility. Doing so allows us to use reducibility in more refined ways, such as for proving that certain languages are not Turing-recognizable and for applications in complexity theory.

The notion of reducing one problem to another may be defined formally in one of several ways. The choice of which one to use depends on the application. Our choice is a simple type of reducibility called ***mapping reducibility***.[2]

Roughly speaking, being able to reduce problem A to problem B by using a mapping reducibility means that a computable function exists that converts instances of problem A to instances of problem B. If we have such a conversion function, called a *reduction*, we can solve A with a solver for B. The reason is that any instance of A can be solved by first using the reduction to convert it to an instance of B and then applying the solver for B. A precise definition of mapping reducibility follows shortly.

COMPUTABLE FUNCTIONS

A Turing machine computes a function by starting with the input to the function on the tape and halting with the output of the function on the tape.

DEFINITION 5.12

A function $f: \Sigma^* \longrightarrow \Sigma^*$ is a ***computable function*** if some Turing machine M, on every input w, halts with just $f(w)$ on its tape.

EXAMPLE 5.13

All usual arithmetic operations on integers are computable functions. For example, we can make a machine that takes input $\langle m, n \rangle$ and returns $m + n$, the sum of m and n. We don't give any details here, leaving them as exercises. ∎

EXAMPLE 5.14

Computable functions may be transformations of machine descriptions. For example, one computable function f takes input w and returns the description of a Turing machine $\langle M' \rangle$ if $w = \langle M \rangle$ is an encoding of a Turing machine M. The machine M' is a machine that recognizes the same language as M, but never attempts to move its head off the left-hand end of its tape. The function f accomplishes this task by adding several states to the description of M. The function returns ε if w is not a legal encoding of a Turing machine. ∎

---

[2]It is called ***many-one reducibility*** in some other textbooks.

FORMAL DEFINITION OF MAPPING REDUCIBILITY

Now we define mapping reducibility. As usual we represent computational problems by languages.

DEFINITION 5.15 ....

Language A is ***mapping reducible*** to language B, written $A \leq_m B$, if there is a computable function $f : \Sigma^* \longrightarrow \Sigma^*$, where for every w,

$$w \in A \Longleftrightarrow f(w) \in B.$$

The function f is called the ***reduction*** of A to B.

The following figure illustrates mapping reducibility.

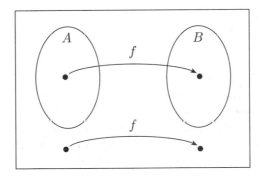

FIGURE 5.6
Function f reducing A to B

A mapping reduction of A to B provides a way to convert questions about membership testing in A to membership testing in B. To test whether $w \in A$, we use the reduction f to map w to $f(w)$ and test whether $f(w) \in B$. The term *mapping reduction* comes from the function or mapping that provides the means of doing the reduction.

If one problem is mapping reducible to a second, previously solved problem, we can thereby obtain a solution to the original problem. We capture this idea in the following theorem.

THEOREM 5.16 ....

If $A \leq_m B$ and B is decidable, then A is decidable.

PROOF We let M be the decider for B and f be the reduction from A to B. We describe a decider N for A as follows.

$N =$ "On-input w:

1. Compute $f(w)$.
2. Run M on input $f(w)$ and output whatever M outputs."

Clearly, if $w \in A$, then $f(w) \in B$ because f is a reduction from A to B. Thus M accepts $f(w)$ whenever $w \in A$. Therefore N works as desired.

COROLLARY **5.17**

If $A \leq_{\mathrm{m}} B$ and A is undecidable, then B is undecidable.

Now we revisit some of our earlier proofs that used the reducibility method to get examples of mapping reducibilities.

EXAMPLE **5.18**

In Theorem 5.1 we used a reduction from A_{TM} to prove that $HALT_{\mathsf{TM}}$ is undecidable. This reduction showed how a decider for $HALT_{\mathsf{TM}}$ could be used to give a decider for A_{TM}. We can demonstrate a mapping reducibility from A_{TM} to $HALT_{\mathsf{TM}}$ as follows. To do so we must present a computable function f that takes input of the form $\langle M, w \rangle$ and returns output of the form $\langle M', w' \rangle$, where

$$\langle M, w \rangle \in A_{\mathsf{TM}} \text{ if and only if } \langle M', w' \rangle \in HALT_{\mathsf{TM}}.$$

The following machine F computes a reduction f.

$F =$ "On input $\langle M, w \rangle$:

1. Construct the following machine M'.
   $M' =$ "On input x:
   1. Run M on x.
   2. If M accepts, *accept*.
   3. If M rejects, enter a loop."
2. Output $\langle M', w \rangle$."

EXAMPLE **5.19**

The proof of the undecidability of the Post correspondence problem in Theorem 5.11 contains two mapping reductions. First, it shows that $A_{\mathsf{TM}} \leq_{\mathrm{m}} MPCP$ and then it shows that $MPCP \leq_{\mathrm{m}} PCP$. In both cases we can easily obtain the actual reduction function and show that it is a mapping reduction. As Exercise 5.6 shows, mapping reducibility is transitive, so these two reductions together imply that $A_{\mathsf{TM}} \leq_{\mathrm{m}} PCP$.

EXAMPLE **5.20**

A mapping reduction from E_{TM} to EQ_{TM} lies in the proof of Theorem 5.4. In this case the reduction f maps the input $\langle M \rangle$ to the output $\langle M, M_1 \rangle$, where M_1 is the machine that rejects all inputs.

EXAMPLE **5.21**

The proof of Theorem 5.2 showing that E_{TM} is undecidable illustrates the difference between the formal notion of mapping reducibility that we have defined in this section and the informal notion of reducibility that we used earlier in this chapter. The proof shows that E_{TM} is undecidable by reducing A_{TM} to it. Let's see whether we can convert this reduction into a mapping reduction.

From the original reduction we may easily construct a function f that takes input $\langle M, w \rangle$ and produces output $\langle M_1 \rangle$, where M_1 is the Turing machine described in that proof. But M accepts w if and only if $L(M_1)$ is *not* empty so f is a mapping reduction from A_{TM} to $\overline{E_{\mathsf{TM}}}$. It still shows that E_{TM} is undecidable because decidability is not affected by complementation, but it doesn't give a mapping reduction from A_{TM} to E_{TM}. In fact, no such reduction exists, as you are asked to show in Exercise 5.5.

The sensitivity of mapping reducibility to complementation is important in the use of reducibility to prove nonrecognizability of certain languages. We can also use mapping reducibility to show that problems are not Turing-recognizable. The following theorem is analogous to Theorem 5.16.

THEOREM **5.22**

If $A \leq_{\mathrm{m}} B$ and B is Turing-recognizable, then A is Turing-recognizable.

The proof is the same as that of Theorem 5.16, except than M and N are recognizers instead of deciders.

COROLLARY **5.23**

If $A \leq_{\mathrm{m}} B$ and A is not Turing-recognizable, then B is not Turing-recognizable.

In a typical application of this corollary, we let A be $\overline{A_{\mathsf{TM}}}$, the complement of A_{TM}. We know that $\overline{A_{\mathsf{TM}}}$ is not Turing-recognizable from Corollary 4.17. The definition of mapping reducibility implies that $A \leq_{\mathrm{m}} B$ means the same as $\overline{A} \leq_{\mathrm{m}} \overline{B}$. To prove that B isn't recognizable we may show that $A_{\mathsf{TM}} \leq_{\mathrm{m}} \overline{B}$. We can also use mapping reducibility to show that certain problems are neither Turing-recognizable nor co-Turing-recognizable as in the following theorem.

THEOREM   5.24 ....

EQ_{TM} is neither Turing-recognizable nor co-Turing-recognizable.

PROOF   First we show that EQ_{TM} is not Turing-recognizable. We do so by showing that A_{TM} is reducible to $\overline{EQ_{TM}}$. The reducing function f works as follows.

$F =$ "On input $\langle M, w \rangle$ where M is a TM and w a string:

1. Construct the following two machines M_1 and M_2.
   $M_1 =$ "On any input:
      1. *Reject.*"
   $M_2 =$ "On any input:
      1. Run M on w. If it accepts, *accept.*"
2. Output $\langle M_1, M_2 \rangle$."

Here, M_1 accepts nothing. If M accepts w, M_2 accepts everything, and so the two machines are not equivalent. Conversely, if M doesn't accept w, M_2 accepts nothing, and they are equivalent. Thus f reduces A_{TM} to $\overline{EQ_{TM}}$, as desired.

To show that $\overline{EQ_{TM}}$ is not Turing-recognizable we give a reduction from A_{TM} to the complement of $\overline{EQ_{TM}}$, namely, EQ_{TM}. Hence we show that $A_{TM} \leq_m EQ_{TM}$. The following TM G computes the reducing function g.

$G =$ "The input is $\langle M, w \rangle$ where M is a TM and w a string.

1. Construct the following two machines M_1 and M_2:
   $M_1 =$ "On any input:
      1. *Accept.*"
   $M_2 =$ "On any input:
      1. Run M on w.
      2. If it accepts, *accept.*"
2. Output $\langle M_1, M_2 \rangle$."

The only difference between f and g is in machine M_1. In f, machine M_1 always rejects, whereas in g it always accepts. In both f and g, M accepts w if and only if M_2 always accepts. In g, M accepts w if and only if M_1 and M_2 are equivalent. That is why g is a reduction from A_{TM} to EQ_{TM}.

....

EXERCISES

5.1 Show that EQ_{CFG} is undecidable.

5.2 Show that EQ_{CFG} is co-Turing-recognizable.

5.3 Find a match in the following instance of the PCP.

$$\left\{ \left[\frac{\mathsf{ab}}{\mathsf{abab}} \right], \left[\frac{\mathsf{b}}{\mathsf{a}} \right], \left[\frac{\mathsf{aba}}{\mathsf{b}} \right], \left[\frac{\mathsf{aa}}{\mathsf{a}} \right] \right\}$$

5.4 If $A \leq_m B$ and B is a regular language, does that imply that A is a regular language? Why or why not?

5.5 Show that A_{TM} is not mapping reducible to E_{TM}.

5.6 Show that $\leq_m$ is a transitive relation.

5.7 Show that if A is Turing-recognizable and $A \leq_m \overline{A}$, then A is decidable.

5.8 In the proof of Theorem 5.11 we modified the Turing machine M so that it never tries to move its head off the left-hand end of the tape. Suppose that we did not make this modification to M. How would we have to modify the PCP construction to handle this case?

PROBLEMS

5.9 Show that all Turing-recognizable problems mapping reduce to A_{TM}.

5.10 Let $J = \{w \mid w = 0x \text{ for some } x \in A_{\mathsf{TM}} \text{ or } w = 1y \text{ for some } y \in \overline{A_{\mathsf{TM}}} \}$. Show that neither J nor $\overline{J}$ is Turing-recognizable.

5.11 Give an example of an undecidable language B, where $B \leq_m \overline{B}$.

5.12 Let $S = \{\langle M \rangle \mid M \text{ is a TM that accepts } w^{\mathcal{R}} \text{ whenever it accepts } w\}$. Show that S is undecidable.

5.13 A **useless state** in a Turing machine is one that is never entered on any input string. Consider the problem of testing whether a Turing machine has any useless states. Formulate this problem as a language and show that it is undecidable.

5.14 Consider the problem of testing whether a Turing machine M on an input w ever attempts to move its head left when its head is on the left-most tape cell. Formulate this problem as a language and show that it is undecidable.

5.15 Consider the problem of testing whether a Turing machine M on a input w ever attempts to move its head left at any point during its computation on w. Formulate this problem as a language and show that it *is* decidable.

5.16 Consider the problem of testing whether a two-tape Turing machine ever writes a nonblank symbol on its second tape. Formulate this problem as a language, and show that it is undecidable.

5.17 Show that the PCP is decidable over a unary alphabet, that is, over the alphabet $\Sigma = \{1\}$.

5.18 Show that the PCP is undecidable over a binary alphabet, that is, over the alphabet $\Sigma = \{0,1\}$.

5.19 Let $AMBIG_{CFG} = \{\langle G \rangle | \; G \text{ is an ambiguous CFG}\}$. Show that $AMBIG$ is undecidable. (Hint: Use a reduction from PCP. Given an instance

$$P = \left\{ \left[\frac{t_1}{b_1} \right], \; \left[\frac{t_2}{b_2} \right], \; \cdots, \; \left[\frac{t_k}{b_k} \right] \right\},$$

of the PCP, construct an CFG G with the rules

$$
\begin{aligned}
S &\rightarrow T \mid B \\
T &\rightarrow t_1 T \mathtt{a}_1 \mid \cdots \mid t_k T \mathtt{a}_k \mid \varepsilon \\
B &\rightarrow b_1 B \mathtt{a}_1 \mid \cdots \mid b_k B \mathtt{a}_k \mid \varepsilon,
\end{aligned}
$$

where $\mathtt{a}_1, \ldots, \mathtt{a}_k$ are new terminal symbols. Prove that this reduction works.)

5.20 Define a *two headed finite automaton* (2DFA) to be a deterministic finite automaton that has two read-only, bidirectional heads that start at the left-hand end of the input tape and can be independently controlled to move in either direction. The tape of a 2DFA is finite and is just large enough to contain the input plus two additional blank tape cells, one on the left-hand end and one on the right-hand end, that serve as delimiters. A 2DFA accepts its input by entering a special halt state. For example, a 2DFA can recognize the language $\{a^n b^n c^n | \; n \geq 0\}$.

    a. Let $A_{2DFA} = \{\langle M, x \rangle | \; M \text{ is a 2DFA and } M \text{ accepts } x\}$. Show that A_{2DFA} is decidable.

    b. Let $E_{2DFA} = \{\langle M \rangle | \; M \text{ is a 2DFA and } L(M) = \emptyset\}$. Show that E_{2DFA} is not decidable.

5.21 A *two dimensional finite automaton* (2DIM-DFA) is defined as follows. The input is an $m \times n$ rectangle, for any $m, n \geq 2$. The squares along the boundary of the rectangle contain the symbol # and the internal squares contain symbols over the input alphabet Σ. The transition function is a mapping $Q \times \Sigma \rightarrow Q \times \{\mathrm{L, R, U, D}\}$ to indicate the next state and the new head position (Left, Right, Up, Down). The machine accepts when it enters one of the designated accept states. It rejects if it tries to move off the input rectangle or if it never halts. Two such machines are equivalent if they accept the same rectangles. Consider the problem of testing whether two of these machines are equivalent. Formulate this problem as a language, and show that it is undecidable.

****5.22** **Rice's Theorem.** Let P be any problem about Turing machines that satisfies the following two properties. As usual we express P as a language.

    a. For any TMs M_1 and M_2, where $L(M_1) = L(M_2)$, we have $\langle M_1 \rangle \in P$ iff $\langle M_2 \rangle \in P$. In other words, the membership of a TM M in P depends only on the language of M.

    b. There exist TMs M_1 and M_2, where $\langle M_1 \rangle \in P$ and $\langle M_2 \rangle \notin P$. In other words, P is nontrivial—it holds for some, but not all, TMs.

Show that P is undecidable.

5.23 Show that both conditions in Problem 5.22 are necessary for proving that P is undecidable.

6

$$\cdots\cdots\cdots\cdots\cdots\cdots\cdots\cdots\cdots\cdots\cdots\cdots\cdots\cdots\cdots\cdots\cdots$$

ADVANCED TOPICS IN COMPUTABILITY THEORY

In this chapter we delve into several deeper aspects of computability theory. The four topics we discuss in this chapter are (1) the recursion theorem, (2) logical theories, (3) Turing reducibility, and (4) descriptive complexity.

Each section is mainly independent of the others, except for an application of the recursion theorem at the end of the section on logical theories. Part Three of this book doesn't depend on any material from this chapter.

6.1

THE RECURSION THEOREM

The recursion theorem is a mathematical result that plays an important role in advanced work in the theory of computability. It has connections to mathematical logic, the theory of self-reproducing systems, and even computer viruses.

To introduce the recursion theorem, we consider a paradox that arises in the study of life. It concerns the possibility of making machines that can construct replicas of themselves. The paradox can be summarized in the following manner.

1. Living things are machines.
2. Living things can self-reproduce.
3. Machines cannot self-reproduce.

Statement 1 is a tenet of modern biology. We believe that organisms operate in a mechanistic way. Statement 2 is obvious. The ability to self-reproduce is an essential characteristic of every biological species.

For statement 3, we make the following argument that machines cannot self-reproduce. Consider a machine that constructs other machines, such as an automated factory that produces cars. Raw materials go in at one end, the manufacturing robots follow a set of instructions, and then completed vehicles come out the other end.

We claim that the factory must be more complex than the cars produced, in the sense that designing the factory would be more difficult than designing a car. This claim must be true because the factory itself has the car's design within it, in addition to the design of all the manufacturing robots. The same reasoning applies to any machine A that constructs a machine B: A must be *more* complex than B. But a machine cannot be more complex than itself. Consequently, no machine can construct itself, and thus self-reproduction is impossible.

How can we resolve this paradox? The answer is simple: Step 3 is incorrect. Making machines that reproduce themselves *is* possible. The recursion theorem demonstrates how.

SELF-REFERENCE

Let's begin by making a Turing machine that ignores its input and prints out a copy of its own description. We call this machine $SELF$. To help describe $SELF$, we need the following lemma.

LEMMA 6.1 ....

There is a computable function $q: \Sigma^* \longrightarrow \Sigma^*$, where, for any string w, $q(w)$ is the description of a Turing machine P_w that prints out w and then halts.

PROOF   Once we understand the statement of this lemma, the proof is easy. Obviously, we can take any string w and construct from it a Turing machine that has w built into a table so that the machine can simply output w when started. The following TM computes $q(w)$.

$Q = $ "On input string w.
  1. Construct the following Turing machine P_w:
     $P_w = $ "On any input:
       1. Erase input.
       2. Write w on the tape.
       3. Halt."
  2. Output $\langle P_w \rangle$."

....

The Turing machine $SELF$ is in two parts, called A and B. We think of A and B as being two separate procedures that go together to make up $SELF$. We want $SELF$ to print out $\langle SELF \rangle = \langle AB \rangle$.

Part A runs first and upon completion passes control to B. The job of A is to print out a description of B, and conversely the job of B is to print out a description of A. The result is the desired description of $SELF$. The jobs are similar, but they are carried out differently. We show how to get part A first.

For A we use the machine $P_{\langle B \rangle}$, described by $q(\langle B \rangle)$, which is the result of applying the function q to $\langle B \rangle$. Thus part A is a Turing machine that prints out $\langle B \rangle$. Our description of A depends on having a description of B. So we can't complete the description of A until we construct B.

Now for part B. We might be tempted to define B with $q(\langle A \rangle)$, but that doesn't make sense! Doing so would define B in terms of A, which in turn is defined in terms of B. That would be a *circular* definition of an object in terms of itself, a logical transgression. Instead, we define B so that it prints A by using a different strategy: B *computes* A from the output that A produces.

We defined $\langle A \rangle$ to be $q(\langle B \rangle)$. Now comes the tricky part: If B can obtain $\langle B \rangle$, it can apply q to that and obtain $\langle A \rangle$. But how does B obtain $\langle B \rangle$? It was left on the tape when A finished! So B only needs to look at the tape to obtain $\langle B \rangle$. Then after computing $q(\langle B \rangle) = \langle A \rangle$, B adds that to the front of the tape. Finally, the tape contains $\langle AB \rangle = \langle SELF \rangle$. In summary, we have:

$$A = P_{\langle B \rangle}$$

and

$B =$ "On input $\langle M \rangle$, where M is a portion of a TM:
1. Compute $q(\langle M \rangle)$.
2. Combine the result with $\langle M \rangle$ to make a complete TM description.
3. Print this description and halt."

This completes the construction of $SELF$, for which a schematic diagram is presented in the following figure.

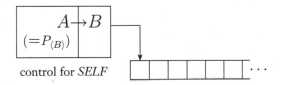

FIGURE 6.1
Schematic of $SELF$, a TM that prints its own description

If we now run *SELF* we observe the following behavior.

1. First *A* runs. It prints $\langle B \rangle$ on the tape.
2. *B* starts. It looks at the tape and finds its input, $\langle B \rangle$.
3. *B* calculates $q(\langle B \rangle) = \langle A \rangle$ and combines that with $\langle B \rangle$ into a TM description, $\langle SELF \rangle$.
4. *B* prints this description and halts."

We can easily implement this construction in any programming language to obtain a program that outputs a copy of itself. We can even do so in plain English. Suppose that we want to give an English sentence that commands the reader to print a copy of the same sentence. One way to do so is to say:

Print out this sentence.

This sentence has the desired meaning because it directs the reader to print a copy of the sentence itself. However, it doesn't have an obvious translation into a programming language because the self-referential word "this" in the sentence usually has no counterpart. But no self-reference is needed to make such a sentence. Consider the following alternative.

Print out two copies of the following, the second one in quotes:
"Print out two copies of the following, the second one in quotes:"

In this sentence, the self-reference is replaced with the same construction used to make the TM *SELF*. Part *B* of the construction is the clause:

Print out two copies of the following, the second one in quotes:

Part *A* is the same, with quotes around it. *A* provides a copy of *B* to *B* so *B* can process that copy as the TM does.

The recursion theorem provides the ability to implement the self-referential *this* into any programming language. With it, any program has the ability to refer to its own description, which has certain applications, as you will see. Before getting to that we give a statement of the recursion theorem itself. The recursion theorem extends the technique we used in constructing *SELF* so that a program can obtain its own description and then go on to compute with it, instead of merely printing it out.

THEOREM 6.2 ···

Recursion Theorem   Let T be a Turing machine that computes a function $t \colon \Sigma^* \times \Sigma^* \longrightarrow \Sigma^*$. There is a Turing machine R that computes a function $r \colon \Sigma^* \longrightarrow \Sigma^*$, where for every w,

$$r(w) = t(\langle R \rangle, w).$$

The statement of this theorem seems a bit technical, but it actually represents something quite simple. To make a Turing machine that can obtain its own description and then compute with it, we need only make a machine, called T in the statement, that takes an extra input that receives the description of the machine. Then the recursion theorem produces a new machine R, which operates exactly as T does but with R's description filled in automatically.

PROOF   The proof is similar to the construction of $SELF$. We construct a TM R in three parts, A, B, and T, where T is given by the statement of the theorem.

Here, A is the Turing machine $P_{\langle BT \rangle}$ described by $q(\langle BT \rangle)$. After A runs, the tape contains $\langle BT \rangle$.

Again, B is a procedure that examines its tape and applies q to its contents. The result is $\langle A \rangle$. Then B combines A, B, and T into a single machine, writes its description on the tape, and passes control to T.

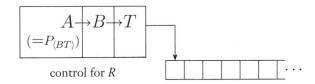

control for R

FIGURE   6.2
Schematic of R

TERMINOLOGY FOR THE RECURSION THEOREM

The recursion theorem states that Turing machines have the capability to obtain their own description and then go on to compute with it. At first glance this capability may seem to be useful only for frivolous tasks such as making a machine that prints a copy of itself. But, as we demonstrate, the recursion theorem is a handy tool for solving certain problems concerning the theory of algorithms.

You can use the recursion theorem in the following way when designing Turing machine algorithms. If you are designing a machine M, you can include the phrase "obtain own description $\langle M \rangle$" in the informal description of M's algorithm. Upon having obtained its own description M can then go on to use it as it would use any other computed value. For example, M might simply print out $\langle M \rangle$, then count the number of states in $\langle M \rangle$, or simulate $\langle M \rangle$.

To illustrate this method we use the recursion theorem to describe the machine $SELF$.

$SELF = $ "On any input:
  1. Obtain, via the recursion theorem, own description $\langle SELF \rangle$.
  2. Print $\langle SELF \rangle$."

APPLICATIONS

A *computer virus* is a computer program that is designed to spread itself among computers. Aptly named, it has much in common with a biological virus. Computer viruses are inactive when standing alone as a piece of code, but when placed appropriately in a host computer, thereby "infecting" it, they can become activated and transmit copies of themselves to other accessible machines. Various media can transmit viruses, including the internet and transferable disks. In order to carry out its primary task of self-replication, a virus may contain the construction described in the proof of the recursion theorem.

Let's now consider three theorems whose proofs use the recursion theorem. An additional application appears in the proof of Theorem 6.15 in Section 6.2.

First we return to the proof of the undecidability of A_{TM}. Recall that we earlier proved it in Theorem 4.9, using Cantor's diagonal method. The recursion theorem gives us a new and simpler proof.

THEOREM 6.3 ....

A_{TM} is undecidable.

PROOF   We assume that Turing machine H decides A_{TM}, for the purposes of obtaining a contradiction. We construct the following machine B.

$B = $ "On input w:

    1. Obtain, via the recursion theorem, own description $\langle B \rangle$.

    2. Run H on input $\langle B, w \rangle$.

    3. Do the opposite of what H says. That is, *accept* if H rejects and *reject* if H accepts."

Running B on input w does the opposite of what H declares it does. Therefore H cannot be deciding A_{TM}. Done!

....

The following is another application of the recursion theorem.

DEFINITION 6.4 ....

If M is a Turing machine, then we say that the *length* of the description $\langle M \rangle$ of M is the number of symbols in the string describing M. Say that M is **minimal** if there is no Turing machine equivalent to M that has a shorter description. Let

$$MIN_{TM} = \{\langle M \rangle |\ M \text{ is a minimal TM}\}.$$

THEOREM 6.5 ....

MIN_{TM} is not Turing-recognizable.

PROOF   Assume that some TM E enumerates MIN_{TM} and obtain a contradiction. We construct the following TM C.

$C = $ "On input w:

    1.   Obtain, via the recursion theorem, own description $\langle C \rangle$.

    2.   Run the enumerator E until a machine D appears with a longer description than that of C.

    3.   Simulate D on input w."

Because MIN_{TM} is infinite, E's list must contain a TM with a longer description than C's description. Therefore step 2 of C eventually terminates with some TM D that is longer than C. Then C simulates D and so is equivalent to it. Because C is shorter than D and is equivalent to it, D cannot be minimal. But D appears on the list that E produces. Thus we have a contradiction.

....

Our final application of the recursion theorem is a type of fixed-point theorem. A *fixed point* of a function is a value that isn't changed by application of the function. In this case we consider functions that are computable transformations of Turing machine descriptions. We show that for any such transformation some Turing machine exists whose behavior is unchanged by the transformation. This theorem is sometimes called the fixed-point version of the recursion theorem.

THEOREM **6.6**   ....

Let $t \colon \Sigma^* \longrightarrow \Sigma^*$ be a computable function. Then there is a Turing machine F wherein $t(\langle F \rangle)$ describes a Turing machine equivalent to F.

In this theorem t plays the role of the transformation, and F is the fixed point.

PROOF   Let F be the following Turing machine.

$F = $ "On input w:

    1.   Obtain, via the recursion theorem, own description $\langle F \rangle$.

    2.   Compute $t(\langle F \rangle)$ to obtain the description of a TM G.

    3.   Simulate G on w."

Clearly, $\langle F \rangle$ and $t(\langle F \rangle) = \langle G \rangle$ describe equivalent Turing machines because F simulates G.

....

6.2 ■

DECIDABILITY OF LOGICAL THEORIES

Mathematical logic is the branch of mathematics that investigates mathematics itself. It addresses questions such as: What is a theorem? What is a proof? What is truth? Can an algorithm decide which statements are true? Are all true statements provable? We'll touch on a few of these topics in our brief introduction to this rich and fascinating subject.

We focus on the problem of determining whether mathematical statements are true or false and investigate the decidability of this problem. The answer will depend on the domain of mathematics from which the statements are drawn. We examine two domains: one for which we can give an algorithm to decide truth and another for which this problem is undecidable.

First we need to set up a precise language to formulate these problems. Our intention is to be able to consider mathematical statements such as

1. $\forall q \, \exists p \, \forall x,y \, \big[p > q \wedge (x,y > 1 \rightarrow xy \neq p) \big]$,
2. $\forall a,b,c,n \, \big[(a,b,c > 0 \wedge n > 2) \rightarrow a^n + b^n \neq c^n \big]$, and
3. $\forall q \, \exists p \, \forall x,y \, \big[p > q \wedge (x,y > 1 \rightarrow (xy \neq p \wedge xy \neq p+2)) \big]$.

Statement 1 says that infinitely many prime numbers exist, and has been known to be true since the time of Euclid, about 2,300 years ago. Statement 2 is known as *Fermat's Last Theorem* and has been known to be true only since Andrew Wiles proved it a few years ago. Finally, statement 3 says that infinitely many prime pairs[1] exist. Known as the *twin prime conjecture*, it remains unsolved.

To consider whether we could automate the process of determining which of these statements are true, we treat such statements merely as strings and define a language consisting of those statements which are true. Then we ask whether this language is decidable.

To make this a bit more precise, let's describe the form of the alphabet of this language:

$$\{\wedge, \vee, \neg, (,), \forall, x, \exists, R_1, \dots, R_k\}.$$

The symbols $\wedge$, $\vee$, and $\neg$, are called **Boolean operations**; "(" and ")" are the **parentheses**; the symbols $\forall$ and $\exists$ are called **quantifiers**; the symbol x is used to denote **variables**;[2] and the symbols $R_1, \dots, R_l$ are called **relations**.

A **formula** is a well-formed string over this alphabet. For completeness, we'll sketch the technical but obvious definition of a **well-formed formula** here, but feel free to skip this part and go on to the next paragraph. A string of the form

---

[1] **Prime pairs** are primes that differ by 2.
[2] If we need to write several variables in a formula, we use the symbols w, y, z, or x_1, x_2, x_3, and so on. We don't list all the infinitely many possible variables in the alphabet to keep the alphabet finite. Instead, we list only the variable symbol x, and use strings of x's to indicate other variables, as in xx for x_2, xxx for x_3, and so on.

$R_i(x_1, \ldots, x_j)$ is an *atomic formula*. The value j is the *arity* of the relation symbol R_i. All appearances of the same relation symbol in a well-formed formula must have the same arity. Subject to this requirement a string ϕ is a formula if it

1. is an atomic formula,
2. has the form $\phi_1 \wedge \phi_2$ or $\phi_1 \vee \phi_2$ or $\neg \phi_1$, where ϕ_1 and ϕ_2 are smaller formulas, or
3. has the form $\exists x_i \, [\, \phi_1 \,]$ or $\forall x_i \, [\, \phi_1 \,]$, where ϕ_1 is a smaller formula.

A quantifier may appear anywhere in a mathematical statement. Its *scope* is the fragment of the statement appearing within the matched pair of parentheses or brackets following the quantified variable. We assume that all formulas are in *prenex normal form*, where all quantifiers appear in the front of the formula. A variable that isn't bound within the scope of a quantifier is called a *free variable*. A formula with no free variables is called a *sentence* or *statement*.

EXAMPLE **6.7**

Among the following examples of formulas, only the last one is a sentence.

1. $R_1(x_1) \wedge R_2(x_1, x_2, x_3)$
2. $\forall x_1 \, \big[\, R_1(x_1) \wedge R_2(x_1, x_2, x_3) \,\big]$
3. $\forall x_1 \, \exists x_2 \, \exists x_3 \, \big[\, R_1(x_1) \wedge R_2(x_1, x_2, x_3) \,\big].$

Having established the syntax of formulas, let's discuss their meanings. The Boolean operations and the quantifiers have their usual meanings, but to determine the meaning of the variables and relation symbols we need to specify two items. One is the *universe* over which the variables may take values. The other is an assignment of specific relations to the relation symbols. As we described in Section 0.2 on page 8 a relation is a function from k-tuples over the universe to $\{\text{TRUE}, \text{FALSE}\}$. The arity of a relation symbol must match that of its assigned relation.

A universe together with an assignment of relations to relation symbols is called a *model*.[3] Formally we say that a model $\mathcal{M}$ is a tuple $(U, P_1, \ldots, P_k)$, where U is the universe and P_1 through P_k are the relations assigned to symbols R_1 through R_k. We sometimes refer to the *language of a model* to be the collection of formulas that use only the relation symbols the model assigns and that use each relation symbol with the correct arity. If ϕ is a sentence in the language of a model, ϕ is either true or false in that model. If ϕ is true in a model $\mathcal{M}$, we say that $\mathcal{M}$ is a model of ϕ.

If you feel overwhelmed by these definitions, concentrate on our objective in stating them. We want to set up a precise language of mathematical statements so that we can ask whether an algorithm can determine which are true and which are false. The following examples should be helpful.

---

[3]A model is also variously called an *interpretation* or *structure*.

EXAMPLE 6.8 ....

Let ϕ be the sentence $\forall x\, \forall y\, \big[\, R_1(x,y) \vee R_1(y,x)\,\big]$. Let model $\mathcal{M}_1 = (\mathcal{N}, \leq)$ be the model whose universe is the natural numbers and which assign the "less than or equal" relation to the symbol R_1. Obviously, ϕ is true in model $\mathcal{M}_1$ because either $a \leq b$ or $b \leq a$ for any two natural numbers a and b. However, if $\mathcal{M}_2$ assigned "less than" instead of "less than or equal" to R_1, then ϕ would not be true because it fails when x and y are equal.

   If we know in advance which relation will be assigned to R_i, we may use the customary symbol for that relation in place of R_i with infix notation rather than prefix notation if customary for that symbol. Thus with model $\mathcal{M}_1$ in mind, we could write ϕ as $\forall x\, \forall y\, \big[\, x{\leq}y \vee y{\leq}x\,\big]$.

EXAMPLE 6.9 ....

As a second example, let $\mathcal{M}_1$ be the model whose universe is the real numbers $\mathcal{R}$ and which assigns the relation $PLUS$ to R_1, where $PLUS(a,b,c) = \text{TRUE}$ whenever $a + b = c$. Then $\mathcal{M}_1$ is a model of $\psi = \forall y\, \exists x\, \big[\, R_1(x,x,y)\,\big]$. However, if $\mathcal{N}$ were used for the universe instead of $\mathcal{R}$ in $\mathcal{M}_2$, the sentence would be false.

   As in the previous example, we may write ψ as $\forall y\, \exists x\, \big[\, x + x = y\,\big]$ in place of $\forall y\, \exists x\, \big[\, R_1(x,x,y)\,\big]$ when we know in advance that we will be assigning the addition relation to R_1.

   As Exercise 6.9 illustrates, we can represent functions such as the addition function by relations. Moreover, we can represent constants such as 0 and 1 by relations similarly.

   Now we make one final definition in preparation for the next section. If $\mathcal{M}$ is a model, we let the ***theory of*** $\mathcal{M}$, written $\text{Th}(\mathcal{M})$, be the collection of true sentences in the language of that model.

A DECIDABLE THEORY

Number theory is one of the oldest branches of mathematics and also one of its most difficult. Many innocent looking statements about the natural numbers and the plus and times operations have confounded mathematicians for centuries, such as the twin prime conjecture mentioned earlier.

   In one of the celebrated developments in mathematical logic, Alonzo Church, building on the work of Kurt Gödel, showed that no algorithm can decide in general whether statements in number theory are true or false. Formally, we write $(\mathcal{N}, +, \times)$ to be the model whose universe is the natural numbers[4] with the usual $+$ and $\times$ relations. Church showed that $\text{Th}(\mathcal{N}, +, \times)$, the theory of this model, is undecidable.

   Before looking at this undecidable theory, let's examine one that is decidable. Let $(\mathcal{N}, +)$ be the same model, except without the $\times$ relation. Its theory

---

[4]For convenience in this section, we change our usual definition of $\mathcal{N}$ to be $\{0, 1, 2, \dots\}$.

is $\mathrm{Th}(\mathcal{N}, +)$. For example, the formula $\forall x \, \exists y \, [\, x + x = y \,]$ is true and is therefore a member of $\mathrm{Th}(\mathcal{N}, +)$, but the formula $\exists y \forall x \, [\, x + x = y \,]$ is false and is therefore not a member.

THEOREM 6.10

$\mathrm{Th}(\mathcal{N}, +)$ is decidable.

PROOF IDEA   This proof is an interesting and nontrivial application of the theory of finite automata that we presented in Chapter 1. One fact about finite automata that we use appears in Problem 1.25 on page 88 where you were asked to show that they are capable of doing addition if the input is presented in a special form. The input describes three numbers in parallel by representing one bit of each number in a single symbol from an eight-symbol alphabet. Here we use a generalization of this method to present i-tuples of numbers in parallel using an alphabet with 2^i symbols.

We give an algorithm that can test whether its input, a sentence ϕ in the language of $(\mathcal{N}, +)$, is true in that model. Let

$$\phi = Q_1 x_1 \, Q_2 x_2 \, \cdots \, Q_l x_l \, [\, \psi \,],$$

where $Q_1, \ldots, Q_l$ each represent either $\exists$ or $\forall$ and ψ is a formula without quantifiers that has variables $x_1, \ldots, x_l$. For each i from 0 to l, define formula ϕ_i to be

$$\phi_i = Q_{i+1} x_{i+1} \, Q_{i+2} x_{i+2} \, \cdots \, Q_l x_l \, [\, \psi \,].$$

Thus $\phi_0 = \phi$ and $\phi_l = \psi$.

Formula ϕ_i has i free variables. For $a_1, \ldots, a_i \in \mathcal{N}$ write $\phi_i(a_1, \ldots, a_i)$ to be the sentence obtained by substituting the constants $a_1, \ldots, a_i$ for the variables $x_1, \ldots, x_i$ in ϕ_i.

For each i from 0 to l, the algorithm constructs a finite automaton A_i that recognizes the collection of strings representing i-tuples of numbers that make ϕ_i true. The algorithm begins by constructing A_l directly, using a generalization of the method in the solution to Problem 1.25. Then, for each i from l down to 1, it uses A_i to construct A_{i-1}. Finally, once the algorithm has A_0, it tests whether A_0 accepts the empty string. If it does, ϕ is true and the algorithm accepts.

PROOF   For $i > 0$ define the alphabet

$$\Sigma_i = \left\{ \begin{bmatrix} 0 \\ \vdots \\ 0 \\ 0 \end{bmatrix}, \begin{bmatrix} 0 \\ \vdots \\ 0 \\ 1 \end{bmatrix}, \begin{bmatrix} 0 \\ \vdots \\ 1 \\ 0 \end{bmatrix}, \begin{bmatrix} 0 \\ \vdots \\ 1 \\ 1 \end{bmatrix}, \ldots, \begin{bmatrix} 1 \\ \vdots \\ 1 \\ 1 \end{bmatrix} \right\}.$$

Hence Σ_i contains all size i columns of 0s and 1s. A string over Σ_i^* represents i binary integers (reading across the rows). We also define $\Sigma_0 = \{[\,]\}$, where $[\,]$ is a symbol.

We now present an algorithm that decides $\mathrm{Th}(\mathcal{N}, +)$. On input ϕ where ϕ is a sentence, the algorithm operates as follows. Write ϕ and define ϕ_i for each i

from 0 to l, as in the proof idea. For each such i construct a finite automaton A_i from ψ that accepts strings over Σ_i^* corresponding to i-tuples $a_1, \ldots, a_i$ whenever $\psi(a_1, \ldots, a_i)$ is true.

To construct the first machine A_l, observe that $\phi_l = \psi$ is a Boolean combination of atomic formulas. An atomic formula in the language of $\mathrm{Th}(\mathcal{N}, +)$ is a single addition. Finite automata can be constructed to compute any of these individual relations corresponding to a single addition and then combined to give the automaton A_l. Doing so involves the use of the regular language closure constructions for union, intersection, and complementation to compute Boolean combinations of the atomic formulas.

Next, we show how to construct A_i from A_{i+1}. If $\phi_i = \exists x_i\ \phi_{i+1}$, we construct A_i to operate as A_{i+1} operates, except that it nondeterministically guesses the value of a_{i+1} instead of receiving it as part of the input.

More precisely, A_i contains a state for each A_{i+1} state, and a new start state. Every time A_i reads a symbol

$$\begin{bmatrix} b_1 \\ \vdots \\ b_{i-1} \\ b_i \end{bmatrix},$$

where every $b_i \in \{0,1\}$ is a bit of the number a_i, it nondeterministically guesses $z \in \{0,1\}$ and simulates A_{i+1} on the input symbol

$$\begin{bmatrix} b_1 \\ \vdots \\ b_{i-1} \\ b_i \\ z \end{bmatrix}.$$

Initially, A_i nondeterministically guesses the leading bits of z corresponding to suppressed leading 0s in b_1 through b_i by nondeterministically branching from its new start state to all states that A_{i+1} could reach from its start state with input strings of the symbols

$$\left\{ \begin{bmatrix} 0 \\ \vdots \\ 0 \\ 0 \end{bmatrix}, \begin{bmatrix} 0 \\ \vdots \\ 0 \\ 1 \end{bmatrix} \right\}$$

in Σ_{i+1}. Clearly, A_i accepts its input $(a_1, \ldots, a_i)$ if some a_{i+1} exists where A_{i+1} accepts $(a_1, \ldots, a_{i+1})$.

If $\phi_i = \forall x_i\ \phi_{i+1}$, it is equivalent to $\neg \exists x_i \neg\ \phi_{i+1}$. Thus we can construct the finite automaton that recognizes the complement of the language of A_{i+1} then apply the preceding construction for the $\exists$ quantifier, and finally apply complementation once again to obtain A_i.

Finite automaton A_0 accepts any input iff ϕ_0 is true. So the final step of the algorithm tests whether A_0 accepts ε. If it does, ϕ is true and the algorithm accepts; otherwise, it rejects.

AN UNDECIDABLE THEORY

As we mentioned earlier, $\mathrm{Th}(\mathcal{N}, +, \times)$ is an undecidable theory. No algorithm exists for deciding the truth or falsity of mathematical statements, even when restricted to the language of $(\mathcal{N}, +, \times)$. This theorem has great importance philosophically because it demonstrates that mathematics cannot be mechanized. We state this theorem, but give only a brief sketch of its proof.

THEOREM 6.11 ....

$\mathrm{Th}(\mathcal{N}, +, \times)$ is undecidable.

Though it contains many details, the proof of this theorem is not difficult conceptually. It follows the pattern of the other proofs of undecidability presented in Chapter 4. We show that $\mathrm{Th}(\mathcal{N}, +, \times)$ is undecidable by reducing A_{TM} to it, using the computation history method as described on page 176. The existence of the reduction depends on the following lemma.

LEMMA 6.12 ....

Let M be a Turing machine and w a string. We can construct from M and w a formula $\phi_{M,w}$ in the language of $\mathrm{Th}(\mathcal{N}, +, \times)$ that contains a single free variable x, whereby the sentence $\exists x\, \phi_{M,w}$ is true iff M accepts w.

....

PROOF IDEA Formula $\phi_{M,w}$ "says" that x is a (suitably encoded) accepting computation history of M on w. Of course, x actually is just a rather large integer, but it represents a computation history in a form that can be checked by using the $+$ and $\times$ operations.

The actual construction of $\psi_{M,w}$ is too complicated to present here. It extracts individual symbols in the computation history with the $+$ and $\times$ operations to check the start configuration for M on w, that each configuration legally follows from the one preceding it, and finally that the last configuration is accepting.

PROOF OF THEOREM 6.11 We give a mapping reduction from A_{TM} to $\mathrm{Th}(\mathcal{N}, +, \times)$. The reduction constructs the formula $\phi_{M,w}$ from the input $\langle M, w \rangle$ using Lemma 6.12. Then, it outputs the sentence $\exists x\, \phi_{M,w}$.

....

Next, we sketch the proof of Kurt Gödel's celebrated *incompleteness theorem*. Informally, this theorem says that, in any reasonable system of formalizing the notion of provability in number theory, some true statements are unprovable.

Loosely speaking, the ***formal proof*** π of a statement ϕ is a sequence of statements, $S_1, S_2, \ldots, S_l$, where $S_l = \phi$. Each S_i follows from the preceding statements and certain basic axioms about numbers, using simple and precise rules of implication. We don't have space to define the concept of proof, but for our purposes assuming the following two reasonable properties of proofs will be enough.

1. The correctness of a proof of a statement can be checked by machine. Formally, $\{\langle \phi, \pi \rangle \mid \pi$ is a proof of $\phi\}$ is decidable.
2. The system of proofs is *sound*. That is, if a statement is provable (i.e., has a proof), it is true.

If a system of provability satisfies these two conditions, the following three theorems hold.

THEOREM 6.13 ....

The collection of provable statements in $\mathrm{Th}(\mathcal{N}, +, \times)$ is Turing-recognizable.

PROOF   The following algorithm P accepts its input ϕ if ϕ is provable. Algorithm P tests each string as a candidate for a proof π of ϕ, using the proof checker assumed in provability property 1. If it finds that any of these candidates is a proof, it accepts.

....

Now we can use the preceding theorem to prove our version of the incompleteness theorem.

THEOREM 6.14 ....

Some true statement in $\mathrm{Th}(\mathcal{N}, +, \times)$ is not provable.

PROOF   We give a proof by contradiction. We assume to the contrary that all true statements are provable. Using this assumption, we describe an algorithm D that decides whether statements are true, contradicting Theorem 6.11.

On input ϕ algorithm D operates by running algorithm P given in the proof of Theorem 6.13 in parallel on inputs ϕ and $\neg\phi$. One of these two statements is true and thus by our assumption is provable. Therefore P must halt on one of the two inputs. By provability property 2, if ϕ is provable, then ϕ is true, and if $\neg\phi$ is provable, then ϕ is false. So algorithm D can decide the truth or falsity of ϕ.

....

In the final theorem of this section we use the recursion theorem to give an explicit sentence in the language of $(\mathcal{N}, +, \times)$ that is true but not provable. Theorem 6.14 demonstrates the existence of such a sentence but doesn't actually describe one, as we do now.

THEOREM 6.15 ....

The sentence $\psi_{\mathrm{unprovable}}$, as described in the proof of this theorem, is unprovable.

....

PROOF IDEA   Construct a sentence that says: "This sentence is not provable," using the recursion theorem to obtain the self-reference.

PROOF   Let S be a TM that operates as follows.

$S = $ "On any input:
1. Obtain own description $\langle S \rangle$ via the recursion theorem.
2. Construct the sentence $\psi = \neg \exists c \left[\phi_{S,0} \right]$, using Lemma 6.12.
3. Run algorithm P from the proof of Theorem 6.13 on input ψ.
4. If the preceding step accepts, *accept*. If it halts and rejects, *reject*."

Let $\psi_{\text{unprovable}}$ be the sentence ψ described in stage 2 of algorithm S. That sentence is true iff S doesn't accept 0 (the string 0 was selected arbitrarily).

If S finds a proof of $\psi_{\text{unprovable}}$, S accepts 0, and the sentence would thus be false. A false sentence cannot be provable, so this situation cannot occur. The only remaining possibility is that S fails to find a proof of $\psi_{\text{unprovable}}$ and so S doesn't accept 0. But then $\psi_{\text{unprovable}}$ is true, as we claimed.

6.3

TURING REDUCIBILITY

We introduced the reducibility concept in Chapter 5 as a way of using a solution to one problem to solve other problems. Thus, if A is reducible to B, and we find a solution to B, we can obtain a solution to A. Subsequently, we described *mapping reducibility*, a specific form of reducibility. But does mapping reducibility capture our intuitive concept of reducibility in the most general way? It doesn't.

For example, consider the two languages A_{TM} and $\overline{A_{\text{TM}}}$. Intuitively, they are reducible to one another because a solution to either could be used to solve the other by simple reversing the answer. However, we know that $\overline{A_{\text{TM}}}$ is *not* mapping reducible to A_{TM} because A_{TM} is Turing-recognizable but $\overline{A_{\text{TM}}}$ isn't. Here we present a very general form of reducibility, called **Turing reducibility**, which captures our intuitive concept of reducibility more closely.

DEFINITION 6.16

An **oracle** for a language B is an external device that is capable of reporting whether any string w is a member of B. An **oracle Turing machine** is a modified Turing machine that has the additional capability of querying an oracle. We write M^B to describe an oracle Turing machine that has an oracle for language B.

We aren't concerned with the way the oracle determines its responses. We use the term oracle to connote a magical ability and consider oracles for languages that aren't decidable by ordinary algorithms, as the following example shows.

EXAMPLE **6.17** ....

Consider an oracle for A_{TM}. An oracle Turing machine with an oracle for A_{TM} can decide more languages than an ordinary Turing machine can. Such a machine can (obviously) decide A_{TM} itself, by querying the oracle about the input. It can also decide E_{TM}, the emptiness testing problem for TMs with the following procedure called $T^{A_{\mathsf{TM}}}$.

$T^{A_{\mathsf{TM}}} =$ "On input $\langle M \rangle$, where M is a TM:
  1. Construct the following TM N:
     $N =$ "On any input:
        1. Run M in parallel in on all strings in Σ^*.
        2. If M halts on any of these strings, *accept*."
  2. Query the oracle to determine whether $\langle N, 0 \rangle \in A_{\mathsf{TM}}$.
  3. If the oracle answers NO, *accept*; if YES, *reject*."

If M's language isn't empty, N will halt on every input, and in particular on input 0. Hence the oracle will answer YES, and $T^{A_{\mathsf{TM}}}$ will reject. Conversely, if M's language is empty, $T^{A_{\mathsf{TM}}}$ will accept. Thus $T^{A_{\mathsf{TM}}}$ decides E_{TM}. We say that E_{TM} is ***decidable relative to*** A_{TM}. That brings us to the definition of Turing reducibility.

DEFINITION **6.18** ....

Language A is ***Turing reducible*** to language B, written $A \leq_{\mathrm{T}} B$, if A is decidable relative to B.

Example 6.17 shows that E_{TM} is Turing reducible to A_{TM}. Turing reducibility satisfies our intuitive concept of reducibility as shown by the following theorem.

THEOREM **6.19** ....

If $A \leq_{\mathrm{T}} B$ and B is decidable, then A is decidable.

PROOF   If B is decidable, then we may replace the oracle for B by an actual procedure that decides B. Thus we may replace the oracle Turing machine that decides A by an ordinary Turing machine that decides A.

....

Turing reducibility is a generalization of mapping reducibility. If $A \leq_{\mathrm{m}} B$ then $A \leq_{\mathrm{T}} B$, because the mapping reduction may be used to give an oracle Turing machine that decides A relative to B.

An oracle Turing machine with an oracle for A_{TM} is very powerful. It can solve many problems that are not solvable by ordinary Turing machines. But even such a powerful machine cannot decide all languages (see Problems 6.21 and 6.22).

6.4 ■

A DEFINITION OF INFORMATION

The concepts *algorithm* and *information* are fundamental in computer science. While the Church–Turing thesis gives a universally applicable definition of algorithm, no equally comprehensive definition of information is known. Instead of a single, universal definition of information, several definitions are used— depending upon the application. In this section we present one way of defining information using computability theory.

We start with an example. Consider the information content of the following two binary sequences:

$$A = 01010101010101010101010101010101010101$$
$$B = 1110010110100011101010000111010011010111$$

Intuitively, sequence A contains little information because it is merely a repetition of the pattern 01 twenty times. In contrast, sequence B appears to contain more information.

We can use this simple example to illustrate the idea behind the definition of information we will present. We define the quantity of information contained in an object to be the size of that object's smallest representation or description. By a description of an object we mean a precise and unambiguous characterization of the object so that we may recreate it from the description alone. Thus sequence A contains little information because it has a small description, whereas sequence B apparently contains more information because it seems to have no concise description.

Why do we consider only the *shortest* description when determining an object's quantity of information? We may always describe an object, such as a string, by placing a copy of the object directly into the description. Thus we can obviously describe the preceding string B with a table that is forty bits long containing a copy of B. This type of description is never shorter than the object itself and doesn't tell us anything about its information quantity. However, a description that is significantly shorter than the object implies that the information contained within can be compressed into a small volume, and so the amount of information can't be very large. Hence the size of the shortest description determines the amount of information.

Now we formalize this intuitive idea. Doing so isn't difficult, but we must do some preliminary work. First, we restrict our attention to objects that are binary strings. Other objects can be represented as binary strings, so this restriction doesn't limit the scope of the theory. Second, we consider only descriptions that are themselves binary strings. By imposing this requirement, we may easily compare the length of the object with the length of its description. In the next section, we consider the type of description that we allow.

MINIMAL LENGTH DESCRIPTIONS

Many types of description language can be used in the definition of information. Selecting which language to use affects the characteristics of the definition. Our description language is based on algorithms.

One way to use algorithms to describe strings is to construct a Turing machine that prints out the string when it is started on a blank tape and then represent that Turing machine itself as a string. Thus the string representing the Turing machine is a description of the original string. A drawback to this approach is that a Turing machine cannot represent a table of information concisely with its transition function. Representing a string of n bits might use n states and n rows in the transition function table. That would result in a description that is excessively long for our purpose. Instead, we use the following more concise description language.

We describe a binary string x with a Turing machine M and a binary input w to M. The length of the description is the combined length of representing M and w. We write this description with our usual notation for encoding several objects into a single binary string $\langle M, w \rangle$. But here we must pay additional attention to the encoding operation $\langle \cdot, \cdot \rangle$ because we need to produce a concise result. We define the string $\langle M, w \rangle$ to be $\langle M \rangle w$, where we simply concatenate the binary string w onto the end of the binary encoding of M. The encoding $\langle M \rangle$ of M may be done in any standard way, except for the subtlety that we describe in the next paragraph. (Don't worry about this subtle point on your first reading of this material. For now, skip past the next paragraph and Figure 6.3.)

Concatenating w onto the end of $\langle M \rangle$ to yield a description of x might run into trouble if the point at which $\langle M \rangle$ ends and w begins is not discernible from the description itself. Otherwise, several ways of partitioning the description $\langle M \rangle w$ into a syntactically correct TM and an input may occur, and then the description would be ambiguous and hence invalid. We avoid this problem by ensuring that we can locate the separation between $\langle M \rangle$ and w in $\langle M \rangle w$. One way to do so is to write each bit of $\langle M \rangle$ twice, writing 0 as 00 and 1 as 11, and then follow it with 01 to mark the separation point. We illustrate this idea in the following figure, depicting the description $\langle M, w \rangle$ of some string x.

$$\langle M, w \rangle = \underbrace{11001111001100 \cdots 1100}_{\langle M \rangle} \overbrace{01}^{\text{delimiter}} \underbrace{01101011 \cdots 010}_{w}$$

FIGURE 6.3
Example of the format of the description $\langle M, w \rangle$ of some string x

Now that we have fixed our description language we are ready to define our measure of the quantity of information in a string.

DEFINITION   6.20 ....

Let x be a binary string. The ***minimal description*** of x, written $d(x)$, is the short-est string $\langle M, w \rangle$ where TM M on input w halts with x on its tape. If several such strings exist, select the lexicographically first among them. The ***descriptive com-plexity***[5] of x, written $K(x)$, is

$$K(x) = |d(x)|.$$

In other words, $K(x)$ is the length of the minimal description of x. The defini-tion of $K(x)$ is intended to capture our intuition for the amount of information in the string x. Next we establish some simple results about descriptive complexity.

THEOREM   6.21 ....

$\exists c\, \forall x\, \big[K(x) \le |x| + c \big].$

This theorem says that the descriptive complexity of a string is at most a fixed constant more than its length. The constant is a universal one, not dependent on the string.

PROOF   To prove an upper bound on $K(x)$ as this theorem claims, we only need to demonstrate some description of x which is no longer than the stated bound. Then the minimal description of x may be shorter than the demonstrated description, but not longer.

Consider the following description of the string x. Let M be a Turing machine that halts as soon as it is started. This machine computes the identity function—its output is the same as its input. A description of x is simply $\langle M \rangle x$. Letting c be the length of $\langle M \rangle$ completes the proof.

....

Theorem 6.21 illustrates how we use the input to the Turing machine to rep-resent information that would require a significantly larger description if stored instead using the machine's transition function. It conforms with our intuition that the amount of information contained by a string cannot be (substantially) more than its length. Similarly, intuition says that the information contained by the string xx is not significantly more than the information contained by x. The following theorem verifies this fact.

THEOREM   6.22 ....

$\exists c\, \forall x\, \big[K(xx) \le K(x) + c \big].$

-----

[5]***Descriptive complexity*** is called ***Kolmogorov complexity*** or ***Kolmogorov–Chaitin com-plexity*** in some treatments.

PROOF   Consider the following Turing machine M, which expects an input of the form $\langle N, w \rangle$, where N is a Turing machine and w is an input for it.

$M = $ "On input $\langle N, w \rangle$ where N is a TM and w is a string:

  1. Run N on w until it halts and produces an output string s.
  2. Output the string ss."

A description of xx is $\langle M \rangle d(x)$. Recall that $d(x)$ is a minimal description of x. The length of this description is $|\langle M \rangle| + |d(x)|$, which is $c + \mathrm{K}(x)$ where c is the length of $\langle M \rangle$.

Next we examine how the descriptive complexity of the concatenation xy of two strings x and y is related to their individual complexities. Theorem 6.21 might lead us to believe that the complexity of the concatenation is at most the sum of the individual complexities (plus a fixed constant), but the cost of combining two descriptions leads to a greater bound, as described in the following theorem.

THEOREM 6.23 ···

$$\exists c \, \forall x, y \, \big[\mathrm{K}(xy) \le 2\mathrm{K}(x) + \mathrm{K}(y) + c \big].$$

PROOF   We construct a TM M that breaks its input w into two separate descriptions. The bits of the first description $d(x)$ are all doubled and terminated with string 01 before the second description $d(y)$ appears, as described in the text preceding Figure 6.3. Once both descriptions are obtained, they are run to obtain the strings x and y and the output xy is produced.

The length if this description of xy is clearly twice the complexity of x plus the complexity of y plus a fixed constant for describing M. This sum is

$$2\mathrm{K}(x) + \mathrm{K}(y) + c,$$

and the proof is complete.

We may improve this theorem somewhat by using a more efficient method of indicating the separation between the two descriptions. One way avoids doubling the bits of $d(x)$. Instead we prepend the length of $\mathrm{K}(x)$ as a binary integer that has been doubled to differentiate it from $d(x)$. The description still contains enough information to decode it into the two descriptions of x and y, and it now has length at most

$$2 \log(\mathrm{K}(x)) + \mathrm{K}(x) + \mathrm{K}(y) + c.$$

Further small improvements are possible. However, as Problem 6.18 asks you to show, we cannot reach the bound $\mathrm{K}(x) + \mathrm{K}(y) + c$.

OPTIMALITY OF THE DEFINITION

Now that we have established some of the elementary properties of descriptive complexity and you have had a chance to develop some intuition, we discuss some features of the definitions.

Our definition of $K(x)$ has an optimality property among all possible ways of defining descriptive complexity with algorithms. Suppose that we consider a general *description language* to be any computable function $p: \Sigma^* \longrightarrow \Sigma^*$ and define the minimal description of x with respect to p, written $d_p(x)$, to be the lexicographically shortest string s where $p(s) = x$. Then we define $K_p(x) = |d_p(x)|$.

For example, consider a programming language such as LISP (encoded into binary) as the description language. Then $d_{\text{LISP}}(x)$ would be the minimal LISP program that outputs s, and $K_{\text{LISP}}(x)$ would be the length of the minimal program.

The following theorem shows that any description language of this type is not significantly more concise than the language of Turing machines and inputs that we originally defined.

THEOREM   **6.24**   ....

For any description language p, a fixed constant c exists that depends only on p, where

$$\forall x \left[K(x) \le K_p(x) + c \right].$$

....

PROOF IDEA   We illustrate the idea of this proof by using the LISP example. Suppose that s has a short description in LISP. Let M be a TM that can interpret LISP and use the LISP program for x as M's input. Then $\langle M, w \rangle$ is a description of x that is only a fixed amount larger than the LISP description of x. The extra length is for the LISP interpreter M.

PROOF   Take any description language p and consider the following Turing machine M.

$M = $ "On input w:

    1. Output $p(w)$."

Then $\langle M \rangle d_p(x)$ is a description of x whose length is at most a fixed constant greater than $K_p(x)$. The constant is the length of $\langle M \rangle$.

....

INCOMPRESSIBLE STRINGS AND RANDOMNESS

Theorem 6.21 shows that a string's minimal description is never much longer than the string itself. Of course for some strings, the minimal description may be much shorter if the information in the string appears sparsely or redundantly. Do some strings lack short descriptions? In other words, is the minimal description of some strings actually as long as the string itself? We show that such strings exist. These strings can't be described any more concisely than simply writing them out explicitly.

DEFINITION 6.25

Let x be a string. Say that x is *c-compressible* if

$$K(x) \leq |x| - c.$$

If x is not c-compressible, say that x is *incompressible by c*. If x is incompressible by 1, say that x is *incompressible*.

In other words, if x has a description that is c bits shorter than its length, x is c-compressible. If not, x is incompressible by c. Finally, if x doesn't have any description shorter than itself, x is incompressible. We first show that incompressible strings exist, and then we discuss their interesting properties. In particular, we show that incompressible strings look like strings that are obtained from random coin tosses.

THEOREM 6.26

Incompressible strings of every length exist.

PROOF IDEA   The number of strings of length n is greater than the number of descriptions of length less than n. Each description describes at most one string. Therefore some string of length n is not described by any description of length less than n. That string is incompressible.

PROOF   The number of binary strings of length n is 2^n. Each description is a nonempty binary string, so the number of descriptions of length less than n is at most the sum of the number of strings of each length up to $n - 1$, or

$$\sum_{0 \leq i \leq n-1} 2^i = 1 + 2 + 4 + 8 + \cdots + 2^{n-1} = 2^n - 1.$$

So, the number of short descriptions is less than the number of strings of length n. Therefore at least one string of length n is incompressible.

COROLLARY 6.27

At least $2^n - 2^{n-c+1} + 1$ strings of length n are incompressible by c.

PROOF   As in Theorem 6.26, at most $2^{n-c+1} - 1$ strings of length n are c-compressible, because at most that many descriptions of length at most $n - c$ exist. The remaining $2^n - (2^{n-c+1} - 1)$ are incompressible by c.

Incompressible strings have many properties that we would expect to find in randomly chosen strings. For example, we can show that any incompressible string of length n has roughly an equal number of 0s and 1s, and that the length of its longest run of 0s is $O(\log n)$, as we would expect to find in a random string of that length. Proving such statements would take us too far afield into combinatorics and probability, but we will prove a theorem that forms the basis for these statements.

That theorem shows that any computable property that holds for "almost all" strings also holds for all sufficiently long incompressible strings. As we mentioned in Section 0.2, a ***property*** of strings is simply a function f that maps strings to $\{\text{TRUE}, \text{FALSE}\}$. We say that a property ***holds for almost all strings*** if the fraction of strings of length n on which it is FALSE approaches 0 as n grows large. A randomly chosen long string is likely to satisfy a computable property that holds for almost all strings. Therefore random strings and incompressible strings share such properties.

THEOREM 6.28 ···

Let f be a computable property that holds for almost all strings. Then, for any $b > 0$, the property f is FALSE on only finitely many strings that are incompressible by b.

PROOF   Let M be the following algorithm.

$M = $ "On input i, a binary integer:
  1. Find the ith string s where $f(s) = $ FALSE, considering the strings ordered lexicographically.
  2. Output string s."

We can use M to obtain short descriptions of strings that fail to have property f as follows. Let x be such a string. Let i_x be the index of x on a list of all strings that fail to have property f, ordered by length and lexicographically within each length. Then $\langle M, i_x \rangle$ is a description of x. The length of this description is $|i_x| + c$, where c is the length of $\langle M \rangle$.

Fix any number $b > 0$. Select n such that at most a $1/2^{b+c}$ fraction of strings of length n or less fail property f. All sufficiently large n satisfy this condition because f holds for almost all strings. Then

$$i_x \le \frac{2^n}{2^{b+c}} = 2^{n-b-c}.$$

Therefore $|i_x| \le n-b-c$, so the length of $\langle M, i_x \rangle$ is at most $(n-b-c)+c = n-b$, which implies that

$$\mathrm{K}(x) \le n - b.$$

Thus every sufficiently long x that fails f is compressible by b. Hence, only finitely many strings that fail f are incompressible by b, and the theorem is proved.

···

At this point exhibiting some examples of incompressible strings would be appropriate. However, as Problem 6.15 asks you to show, the K measure of complexity is not computable. Furthermore, no algorithm can decide in general whether strings are incompressible, by Problem 6.16. Indeed, by Problem 6.17, no infinite subset of them is Turing-recognizable. So we have no way to obtain long incompressible strings and would have no way to check that a string is incompressible even if we had one. The following theorem describes certain strings that are nearly incompressible, although it doesn't provide a way to exhibit them explicitly.

THEOREM **6.29**

For some constant b, for every string x, the minimal description $d(x)$ of x is incompressible by b.

PROOF Consider the following TM M:

$M = $ "On input $\langle R, y \rangle$, where R is a TM and y is a string:

 1. Run R on y and *reject* if its output is not of the form $\langle S, z \rangle$.
 2. Run S on z and halt with its output on the tape."

Let b be $|\langle M \rangle| + 1$. We show that b satisfies the theorem. Suppose to the contrary that $d(x)$ is b-compressible for some string x. Then

$$|d(d(x))| \leq |d(x)| - b.$$

But then $\langle M \rangle d(d(x))$ is a description of x whose length is at most

$$|\langle M \rangle| + |d(d(x))| \leq (b - 1) + (|d(x)| - b) = |d(x)| - 1.$$

This description of x is shorter than $d(x)$, contradicting the latter's minimality.

EXERCISES

 6.1 Give an example in the spirit of the recursion theorem of a program in a real programming language (or a reasonable approximation thereof) that prints itself out.

 6.2 Show that any infinite subset of MIN_{TM} is not Turing-recognizable.

 6.3 Show that if $A \leq_{\text{T}} B$ and $B \leq_{\text{T}} C$ then $A \leq_{\text{T}} C$.

 6.4 Is the statement $\exists x \, \forall y \, [\, x + y = y \,]$ a member of $\text{Th}(\mathcal{N}, +)$? Why or why not? What about the statement $\exists x \, \forall y \, [\, x + y = x \,]$?

PROBLEMS

6.5 Describe two different Turing machines, M and N, where, when started on any input, M outputs $\langle N \rangle$ and N outputs $\langle M \rangle$.

6.6 In the fixed-point version of the recursion theorem (Theorem 6.6) let the transformation t be a function that interchanges the states q_{accept} and q_{reject} in Turing machine descriptions. Give an example of a fixed point for t.

6.7 Show that for any two languages A and B a language J exists where $A \leq_T J$ and $B \leq_T J$.

****6.8** Prove that there exist two languages A and B that are Turing-incomparable, that is, where $A \not\leq_T B$ and $B \not\leq_T A$.

6.9 Give a model of the sentence

$$\phi_{\text{eq}} = \quad \forall x \, \big[\, R_1(x, x) \, \big] \\ \wedge \, \forall x, y \big[\, R_1(x, y) \leftrightarrow R_1(y, x) \, \big] \\ \wedge \, \forall x, y, z \big[\, (R_1(x, y) \wedge R_1(y, z)) \rightarrow R_1(x, z) \, \big].$$

****6.10** Let ϕ_{eq} be defined as in Problem 6.9. Give a model of the sentence

$$\phi_{\text{lt}} = \quad \phi_{\text{eq}} \\ \wedge \, \forall x \, \big[\, R_1(x, x) \rightarrow \neg R_2(x, x) \, \big] \\ \wedge \, \forall x, y \, \big[\, \neg R_1(x, y) \rightarrow (R_2(x, y) \oplus R_2(y, x)) \, \big] \\ \wedge \, \forall x, y, z \, \big[\, (R_2(x, y) \wedge R_2(y, z)) \rightarrow R_2(x, z) \, \big] \\ \wedge \, \forall x \, \exists y \, \big[\, R_2(x, y) \, \big].$$

6.11 Let $(\mathcal{N}, <)$ be the model with universe $\mathcal{N}$ and the "less than" relation. Show that $\text{Th}(\mathcal{N}, <)$ is decidable.

6.12 For each $m > 1$ let $\mathcal{Z}_m = \{0, 1, 2, \dots, m - 1\}$ and let $\mathcal{F}_m = (\mathcal{Z}_m, +, \times)$ be the model whose universe is $\mathcal{Z}_m$ and which has relations corresponding to the $+$ and $\times$ relations computed modulo m. Show that for each m the theory $\text{Th}(\mathcal{F}_m)$ is decidable.

6.13 Show how to compute the descriptive complexity of strings $K(x)$ with an oracle for A_{TM}.

6.14 Use the result of Problem 6.13 to give a function f that is computable with an oracle for A_{TM}, where for each n, $f(n)$ is an incompressible string of length n.

6.15 Show that the function $K(x)$ is not a computable function.

6.16 Show that the set of incompressible strings is undecidable.

6.17 Show that the set of incompressible strings contains no infinite Turing-recognizable subset.

****6.18** Show that for any c, some strings x and y exist, where $K(xy) > K(x) + K(y) + c$.

****6.19** Let A and B be two disjoint languages. Say that language C *separates* A and B if $A \subseteq C$ and $B \subseteq \overline{C}$. Describe two disjoint Turing-recognizable languages that aren't separable by any decidable language.

6.20 Recall the Post correspondence problem that we defined in Section 5.2 and its associated language PCP. Show that PCP is decidable relative to A_{TM}.

6.21 In Corollary 4.15 we showed that the set of all languages is uncountable. Use this result to prove that languages exist that are not recognizable by an oracle Turing machine with oracle for A_{TM}.

6.22 Let

$$Z = \{\langle M, w\rangle|\ M \text{ is an oracle TM and } M^{A_{\mathsf{TM}}} \text{ accepts } w\}.$$

Use a proof by diagonalization to show that an oracle TM with an oracle for A_{TM} can't decide Z.

PART THREE

COMPLEXITY THEORY

7

TIME COMPLEXITY

Even when a problem is decidable and thus computationally solvable in principle, it may not be solvable in practice if the solution requires an inordinate amount of time or memory. In this final part of the book we introduce computational complexity theory—an investigation of the time, memory, or other resources required for solving computational problems. We begin with time.

Our objective in this chapter is to present the basics of time complexity theory. First we introduce a way of measuring the time used to solve a problem. Then we show how to classify problems according to the amount of time required. After that we discuss the possibility that certain decidable problems require enormous amounts of time and how to determine when you are faced with such a problem.

7.1

MEASURING COMPLEXITY

Let's begin with an example. Take the language $A = \{0^k 1^k | k \geq 0\}$. Obviously A is a decidable language. How much time does a single-tape Turing machine need to decide A? We examine the following single-tape TM M_1 for A. We give the Turing machine description at a low level, including the actual head motion on the tape, so that we can count the number of steps that M_1 uses when it runs.

M_1 = "On input string w:

1. Scan across the tape and *reject* if a 0 is found to the right of a 1.
2. Repeat the following if both 0s and 1s remain on the tape.
3.   Scan across the tape, crossing off a single 0 and a single 1.
4. If 0s still remain after all the 1s have been crossed off, or if 1s still remain after all the 0s have been crossed off, *reject*. Otherwise, if neither 0s nor 1s remain on the tape, *accept*."

We *analyze* the algorithm for Turing machine M_1 deciding A to determine how much time it uses.

The number of steps that an algorithm uses on a particular input may depend on several parameters. For instance, if the input is a graph, the number of steps may depend on the number of nodes, the number of edges, and the maximum degree of the graph, or some combination of these and/or other factors. For simplicity we compute the running time of an algorithm purely as a function of the length of the string representing the input and don't consider any other parameters. In ***worst-case analysis***, the form we consider here, we consider the longest running time of all inputs of a particular length. In ***average-case analysis*** we consider the average of all the running times of inputs of a particular length.

DEFINITION 7.1

Let M be a deterministic Turing machine that halts on all inputs. The ***running time*** or ***time complexity*** of M is the function $f: \mathcal{N} \longrightarrow \mathcal{N}$, where $f(n)$ is the maximum number of steps that M uses on any input of length n. If $f(n)$ is the running time of M, we say that M runs in time $f(n)$ and that M is an $f(n)$ time Turing machine.

BIG-O AND SMALL-O NOTATION

Because the exact running time of an algorithm often is a complex expression, we usually just estimate it. In one convenient form of estimation, called ***asymptotic analysis***, we seek to understand the running time of the algorithm when it is run on large inputs. We do so by considering only the highest order term of the expression for the running time of the algorithm, disregarding both the coefficient of that term and any lower order terms, because the highest order term dominates the other terms on large inputs.

For example, the function $f(n) = 6n^3 + 2n^2 + 20n + 45$ has four terms, and the highest order term is $6n^3$. Disregarding the coefficient 6, we say that f is asymptotically at most n^3. The ***asymptotic notation*** or ***big-O notation*** for describing this relationship is $f(n) = O(n^3)$. We formalize this notion in the following definition. Let $\mathcal{R}^+$ be the set of real numbers greater than 0.

DEFINITION 7.2

Let f and g be two functions $f, g: \mathcal{N} \longrightarrow \mathcal{R}^+$. Say that $f(n) = O(g(n))$ if positive integers c and n_0 exist so that for every integer $n \geq n_0$

$$f(n) \leq c\, g(n).$$

When $f(n) = O(g(n))$ we say that $g(n)$ is an ***upper bound*** for $f(n)$, or more precisely, that $g(n)$ is an ***asymptotic upper bound*** for $f(n)$, to emphasize that we are suppressing constant factors.

Intuitively, $f(n) = O(g(n))$ means that f is less than or equal to g if we disregard differences up to a constant factor. You may think of O as representing a suppressed constant. In practice, most functions f that you are likely to encounter have an obvious highest order term h. In that case write $f(n) = O(g(n))$, where g is h without its coefficient.

EXAMPLE 7.3

Let $f_1(n)$ be the function $5n^3 + 2n^2 + 22n + 6$. Then, selecting the highest order term $5n^3$ and disregarding its coefficient 5 gives $f_1(n) = O(n^3)$.

Let's verify that this result satisfies the formal definition. We do so by letting c be 6 and n_0 be 10. Then, $5n^3 + 2n^2 + 22n + 6 \leq 6n^3$ for every $n \geq 10$.

In addition, $f_1(n) = O(n^4)$ because n^4 is larger than n^3 and so is still an asymptotic upper bound on f_1.

However, $f_1(n)$ is not $O(n^2)$. Regardless of the values we assign to c and n_0, the definition remains unsatisfied in this case.

EXAMPLE 7.4

The big-O interacts with logarithms in a particular way. Usually when we use logarithms we must specify the base, as in $x = \log_2 n$. The base 2 here indicates that this equality is equivalent to the equality $2^x = n$. Changing the value of the base b changes the value of $\log_b n$ by a constant factor, owing to the identity $\log_b n = \log_2 n / \log_2 b$. Thus, when we write $f(n) = O(\log n)$, specifying the base is no longer necessary because we are suppressing constant factors anyway.

Let $f_2(n)$ be the function $3n \log_2 n + 5n \log_2 \log_2 n + 2$. In this case we have $f_2(n) = O(n \log n)$ because $\log n$ dominates $\log \log n$.

Big-O notation also appears in arithmetic expressions such as the expression $f(n) = O(n^2) + O(n)$. In that case each occurrence of the O symbol represents a different suppressed constant. Because the $O(n^2)$ term dominates the $O(n)$ term, that expression is equivalent to $f(n) = O(n^2)$. When the O symbol occurs in an exponent as in the expression $f(n) = 2^{O(n)}$, the same idea applies. This expression represents an upper bound of 2^{cn} for some constant c.

The expression $f(n) = 2^{O(\log n)}$ occurs in some analyses. Using the identity $n = 2^{\log_2 n}$ and thus that $n^c = 2^{c \log_2 n}$, we see that $2^{O(\log n)}$ represents an upper bound of n^c for some c. The expression $n^{O(1)}$ represents the same bound in a different way, because the expression $O(1)$ represents a value that is never more than a fixed constant.

Frequently we derive bounds of the form n^c for c greater than 0. Such bounds are called ***polynomial bounds***. Bounds of the form $2^{(n^\delta)}$ are called ***exponential bounds*** when δ is a real number greater than 0.

Big-O notation has a companion called ***small-o notation***. Big-O notation gives a way to say that one function is asymptotically *no more than* another. To say that one function is asymptotically *less than* another we use small-o notation. The difference between the big-O and small-o notations is analogous to the difference between $\leq$ and $<$.

DEFINITION 7.5 ···

Let f and g be two functions $f, g \colon \mathcal{N} \longrightarrow \mathcal{R}^+$. Say that $f(n) = o(g(n))$ if

$$\lim_{n \to \infty} \frac{f(n)}{g(n)} = 0.$$

In other words, $f(n) = o(g(n))$ means that, for any real number $c > 0$, a number n_0 exists, where $f(n) < c\, g(n)$ for all $n \geq n_0$.

EXAMPLE 7.6 ··

The following are easy to check.

1. $\sqrt{n} = o(n)$.
2. $n = o(n \log \log n)$.
3. $n \log \log n = o(n \log n)$.
4. $n \log n = o(n^2)$.
5. $n^2 = o(n^3)$.

However, $f(n)$ is never $o(f(n))$. ∎

ANALYZING ALGORITHMS

Let's analyze the algorithm we gave for the language $A = \{0^k 1^k | \ k \geq 0\}$. We repeat it here for convenience.

$M_1 =$ "On input string w:

1. Scan across the tape and *reject* if a 0 is found to the right of a 1.
2. Repeat the following if both 0s and 1s remain on the tape.
3.   Scan across the tape, crossing off a single 0 and a single 1.
4. If 0s still remain after all the 1s have been crossed off, or if 1s still remain after all the 0s have been crossed off, *reject*. Otherwise, if neither 0s nor 1s remain on the tape, *accept*."

To analyze M_1 we consider each of its three stages separately. In stage 1, the machine scans across the tape to verify that the input is of the form 0*1*. Performing this scan uses n steps. Repositioning the head at the left-hand end of the tape uses another n steps. So the total used in this stage is $2n$ steps. In big-O notation we say that this stage uses $O(n)$ steps. Note that we didn't mention the repositioning of the tape head in the machine description. Using asymptotic notation allows us to omit details of the machine description that affect the running time by at most a constant factor.

In stages 2 and 3, the machine repeatedly scans the tape and crosses off a 0 and 1 on each scan. Each scan uses $O(n)$ steps. Because each scan crosses off two symbols, at most $n/2$ scans can occur. So the total time taken by stages 2 and 3 is $(n/2)O(n) = O(n^2)$ steps.

In stage 4 the machine makes a single scan to decide whether to accept or reject. The time taken in this stage is at most $O(n)$.

Thus the total time of M_1 on an input of length n is $O(n) + O(n^2) + O(n)$, or $O(n^2)$. In other words, its running time is $O(n^2)$, which completes the time analysis of this machine.

Let's set up some notation for classifying languages according to their time requirements.

DEFINITION   **7.7** ....

Let $t\colon \mathcal{N} \longrightarrow \mathcal{N}$ be a function. Define the *time complexity class*, $\mathrm{TIME}(t(n))$, to be

$$\mathrm{TIME}(t(n)) = \{L| \ L \text{ is a language decided by a } O(t(n)) \text{ time Turing machine}\}.$$

Recall the language $A = \{0^k 1^k | \ k \geq 0\}$. The preceding analysis shows that $A \in \mathrm{TIME}(n^2)$ because M_1 decides A in time $O(n^2)$ and $\mathrm{TIME}(n^2)$ contains all languages that can be decided in $O(n^2)$ time.

Is there a machine that decides A asymptotically more quickly? In other words, is A in $\mathrm{TIME}(t(n))$ for $t(n) = o(n^2)$? We can improve the running time by crossing off two 0s and two 1s on every scan instead of just one because doing so cuts the number of scans by half. But that improves the running time only by a factor of 2 and doesn't affect the asymptotic running time. The following machine, M_2, uses a different method to decide A asymptotically faster. It shows that $A \in \text{TIME}(n \log n)$.

M_2 = "On input string w:

1. Scan across the tape and *reject* if a 0 is found to the right of a 1.
2. Repeat the following as long as some 0s and some 1s remain on the tape.
3. Scan across the tape, checking whether the total number of 0s and 1s remaining is even or odd. If it is odd, *reject*.
4. Scan again across the tape, crossing off every other 0 starting with the first 0, and then crossing off every other 1 starting with the first 1.
5. If no 0s and no 1s remain on the tape, *accept*. Otherwise, *reject*."

Before analyzing M_2, let's verify that it actually decides A. On every scan performed in stage 4, the total number of 0s remaining is cut in half and any remainder is discarded. Thus, if we started with 13 0s, after stage 4 is executed a single time only 6 0s remain. After subsequent executions of this stage, 3, then 1, and then 0 remain. This stage has the same effect on the number of 1s.

Now we examine the even/odd parity of the number of 0s and the number of 1s at each execution of stage 3. Consider again starting with 13 0s and 13 1s. The first execution of stage 3 finds an odd number of 0s (because 13 is an odd number) and an odd number of 1s. On subsequent executions an even number (6) occurs, then an odd number (3), and an odd number (1). We do not execute this stage on 0 0s or 0 1s because of the condition on the repeat loop specified in stage 2. For the sequence of parities found (odd, even, odd, odd) if we replace the evens with 0s and the odds with 1s and then reverse the sequence, we obtain 1101, the binary representation of 13, or the number of 0s and 1s at the beginning. The sequence of parities always gives the reverse of the binary representation.

When stage 3 checks to determine that the total number of 0s and 1s remaining is even, it actually is checking on the agreement of the parity of the 0s with the parity of the 1s. If all parities agree, the binary representations of the numbers of 0s and of 1s agree, and so the two numbers are equal.

To analyze the running time of M_2, we first observe that every stage takes $O(n)$ time. We then determine the number of times that each is executed. Stages 1 and 5 are executed once, taking a total of $O(n)$ time. Stage 4 crosses off at least half the 0s and 1s each time it is executed, so at most $1 + \log_2 n$ iterations occur before all get crossed off. Thus the total time of stages 2, 3, and 4 is $(1 + \log_2 n)O(n)$, or $O(n \log n)$. The running time of M_2 is $O(n) + O(n \log n) = O(n \log n)$.

Earlier we showed that $A \in \text{TIME}(n^2)$, but now we have a better bound, namely, $A \in \text{TIME}(n \log n)$. This result cannot be further improved on single-tape Turing machines. In fact, any language that can be decided in $o(n \log n)$ time on a single-tape Turing machine is regular, though we won't prove this result.

We can decide the language A in $O(n)$ time (also called **linear time**) if the Turing machine has a second tape. The following two-tape TM M_3 decides A in linear time.

$M_3 = $ "On input string w:

1. Scan across the tape and *reject* if a 0 is found to the right of a 1.
2. Scan across the 0s on Tape 1 until the first 1. At the same time, copy the 0s onto Tape 2.
3. Scan across the 1s on Tape 1 until the end of the input. For each 1 read on Tape 1, cross off a 0 on Tape 2. If all 0s are crossed off before all the 1s are read, *reject*.
4. If all the 0s have now been crossed off, *accept*. If any 0s remain, *reject*."

Machine M_3 operates differently from the previous machines for A. It simply copies the 0s to its second tape and then matches them against the 1s.

This machine is simple to analyze. Each of the four stages obviously uses $O(n)$ steps, so the total running time is $O(n)$ and thus linear. Note that this running time is the best possible because n steps are necessary just to read the input.

Let's summarize what we have shown about the time complexity of A. We produced a single-tape TM M_1 that decides A in $O(n^2)$ time and a faster single tape TM M_2 that decides A in $O(n \log n)$ time. We claimed (without proof) that no single-tape TM can do it more quickly. Then we exhibited a two-tape TM M_3 that decides A in $O(n)$ time. Hence the time complexity of A on a single-tape TM is $O(n \log n)$ and on a two-tape TM it is $O(n)$. Note that the complexity of A depends on the model of computation selected.

This discussion highlights an important difference between complexity theory and computability theory. In computability theory, the Church–Turing thesis implies that all reasonable models of computation are equivalent, that is, they all decide the same class of languages. In complexity theory, the choice of model affects the time complexity of languages. Languages that are decidable in, say, linear time on one model aren't necessarily decidable in linear time on another.

In complexity theory, we want to classify computational problems according to the amount of time required for solution. But with which model do we measure time? The same language may have different time requirements on different models.

Fortunately, time requirements don't differ greatly for typical deterministic models. So, if our classification system isn't very sensitive to relatively small differences in complexity, the deterministic model chosen isn't crucial. We discuss this idea further in the next several sections.

COMPLEXITY RELATIONSHIPS AMONG MODELS

Here we examine how the choice of computational model can affect the time complexity of languages. We consider three models: the single-tape Turing machine; the multitape Turing machine; and the nondeterministic Turing machine.

THEOREM **7.8** ....

Let $t(n)$ be a function, where $t(n) \geq n$. Then every $t(n)$ time multitape Turing machine has an equivalent $O(t^2(n))$ time single-tape Turing machine.

....

PROOF IDEA The idea behind the proof of this theorem is quite simple. Recall that in Theorem 3.8 we showed how to convert any multitape TM into a single-tape TM that simulates it. Now we analyze that simulation to determine how much additional time it requires. We show that simulating each step of the multitape machine uses at most $O(t(n))$ steps on the single-tape machine. Hence the total time used is $O(t^2(n))$ steps.

PROOF Let M be a k-tape TM that runs in $t(n)$ time. We construct a single-tape TM S that runs in $O(t^2(n))$ time.

Machine S operates by simulating M, as described in Theorem 3.8. To review that simulation, recall that S uses its single tape to represent the contents on all k of M's tapes. The tapes are stored consecutively, with the positions of M's heads marked on the appropriate squares.

Initially, S puts its tape into the format that represents all the tapes of M and then simulates M's steps. To simulate one step, S scans all the information stored on its tape to determine the symbols under M's tape heads. Then S makes another pass over its tape to update the tape contents and head positions. If one of M's heads moves rightward onto the previously unread portion of its tape, S must increase the amount of space allocated to this tape. It does so by shifting a portion of its own tape one cell to the right.

Now we analyze this simulation. For each step of M, machine S makes two passes over the active portion of its tape. The first obtains the information necessary to determine the next move and the second carries it out. The length of the active portion of S's tape determines how long S takes to scan it, so we must determine an upper bound on this length. To do so we take the sum of the lengths of the active portions of M's k tapes. Each of these active portions has length at most $t(n)$ because M uses $t(n)$ tape cells in $t(n)$ steps if the head moves rightward at every step and even fewer if a head ever moves leftward. Thus a scan of the active portion of S's tape uses $O(t(n))$ steps.

To simulate each of M's steps, S performs two scans and possibly up to k rightward shifts. Each uses $O(t(n))$ time, so the total time for S to simulate one of M's steps is $O(t(n))$.

Now we bound the total time used by the simulation. The initial stage, where S puts its tape into the proper format, uses $O(n)$ steps. Afterward, S simulates each of the $t(n)$ steps of M, using $O(t(n))$ steps, so this part of the simulation uses $t(n) \times O(t(n)) = O(t^2(n))$ steps. Therefore the entire simulation uses is $O(n) + O(t^2(n))$ steps.

We have assumed that $t(n) \geq n$ (a reasonable assumption because M could not even read the entire input in less time). Therefore the running time of S is $O(t^2(n))$ and the proof is complete.

....

Next, we consider the analogous theorem for nondeterministic single-tape Turing machines. We show that any language that is decidable on such a machine is decidable on a deterministic single-tape Turing machine that requires significantly more time. Before doing so, we must define the running time of a nondeterministic Turing machine. Recall that a nondeterministic Turing machine is a decider if all its computation branches halt on all inputs.

DEFINITION 7.9

Let N be a nondeterministic Turing machine that is a decider. The ***running time*** of N is the function $f \colon \mathcal{N} \longrightarrow \mathcal{N}$, where $f(n)$ is the maximum number of steps that N uses on any branch of its computation on any input of length n, as shown in the following figure.

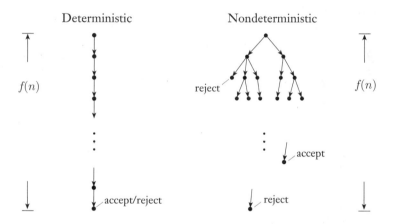

FIGURE 7.1
Measuring deterministic and nondeterministic time

The definition of the running time of a nondeterministic Turing machine is not intended to correspond to any real-world computing device. Rather, it is a useful mathematical definition that assists in characterizing the complexity of an important class of computational problems, as we demonstrate shortly.

THEOREM 7.10

Let $t(n)$ be a function, where $t(n) \geq n$. Then every $t(n)$ time nondeterministic single-tape Turing machine has an equivalent $2^{O(t(n))}$ time deterministic single-tape Turing machine.

PROOF   Let N be a nondeterministic TM running in $t(n)$ time. We construct a deterministic TM D that simulates N as in the proof of Theorem 3.10 by searching N's nondeterministic computation tree. Now we analyze that simulation.

On an input of length n, every branch of N's nondeterministic computation tree has a length of at most $t(n)$. Every node in the tree can have at most b children, where b is the maximum number of legal choices given by N's transition function. Thus the total number of leaves in the tree is at most $b^{t(n)}$.

The simulation proceeds by exploring this tree breadth first. In other words, it visits all nodes at depth d before going on to any of the nodes at depth $d + 1$. The algorithm given in the proof of Theorem 3.10 inefficiently starts at the root and travels down to a node whenever it visits that node, but eliminating this inefficiency doesn't alter the statement of the current theorem, so we leave it as is. The total number of nodes in the tree is less than twice the maximum number of leaves, so we bound it by $O(b^{t(n)})$. The time for starting from the root and traveling down to a node is $O(t(n))$. Therefore the running time of D is $O(t(n)b^{t(n)}) = 2^{O(t(n))}$.

As described in Theorem 3.10, the TM D has three tapes. Converting to a single-tape TM at most squares the running time, by Theorem 7.8. Thus the running time of the single-tape simulator is $\left(2^{O(t(n))}\right)^2 = 2^{O(2t(n))} = 2^{O(t(n))}$, and the theorem is proved.

7.2

THE CLASS P

Theorems 7.8 and 7.10 illustrate an important distinction. On the one hand, we demonstrated at most a square or *polynomial* difference between the time complexity of problems measured on deterministic single-tape and multitape Turing machines. On the other hand, we showed at most an *exponential* difference between the time complexity of problems on deterministic and nondeterministic Turing machines.

POLYNOMIAL TIME

For our purposes, polynomial differences in running time are considered to be small, whereas exponential differences are considered to be large. Let's look at why we chose to make this separation between polynomials and exponentials rather than between some other classes of functions.

First, note the dramatic difference between the growth rate of typically occurring polynomials such as n^3 and typically occurring exponentials such as 2^n. For example, let n be 1000, the size of a reasonable input to an algorithm. In that case, n^3 is 1 billion, a large, but manageable number, whereas 2^n is a number much larger than the number of atoms in the universe. Polynomial time algorithms are fast enough for many purposes, but exponential time algorithms rarely are useful.

Exponential time algorithms typically arise when we solve problems by searching through a space of solutions, called **brute-force search**. For example, one way to factor a number into its constituent primes is to search through all potential divisors. The size of the search space is exponential, so this search uses exponential time. Sometimes, brute-force search may be avoided through a deeper understanding of a problem, which may reveal a polynomial time algorithm of greater utility.

All reasonable deterministic computational models are **polynomially equivalent**. That is, any one of them can simulate another with only a polynomial increase in running time. When we say that all reasonable deterministic models are polynomially equivalent, we do not attempt to define *reasonable*. However, we have in mind a notion broad enough to include models that closely approximate running times on actual computers. For example, Theorem 7.8 shows that the deterministic single-tape and multitape Turing machine models are polynomially equivalent.

From here on we focus on aspects of time complexity theory that are unaffected by polynomial differences in running time. We consider such differences to be insignificant and ignore them. Doing so allows us develop the theory in a way that doesn't depend on the selection of a particular model of computation. Remember, our aim is to present the fundamental properties of *computation*, rather than properties of Turing machines or any other special model.

You may feel that disregarding polynomial differences in running time is absurd. Real programmers certainly care about such differences and work hard just to make their programs run twice as quickly. However, we disregarded constant factors a while back when we introduced asymptotic notation. Now we propose to disregard the much greater polynomial differences, such as that between time n and time n^3.

Our decision to disregard polynomial differences doesn't imply that we consider such differences unimportant. On the contrary, we certainly do consider the difference between time n and time n^3 to be an important one. But some questions, such as the polynomiality or nonpolynomiality of the factoring problem, do not depend on polynomial differences and are important, too. We merely choose to focus on this type of question here. Ignoring the trees to see the forest doesn't mean that one is more important than the other—it just gives a different perspective.

Now we come to an important definition in complexity theory.

DEFINITION 7.11 ···

P is the class of languages that are decidable in polynomial time on a deterministic single-tape Turing machine. In other words,

$$P = \bigcup_k \text{TIME}(n^k).$$

The class P plays a central role in our theory and is important because

1. P is invariant for all models of computation that are polynomially equivalent to the deterministic single-tape Turing machine, and

2. P roughly corresponds to the class of problems that are realistically solvable on a computer.

Item 1 indicates that P is a mathematically robust class. It isn't affected by the particulars of the model of computation that we are using.

Item 2 indicates that P is relevant from a practical standpoint. When a problem is in P, we have a method of solving it that runs in time n^k for some constant k. Whether this running time is practical depends on k and on the application. Of course, a running time of n^{100} is unlikely to be of any practical use. Nevertheless, calling polynomial time the threshold of practical solvability has proven to be useful. Once a polynomial time algorithm has been found for a problem that formerly appeared to require exponential time, some key insight into it has been gained, and further reductions in its complexity usually follow, often to the point of actual practical utility.

EXAMPLES OF PROBLEMS IN P

When we present a polynomial time algorithm we give a high-level description of it without reference to features of a particular computational model. Doing so avoids tedious details of tapes and head motions. We need to follow certain conventions when describing an algorithm so that we can analyze it for polynomiality.

We describe algorithms with numbered stages. The notion of a stage of an algorithm is analogous to a step of a Turing machine, though of course, implementing one stage of an algorithm on a Turing machine, in general, will require many Turing machine steps.

When we analyze an algorithm to show that it runs in polynomial time, we need to do two things. First, we have to give a polynomial upper bound (usually in big-O notation) on the number of stages that the algorithm uses when it runs on an input of length n. Then, we have to examine the individual stages in the description of the algorithm to be sure that each can be implemented in polynomial time on a reasonable deterministic model. We choose the stages when we describe the algorithm to make this second part of the analysis easy to do. When both tasks have been completed, we can conclude that the algorithm runs in polynomial time because we have demonstrated that it runs for a polynomial number of stages, each of which can be done in polynomial time, and the composition of polynomials is a polynomial.

One point that requires attention is the encoding method used for problems. We continue to use the bracket notation $\langle \cdot \rangle$ to indicate a reasonable encoding of one or more objects into a string, without specifying any particular encoding method. Now, a reasonable method is one that allows for polynomial time encoding and decoding of objects into natural internal representations or into other reasonable encodings. Familiar encoding methods for graphs, automata, and the like all are reasonable. But note that unary notation for encoding numbers (as in the number 17 encoded by the unary string 11111111111111111) isn't reasonable because it is exponentially larger than truly reasonable encodings, such as base k notation for any $k \geq 2$.

Many computational problems you encounter in this chapter contain encodings of graphs. One reasonable encoding of a graph is a list of its nodes and edges. Another is the **_adjacency matrix_**, where the (i, j)th entry is 1 if there is an edge from node i to node j and 0 if not. When we analyze algorithms on graphs, the running time may be computed in terms of the number or nodes instead of the size of the graph representation. In reasonable graph representations, the size of the representation is a polynomial in the number of nodes. Thus, if we analyze an algorithm and show that its running time is polynomial (or exponential) in the number of nodes, we know that it is polynomial (or exponential) in the size of the input.

The first problem concerns directed graphs. A directed graph G contains nodes s and t, as shown in the following figure. The *PATH* problem is to determine whether a directed path exists from s to t. Let

$$PATH = \{\langle G, s, t\rangle|\ G \text{ is a directed graph that has a directed path from } s \text{ to } t\}.$$

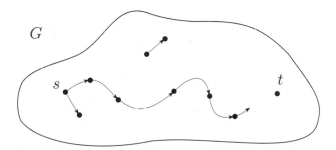

FIGURE **7.2**
The *PATH* problem: Is there a path from s to t?

THEOREM **7.12** ···

$PATH \in \text{P}$.

PROOF IDEA   We prove this theorem by presenting a polynomial time algorithm that decides *PATH*. Before describing that algorithm, let's observe that a brute-force algorithm for this problem isn't fast enough.

A brute-force algorithm for *PATH* proceeds by examining all potential paths in G and determining whether any is a directed path from s to t. A potential path is a sequence of nodes in G having a length of at most m, where m is the number of nodes in G. (If any directed path exists from s to t, one having a length of at most m exists because repeating a node never is necessary.) But the number of such potential paths is m^m, which is exponential in the number of nodes in G. Therefore this brute-force algorithm uses exponential time.

To get a polynomial time algorithm for *PATH* we must do something that avoids brute force. One way is to use a graph-searching method such as breadth-first search. Here, we successively mark all nodes in D that are reachable from s by directed paths of length 1, then 2, then 3, through m. Bounding the running time of this strategy by a polynomial is easy.

PROOF   A polynomial time algorithm M for *PATH* operates as follows.

$M =$ "On input $\langle G, s, t \rangle$ where G is a directed graph with nodes s and t:
1. Place a mark on node s.
2. Repeat the following until no additional nodes are marked.
3.   Scan all the edges of G. If an edge (a, b) is found going from a marked node a to an unmarked node b, mark node b.
4. If t is marked, *accept*. Otherwise, *reject*."

Now we analyze this algorithm to show that it runs in polynomial time. Obviously, stages 1 and 4 are executed only once. Stage 3 runs at most m times because each time except the last it marks an additional node in G. Thus the total number of stages used is at most $1 + 1 + m$, giving a polynomial in the size of G.

Stages 1 and 4 of M are easily implemented in polynomial time on any reasonable deterministic model. Stage 3 involves a scan of the input and a test of whether certain nodes are marked, which also is easily implemented in polynomial time. Hence M is a polynomial time algorithm for *PATH*.

Let's turn to another example of a polynomial time algorithm. Say that two numbers are ***relatively prime*** if 1 is the largest integer that evenly divides them both. For example, 10 and 21 are relatively prime, even though neither of them is a prime number by itself, whereas 10 and 22 are not relatively prime because both are divisible by 2. Let *RELPRIME* be the problem of testing whether two numbers are relatively prime. Thus

$$RELPRIME = \{\langle x, y \rangle | \ x \text{ and } y \text{ are relatively prime}\}.$$

THEOREM 7.13 ⋯⋯⋯⋯⋯⋯⋯⋯⋯⋯⋯⋯⋯⋯⋯⋯⋯⋯⋯⋯⋯⋯⋯⋯⋯⋯⋯⋯⋯⋯

RELPRIME ∈ P.

⋯⋯

PROOF IDEA   One algorithm that solves this problem searches through all possible divisors of both numbers and accepts if none are greater than 1. However, the magnitude of a number represented in binary, or in any other base k notation for $k \geq 2$, is exponential in the length of its representation. Therefore this brute-force algorithm searches through an exponential number of potential divisors and has an exponential running time.

Instead, we solve this problem with an ancient numerical procedure, called the ***Euclidean algorithm***, for computing the greatest common divisor. The ***greatest common divisor*** of two natural numbers x and y, written $\gcd(x, y)$, is the largest integer that evenly divides both x and y. For example, $\gcd(18, 24) = 6$. Obviously, x and y are relatively prime iff $\gcd(x, y) = 1$. We describe the Euclidean algorithm as algorithm E in the proof. It uses the mod function, where $x \bmod y$ is the remainder after the integer division of x by y.

PROOF   The Euclidean algorithm, E, is as follows.

$E = $ "On input $\langle x, y \rangle$, where x and y are natural numbers in binary:
  1. Repeat until $y = 0$.
  2.   Assign $x \leftarrow x \bmod y$.
  3.   Exchange x and y.
  4. Output x."

Algorithm R solves *RELPRIME*, using E as a subroutine.

$R = $ "On input $\langle x, y \rangle$, where x and y are natural numbers in binary:
  1. Run E on $\langle x, y \rangle$.
  2. If the result is 1, *accept*. Otherwise, *reject*."

Clearly, if E runs correctly in polynomial time, so does R and hence we only need to analyze E for time and correctness. The correctness of this algorithm is well known so we won't discuss it further here.

To analyze the time complexity of E, we first show that every execution of stage 2 (except possibly the first), cuts the value of x by at least half. After stage 2 is executed, $x < y$ because of the nature of the mod function. After stage 3, $x > y$ because the two have been exchanged. Thus, when stage 2 is subsequently executed, $x > y$. If $x/2 \geq y$, then $x \bmod y < y \leq x/2$ and x drops by at least half. If $x/2 < y$, then $x \bmod y = x - y < x/2$ and x drops by at least half.

The values of x and y are exchanged every time stage 3 is executed, so each of the original values of x and y are reduced by at least half every other time through the loop. Thus the maximum number of times that stages 2 and 3 are executed is the lesser of $\log_2 x$ and $\log_2 y$. These logarithms are proportional to the lengths of the representations, giving the number of stages executed as $O(n)$. Each stage of E uses only polynomial time, so the total running time is polynomial.

⋯⋯

The final example of a polynomial time algorithm shows that every context-free language is decidable in polynomial time.

THEOREM **7.14** ....

Every context-free language is a member of P.

....

PROOF IDEA In Theorem 4.8 we proved that every CFL is decidable. To do so we gave an algorithm for each CFL that decides it. If that algorithm runs in polynomial time, the current theorem follows as a corollary. Let's recall that algorithm and find out whether it runs quickly enough.

Let L be a CFL generated by CFG G that is in Chomsky normal form. From Problem 2.19, any derivation of a string w has $2n - 1$ steps, where n is the length of w because G is in Chomsky normal form. The decider for L works by trying all possible derivations with $2n - 1$ steps when its input is a string of length n. If any of these is a derivation of w, the decider accepts; if not, it rejects.

A quick analysis of this algorithm shows that it doesn't run in polynomial time. The number of derivations with k steps may be exponential in k, so this algorithm may require exponential time.

To get a polynomial time algorithm we introduce a powerful technique called **dynamic programming**. This technique uses the accumulation of information about smaller subproblems to solve larger problems. We record the solution to any subproblem so that we need to solve it only once. We do so by making a table of all subproblems and entering their solutions systematically as we find them.

In this case, we consider the subproblems of determining whether each variable in G generates each substring of w. The algorithm enters the solution to this subproblem in an $n \times n$ table. For $i \leq j$ the (i, j)th entry of the table contains the collection of variables that generate the substring $w_i w_{i+1} \cdots w_j$. For $i > j$ the table entries are unused.

The algorithm fills in the table entries for each substring of w. First it fills in the entries for the substrings of length 1, then those of length 2, and so on. It uses the entries for the shorter lengths to assist in determining the entries for the longer lengths.

For example, suppose that the algorithm has already determined which variables generate all substrings up to length k. To determine whether a variable A generates a particular substring of length $k + 1$ the algorithm splits that substring into two nonempty pieces in the k possible ways. For each split, the algorithm examines each rule $A \rightarrow BC$ to determine whether B generates the first piece and C generates the second piece, using table entries previously computed. If both B and C generate the respective pieces, A generates the substring and so is added to the associated table entry. The algorithm starts the process with the strings of length 1 by examining the table for the rules $A \rightarrow \mathtt{b}$.

PROOF The following algorithm D implements the proof idea. Let G be a CFG in Chomsky normal form generating the CFG L. Assume that S is the start variable. (Recall that the empty string is handled specially in a Chomsky normal form grammar. The algorithm handles the special case in which $w = \varepsilon$ in stage 1.) Comments appear inside double brackets.

$D =$ "On input $w = w_1 \cdots w_n$:
   1. If $w = \varepsilon$ and $S \rightarrow \varepsilon$ is a rule, *accept*.   [[handle $w = \varepsilon$ case]]
   2. For $i = 1$ to n,   [[examine each substring of length 1]]
   3.   For each variable A,
   4.   Test whether $A \rightarrow$ b is a rule, where b $= w_i$.
   5.   If so, place A in $table(i, i)$.
   6. For $l = 2$ to n,   [[l is the length of the substring]]
   7.   For $i = 1$ to $n - l + 1$,   [[i is the start position of the substring]]
   8.   Let $j = i + l - 1$,   [[j is the end position of the substring]]
   9.   For $k = i$ to $j - 1$,   [[k is the split position]]
  10.   For each rule $A \rightarrow BC$,
  11.   If $table(i, k)$ contains B and $table(k+1, j)$ contains C, put A in $table(i, j)$.
  12. If S is in $table(1, n)$, *accept*. Otherwise, *reject*."

Now we analyze D. Each stage is easily implemented to run in polynomial time. Stages 4 and 5 run at most nv times, where v is the number of variables in G and is a fixed constant independent of n; hence these stages run $O(n)$ times. Stage 6 runs at most n times. Each time stage 6 runs, stage 7 runs at most n times. Each time stage 7 runs, stages 8 and 9 run at most n times. Each time stage 9 runs, stage 10 runs r times, where r is the number of rules of G and is another fixed constant. Thus stage 11, the inner loop of the algorithm, runs $O(n^3)$ times. Summing the total shows that the running time of D is $O(n^3)$.

7.3

THE CLASS NP

As we observed in Section 7.2, we can avoid brute-force search in many problems and obtain polynomial time solutions. However, attempts to avoid brute force in certain other problems, including many interesting and useful ones, haven't been successful, and polynomial time algorithms that solve them aren't known to exist.

Why have we been unsuccessful in finding polynomial time algorithms for these problems? We don't know the answer to this important question. Perhaps these problems have, as yet undiscovered, polynomial time algorithms that rest on unknown principles. Or possibly some of these problems simply *cannot* be solved in polynomial time. They may be intrinsically difficult.

One remarkable discovery concerning this question shows that the complexities of many problems are linked. The discovery of a polynomial time algorithm for one such problem can be used to solve an entire class of problems. To understand this phenomenon, let's begin with an example.

A *Hamiltonian path* in a directed graph G is a directed path that goes through each node once. We consider the problem of testing whether a directed graph contains a Hamiltonian path connecting two specified nodes, as shown in the following figure. Let

$$HAMPATH = \{\langle G, s, t\rangle |\ G \text{ is a directed graph}$$
$$\text{with a Hamiltonian path from } s \text{ to } t\}.$$

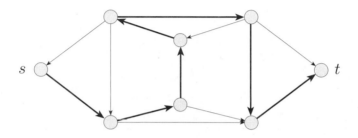

FIGURE 7.3
A Hamiltonian path goes through every node exactly once

We can easily obtain an exponential time algorithm for the *HAMPATH* problem by modifying the brute-force algorithm for *PATH* given in Theorem 7.12. We need only add a check to verify that the potential path is Hamiltonian. No one knows whether *HAMPATH* is solvable in polynomial time.

The *HAMPATH* problem does have a feature called *polynomial verifiability* that is important for understanding its complexity. Even though we don't know of a fast (i.e., polynomial time) way to determine whether a graph contains a Hamiltonian path, if such a path were discovered somehow (perhaps using the exponential time algorithm), we could easily convince someone else of its existence, simply by presenting it. In other words, *verifying* the existence of a Hamiltonian path may be much easier than *determining* its existence.

Another polynomially verifiable problem is compositeness. Recall that a natural number is *composite* if it is the product of two integers greater than 1 (i.e., a composite number is one that is not a prime number). Let

$$COMPOSITES = \{x|\ x = pq,\ \text{for integers } p, q > 1\}.$$

Although we don't know of a polynomial time algorithm for deciding this problem, we can easily verify that a number is composite—all that is needed is a divisor of that number.

Some problems may not be polynomially verifiable. For example, take $\overline{HAMPATH}$, the complement of the *HAMPATH* problem. Even if we could determine (somehow) that a graph did *not* have a Hamiltonian path, we don't know of a way for someone else to verify its nonexistence without using the same exponential time algorithm for making the determination in the first place. A formal definition follows.

DEFINITION 7.15 ....

A *verifier* for a language A is an algorithm V, where

$$A = \{w|\ V \text{ accepts } \langle w, c \rangle \text{ for some string } c\}.$$

We measure the time of a verifier only in terms of the length of w, so a *polynomial time verifier* runs in polynomial time in the length of w. A language A is *polynomially verifiable* if it has a polynomial time verifier.

A verifier uses additional information, represented by the symbol c in Definition 7.15, to verify that a string w is a member of A. This information is called a *certificate*, or *proof*, of membership in A. Observe that, for polynomial verifiers, the certificate has polynomial length (in the length of w) because that is all the verifier can access in its time bound. Let's apply this definition to the languages *HAMPATH* and *COMPOSITES*.

For the *HAMPATH* problem, a certificate for a string $\langle G, s, t \rangle \in HAMPATH$ simply is the Hamiltonian path from s to t. For the *COMPOSITES* problem, a certificate for the composite number x simply is one of its divisors. In both cases the verifier can check in polynomial time that the input is in the language when it is given the certificate.

DEFINITION 7.16 ....

NP is the class of languages that have polynomial time verifiers.

The class NP is important because it contains many problems of practical interest. From the preceding discussion, both *HAMPATH* and *COMPOSITES* are members of NP. The term NP comes from *nondeterministic polynomial time* and is derived from an alternative characterization by using nondeterministic polynomial time Turing machines.

The following is a nondeterministic Turing machine (NTM) that decides the *HAMPATH* problem in nondeterministic polynomial time. Recall that in Definition 7.9 we defined the time of a nondeterministic machine to be the time used by the longest computation branch.

N_1 = "On input $\langle G, s, t \rangle$, where G is a directed graph with nodes s and t:

1. Write a list of m numbers, $p_1, \ldots, p_m$, where m is the number of nodes in G. Each number in the list is nondeterministically selected to be between 1 and m.

2. Check for repetitions in the list. If any are found, *reject*.

3. Check whether $s = p_1$ and $t = p_m$. If either fail, *reject*.

4. For each i between 1 and $m - 1$, check whether (p_i, p_{i+1}) is an edge of G. If any are not, *reject*. Otherwise, all tests have been passed, so *accept*."

To analyze this algorithm and verify that it runs in nondeterministic polynomial time, we examine each of its stages. In stage 1, the nondeterministic selection clearly runs in polynomial time. In stages 2 and 3, each part is a simple check, so together they run in polynomial time. Finally, stage 4 also clearly runs in polynomial time. Thus this algorithm runs in nondeterministic polynomial time.

THEOREM 7.17 ....

A language is in NP iff it is decided by some nondeterministic polynomial time Turing machine.

....

PROOF IDEA We show how to convert a polynomial time verifier to an equivalent polynomial time NTM and vice versa. The NTM simulates the verifier by guessing the certificate. The verifier simulates the NTM by using the accepting branch as the certificate.

PROOF For the forward direction of this theorem, let $A \in$ NP and show that A is decided by a polynomial time NTM N. Let V be the polynomial time verifier for A that exists by the definition of NP. Assume that V is a TM that runs in time n^k and construct N as follows.

N = "On input w of length n.

1. Nondeterministically select string c of length n^k.

2. Run V on input $\langle w, c \rangle$.

3. If V accepts, *accept*; otherwise, *reject*."

To prove the other direction of the theorem, assume that A is decided by a polynomial time NTM N and construct a polynomial time verifier V as follows.

V = "On input $\langle w, c \rangle$, where w and c are strings:

1. Simulate N on input w, treating each symbol of c as a description of the nondeterministic choice to make at each step (as in the proof of Theorem 3.10).

2. If this branch of N's computation accepts, *accept*; otherwise, *reject*."

....

We define the nondeterministic time complexity class $\mathrm{NTIME}(t(n))$ as analogous to the deterministic time complexity class $\mathrm{TIME}(t(n))$.

DEFINITION 7.18

$$\mathrm{NTIME}(t(n)) = \{L|\ L \text{ is a language decided by a } O(t(n)) \text{ time}$$
$$\text{nondeterministic Turing machine}\}.$$

COROLLARY 7.19

$\mathrm{NP} = \bigcup_k \mathrm{NTIME}(n^k)$.

The class NP is insensitive to the choice of reasonable nondeterministic computational model because all such models are polynomially equivalent. When describing and analyzing nondeterministic polynomial time algorithms, we follow the preceding conventions for deterministic polynomial time algorithms. Each stage of a nondeterministic polynomial time algorithm must have an obvious implementation in nondeterministic polynomial time on a reasonable nondeterministic computational model. We analyze the algorithm to show that every branch uses at most polynomially many stages.

EXAMPLES OF PROBLEMS IN NP

A *clique* in an undirected graph is a subgraph, wherein every two nodes are connected by an edge. A *k-clique* is a clique that contains k nodes. The following figure illustrates a graph having a 5-clique.

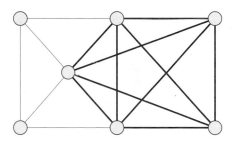

FIGURE 7.4
A graph with a 5-clique

The clique problem is to determine whether a graph contains a clique of a specified size. Let

$CLIQUE = \{\langle G, k \rangle|\ G \text{ is an undirected graph with a } k\text{-clique}\}$.

THEOREM **7.20** ....

CLIQUE is in NP.

....

PROOF IDEA The clique is the certificate.

PROOF The following is a verifier V for *CLIQUE*.

V = "On input $\langle\langle G, k\rangle, c\rangle$:
1. Test whether c is a set of k nodes in G
2. Test whether G contains all edges connecting nodes in c.
3. If both pass, *accept*; otherwise, *reject*."

ALTERNATIVE PROOF If you prefer to think of NP in terms of nondeterministic polynomial time Turing machines, you may prove this theorem by giving one that decides *CLIQUE*. Observe the similarity between the two proofs.

N = "On input $\langle G, k\rangle$, where G is a graph:
1. Nondeterministically select a subset c of k nodes of G.
2. Test whether G contains all edges connecting nodes in c.
3. If yes, *accept*; otherwise, *reject*."

....

Next we consider the *SUBSET-SUM* problem concerning integer arithmetic. In this problem we have a collection of numbers, $x_1, \ldots, x_k$ and a target number t. We want to determine whether the collection contains a subcollection that adds up to t. Thus

$$SUBSET\text{-}SUM = \{\langle S, t\rangle | \ S = \{x_1, \ldots, x_k\} \text{ and for some}$$
$$\{y_1, \ldots, y_l\} \subseteq \{x_1, \ldots, x_k\}, \text{ we have } \Sigma y_i = t\}.$$

For example, $\langle\{4, 11, 16, 21, 27\}, 25\rangle \in SUBSET\text{-}SUM$ because $4 + 21 = 25$. Note that $\{x_1, \ldots, x_k\}$ and $\{y_1, \ldots, y_l\}$ are considered to be **multisets** and so allow repetition of elements.

THEOREM **7.21** ....

SUBSET-SUM is in NP.

....

PROOF IDEA The subset is the certificate.

PROOF   The following is a verifier V for *SUBSET-SUM*.

$V =$ "On input $\langle\langle S, t \rangle, c \rangle$:
1. Test whether c is a collection of numbers that sum to t.
2. Test whether S contains all the numbers in c.
3. If both pass, *accept*; otherwise, *reject*."

ALTERNATIVE PROOF   We can also prove this theorem by giving a nondeterministic polynomial time Turing machine for *SUBSET-SUM* as follows.

$N =$ "On input $\langle S, t \rangle$:
1. Nondeterministically select a subset c of the numbers in S.
2. Test whether c is a collection of numbers that sum to t.
3. If both pass, *accept*; otherwise, *reject*."

Observe that the complements of these sets, $\overline{CLIQUE}$ and $\overline{SUBSET\text{-}SUM}$, are not obviously members of NP. Verifying that something is *not* present seems to be more difficult than verifying that it *is* present. We make a separate complexity class, called coNP, which contains the languages that are complements of languages in NP. We don't know whether coNP is different from NP.

THE P VERSUS NP QUESTION

As we have been saying, NP is the class of languages that are solvable in polynomial time on a nondeterministic Turing machine, or, equivalently, it is the class of languages whereby membership in the language can be verified in polynomial time. P is the class of languages where membership can be tested in polynomial time. We summarize this information as follows, where we loosely refer to polynomial time solvable as solvable "quickly."

P = the class of languages where membership can be *decided* quickly.

NP = the class of languages where membership can be *verified* quickly.

We have presented examples of languages, such as *HAMPATH* and *CLIQUE*, that are members of NP but that are not known to be in P. The power of polynomial verifiability seems to be much greater than that of polynomial decidability. But, hard as it may be to imagine, P and NP could be equal. We are unable to *prove* the existence of a single language in NP that is not in P.

The question of whether P = NP is one of the greatest unsolved problems in theoretical computer science and contemporary mathematics. If these classes were equal, any polynomially verifiable problem would be polynomially decidable. Most researchers believe that the two classes are not equal because people have invested enormous effort to find polynomial time algorithms for certain problems in NP, without success. Researchers also have tried proving that the classes are unequal, but that would entail showing that no fast algorithm exists to replace brute-force search. Doing so is presently beyond scientific reach. The following figure shows the two possibilities.

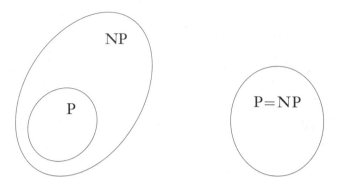

One of these two possibilities is correct

The best method known for solving languages in NP deterministically uses exponential time. In other words, we can prove that

$$NP \subseteq EXPTIME = \bigcup_{k} TIME(2^{n^{k}}),$$

but we don't know whether NP is contained in a smaller deterministic time complexity class.

7.4

NP-COMPLETENESS

One important advance on the P versus NP question came in the early 1970s with the work of Stephen Cook and Leonid Levin. They discovered certain problems in NP whose individual complexity is related to that of the entire class. If a polynomial time algorithm exists for any of these problems, all problems in NP would be polynomial time solvable. These problems are called *NP-complete*. The phenomenon of NP-completeness is important for both theoretical and practical reasons.

On the theoretical side, a researcher trying to show that P is unequal to NP may focus on an NP-complete problem. If any problem in NP requires more than polynomial time, an NP-complete one does. Furthermore, a researcher attempting to prove that P equals NP only needs to find a polynomial time algorithm for an NP-complete problem to achieve this goal.

On the practical side, the phenomenon of NP-completeness may prevent wasting time searching for a nonexistent polynomial time algorithm to solve a particular problem. Even though we may not have the necessary mathematics to prove that the problem is unsolvable in polynomial time, we believe that P is unequal to NP, so proving that a problem is NP-complete is strong evidence of its nonpolynomiality.

The first NP-complete problem that we present is called the *satisfiability problem*. Recall that variables that can take on the values TRUE and FALSE are called *Boolean variables* (see Section 0.2). Usually, we represent TRUE by 1 and FALSE by 0. The *Boolean operations* AND, OR, and NOT, represented by the symbols $\wedge$, $\vee$, and $\neg$, respectively, are described in the following list. We use the overbar as a shorthand for the $\neg$ symbol, so $\overline{x}$ means $\neg\,x$.

$$
\begin{array}{lll}
0 \wedge 0 = 0 & 0 \vee 0 = 0 & \overline{0} = 1 \\
0 \wedge 1 = 0 & 0 \vee 1 = 1 & \overline{1} = 0 \\
1 \wedge 0 = 0 & 1 \vee 0 = 1 & \\
1 \wedge 1 = 1 & 1 \vee 1 = 1 &
\end{array}
$$

A *Boolean formula* is an expression involving Boolean variables and operations. For example,

$$\phi = (\overline{x} \wedge y) \vee (x \wedge \overline{z})$$

is a Boolean formula. A Boolean formula is *satisfiable* if some assignment of 0s and 1s to the variables makes the formula evaluate to 1. The preceding formula is satisfiable because the assignment $x = 0$, $y = 1$, and $z = 0$ makes ϕ evaluate to 1. We say the assignment *satisfies* ϕ. The *satisfiability problem* is to test whether a Boolean formula is satisfiable. Let

$$SAT = \{\langle\phi\rangle|\ \phi \text{ is a satisfiable Boolean formula}\}.$$

Now we state the Cook–Levin theorem which links the complexity of the *SAT* problem to the complexities of all problems in NP.

THEOREM **7.22** ···

Cook–Levin theorem $SAT \in P$ iff P $=$ NP.

Next, we develop the method that is central to the proof of the Cook–Levin theorem.

POLYNOMIAL TIME REDUCIBILITY

In Chapter 5 we defined the concept of reducing one problem to another. When problem A reduces to problem B, a solution to B can be used to solve A. Now we define a version of reducibility that takes the efficiency of computation into account. When problem A is *efficiently* reducible to problem B, an efficient solution to B can be used to solve A efficiently.

DEFINITION **7.23** ···

A function $f : \Sigma^* \longrightarrow \Sigma^*$ is a ***polynomial time computable function*** if some polynomial time Turing machine M exists that halts with just $f(w)$ on its tape, when started on any input w.

DEFINITION **7.24** ···

Language A is ***polynomial time mapping reducible***,[1] or simply ***polynomial time reducible***, to language B, written $A \leq_{\mathrm{P}} B$, if a polynomial time computable function $f : \Sigma^* \longrightarrow \Sigma^*$ exists, where for every w,

$$w \in A \iff f(w) \in B.$$

The function f is called the ***polynomial time reduction*** of A to B.

Polynomial time reducibility is the efficient analog to mapping reducibility as defined in Section 5.3. Other forms of efficient reducibility are available, but polynomial time reducibility is a simple form that is adequate for our purposes so we won't discuss the others here. The following figure illustrates polynomial time reducibility.

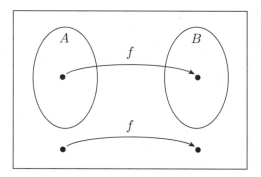

FIGURE **7.6**
Polynomial time function f reducing A to B

As with an ordinary mapping reduction, a polynomial time reduction of A to B provides a way to convert membership testing in A to membership testing in B, but now the conversion is done efficiently. To test whether $w \in A$, we use the reduction f to map w to $f(w)$ and test whether $f(w) \in B$.

If one language is polynomial time reducible to a language already known to have a polynomial time solution, we obtain a polynomial time solution to the original language, as in the following theorem.

---

[1]It is called ***polynomial time many-one reducibility*** in some other textbooks.

THEOREM **7.25**

If $A \leq_P B$ and $B \in P$, then $A \in P$.

PROOF   Let M be the polynomial time algorithm deciding B and f be the polynomial time reduction from A to B. We describe a polynomial time algorithm N deciding A as follows.

$N = $ "On input w:
1.   Compute $f(w)$.
2.   Run M on input $f(w)$ and output whatever M outputs."

If $w \in A$, then $f(w) \in B$ because f is a reduction from A to B. Thus M accepts $f(w)$ whenever $w \in A$. Moreover, N runs in polynomial time because each of its two stages runs in polynomial time. Note that stage 2 runs in polynomial time because the composition of two polynomials is a polynomial.

Before demonstrating a polynomial time reduction we introduce *3SAT*, a special case of the satisfiability problem whereby all formulas are in a special form. A *literal* is a Boolean variable or a negated Boolean variable, as in x or $\overline{x}$. A *clause* is several literals connected with $\vee$s, as in $(x_1 \vee \overline{x_2} \vee \overline{x_3} \vee x_4)$. A Boolean formula is in *conjunctive normal form*, called a *cnf-formula*, if it comprises several clauses connected with $\wedge$s, as in

$$(x_1 \vee \overline{x_2} \vee \overline{x_3} \vee x_4) \wedge (x_3 \vee \overline{x_5} \vee x_6) \wedge (x_3 \vee \overline{x_6}).$$

It is a *3cnf-formula* if all the clauses have three literals, as in

$$(x_1 \vee \overline{x_2} \vee \overline{x_3}) \wedge (x_3 \vee \overline{x_5} \vee x_6) \wedge (x_3 \vee \overline{x_6} \vee x_4) \wedge (x_4 \vee x_5 \vee x_6).$$

Let *3SAT* $= \{\langle\phi\rangle|\ \phi$ is a satisfiable 3cnf-formula$\}$. In a satisfiable cnf-formula, each clause must contain at least one literal that is assigned 1.

The following theorem presents a polynomial time reduction from the *3SAT* problem to the *CLIQUE* problem.

THEOREM **7.26**

3SAT is polynomial time reducible to *CLIQUE*.

PROOF IDEA   The polynomial time reduction f that we demonstrate from *3SAT* to *CLIQUE* converts formulas to graphs. In the constructed graphs, cliques of a specified size correspond to satisfying assignments of the formula. Structures within the graph are designed to mimic the behavior of the variables and clauses.

PROOF   Let ϕ be a formula with k clauses such as

$$\phi = (a_1 \vee b_1 \vee c_1) \wedge (a_2 \vee b_2 \vee c_2) \wedge \quad \cdots \quad \wedge (a_k \vee b_k \vee c_k).$$

The reduction f generates the string $\langle G, k \rangle$, where G is an undirected graph defined as follows.

The nodes in G are organized into k groups of three nodes each called the **triples**, $t_1, \ldots, t_k$. Each triple corresponds to one of the clauses in ϕ, and each node in a triple corresponds to a literal in the associated clause. Label each node of G with its corresponding literal in ϕ.

The edges of G connect all but two types of pairs of nodes in G. No edge is present between nodes in the same triple and no edge is present between two nodes with contradictory labels, as in x_2 and $\overline{x_2}$. The following figure illustrates this construction when $\phi = (x_1 \vee x_1 \vee x_2) \wedge (\overline{x_1} \vee \overline{x_2} \vee \overline{x_2}) \wedge (\overline{x_1} \vee x_2 \vee x_2)$.

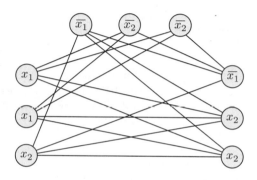

FIGURE **7.7**
The graph that the reduction produces from
$\phi = (x_1 \vee x_1 \vee x_2) \wedge (\overline{x_1} \vee \overline{x_2} \vee \overline{x_2}) \wedge (\overline{x_1} \vee x_2 \vee x_2)$

Now we demonstrate why this construction works. We show that ϕ is satisfiable iff G has a k-clique.

Suppose that ϕ has a satisfying assignment. In that satisfying assignment, at least one literal is true in every clause. In each triple of G, we select one node corresponding to a true literal in the satisfying assignment. If more than one literal is true in a particular clause, we choose one of the true literals arbitrarily. The nodes just selected form a k-clique. The number of nodes selected is k, because we chose one for each of the k triples. Each pair of selected nodes is joined by an edge because no pair fits one of the exceptions described previously. They could not be from the same triple because we selected only one node per triple. They could not have contradictory labels because the associated literals were both true in the satisfying assignment. Therefore G contains a k-clique.

Suppose that G has a k-clique. No two of the clique's nodes occur in the same triple because nodes in the same triple aren't connected by edges. Therefore each of the k triples contains exactly one of the k clique nodes. We assign truth values to the variables of ϕ so that each literal labeling a clique node is made true. Doing so is always possible because two nodes labeled in a contradictory way are not connected by an edge and hence both can't be in the clique. This assignment to the variables satisfies ϕ because each triple contains a clique node and hence each clause contains a literal that is assigned TRUE. Therefore ϕ is satisfiable.

....

Theorems 7.25 and 7.26 tell us that, if *CLIQUE* is solvable in polynomial time, so is *3SAT*. At first glance, this connection between these two problems appears quite remarkable because, superficially, they are rather different. But polynomial time reducibility allows us to link their complexities. Now we turn to a definition that will allow us to similarly link the complexities of an entire class of problems.

DEFINITION OF NP-COMPLETENESS

DEFINITION **7.27** ....

A language B is **NP-complete** if it satisfies two conditions:

1. B is in NP, and
2. every A in NP is polynomial time reducible to B.

THEOREM **7.28** ....

If B is NP-complete and $B \in \mathrm{P}$, then $\mathrm{P} = \mathrm{NP}$.

PROOF   This theorem follows directly from the definition of polynomial time reducibility.

....

THEOREM **7.29** ....

If B is NP-complete and $B \leq_\mathrm{P} C$ for C in NP, then C is NP-complete.

PROOF   We already know that C is in NP, so we must show that every A in NP is polynomial time reducible to C. Because B is NP-complete, every language in NP is polynomial time reducible to B, and B in turn is polynomial time reducible to C. Polynomial time reductions compose; that is, if A is polynomial time reducible to C and C is polynomial time reducible to B, then A is polynomial time reducible to B. Hence every language in NP is polynomial time reducible to C.

....

THE COOK-LEVIN THEOREM

Once we have one NP-complete problem, we may obtain others by polynomial time reduction from it. However, establishing the first NP-complete problem is more difficult. Now we do so by proving that *SAT* is NP-complete.

THEOREM **7.30** ....

SAT is NP-complete.[2]

This theorem restates Theorem 7.22, the Cook–Levin theorem, in another form.

....

PROOF IDEA   Showing that *SAT* is in NP is easy, and we do so shortly. The hard part of the proof is showing that any language in NP is polynomial time reducible to *SAT*.

To do so we construct a polynomial time reduction for each language A in NP to *SAT*. The reduction for A takes a string w and produces a Boolean formula ϕ that simulates the NP machine for A on input w. If the machine accepts, ϕ has a satisfying assignment that corresponds to the accepting computation. If the machine doesn't accept, no assignment satisfies ϕ. Therefore, w is in A if and only if ϕ is satisfiable.

Actually constructing the reduction to work in this way is a conceptually simple task, though we must cope with many details. A Boolean formula may contain the Boolean operations AND, OR, and NOT, and these operations form the basis for the circuitry used in electronic computers. Hence, the fact that we can design a Boolean formula to simulate a Turing machine isn't surprising. The details are in the implementation of this idea.

PROOF   First, we show that *SAT* is in NP. A nondeterministic polynomial time machine can guess an assignment to a given formula ϕ and accept if the assignment satisfies ϕ.

Next, we take any language A in NP and show that A is polynomial time reducible to *SAT*. Let N be a nondeterministic Turing machine that decides A in n^k time for some constant k. (For convenience we actually assume that N runs in time $n^k - 3$, but only those readers interested in details should worry about this minor point.) The following notion helps to describe the reduction.

A ***tableau*** for N on w is an $n^k \times n^k$ table whose rows are the configurations of a branch of the computation of N on input w, as shown in the following figure. For convenience later we assume that each configuration starts and ends with a # symbol, so the first and last columns of a tableau are all #s. The first row of the tableau is the starting configuration of N on w, and each row follows the previous one according to N's transition function. A tableau is ***accepting*** if any row of the tableau is an accepting configuration.

---

[2]An alternative proof of this theorem appears in Section 9.3 on page 321.

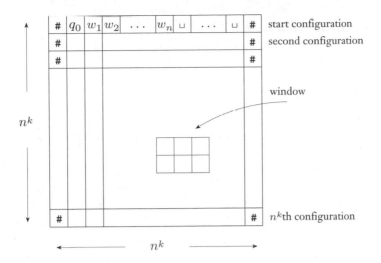

start configuration
second configuration
window
n^kth configuration

FIGURE 7.8
A tableau is an $n^k \times n^k$ table of configurations

Every accepting tableau for N on w corresponds to a computation branch of N on w. Thus the problem of determining whether N accepts w is equivalent to the problem of determining whether an accepting tableau for N on w exists.

Now we get to the description of the polynomial time reduction f from A to SAT. On input w, the reduction produces a formula ϕ. We begin by describing the variables of ϕ. Say that Q and Γ are the state set and tape alphabet of N. Let $C = Q \cup \Gamma \cup \{\#\}$. For each i and j between 1 and n^k and for each s in C we have a variable, $x_{i,j,s}$.

Each of the $(n^k)^2$ entries of a tableau is called a **cell**. The cell in row i and column j is called $cell[i,j]$ and contains a symbol from C. We represent the contents of the cells with the variables of ϕ. If $x_{i,j,s}$ takes on the value 1, it means that $cell[i,j]$ contains an s.

Now we design ϕ so that a satisfying assignment to the variables does correspond to an accepting tableau for N on w. The formula ϕ is the AND of four parts $\phi_{\text{cell}} \wedge \phi_{\text{start}} \wedge \phi_{\text{move}} \wedge \phi_{\text{accept}}$ and we describe each one in turn.

As we mentioned previously, turning variable $x_{i,j,s}$ on corresponds to placing symbol s in $cell[i,j]$. The first thing we must guarantee in order to obtain a correspondence between an assignment and a tableau is that the assignment turns on exactly one variable for each cell. Formula ϕ_{cell} ensures this requirement by expressing it in terms of Boolean operations:

$$\phi_{\text{cell}} = \bigwedge_{1 \le i,j \le n^k} \left[\left(\bigvee_{s \in C} x_{i,j,s} \right) \wedge \left(\bigwedge_{\substack{s,t \in C \\ s \ne t}} (\overline{x_{i,j,s}} \vee \overline{x_{i,j,t}}) \right) \right].$$

The symbols $\bigwedge$ and $\bigvee$ stand for iterated AND and OR. For example, the fragment of the preceding formula

$$\bigvee_{s \in C} x_{i,j,s}$$

is shorthand for

$$x_{i,j,s_1} \vee x_{i,j,s_2} \vee \cdots \vee x_{i,j,s_l}$$

where $C = \{s_1, s_2, \ldots, s_l\}$. Hence, ϕ_{cell} is actually a large expression that contains a fragment for each cell in the tableau because i and j range from 1 to n^k. The first part of each fragment says that at least one variable is turned on in the corresponding cell. The second part of each fragment says that no more than one variable is turned on (literally, it says that in each pair of variables, at least one is turned off) in the corresponding cell. These fragments are connected by $\wedge$ operations.

The first part of ϕ_{cell} inside the square brackets stipulates that at least one variable that is associated to each cell is on, whereas the second part stipulates that no more than one variable is on for each cell. Any assignment to the variables that satisfies ϕ and therefore ϕ_{cell} must have exactly one variable on for every cell. Thus any satisfying assignment specifies one symbol in each cell of the table. Parts ϕ_{start}, ϕ_{move}, and ϕ_{accept} ensure that the table is actually an accepting tableau as follows.

Formula ϕ_{start} ensures that the first row of the table is the starting configuration of N on w by explicitly stipulating that the corresponding variables are on:

$$\phi_{\text{start}} = x_{1,1,\#} \wedge x_{1,2,q_0} \wedge$$
$$x_{1,3,w_1} \wedge x_{1,4,w_2} \wedge \ldots \wedge x_{1,n+2,w_n} \wedge$$
$$x_{1,n+3,\sqcup} \wedge \ldots \wedge x_{1,n^k-1,\sqcup} \wedge x_{1,n^k,\#} \,.$$

Formula ϕ_{accept} guarantees that an accepting configuration occurs in the tableau. It ensures that q_{accept}, the symbol for the accept state, appears in one of the cells of the tableau, by stipulating that one of the corresponding variables is on:

$$\phi_{\text{accept}} = \bigvee_{1 \leq i,j \leq n^k} x_{i,j,q_{\text{accept}}} \,.$$

Finally, formula ϕ_{move} guarantees that each row of the table corresponds to a configuration that legally follows the preceding row's configuration according to N's rules. It does so by ensuring that each 2×3 window of cells is legal. We say that a 2×3 window is *legal* if that window does not violate the actions specified by M's transition function. In other words, a window is legal if it might appear when one configuration correctly follows another.[3]

---

[3]We could give a precise definition of *legal window* here, in terms of the transition function. But doing so is quite tedious and would be distracting from the main thrust of the proof argument. Anyone desiring more precision should refer to the related analysis in the proof of Theorem 5.11, the undecidability of the Post Correspondence Problem.

For example, say that a, b, and c are members of the tape alphabet and q_1 and q_2 are states of M. Assume that when in state q_1 with the head reading an a, M writes a b, stays in state q_1 and moves right, and that when in state q_1 with the head reading an b, M nondeterministically either

1. writes a c, enters q_2 and moves to the left, or
2. writes an a, enters q_2 and moves to the right.

Expressed formally, $\delta(q_1, \texttt{a}) = \{(q_1,\texttt{b},\text{R})\}$ and $\delta(q_1, \texttt{b}) = \{(q_2,\texttt{c},\text{L}), (q_2,\texttt{a},\text{R})\}$. Examples of legal windows for this machine are shown in the following figure.

(a)

a	q_1	b
q_2	a	c

(b)

a	q_1	b
a	a	q_2

(c)

a	a	q_1
a	a	b

(d)

#	b	a
#	b	a

(e)

a	b	a
a	b	q_2

(f)

b	b	b
c	b	b

FIGURE 7.9
Examples of legal windows

In Figure 7.9, windows (a) and (b) are legal because the transition function allows M to move in the indicated way. Window (c) is legal because, with q_1 appearing on the right side of the top row, we don't know what symbol the head is over. That symbol could be an a, and q_1 might change it to a b and move to the right. That possibility would give rise to this window, so it doesn't violate M's rules. Window (d) is obviously legal because the top and bottom are identical, which would occur if the head weren't adjacent to the location of the window. Note that # may appear on the left or right of both the top and bottom rows in a legal window. Window (e) is legal because state q_1 reading a b might have been immediately to the right of the top row, and it would then have moved to the left in state q_2 to appear on the right-hand end of the bottom row. Finally, window (f) is legal because state q_1 might have been immediately to the left of the top row and it might have changed the b to a c and moved to the left.

The windows shown in the following figure aren't legal for machine M.

(a)

a	b	a
a	a	a

(b)

a	q_1	b
q_1	a	a

(c)

b	q_1	b
q_2	b	q_2

FIGURE 7.10
Examples of illegal windows

In window (a) the central symbol in the top row can't change because a state wasn't adjacent to it. Window (b) isn't legal because the transition function specifies that the b gets changed to a c but not to an a. Window (c) isn't legal because two states appear in the bottom row.

CLAIM **7.31** ....

If the top row of the table is the start configuration and every window in the table is legal, each row of the table is a configuration that legally follows the preceding one.

We prove this claim by considering any two adjacent configurations in the table, called the upper configuration and the lower configuration. In the upper configuration, every cell that isn't adjacent to a state symbol and that doesn't contain the boundary symbol #, is the center top cell in a window whose top row contains no states. Therefore that symbol must appear unchanged in the center bottom of the window. Hence it appears in the same position in the bottom configuration.

The window containing the state symbol in the center top cell guarantees that the corresponding three positions are updated consistently with the transition function. Therefore, if the upper configuration is a legal configuration, so is the lower configuration, and the lower one follows the upper one according to M's rules. Note that this proof, though straightforward, depends crucially on our choice of a 2×3 window size, as Exercise 7.32 shows.

Now we return to the construction of ϕ_{move}. It stipulates that all the windows in the tableau are legal. Each window contains six cells, which may be set in a fixed number of ways to yield a legal window. Formula ϕ_{move} says that the settings of those six cells must be one of these ways, or

$$\phi_{\text{move}} = \bigwedge_{1 \le i,j \le n^k} \left(\text{the } (i,j) \text{ window is legal} \right)$$

We replace the text "the (i,j) window is legal" in this formula with the following formula. We write the contents of six cells of a window as $a_1, \ldots, a_6$.

$$\bigvee_{\substack{a_1, \ldots, a_6 \\ \text{is a legal window}}} \left(x_{i-1,j,a_1} \wedge x_{i,j,a_2} \wedge x_{i+1,j,a_3} \wedge x_{i-1,j+1,a_4} \wedge x_{i,j+1,a_5} \wedge x_{i+1,j+1,a_6} \right)$$

Next we analyze the complexity of the reduction to show that it operates in polynomial time. To do so we examine the size of ϕ. Recall that the tableau is an $n^k \times n^k$ table, so it contains n^{2k} cells. Each cell has l variables associated with it, where l is the number of symbols in C. Because l depends only on M and not on n, the total number of variables is $O(n^{2k})$.

Formula ϕ_{cell} contains a fixed-size fragment of the formula for each cell of the tableau, so its size is $O(n^{2k})$. Formula ϕ_{start} has a fragment for each cell in the top row, so its size is $O(n^k)$. Formulas ϕ_{move} and ϕ_{accept} each contain a fixed-size fragment of the formula for each cell of the tableau, so their size is $O(n^{2k})$.

Thus ϕ's total size is $O(n^{2k})$. That result is good because the size of ϕ is polynomial in n. If it were more than polynomial, the reduction wouldn't have any chance of generating it in polynomial time. (Actually our estimates are low by a factor of $O(\log n)$ because each variable has indices that can range up to n^k and so may require $O(\log n)$ symbols to write into the formula, but this additional factor doesn't change the polynomiality of the result.)

To see that we can generate the formula in polynomial time, observe its highly repetitive nature. Each component of the formula is composed of many nearly identical fragments, which differ only at the indices in a simple way. Therefore we may easily construct a reduction that produces ϕ in polynomial time from the input w.

Thus we have concluded the proof of the Cook–Levin theorem, showing that *SAT* is NP-complete. Showing the NP-completeness of other languages generally doesn't require such a lengthy proof. Instead NP-completeness can be proved with a polynomial time reduction from a language that is already known to be NP-complete. We can use *SAT* for this purpose, but using *3SAT*, the special case of *SAT* that we defined on page 251, is usually easier. Recall that the formulas in *3SAT* are in conjunctive normal form (cnf) with three literals per clause. First, we must show that *3SAT* itself is NP-complete. We prove this as a corollary to Theorem 7.30.

COROLLARY 7.32

3SAT is NP-complete.

PROOF   Obviously *3SAT* is in NP, so we only need to prove that all languages in NP reduce to *3SAT* in polynomial time. One way to do so is by showing that *SAT* polynomial time reduces to *3SAT*. Instead, we modify the proof of Theorem 7.30 so that it directly produces a formula in conjunctive normal form with three literals per clause.

Theorem 7.30 produces a formula that is already almost in conjunctive normal form. Formula ϕ_{cell} is a big AND of subformulas, each of which contains a big OR and a big AND of ORs. Thus ϕ_{cell} is an AND of clauses and so is already in cnf. Formula ϕ_{start} is a big AND of variables. Taking each of these variables to be a clause of size 1 we see that ϕ_{start} is in cnf. Formula ϕ_{accept} is a big OR of variables and is thus a single clause. Formula ϕ_{move} is the only one that isn't already in cnf, but we may easily convert it into a formula that is in cnf as follows.

Recall that ϕ_{move} is a big AND of subformulas, each of which is an OR of ANDs that describes all possible legal windows. The distributive laws, as described in Chapter 0, state that we can replace an OR of ANDs with an equivalent AND of ORs. Doing so may significantly increase the size of each subformula, but can only increase the total size of ϕ_{move} by a constant factor because the size of each subformula depends only on N. The result is a formula which is in conjunctive normal form.

Now that we have written the formula in cnf, we convert it to one with three literals per clause. In each clause that currently has one or two literals, we replicate one of the literals until the total number is three. In each clause that has more than three literals, we split it into several clauses and add additional variables to preserve the satisfiability or nonsatisfiability of the original.

For example, we replace clause $(a_1 \lor a_2 \lor a_3 \lor a_4)$ wherein each a_i is a literal with the two clause expression $(a_1 \lor a_2 \lor z) \land (\overline{z} \lor a_3 \lor a_4)$ wherein z is a new variable. If some setting of the a_i's satisfies the original clause, we can find some setting of z so that the two new clauses are satisfied. In general, if the clause contains l literals,

$$(a_1 \lor a_2 \lor \cdots \lor a_l),$$

we can replace it with the $l - 2$ clauses

$$(a_1 \lor a_2 \lor z_1) \land (\overline{z_1} \lor a_3 \lor z_2) \land (\overline{z_2} \lor a_4 \lor z_3) \land \cdots \land (\overline{z_{l-3}} \lor a_{l-1} \lor a_l).$$

We may easily verify that the new formula is satisfiable if and only if the original formula was, so the proof is complete.

....

7.5

ADDITIONAL NP-COMPLETE PROBLEMS

In this section we present additional theorems showing that various languages are NP-complete. Our general strategy is to exhibit a polynomial time reduction from *3SAT* to the language in question, though we sometimes reduce from other NP-complete languages when that is more convenient.

When constructing a polynomial time reduction from *3SAT* to a language, we look for structures in that language that can simulate the variables and clauses in Boolean formulas. Such structures are sometimes called **gadgets**. For example, in the reduction from *3SAT* to *CLIQUE* presented in Theorem 7.26, individual nodes simulate variables and triples of nodes simulate clauses. An individual node may or may not be a member of the clique, which corresponds to a variable that may or may not be true in a satisfying assignment. Each clause must contain a literal that is assigned true and that corresponds to the way each triple must contain a node in the clique if the target size is to be reached. The following corollary to Theorem 7.26 states that *CLIQUE* is NP-complete.

COROLLARY **7.33** ....

CLIQUE is NP-complete.

THE VERTEX COVER PROBLEM

If G is an undirected graph, a **vertex cover** of G is a subset of the nodes where every edge of G touches one of those nodes. The vertex cover problem asks for the size of the smallest vertex cover. Let

$$VERTEX\text{-}COVER = \{\langle G, k\rangle|\ G \text{ is an undirected graph that}$$
$$\text{has a } k\text{-node vertex cover}\}.$$

THEOREM 7.34 ⋯⋯⋯⋯⋯⋯⋯⋯⋯⋯⋯⋯⋯⋯⋯⋯⋯⋯⋯⋯⋯⋯⋯⋯⋯⋯⋯⋯⋯

$VERTEX\text{-}COVER$ is NP-complete.

PROOF We give a reduction from $3SAT$ to $VERTEX\text{-}COVER$ that operates in polynomial time. The reduction maps a Boolean formula ϕ to a graph G and a value k. Each edge in G must touch at least one node in the vertex cover, so a natural gadget for a variable is a single edge. Setting that variable to TRUE corresponds to selecting the left node for the vertex cover, whereas FALSE corresponds to the right node. We label the two nodes in the gadget for variable for x by x and $\overline{x}$.

The gadgets for the clauses are a bit more complex. Each clause gadget is a triple of three nodes that are labeled with the three literals of the clause. These three nodes are connected to each other and to the nodes in the variables gadgets that have the identical labels. Thus the total number of nodes that appear in G is $2m + 3l$, where ϕ has m variables and l clauses. Let k be $m + 2l$.

For example, if $\phi = (x_1 \vee x_1 \vee x_2) \wedge (\overline{x_1} \vee \overline{x_2} \vee \overline{x_2}) \wedge (\overline{x_1} \vee x_2 \vee x_2)$, the reduction produces $\langle G, k\rangle$ from ϕ, where $k = 8$ and G takes the form shown in the following figure.

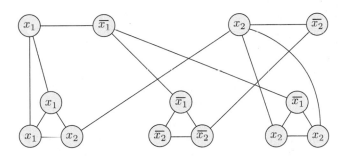

FIGURE 7.11
The graph that the reduction produces from
$\phi = (x_1 \vee x_1 \vee x_2) \wedge (\overline{x_1} \vee \overline{x_2} \vee \overline{x_2}) \wedge (\overline{x_1} \vee x_2 \vee x_2)$

To prove that this reduction works, we need to show that ϕ is satisfiable if and only if G has a vertex cover with k nodes. We start with a satisfying assignment. We put the nodes of the variable gadgets that correspond to the true literals in the assignment into the vertex cover. Then, we select one true literal in every clause and put the remaining two nodes from every clause gadget into the vertex cover. Now, we have a total of k nodes. They cover all edges because every variable gadget edge is clearly covered, all three edges within every clause gadget are covered, and all edges between variable and clause gadgets are covered. Hence G has a vertex cover with k nodes.

Second, if G has a vertex cover with k nodes we show that ϕ is satisfiable by constructing the satisfying assignment. The vertex cover must contain one node in each variable gadget and two in every clause gadget in order to cover the edges of the variable gadgets and the three edges within the edge gadgets. That accounts for all the nodes, so none are left over. We take the nodes of the variable gadgets that are in the vertex cover and assign the corresponding literals true. That assignment satisfies ϕ because each of the three edges connecting the variable gadgets with each clause gadget is covered and only two nodes of the clause gadget are in the vertex cover. Therefore one of the edges must be covered by a node from a variable gadget and so that assignment satisfies the corresponding clause.

THE HAMILTONIAN PATH PROBLEM

Recall that the Hamiltonian path problem asks whether the input graph contains a path from s to t that goes through every node exactly once.

THEOREM **7.35**

HAMPATH is NP-complete.

PROOF IDEA To show that *HAMPATH* is NP-complete we must demonstrate two things: (1) that *HAMPATH* is in NP; and (2) that every language A in NP is polynomial time reducible to *HAMPATH*. The first we did in Section 7.3. To do the second we show that a known NP-complete problem, *3SAT*, is polynomial time reducible to *HAMPATH*. We give a way to convert 3cnf-formulas into graphs in which Hamiltonian paths correspond to satisfying assignments of the formula. The graphs contain gadgets that mimic variables and clauses. The variable gadget is a diamond structure that can be traversed in either of two ways, corresponding to the two truth settings. The clause gadget is a node. Ensuring that the path goes through each clause gadget corresponds to ensuring that each clause is satisfied in the satisfying assignment.

PROOF   We have previously shown that *HAMPATH* is in NP, so all that remains to be done is to show *3SAT* $\leq_P$ *HAMPATH*. For each 3cnf-formula ϕ we show how to construct a directed graph G with two nodes, s and t, where a Hamiltonian path exists between s and t iff ϕ is satisfiable.

We start the construction with a 3cnf-formula ϕ containing k clauses,

$$\phi = (a_1 \vee b_1 \vee c_1) \wedge (a_2 \vee b_2 \vee c_2) \wedge \cdots \wedge (a_k \vee b_k \vee c_k).$$

where each a, b, and c is a literal x_i or $\overline{x_i}$. Let $x_1, \ldots, x_l$ be the l variables of ϕ.

Now we show how to convert ϕ into a graph G. The graph G that we construct has various parts to represent the structures (variables and clauses) that appear in ϕ.

We represent each variable x_i with a diamond-shaped structure that contains a horizontal row of nodes, as shown in the following figure. Later we specify the number of nodes that appear in the horizontal row.

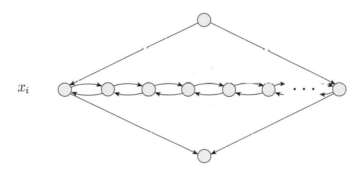

FIGURE   7.12
Representing the variable x_i as a diamond structure

We represent each clause of ϕ as a single node, as follows.

FIGURE   7.13
Representing the clause c_j as a node

The following figure depicts the global structure of G. It shows all the elements of G and their relationships, except the edges that represent the relationship of the variables to the clauses that contain them.

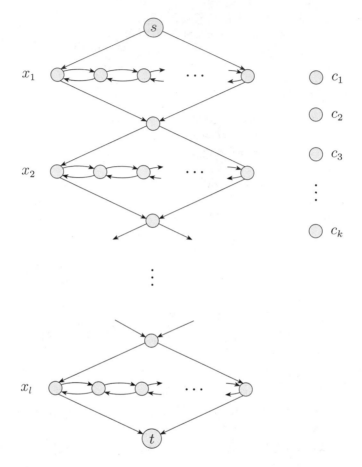

FIGURE **7.14**
The high-level structure of G

Next we show how to connect the diamonds representing the variables to the nodes representing the clauses. Each diamond structure contains a horizontal row of nodes connected by edges running in both directions. The horizontal row contains $2k$ nodes in addition to the two nodes on the ends belonging to the diamond. These nodes are grouped into adjacent pairs, one for each clause, as shown in the following figure.

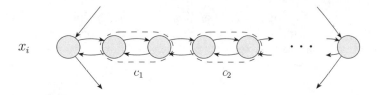

FIGURE **7.15**
The horizontal nodes in a diamond structure

If variable x_i appears in clause c_j, we add the following two edges from the jth pair in the ith diamond to the jth clause node.

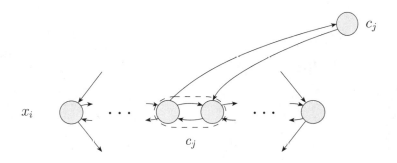

FIGURE **7.16**
The additional edges when clause c_j contains x_i

If $\overline{x_i}$ appears in clause c_j, we add the following two edges from the jth pair in the ith diamond to the jth clause node.

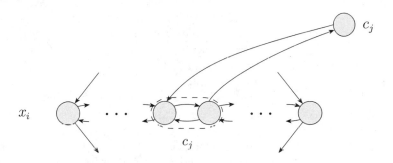

FIGURE **7.17**
The additional edges when clause c_j contains $\overline{x_i}$

After we add all the edges corresponding to each occurrence of x_i or $\overline{x_i}$ in each clause, the construction of G is complete. To show that this construction works, we argue that, if ϕ is satisfiable, a Hamiltonian path exists from s to t and, conversely, if such a path exists, ϕ is satisfiable.

Suppose that ϕ is satisfiable. To demonstrate a Hamiltonian path from s to t, we first ignore the clause nodes. The path begins at s, goes through each diamond in turn, and ends up at t. To hit the horizontal nodes in a diamond, the path either zig-zags from left to right or zag-zigs from right to left, the satisfying assignment to ϕ determines which. If x_i is assigned TRUE, zig-zag through the corresponding diamond. If x_i is assigned FALSE, zag-zig. We show both possibilities in the following figure.

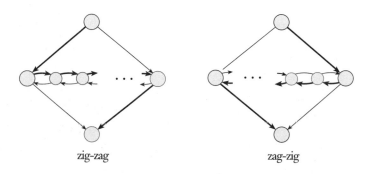

zig-zag   zag-zig

FIGURE **7.18**
Zig-zagging and zag-zigging through a diamond, as determined by the satisfying assignment

So far this path covers all the nodes in G except the clause nodes. We can easily include them by adding detours at the horizontal nodes. In each clause, select one of the literals assigned TRUE by the satisfying assignment.

If we selected x_i in clause c_j, we can detour at the jth pair in the ith diamond. Doing so is possible because x_i must be TRUE, so the path zig-zags from left to right through the corresponding diamond. Hence the edges to the c_j node are in the correct order to allow a detour and return.

Similarly, if we selected $\overline{x_i}$ in clause c_j, we can detour at the jth pair in the ith diamond. Doing so is possible because x_i must be FALSE, so the path zag-zigs from right to left through the corresponding diamond. Hence the edges to the c_j node again are in the correct order to allow a detour and return. (Note that each true literal in a clause provides an *option* of a detour to hit the clause node. As a result, if several literals in a clause are true, only one detour is taken.) Thus we have constructed the desired Hamiltonian path.

For the reverse direction, if G has a Hamiltonian path from s to t, we demonstrate a satisfying assignment for ϕ. If the Hamiltonian path is *normal*, that is, it goes through the diamonds in order from the top one to the bottom one, except for the detours to the clause nodes, we can easily obtain the satisfying assignment. If the path zig-zags through the diamond, we assign the corresponding variable TRUE, and, if the path zag-zigs, we assign FALSE. Because each clause node appears on the path, by observing the diamond at which the detour to it is taken, we may determine which of the literals in the corresponding clause is TRUE.

All that remains to be done is to show that a Hamiltonian path must be normal. The only way for normality to fail would be for the path to enter a clause from one diamond but return to another, as in the following figure. The path goes from node a_1 to c, but instead of returning to a_2 in the same diamond, it returns to b_2 in a different diamond. But, were this configuration to occur, the path could not contain node a_2 because the only arrows into a_2 are from c, a_1, and a_3. The path cannot enter a_2 from c or a_1 because the path goes elsewhere from these nodes. The path cannot enter a_2 from a_3, because a_3 is the only available node that a_2 points at, so the path must exit a_2 via a_3. Hence a Hamiltonian path must be normal. This reduction obviously operates in polynomial time and the proof is complete.

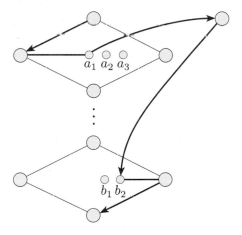

FIGURE   **7.19**
This situation cannot occur

Next we consider an undirected version of the Hamiltonian path problem, called *UHAMPATH*. To show that *UHAMPATH* is NP-complete we give a polynomial time reduction from the directed version of the problem.

....

UHAMPATH is NP-complete.

PROOF   The reduction takes a directed graph G with nodes s and t, and constructs an undirected graph G' with nodes s' and t'. Graph G has a Hamiltonian path from s to t if and only if G' has a Hamiltonian path from s' to t'. We describe G' as follows.

Each node u of G, except for s and t, is replaced by a triple of nodes u^{in}, u^{mid}, and u^{out} in G'. Nodes s and t in G are replaced by nodes s^{out} and t^{in} in G'. Edges of two types appear in G'. First, edges connect u^{mid} with u^{in} and u^{out}. Second, an edge connects u^{out} with u^{in} if an edge goes from u to v in G. That completes the construction of G'.

We can demonstrate that this construction works by showing that G has a Hamiltonian path from s to t if and only if G' has a Hamiltonian path from s^{out} to t^{in}. To show one direction, we observe that a Hamiltonian path P in G,

$$s, u_1, u_2, \ldots, u_k, t,$$

has a corresponding Hamiltonian path P' in G',

$$s^{\text{out}}, u_1^{\text{in}}, u_1^{\text{mid}}, u_1^{\text{out}}, u_2^{\text{in}}, u_2^{\text{mid}}, u_2^{\text{out}}, \ldots, t^{\text{in}}.$$

To show the other direction, we claim that any Hamiltonian path in G' from s^{out} to t^{in} in G' must go from a triple of nodes to a triple of nodes, except for the start and finish, as does the path P' we just described. That would complete the proof because any such path has a corresponding Hamiltonian path in G. We prove the claim by following the path starting at node s^{out}. Observe that the next node in the path must be u_i^{in} for some i because only those nodes are connected to s^{out}. The next node must u_i^{mid}, because no other way is available to include u_i^{mid} in the Hamiltonian path. After u_i^{mid} comes u_i^{out} because that is the only other one to which u_i^{mid} is connected. The next node must be u_j^{in} for some j because no other available node is connected to u_i^{out}. The argument then repeats until t^{in} is reached.

....

THE SUBSET SUM PROBLEM

Recall the *SUBSET-SUM* problem defined on page 246. In that problem, we are given a collection of numbers, $x_1, \ldots, x_k$ together with a target number t, and want to determine whether the collection contains a subcollection that adds up to t. We now show that this problem is NP-complete.

THEOREM **7.37**   ....

SUBSET-SUM is NP-complete.

PROOF IDEA   We have already shown that *SUBSET-SUM* is in NP in Theorem 7.21. We prove that all languages in NP are polynomial time reducible to *SUBSET-SUM* by reducing the NP-complete language *3SAT* to it. Given a 3cnf-formula ϕ we construct an instance of the *SUBSET-SUM* problem that contains a subcollection summing to the target t if and only if ϕ is satisfiable. Call this subcollection T.

To achieve this reduction we find structures of the *SUBSET-SUM* problem that represent variables and clauses. The *SUBSET-SUM* problem instance that we construct contains numbers of large magnitude presented in decimal notation. We represent variables by pairs of numbers and clauses by certain positions in the decimal representations of the numbers.

We represent variable x_i by two numbers, y_i and z_i. We prove that either y_i or z_i must be in T for each i, which establishes the encoding for the truth value of x_i in the satisfying assignment.

Each clause position contains a certain value in the target t, which imposes a requirement on the subset T. We prove that this requirement is the same as the one in the corresponding clause, namely, that one of the literals in that clause is assigned TRUE.

PROOF   We already know that *SUBSET-SUM* $\in$ NP, so we now show that *3SAT* $\leq_P$ *SUBSET-SUM*.

Let ϕ be a Boolean formula with variables $x_1, \ldots, x_l$ and clauses $c_1, \ldots, c_k$. The reduction converts ϕ to an instance of the *SUBSET-SUM* problem $\langle S, t \rangle$, wherein the elements of S and the number t are the rows in the following table expressed in ordinary decimal notation. The rows above the double line are labeled

$$y_1, z_1, y_2, z_2, \ldots, y_l, z_l \quad \text{and} \quad g_1, h_1, g_2, h_2, \ldots, g_k, h_k$$

and comprise the elements of S. The row below the double line is t.

Thus S contains one pair of numbers, y_i, z_i, for each variable x_i in ϕ. The decimal representation of these numbers is in two parts, as indicated in the table. The left-hand part comprises a 1 followed by $l - i$ 0s. The right-hand part contains one digit for each clause, where the jth digit of y_i is 1 if clause c_j contains literal x_i and the jth digit of z_i is 1 if clause c_j contains literal $\overline{x_i}$. Digits not specified to be 1 are 0.

The table is partially filled in to illustrate sample clauses, c_1, c_2, and c_k:

$$(x_1 \lor \overline{x_2} \lor x_3) \land (x_2 \lor x_3 \lor \cdots) \land \cdots \land (\overline{x_3} \lor \cdots \lor \cdots).$$

Additionally, S contains one pair of numbers, g_j, h_j, for each clause c_j. These two numbers are equal and consist of a 1 followed by $j - 1$ 0s.

Finally, the target number t, the bottom row of the table, consists of l 1s followed by k 3s.

	1	2	3	4	$\cdots$	l	c_1	c_2	$\cdots$	c_k
y_1	1	0	0	0	$\cdots$	0	1	0	$\cdots$	0
z_1	1	0	0	0	$\cdots$	0	0	0	$\cdots$	0
y_2		1	0	0	$\cdots$	0	0	1	$\cdots$	0
z_2		1	0	0	$\cdots$	0	1	0	$\cdots$	0
y_3			1	0	$\cdots$	0	1	1	$\cdots$	0
z_3			1	0	$\cdots$	0	0	0	$\cdots$	1
$\vdots$					$\ddots$	$\vdots$	$\vdots$		$\vdots$	$\vdots$
y_l						1	0	0	$\cdots$	0
z_l						1	0	0	$\cdots$	0
g_1							1	0	$\cdots$	0
h_1							1	0	$\cdots$	0
g_2								1	$\cdots$	0
h_2								1	$\cdots$	0
$\vdots$									$\ddots$	$\vdots$
g_k										1
h_k										1
t	1	1	1	1	$\cdots$	1	3	3	$\cdots$	3

Now we show why this construction works. We demonstrate that ϕ is satisfiable if and only if some subset of S sums to t.

Suppose that ϕ is satisfiable. We construct a subset of S as follows. We select y_i if x_i is assigned TRUE in the satisfying assignment and z_i if x_i is assigned FALSE. If we add up what we have selected so far, we obtain a 1 in each of the first l digits because we have selected either y_i or z_i for each i. Furthermore, each of the last k digits is a number between 1 and 3 because each clause is satisfied and so contains between 1 and 3 true literals. Now we further select enough of the g and h numbers to bring each of the last k digits up to 3, thus hitting the target.

Suppose that a subset of S sums to t. We construct a satisfying assignment to ϕ after making several observations. First, all the digits in members of S are either 0 or 1. Furthermore, each column in the table describing S contains at most five 1s. Hence a "carry" into the next column never occurs when a subset of S is added. To get a 1 in each of the first l columns the subset must have either y_i or z_i for each i, but not both.

Now we make the satisfying assignment. If the subset contains y_i, we assign x_i TRUE, otherwise, we assign it FALSE. This assignment must satisfy ϕ because in each of the final k columns the sum is always 3. In column c_j, at most 2 can come from g_j and h_j, so at least 1 in this column must come from some y_i or z_i in the subset. If it is y_i, then x_i appears in c_j and is assigned TRUE, so c_j is satisfied. If it is z_i, then $\overline{x_i}$ appears in c_j and x_i is assigned FALSE, so c_j is satisfied. Therefore ϕ is satisfied.

Finally, we must be sure that the reduction can be carried out in polynomial time. The table has a size of roughly $(k + l)^2$, and each entry is easily calculated for any ϕ. So the total time is $O(n^2)$ easy stages.

EXERCISES

7.1 Answer each part TRUE or FALSE.

    a. $2n = O(n)$.

    b. $n^2 = O(n)$.

    c. $n^2 = O(n \log^2 n)$.

    d. $n \log n = O(n^2)$.

    e. $3^n = 2^{O(n)}$.

    f. $2^{2^n} = O(2^{2^n})$.

7.2 Answer each part TRUE or FALSE.

    a. $n = o(2n)$.

    b. $2n = o(n^2)$.

    c. $2^n = o(3^n)$.

    d. $1 = o(n)$.

    e. $n = o(\log n)$.

    f. $1 = o(1/n)$.

7.3 Which of the following pairs of numbers are relatively prime? Show the calculations that led to your conclusions.

    a. 1274 and 10505

    b. 7289 and 8029

7.4 Fill out the table described in the polynomial time algorithm for context-free language recognition from Theorem 7.14 for string $w = \text{baba}$ and CFG G:

$$S \rightarrow RT$$
$$R \rightarrow TR \mid \text{a}$$
$$T \rightarrow TR \mid \text{b}$$

7.5 Is the following formula satisfiable?

$$(x \vee y) \wedge (x \vee \overline{y}) \wedge (\overline{x} \vee y) \wedge (\overline{x} \vee \overline{y})$$

7.6 Show that P is closed under union, concatenation, and complement.

7.7 Show that NP is closed under union and concatenation.

7.8 Show that primality testing is solvable in polynomial time if we use a unary encoding rather than a binary encoding for numbers. In other words, show that the language $UNARY\text{-}PRIMES = \{1^n | \ n \text{ is prime}\}$ is in P.

7.9 Let $CONNECTED = \{\langle G \rangle | \ G \text{ is a connected undirected graph}\}$. Analyze the algorithm given on page 145 to show that this language is in P.

7.10 A **triangle** in an undirected graph is a 3-clique. Show that $TRIANGLE \in P$, where $TRIANGLE = \{\langle G \rangle | \ G \text{ contains a triangle}\}$.

7.11 Call graphs G and H **isomorphic** if the nodes of G may be reordered so that it is identical to H. Let $ISO = \{\langle G, H \rangle | \ G \text{ and } H \text{ are isomorphic graphs}\}$. Show that $ISO \in NP$.

PROBLEMS

7.12 Let

$$MODEXP = \{\langle a, b, c, p \rangle | \ a, b, c, \text{ and } p \text{ are binary integers}$$
$$\text{such that } a^b \equiv c \pmod{p}\}.$$

Show that $MODEXP \in P$. (Note that the most obvious algorithm doesn't run in polynomial time. Hint: Try it first where b is a power of 2.)

7.13 Show that P is closed under the star operation. (Hint: On input $y = y_1 \cdots y_n$ for $y_i \in \Sigma$, build a table indicating for each $i \leq j$ whether the substring $y_i \cdots y_j \in A^*$ for any $A \in P$.)

7.14 Show that NP is closed under the star operation.

7.15 Let $UNARY\text{-}SSUM$ be the subset sum problem in which all numbers are represented in unary. Why does the NP-completeness proof for $SUBSET\text{-}SUM$ fail to show $UNARY\text{-}SSUM$ is NP-complete? Show that $UNARY\text{-}SSUM \in P$.

7.16 Let G represent an undirected graph and let

$$SPATH = \{\langle G, a, b, k \rangle | \ G \text{ contains a simple path of}$$
$$\text{length at most } k \text{ from } a \text{ to } b\}.$$

and

$$LPATH = \{\langle G, a, b, k \rangle | \ G \text{ contains a simple path of}$$
$$\text{length at least } k \text{ from } a \text{ to } b\}.$$

   a. Show that $SPATH \in P$.

   b. Show that $LPATH$ is NP-complete. You may assume the NP-completeness of $UHAMPATH$, the Hamiltonian path problem for undirected graphs.

7.17 Show that, if P = NP then every language $A \in P$ except $A = \emptyset$ and $A = \Sigma^*$ is NP-complete.

★7.18 Show that $PRIMES = \{n | \ n \text{ is a prime number in binary}\} \in NP$. (Hint: For $p > 1$ the multiplicative group $Z_p^* = \{x | \ x \text{ is relatively prime to } p \text{ and } 1 \leq x < p\}$ is both cyclic and of order $p - 1$ iff p is prime. You may use this fact without proving it.)

7.19 Let $DOUBLE\text{-}SAT = \{\langle \phi \rangle | \ \phi \text{ has at least two satisfying assignments}\}$. Show that $DOUBLE\text{-}SAT$ is NP-complete.

7.20 A *permutation* on the set $\{1, \ldots, k\}$ is a one-to-one, onto function on this set. When p is a permutation, p^t means the composition of p with itself t times. Let

$$PERM\text{-}POWER = \{\langle p, q, t\rangle|\ p = q^t \text{ where } p \text{ and } q \text{ are permutations}$$
$$\text{on } \{1, \ldots, k\} \text{ and } t \text{ is a binary integer}\}.$$

Show that $PERM\text{-}POWER \in \mathrm{P}$. (Note that the most obvious algorithm doesn't run within polynomial time. Hint: First try it where t is a power of 2).

7.21 Let

$$HALF\text{-}CLIQUE = \{\langle G\rangle|\ G \text{ is an undirected graph having a complete subgraph}$$
$$\text{with at least } n/2 \text{ nodes, where } n \text{ is the number of nodes in } G\}.$$

Show that $HALF\text{-}CLIQUE$ is NP-complete.

7.22 Let ϕ be a 3cnf-formula. An $\neq$-*assignment* to the variables of ϕ is one where each clause contains two literals with unequal truth values. In other words an $\neq$-assignment satisfies ϕ without assigning three true literals in any clause.

  a. Show that the negation of any $\neq$-assignment to ϕ is also an $\neq$-assignment.
  b. Let $\neq SAT$ be the collection of 3cnf-formulas that have an $\neq$-assignment. Show that we obtain a polynomial time reduction from $3SAT$ to $\neq SAT$ by replacing each clause c_i

$$(y_1 \vee y_2 \vee y_3)$$

by the two clauses

$$(y_1 \vee y_2 \vee z_i) \text{ and } (\overline{z_i} \vee y_3 \vee b)$$

where z_i is a new variable for each clause c_i and b is a single additional new variable.

  c. Conclude that $\neq SAT$ is NP-complete.

7.23 A *cut* in an undirected graph is a separation of the vertices V into two disjoint subsets S and T. The size of a cut is the number of edges that have one endpoint in S and the other in T. Let

$$MAX\text{-}CUT = \{\langle G, k\rangle|\ G \text{ has a cut of size } k \text{ or more}\}.$$

Show that $MAX\text{-}CUT$ is NP-complete. You may assume the result of Problem 7.22. (Hint: Show that $\neq SAT \leq_{\mathrm{P}} MAX\text{-}CUT$. The variable gadget for variable x is a collection of $3k$ nodes labeled with x and another $3k$ nodes labeled with $\overline{x}$, where k is the number of clauses. All nodes labeled x are connected with all nodes labeled $\overline{x}$. The clique gadget is a triangle of three edges connecting three nodes labeled with the literals appearing in the clique. Do not use the same node in more than one clique gadget. Prove that this reduction works.)

7.24 Recall, in our discussion of the Church–Turing thesis, that we introduced the language $D = \{\langle p\rangle|\ p \text{ is a polynomial in several variables having an integral root}\}$. We stated, but didn't prove, that D is undecidable. In this problem you are to prove a different property of D, namely, that D is NP-hard. A problem is *NP-hard* if all problems in NP are polynomial time reducible to it, even though it may not be in NP itself. So, you must show that all problems in NP are polynomial time reducible to D.

7.25 Let $U = \{\langle M, x, 1^t\rangle |\ M$ is an NTM that accepts input x within t steps$\}$. Show that U is NP-complete.

7.26 You are given a box and a collection of cards as indicated in the following figure. Because of the pegs in the box and the notches in the cards, each card will fit in the box in either of two ways. Each card contains two columns of holes, some of which may not be punched out. The puzzle is solved by placing all the cards in the box so as to completely cover the bottom of the box, (i.e., every hole position is blocked by at least one card that has no hole there.) Let

$$PUZZLE = \{\langle c_1, \ldots, c_k\rangle |\ \text{each } c_i \text{ represents a card}$$
$$\text{and this collection of cards has a solution}\}.$$

Show $PUZZLE$ is NP-complete.

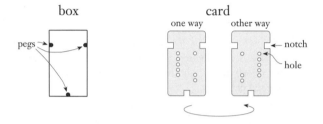

7.27 Let $SET\text{-}SPLITTING = \{\langle S, C\rangle |\ S$ is a finite set and $C = \{C_1, \ldots, C_k\}$ is a collection of subsets of S, for some $k > 0$, such that elements of S can be colored *red* or *blue* so that no C_i has all its elements colored with the same color.$\}$ Show that $SET\text{-}SPLITTING$ is NP-complete.

7.28 Show that, if P = NP, we can factor integers in polynomial time. (Note: NP is a class of *languages* and the factoring problem is a *function*. Thus simply saying that, "because factoring is in NP, you are done" isn't enough.)

7.29 Show that, if P = NP, a polynomial time algorithm exists that, given a Boolean formula ϕ, actually produces a satisfying assignment for ϕ if it is satisfiable.

7.30 Let $MAX\text{-}CLIQUE = \{\langle G, k\rangle |\ $the *largest* clique of G has k vertices$\}$. Whether $MAX\text{-}CLIQUE$ is in NP is unknown. Show that if P = NP, then $MAX\text{-}CLIQUE$ is in P, and a polynomial time algorithm exists that, for a graph G, finds one of its largest cliques.

7.31 Show that ALL_{DFA} is in P.

7.32 In the proof of the Cook–Levin theorem, we defined a window to be a 2×3 rectangle of cells. Show why the proof would have failed if we had used 2×2 windows instead.

7.33 Describe the error in the following fallacious "proof" that P $\neq$ NP. Consider an algorithm for SAT: "On input ϕ, try all possible assignments to the variables. Accept if any satisfy ϕ." This algorithm clearly requires exponential time. Thus SAT has exponential time complexity. Therefore SAT is not in P. Because SAT is in NP, it must be true that P is not equal to NP.

7.34 A *coloring* of a graph is an assignment of colors to its nodes so that no two adjacent nodes are assigned the same color. Let

$$3COLOR = \{\langle G \rangle | \text{ the nodes of } G \text{ can be colored with three colors such that}$$
$$\text{no two nodes joined by an edge have the same color}\}.$$

Show that *3COLOR* is NP-complete. (Hint: Use the following three subgraphs.)

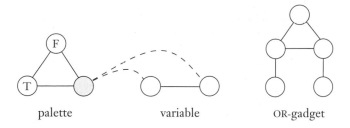

palette   variable   OR-gadget

*7.35 Consider the following algorithm *MINIMIZE*, which takes a DFA M as input and outputs DFA M'.

MINIMIZE = "On input $\langle M \rangle$, where $M = (Q, \Sigma, \delta, q_0, A)$ is a DFA:
1. Remove all states of M that are unreachable from the start state.
2. Construct the following undirected graph G whose nodes are the states of M.
3. Place an edge in G connecting every accept state with every nonaccept state. Add additional edges as follows.
4. Repeat until no new edges are added to G:
5.   For every pair of distinct states q and r of M and every $a \in \Sigma$:
6.   Add the edge (q, r) to G if $(\delta(q, a), \delta(r, a))$ is an edge of G.
7. For each state q, let $[q]$ be the collection of states:
   $[q] = \{r \in Q|$ no edge joins q and r in G, including $r = q\}$.
8. Form a new DFA $M' = (Q', \Sigma, \delta', q_0, A')$ where
   $Q' = \{[q]| q \in Q\}$, (if $[q] = [r]$, only one of them is in Q'),
   $\delta'([q], a) = [\delta(q, a)]$, for every $q \in Q$ and $a \in \Sigma$,
   $q_0' = [q_0]$, and
   $A' = \{[q]| q \in A\}$.
9. Output $\langle M' \rangle$."

  a. Show that M and M' are equivalent.
  b. Show that M' is minimal, that is, no DFA with fewer states recognizes the same language. You may use the result of Problem 1.35 without proof.
  c. Show that *MINIMIZE* operates in polynomial time.

*7.36 For a cnf-formula ϕ with m variables and c clauses, show that you can construct in polynomial time an NFA with $O(cm)$ states that accepts all nonsatisfying assignments, represented as Boolean strings of length m. Conclude that the problem of minimizing NFAs cannot be done in polynomial time unless P $\neq$ NP.

*7.37 A *2cnf-formula* is an AND of clauses, where each clause is an OR of at most two literals. Let $2SAT = \{\langle \phi \rangle | \phi$ is a satisfiable 2cnf-formula$\}$. Show that $2SAT \in$ P.

7.38 Modify the algorithm for context-free language recognition in the proof of Theorem 7.14 to give a polynomial time that produces a parse tree for a string, given the string and a CFG, if that grammar generates the string.

***7.39** The *difference hierarchy* D_iP is defined recursively as follows.

    a. $D_1P = NP$.

    b. $D_iP = \{A|\ A = B \setminus C \text{ for } B \text{ in NP and } C \text{ in } D_{i-1}P\}$.
    (Here $B \setminus C = B \cap \overline{C}$.)

For example, a language in D_2P is the difference of two NP languages. Sometimes D_2P is called DP (and may be written D^P). Let

$$Z = \{\langle G_1, k_1, G_2, k_2\rangle|\ G_1 \text{ has a } k_1\text{-clique and } G_2 \text{ doesn't have a } k_2\text{-clique}\}.$$

Show that Z is complete for DP. In other words, show that every language in DP is polynomial time reducible to Z.

***7.40** Let $MAX\text{-}CLIQUE = \{\langle G, k\rangle|$ the largest clique in G is of size exactly $k\}$. Use the result of Problem 7.39 to show that $MAX\text{-}CLIQUE$ is DP-complete.

8

SPACE COMPLEXITY

In this chapter we consider the complexity of computational problems in terms of the amount of space (or memory) that they require. Time and space are two of the most important considerations when we seek practical solutions to many computational problems. Space complexity shares many of the features of time complexity and serves as a further way of classifying problems according to their computational difficulty.

As we did with time complexity, we need to select a model for measuring the space used by an algorithm. We continue with the Turing machine model for the same reason that we used it to measure time. Turing machines are mathematically simple and close enough to real computers to give meaningful results.

DEFINITION 8.1

Let M be a deterministic Turing machine that halts on all inputs. We define the *space complexity* of M to be the function $f : \mathcal{N} \longrightarrow \mathcal{N}$, where $f(n)$ is the maximum number of tape cells that M scans on any input of length n. If the space complexity of M is $f(n)$, we also say that M runs in space $f(n)$.

If M is a nondeterministic Turing machine wherein all branches halt on all inputs, we define its space complexity $f(n)$ to be the maximum number of tape cells that M scans on any branch of its computation for any input of length n.

As with time complexity, we usually estimate the space complexity of Turing machines using asymptotic notation.

DEFINITION   **8.2** ....

Let $f: \mathcal{N} \longrightarrow \mathcal{N}$ be a function. The ***space complexity classes***, $\text{SPACE}(f(n))$ and $\text{NSPACE}(f(n))$, are defined as follows.

$$\text{SPACE}(f(n)) = \{L \mid L \text{ is a language decided by a } O(f(n)) \text{ space}$$
$$\text{deterministic Turing machine}\}.$$
$$\text{NSPACE}(f(n)) = \{L \mid L \text{ is a language decided by a } O(f(n)) \text{ space}$$
$$\text{nondeterministic Turing machine}\}.$$

EXAMPLE   **8.3** ....

In Chapter 7 we introduced the NP-complete problem *SAT*. Here, we show that *SAT* can be solved with a linear space algorithm. We believe that *SAT* cannot be solved with a polynomial time algorithm, much less with a linear time algorithm, because *SAT* is NP-complete. Space appears to be more powerful than time because space can be reused, whereas time cannot.

$M_1 -$ "On input $\langle \phi \rangle$, where ϕ is a Boolean formula:

1.   For each truth assignment to the variables $x_1, \ldots, x_m$ of ϕ:
2.   Evaluate ϕ on that truth assignment.
3.   If ϕ ever evaluated to 1, *accept*; if not, *reject*."

Machine M_1 clearly runs in linear space because each iteration of the loop can reuse the same portion of the tape. The machine only needs to store the current truth assignment and that can be done with $O(m)$ space. The number of variables m is at most n, the length of the input, so this machine runs in space $O(n)$.   ▪

EXAMPLE   **8.4** ....

Here, we illustrate the nondeterministic space complexity of a language. In the next section we show how determining the nondeterministic space complexity can be useful in determining its deterministic space complexity. Consider the problem of testing whether a nondeterministic finite automaton accepts any strings. Let

$$E_{\text{NFA}} = \{\langle A \rangle \mid A \text{ is a NFA and } L(A) = \emptyset\}.$$

We give a nondeterministic linear space algorithm that decides the complement of this language, $\overline{E_{\text{NFA}}}$. The idea behind this algorithm is to use nondeterminism to guess a string that is accepted by the NFA and to use linear space to keep track of which states the NFA could be in at a particular time. Note that this language is not known to be in NP or in coNP.

$N =$ "On input $\langle M \rangle$ where M is an NFA:

1. Place a marker on the start state of the NFA.
2. Repeat 2^q times, where q is the number of states of M:
3.   Nondeterministically select an input symbol and change the positions of the markers on M's states to simulate reading that symbol.
4. If a marker was ever placed on an accept state, *reject*; otherwise *accept*."

If M accepts any strings, it must accept one of length at most 2^q because in any longer string that is accepted the locations of the markers described in the preceding algorithm would repeat. The section of the string between the repetitions can be removed to obtain a shorter accepted string. Hence N decides E_{NFA}.

The only space needed by this algorithm is for storing the location of the markers, and doing so only requires linear space. Hence the algorithm runs in nondeterministic space $O(n)$. Next, we prove a theorem that provides information about the deterministic space complexity of E_{NFA}.

8.1

SAVITCH'S THEOREM

In this section we present one of the earliest results concerning space complexity, called Savitch's theorem. It shows that deterministic machines can simulate nondeterministic machines by using a surprisingly small amount of space. For time complexity, such a simulation seems to require an exponential increase in time. For space complexity, Savitch's theorem shows that any nondeterministic TM that uses $f(n)$ space can be converted to a deterministic TM that uses only $f^2(n)$ space.

THEOREM 8.5 ....

Savitch's theorem   For any[1] function $f \colon \mathcal{N} \longrightarrow \mathcal{N}$, where $f(n) > n$,

$$\mathrm{NSPACE}(f(n)) \subseteq \mathrm{SPACE}(f^2(n)).$$

....

PROOF IDEA   We need to simulate an $f(n)$ space NTM deterministically. A naive approach is to proceed by trying all the branches of the NTM's computation, one by one. The simulation needs to keep track of which branch it is currently trying so that it is able to go on to the next one. But a branch that uses $f(n)$ space may run for $2^{O(f(n))}$ steps, and each step may be a nondeterministic choice.

---

[1] On page 296, we show that Savitch's theorem also holds whenever $f(n) \geq \log n$.

Exploring the branches sequentially would require recording all of the choices used on a particular branch in order to be able to find the next branch. Therefore this approach may use $2^{O(f(n))}$ space, exceeding our goal of $O(f^2(n))$ space.

Instead, we take a different approach by considering the following more general problem. We are given two configurations of the NTM, c_1 and c_2, together with a number t, and we must test whether the NTM can get from c_1 to c_2 within t steps. We call this problem the **yieldability problem**. By solving the yieldability problem where c_1 is the start configuration, c_2 is the accept configuration, and t is the maximum number of steps that the nondeterministic machine can use, we can determine whether the machine accepts the input.

We give a deterministic, recursive algorithm that solves the yieldability problem. It operates by searching for an intermediate configuration c_m, and recursively testing both whether c_1 can get to c_m within $t/2$ steps and whether c_m can get to c_2 within $t/2$ steps. Reusing the space for each of the two recursive tests allows a significant saving of space.

This algorithm needs space for storing the recursion stack. Each level of the recursion uses $O(f(n))$ space to store a configuration. The depth of the recursion is $\log t$, where t is the maximum time that the nondeterministic machine may use on any branch. We have $t = 2^{O(f(n))}$, so $\log t = O(f(n))$. Hence the deterministic simulation uses $O(f^2(n))$ space.

PROOF Let N be an NTM deciding a language A in space $f(n)$. We construct a deterministic TM M deciding A. Machine M uses the procedure CANYIELD, which tests whether one of N's configurations can yield another within a specified number of steps. This procedure solves the yieldability problem described in the proof idea.

Let w be a string considered as input to N. For configurations c_1 and c_2 of N on w, and integer t, CANYIELD(c_1, c_2, t) outputs *accept* if, when started in configuration c_1, N has some sequence of nondeterministic choices that can cause it to enter configuration c_2 within t steps. If not, CANYIELD outputs *reject*.

CANYIELD = "On input c_1, c_2, and t:

1. If $t = 1$, then test directly whether $c_1 = c_2$ or whether c_1 yields c_2 in one step according to the rules of N. *Accept* if either test succeeds; *reject* if both fail.

2. If $t > 1$, then for each configuration c_m of N on w using space $f(n)$:

3.   Run CANYIELD$(c_1, c_m, \lceil \frac{t}{2} \rceil)$.[2]

4.   Run CANYIELD$(c_m, c_2, \lceil \frac{t}{2} \rceil)$.

5.   If steps 3 and 4 both accept, then *accept*.

6. If haven't yet accepted, *reject*."

Now we define M to simulate N as follows. We first modify N so that when it accepts it clears its tape and moves the head to the leftmost cell, thereby entering a

---

[2] The notation $\lceil \frac{t}{2} \rceil$ represents the "rounding up" of $\frac{t}{2}$ to the next larger integer.

configuration called c_{accept}. Let c_{start} be the start configuration of N on w. Select a constant d so that N has no more than $2^{df(n)}$ configurations using $f(n)$ tape, where n is the length of w. We know that $2^{df(n)}$ provides an upper bound on the running time of any branch of N on w.

$M =$ "On input w:

    1. Output the result of CANYIELD($c_{start}, c_{accept}, 2^{df(n)}$)."

Algorithm CANYIELD obviously solves the yieldability problem, and hence M correctly simulates N. We need to analyze it to see that M works within $O(f^2(n))$ space.

Whenever CANYIELD invokes itself recursively, it stores the values of c_1, c_2, and t on a stack so that these values may be restored upon return from the recursive invocation. Each level of the recursion thus uses $O(f(n))$ additional space. Furthermore, each level of the recursion divides the size of t in half. Initially t starts out equal to $2^{df(n)}$, so the depth of the recursion is $O(\log 2^{df(n)})$ or $O(f(n))$. Therefore the total space used is $O(f^2(n))$, as claimed.

One technical difficulty arises in this argument because algorithm M needs to know the value of $f(n)$ when it calls CANYIELD. We can handle this difficulty by modifying M so that it tries $f(n) = 1, 2, 3, \ldots$ For each value $f(n) = i$, the modified algorithm uses CANYIELD to determine whether the accept configuration is reachable and also to determine whether N uses at least space i by testing whether N can reach any of the configurations of length i from the start configuration. If the accept configuration is reachable, M accepts; if no configuration of length i is reachable, M rejects; and otherwise M continues with $f(n) = i+1$. (We could have handled this difficulty in another way by assuming that M can compute $f(n)$ within $O(f(n))$ space, but then we would need to add that assumption to the statement of the theorem).

8.2

THE CLASS PSPACE

By analogy with the class P we define the class PSPACE for space complexity.

DEFINITION   **8.6**

PSPACE is the class of languages that are decidable in polynomial space on a deterministic Turing machine. In other words,

$$\text{PSPACE} = \bigcup_k \text{SPACE}(n^k).$$

The nondeterministic counterpart, NPSPACE, of the class PSPACE may be defined analogously by using the NSPACE classes. However, Savitch's theorem implies that NPSPACE = PSPACE because the square of any polynomial is still a polynomial.

In Examples 8.3 and 8.4 we showed that SAT is in SPACE(n) and that E_{NFA} is in NSPACE(n) and hence, by Savitch's theorem, in SPACE(n^2). Therefore both languages are in PSPACE.

Let's examine the relationship of PSPACE with P and NP. It is easy to see that P $\subseteq$ PSPACE because a machine that runs quickly cannot use a great deal of space. More precisely, for $t(n) \geq n$, any machine that operates in time $t(n)$ can use at most $t(n)$ space because a machine can explore at most one new cell at each step of its computation. Similarly, NP $\subseteq$ NPSPACE, and so NP $\subseteq$ PSPACE.

Conversely, we can bound the time complexity of a Turing machine in terms of its space complexity. For $f(n) \geq n$, a TM that uses $f(n)$ space can have at most $n\, 2^{O(f(n))}$ different configurations, by a simple generalization of the proof of Lemma 5.7 on page 178. A Turing machine computation that halts may not repeat a configuration. Therefore a Turing machine[3] that uses space $f(n)$ must run in time $n\, 2^{O(f(n))}$, so PSPACE $\subseteq$ EXPTIME $= \bigcup_k$ TIME(2^{n^k}).

We summarize our knowledge of the relationships among the complexity classes defined so far in the series of containments

$$P \subseteq NP \subseteq PSPACE = NPSPACE \subseteq EXPTIME.$$

We don't know whether any of these containments is actually an equality. Someone may yet discover a simulation like the one in Savitch's theorem that merges some of these classes into the same class. However, in Chapter 9 we prove that P $\neq$ EXPTIME. Therefore at least one of the preceding containments is proper, but we are unable to say which! Indeed, most researchers believe that all the containments are proper. The following diagram depicts the relationships among these classes, assuming all are different.

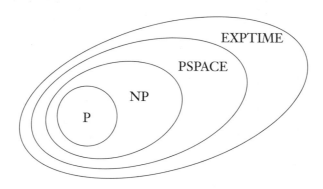

FIGURE **8.1**
Conjectured relationships among P, NP, PSPACE, and EXPTIME

---

[3]The requirement here that $f(n) \geq n$ is generalized later to $f(n) \geq \log n$, when we introduce Turing machines that use sublinear space on page 296.

8.3

PSPACE-COMPLETENESS

In Section 7.4 we introduced the category of NP-complete languages as representing the most difficult languages in NP. Proving that a language is NP-complete is strong evidence that the language is not in P. If it were, P and NP would be equal. In this section we introduce the analogous notion, PSPACE-completeness, for the class PSPACE.

DEFINITION 8.7 ....

A language B is **PSPACE-complete** if it satisfies two conditions:

1. B is in PSPACE, and
2. every A in PSPACE is polynomial time reducible to B.

If B merely satisfies condition 2, we say that it is **PSPACE-hard**.

In defining PSPACE-completeness, we use polynomial time reducibility as given in Definition 7.24. Why don't we define a notion of polynomial *space* reducibility and use that instead of polynomial *time* reducibility? To understand the answer to this important question, consider our motivation for defining complete problems in the first place.

Complete problems are important because they are examples of the most difficult problems in a complexity class. A complete problem is most difficult because any other problem in the class is easily reduced into it, so if we find an easy way to solve the complete problem, we can easily solve all other problems in the class. The reduction must be *easy*, relative to the complexity of typical problems in the class, for this reasoning to apply. If the reduction itself were difficult to compute, an easy solution to the complete problem wouldn't necessarily yield an easy solution to the the problems reducing to it.

Therefore, the rule is: Whenever we define complete problems for a complexity class, the reduction model must be more limited than the model used for defining the class itself.

THE TQBF PROBLEM

Our first example of a PSPACE-complete problem involves a generalization of the satisfiability problem. Recall that a **Boolean formula** is an expression that contains Boolean variables, the constants 0 and 1, and the Boolean operations $\land$, $\lor$, and $\neg$. We now introduce a more general type of Boolean formula.

The **quantifiers** $\forall$ (for all) and $\exists$ (there exists) make frequent appearances in mathematical statements. Writing the statement $\forall x\, \phi$ means that, for *every* value for the variable x, the statement ϕ is true. Similarly, writing the statement $\exists x\, \phi$ means that, for *some* value for the variable x, the statement ϕ is true. Sometimes,

$\forall$ is referred to as the ***universal quantifier*** and $\exists$ is the ***existential quantifier***. We say that the variable x immediately following the quantifier is ***bound*** to the quantifier.

For example, if we consider the natural numbers, the statement $\forall x\, [x + 1 > x]$ means that the successor $x + 1$ of every natural number x is greater than the number itself. Obviously, this statement is true. However, the statement $\exists y\, [y + y = 3]$ obviously is false. When interpreting the meaning of statements involving quantifiers, the ***universe*** from which the values are drawn must be considered. In the preceding cases the universe was the natural numbers, but if we took the real numbers instead, the existentially quantified statement would become true.

Statements may contain several quantifiers, as in $\forall x\, \exists y\, [y > x]$. For the universe of the natural numbers, this statement says that every natural number has another natural number larger than it. The order of the quantifiers is important. Reversing the order, as in the statement $\exists y\, \forall x\, [y > x]$, gives an entirely different meaning, namely, that some natural number is greater than all others. Obviously, the first statement is true and the second is false.

A quantifier may appear anywhere in a mathematical statement. It applies to the fragment of the statement appearing within the matched pair of parentheses or brackets following the quantified variable. This fragment is called the ***scope*** of the quantifier. Often, it is convenient to require that all quantifiers appear at the beginning of the statement and that each quantifier's scope is everything following it. Such statements are said to be in ***prenex normal form***. Any statement may be put into prenex normal form easily. We consider statements in this form only, unless otherwise indicated.

Boolean formulas with quantifiers are called ***quantified Boolean formulas***. For such formulas, the universe is $\{0, 1\}$. For example,

$$\phi = \forall x\, \exists y\, \big[(x \vee y) \wedge (\overline{x} \vee \overline{y}) \big]$$

is a quantified Boolean formula. Here, ϕ is true, but it would be false if the quantifiers $\forall x$ and $\exists y$ were reversed.

When each variable of a formula appears within the scope of some quantifier, the formula is said to be ***fully quantified***. A fully quantified Boolean formula is sometimes called a ***sentence*** and is always either true or false. For example, the preceding formula ϕ is fully quantified. However, if the initial part, $\forall x$, of ϕ were removed, the formula would no longer be fully quantified and would be neither true nor false.

The *TQBF* problem is to determine whether a fully quantified Boolean formula is true or false. We define the language

$$TQBF = \{\langle \phi \rangle \mid \phi \text{ is a true fully quantified Boolean formula}\}.$$

THEOREM 8.8 ....

TQBF is PSPACE-complete.

PROOF IDEA To show that *TQBF* is in PSPACE we give a straightforward algorithm that assigns values to the variables and recursively evaluates the truth of the formula for those values. From that information the algorithm can determine the truth of the original quantified formula.

To show that every language A in PSPACE reduces to *TQBF* in polynomial time, we begin with a polynomial space bounded Turing machine for A. Then we give a polynomial time reduction that maps a string to a quantified Boolean formula ϕ that encodes a simulation of the machine on that input. The formula is true if the machine accepts.

As a first attempt at this construction, let's try to imitate the proof of the Cook–Levin theorem, Theorem 7.22. We can construct a formula ϕ that simulates M on an input w by simulating the circuit representing the computation. A tableau for M on w has width $O(n^k)$, the space used by M, but its height is exponential in n^k, because M can run for exponential time. Thus, if we represent the tableau with a formula directly, we would end up with a formula of exponential size. However, a polynomial time reduction cannot produce an exponential size result, so this attempt fails to show $A \leq_{\mathrm{P}} TQBF$.

Instead, use a technique related to the proof of Savitch's theorem to construct the formula. The formula divides the tableau into halves and employs the universal quantifier to represent each half with the same part of the formula. The result is a much shorter formula.

PROOF First, we give a polynomial space algorithm deciding *TQBF*.

$T =$ "On input $\langle \phi \rangle$, a fully quantified Boolean formula:

1. If ϕ contains no quantifiers, then it is an expression with only constants, so evaluate ϕ and *accept* if it is true; otherwise *reject*.

2. If ϕ equals $\exists x\, \psi$, recursively call T on ψ, first with 0 substituted for x and then with 1 substituted for x. If either result is accept, then *accept*; otherwise *reject*.

3. If ϕ equals $\forall x\, \psi$, recursively call T on ψ, first with 0 substituted for x and then with 1 substituted for x. If both results are accept, then *accept*; otherwise *reject*."

Algorithm T obviously decides *TQBF*. To analyze its space complexity we observe that the depth of the recursion is at most the number of variables. At each level we need only store the value of one variable, so the total space used is $O(m)$, where m is the number of variables that appear in ϕ. Therefore T runs in linear space.

Next, we show that *TQBF* is PSPACE-hard. Let A be a language decided by a TM M in space n^k for some constant k. We give a polynomial time reduction from A to *TQBF*.

The reduction maps a string w to a quantified Boolean formula ϕ that is true if and only if M accepts w. To show how to construct ϕ we solve a more general problem. Using two collections of variables denoted c_1 and c_2 representing two configurations and a number $t > 0$, we construct a formula $\phi_{c_1, c_2, t}$. If we assign

c_1 and c_2 to actual configurations, the formula is true if and only if M can go from c_1 to c_2 in at most t steps. Then we can let ϕ be the formula $\phi_{c_{start}, c_{accept}, h}$, where $h = 2^{df(n)}$ for a constant d, chosen so that M has no more than $2^{df(n)}$ possible configurations on an input of length n.

The formula encodes the contents of tape cells as in the proof of the Cook–Levin theorem. Each cell has several variables associated with it, one for each tape symbol and state, corresponding to the possible settings of that cell. Each configuration has n^k cells and so is encoded by $O(n^k)$ variables.

If $t = 1$, we can easily construct $\phi_{c_1, c_2, t}$. We design the formula to say that either c_1 equals c_2, or c_2 follows from c_1 in a single step of M. We express the equality by writing a Boolean expression saying that each of the variables representing c_1 contains the same Boolean value as the corresponding variable representing c_2. We express the second possibility by using the technique presented in the proof of the Cook–Levin theorem. That is, we can express that c_1 yields c_2 in a single step of M by writing Boolean expressions stating that the contents of each triple of c_1's cells correctly yields the contents of the corresponding triple of c_2's cells.

If $t > 1$, we construct $\phi_{c_1, c_2, t}$ recursively. As a warmup let's try one idea that doesn't quite work and then fix it. Let

$$\phi_{c_1, c_2, t} = \exists m_1 \left[\phi_{c_1, m_1, \lceil \frac{t}{2} \rceil} \wedge \phi_{m_1, c_2, \lceil \frac{t}{2} \rceil} \right].$$

The symbol m_1 represents a configuration of M. Writing $\exists m_1$ is shorthand for $\exists x_1, \ldots, x_l$, where $l = O(n^k)$ and $x_1, \ldots, x_l$ are the variables that encode m_1. So this construction of $\phi_{c_1, c_2, t}$ says that M can go from c_1 to c_2 in at most t steps if some intermediate configuration m_1 exists, whereby M can go from c_1 to m_1 in at most $\lceil \frac{t}{2} \rceil$ steps and then from m_1 to c_2 in at most $\lceil \frac{t}{2} \rceil$ steps. Then we construct the two formulas $\phi_{c_1, m_1, \lceil \frac{t}{2} \rceil}$ and $\phi_{m_1, c_2, \lceil \frac{t}{2} \rceil}$ recursively.

The formula $\phi_{c_1, c_2, t}$ has the correct value; that is, it is TRUE whenever M can go from c_1 to c_2 within t steps. However, it is too big. Every level of the recursion involved in the construction cuts t in half but roughly doubles the size of the formula. Hence we end up with a formula of size roughly t. Initially $t = 2^{df(n)}$, so this method gives an exponentially large formula.

To reduce the size of the formula we use the $\forall$ quantifier in addition to the $\exists$ quantifier. Let

$$\phi_{c_1, c_2, t} = \exists m_1 \, \forall (c_3, c_4) \in \{(c_1, m_1), (m_1, c_2)\} \left[\phi_{c_3, c_4, \lceil \frac{t}{2} \rceil} \right].$$

The introduction of the new variables representing the configurations c_3 and c_4 allows us to "fold" the two recursive subformulas into a single subformula, while preserving the original meaning. By writing $\forall (c_3, c_4) \in \{(c_1, m_1), (m_1, c_2)\}$, we indicate that the variables representing the configurations c_3 and c_4 may take the values of the variables of c_1 and m_1 or of m_1 and c_2, respectively, and that the resulting formula $\phi_{c_3, c_4, \lceil \frac{t}{2} \rceil}$ is true in either case. We may replace the construct $\forall x \in \{y, z\} \, [\ldots]$ by the equivalent construct $\forall x \, [(x = y \vee x = z) \to \ldots]$ to obtain a syntactically correct quantified Boolean formula. Recall that in Section 0.2 we showed that Boolean implication ($\to$) and Boolean equality ($=$) can be expressed in terms of AND and OR.

To calculate to size of the formula $\phi_{c_{start}, c_{accept}, h}$, where $h = 2^{df(n)}$, we note that recursion adds a portion of the formula that is linear in the size of the configurations and thus of size $O(f(n))$. The number of levels of the recursion is $\log(2^{df(n)})$, or $O(f(n))$. Hence the size of the resulting formula is $O(f^2(n))$.

WINNING STRATEGIES FOR GAMES

For the purposes of this section, a ***game*** is loosely defined to be a competition in which two opposing parties each attempt to achieve some goal according to prespecified rules. Games appear in many forms, from board games such as chess to economic and war games that model corporate or societal conflict.

Games are closely related to quantifiers. A quantified statement has a corresponding game; conversely, a game often has a corresponding quantified statement. These correspondences are helpful in several ways. For one, expressing a mathematical statement that uses many quantifiers in terms of the corresponding game may give insight into the statement's meaning. For another, expressing a game in terms of a quantified statement aids in understanding the complexity of the game. To illustrate the correspondence between games and quantifiers, we turn to an artificial game called the ***formula game***.

Let $\phi = \exists x_1 \forall x_2 \exists x_3 \cdots Q x_k [\psi]$ be a quantified Boolean formula in prenex normal form. Here Q represents either a $\forall$ or an $\exists$ quantifier. We associate a game with ϕ as follows. Two players, called Player A and Player E, take turns selecting the values of the variables $x_1, \ldots, x_k$. Player A selects values for the variables that are bound to $\forall$ quantifiers and player E selects values for the variables that are bound to $\exists$ quantifiers. The order of play is the same as that of the quantifiers at the beginning of the formula. At the end of play we use the values that the players have selected for the variables and declare that Player E has won the game if ψ, the part of the formula with the quantifiers stripped off, is now TRUE. Player A has won if ψ is now FALSE.

EXAMPLE **8.9**

Say that ϕ_1 is the formula

$$\exists x_1 \forall x_2 \exists x_3 \left[(x_1 \vee x_2) \wedge (x_2 \vee x_3) \wedge (\overline{x_2} \vee \overline{x_3}) \right].$$

In the formula game for ϕ_1, Player E picks the value of x_1, then Player A picks the value of x_2, and finally Player E picks the value of x_3.

We illustrate a sample play of this game. As usual, we represent the Boolean value TRUE with 1 and FALSE with 0. Say Player E picks $x_1 = 1$, then Player A picks $x_2 = 0$, and finally Player E picks $x_3 = 1$. With these values for x_1, x_2, and x_3, the subformula

$$(x_1 \vee x_2) \wedge (x_2 \vee x_3) \wedge (\overline{x_2} \vee \overline{x_3})$$

is 1, so Player E has won the game. In fact, Player E may always win this game by selecting $x_1 = 1$ and then selecting x_3 to be the negation of whatever Player A selects for x_2. We say that Player E has a ***winning strategy*** for this game. A player has a winning strategy for a game if that player wins when both sides play optimally.

Now let's change the formula slightly to get a game in which Player A has a winning strategy. Let ϕ_2 be the formula

$$\exists x_1 \, \forall x_2 \, \exists x_3 \, \big[(x_1 \vee x_2) \wedge (x_2 \vee x_3) \wedge (x_2 \vee \overline{x_3}) \big].$$

Player A now has a winning strategy because, no matter what Player E selects for x_1, Player A may select $x_2 = 0$, thereby falsifying the part of the formula appearing after the quantifiers, whatever Player E's last move may be.

We next consider the problem of determining which player has a winning strategy in the formula game associated with a particular formula. Let

$$FORMULA\text{-}GAME = \{\langle \phi \rangle | \text{ Player E has a winning strategy in}$$
$$\text{the formula game associated with } \phi\}.$$

THEOREM 8.10 ···

FORMULA-GAME is PSPACE-complete

···

PROOF IDEA   *FORMULA-GAME* is PSPACE-complete for a simple reason, namely, it is the same as *TQBF*. To see that *FORMULA-GAME* = *TQBF*, observe that a formula is TRUE exactly when Player E has a winning strategy in the associated formula game because both possibilities have the same semantic content.

PROOF   The formula $\phi = \exists x_1 \, \forall x_2 \, \exists x_3 \cdots [\psi]$ is TRUE when some setting for x_1 exists such that, for any setting of x_2, a setting of x_3 exists such that, and so on ..., where ψ is TRUE under the settings of the variables. Similarly, Player E has a winning strategy in the game associated with ϕ when Player E can make some assignment to x_1 such that, for any setting of x_2, Player E can make an assignment to x_3 such that, and so on ..., ψ is TRUE under these settings of the variables.

The same reasoning applies when the formula doesn't alternate between existential and universal quantifiers. If ϕ has the form $\forall x_1, x_2, x_3 \, \exists x_4, x_5 \, \forall x_6 \, [\psi]$, Player A would make the first three moves in the formula game to assign values to x_1, x_2, and x_3; then Player E would make two moves to assign x_4 and x_5; and finally Player A would assign a value x_6.

Hence, $\phi \in TQBF$ exactly when $\phi \in FORMULA\text{-}GAME$, and the theorem follows from Theorem 8.8.

···

GENERALIZED GEOGRAPHY

Now that we know that the formula game is PSPACE-complete, we can establish the PSPACE-completeness or PSPACE-hardness of some other games more easily. We'll begin begin with a generalization of the game geography and later discuss games such as chess, checkers, and GO.

Geography is a child's game in which players take turns naming cities from anywhere in the world. Each city chosen must begin with the same letter that ended the previous city's name. Repetition isn't permitted. The game starts with some designated starting city and ends when some player loses because he or she is unable to continue. For example, if the game starts with Peoria, then Amherst might legally follow (because Peoria ends with the letter *a*, and Amherst begins with the letter *a*), then Tucson, then Nashua, and so on until one player gets stuck and thereby loses.

We can model this game with a directed graph whose nodes are the cities of the world. We draw an arrow from one city to another if the first can lead to the second according to the game rules. In other words, the graph contains an edge from a city X to a city Y if city X ends with the same letter that begins city Y. We illustrate a portion of the geography graph in the following figure.

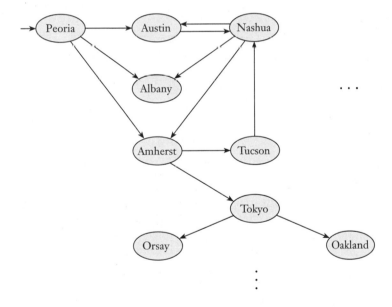

FIGURE **8.2**
Portion of the graph representing the geography game

When the rules of geography are interpreted for this graphic representation, one player starts by selecting the designated start node and then the players take turns alternately by picking nodes that form a simple path in the graph. The requirement that the path be simple (i.e., doesn't use any node more than once) corresponds to the requirement that a city may not be repeated. The first player unable to extend the path loses the game.

In **generalized geography** we take an arbitrary directed graph with a designated start node instead of the graph associated with the actual cities. For example, the following graph is an example of a generalized geography game.

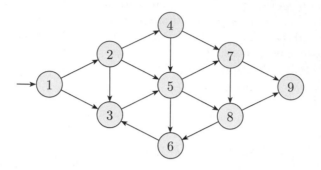

FIGURE 8.3
A sample generalized geography game

Say that Player I is the one who moves first and Player II second. In this example, Player I has a winning strategy as follows. Player I starts at node 1, the designated start node. Node 1 points only at nodes 2 and 3, so Player I's first move must be one of these two choices. He chooses 3. Now Player II must move, but node 3 points only to node 5, so she is forced to select node 5. Then Player I selects 6, from choices 6, 7, and 8. Now Player II must play from node 6, but it points only to node 3, and 3 was previously played. Player II is stuck, and thus Player I wins.

If we change the example by reversing the direction of the edge between nodes 3 and 6, Player II has a winning strategy. Can you see it? If Player I starts out with node 3 as before, Player II responds with 6 and wins immediately, so Player I's only hope is to begin with 2. In that case, however, Player II responds with 4. If Player I now takes 5, Player II wins with 6. If Player I takes 7, Player II wins with 9. No matter what Player I does, Player II can find a way to win, so Player II has a winning strategy.

The problem of determining which player has a winning strategy in a generalized geography game is PSPACE-complete. Let

$$GG = \{\langle G, b \rangle | \text{ Player I has a winning strategy for the generalized}$$
$$\text{geography game played on graph } G \text{ starting at node } b\}.$$

THEOREM 8.11 ....

GG is PSPACE-complete.

PROOF IDEA A recursive algorithm similar to the one used for *TQBF* in Theorem 8.8 determines which player has a winning strategy. This algorithm runs in polynomial space and so $GG \in \text{PSPACE}$.

To prove that GG is PSPACE-hard, we give a polynomial time reduction from *FORMULA-GAME* to *GG*. This reduction converts a formula game to a generalized geography graph so that play on the graph mimics play in the formula game. In effect, the players in the generalized geography game are really playing an encoded form of the formula game.

PROOF The following algorithm decides whether Player I has a winning strategy in instances of generalized geography; in other words, it decides *GG*. We show that it runs in polynomial space.

$M =$ "On input $\langle G, b \rangle$, where G is a directed graph and b is a node of G:

1. Remove node b and all arrows touching it to get a new graph G_1.
2. For each of the nodes $b_1, b_2, \ldots, b_k$ that b originally pointed at, recursively call M on $\langle G_1, b_i \rangle$.
3. If any of these accept, Player II has a winning strategy in the original game, so *reject*. Otherwise, Player II doesn't have a winning strategy, so Player I must; therefore *accept*."

This algorithm clearly decides G. The only space required is for storing the recursion stack. Each level of the recursion adds a single node to the stack, and at most m levels occur, where m is the number of nodes in G. Hence the algorithm runs in linear space.

To establish the PSPACE-hardness of GG, we show that *FORMULA-GAME* is polynomial time reducible to *GG*. The reduction maps the formula

$$\phi = \exists x_1 \, \forall x_2 \, \exists x_3 \, \cdots \, Qx_k \, [\psi]$$

to an instance of the generalized geography $\langle G, b \rangle$. Here we assume for simplicity that ϕ's quantifiers begin and end with $\exists$ and that they strictly alternate between $\exists$ and $\forall$. A formula that doesn't conform to this assumption may be converted to a slightly larger one that does by adding extra quantifiers binding otherwise unused or "dummy" variables. We assume also that ψ is in conjunctive normal form (see Problem 8.13).

The reduction constructs a geography game on a graph G where optimal play mimics optimal play of the formula game on ϕ. Player I in the geography game takes the role of player E in the formula game, and Player II takes the role of Player A.

The structure of graph G is partially shown in Figure 8.4. Play starts at node b, which appears at the top left-hand side of G. Underneath b, a sequence of diamond structures appear, one for each of the variables of ϕ. Before getting to the right-hand side of G, let's see how play proceeds on the left-hand side.

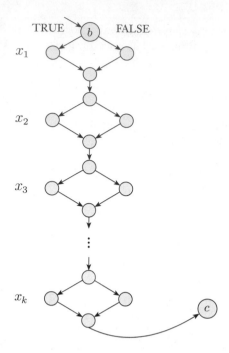

FIGURE **8.4**
Partial structure of the geography game simulating the formula game

Play starts at b. Player I must select one of the two edges going from b. These edges correspond to Player E's possible choices at the beginning of the formula game. The left-hand choice for Player I corresponds to TRUE for Player E in the formula game and the right-hand choice to FALSE. After Player I has selected one of these edges, say, the left-hand one, Player II moves. Only one outgoing edge is present, so this move is forced. Similarly, Player I's next move is forced and play continues from the top of the second diamond. Now two edges again are present, but Player II gets the choice. This choice corresponds to Player A's first move in the formula game. As play continues in this way, Players I and II chose a rightward or leftward path through each of the diamonds.

After play passes through all the diamonds, the head of the path is at the bottom node in the last diamond, and it is Player I's turn because we assumed that the last quantifier is ∃. Player I's next move is forced. Then they are at node c in the figure, and Player II makes the next move.

This point in the geography game corresponds to the end of play in the formula game. The chosen path through the diamonds corresponds to an assignment to ϕ's variables. Under that assignment, if ψ is TRUE, Player E wins the formula game, whereas if ψ is FALSE, Player A wins. The structure on the right-hand side of the figure guarantees that Player I can win if Player E has won and that Player II can win if Player A has won, as follows. At node c, Player II may chose a node corresponding to one of ψ's clauses. Then Player I may chose a node corresponding to a literal in that clause. The nodes corresponding to unnegated literals are connected to the left-hand (TRUE) sides of the diamond for associated variables, and similarly for negated literals and right-hand (FALSE) sides as shown in the following figure.

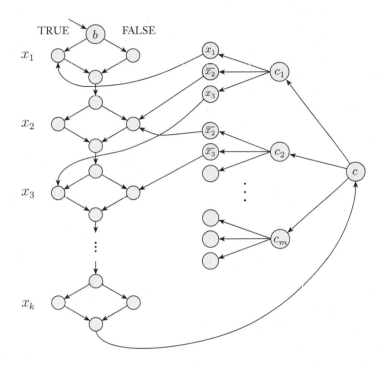

FIGURE   **8.5**

Full structure of the geography game simulating the formula game, where
$\phi = \exists x_1 \, \forall x_2 \cdots Q x_k \, [(x_1 \vee \overline{x_2} \vee x_3) \wedge (\overline{x_2} \vee \overline{x_3} \vee \cdots) \wedge \cdots \wedge (\quad)]$

If ϕ is FALSE, Player II may win by selecting the unsatisfied clause. Any literal that Player I may then pick is FALSE and is connected to the side of the diamond that hasn't yet been played. Thus Player II may play the node in the diamond, but then Player I is unable to move and loses. If ϕ is TRUE, any clause that Player II picks contains a TRUE literal. Player I selects that literal after Player II's move. Because the literal is TRUE, it is connected to the side of the diamond that has already been played, so Player II is unable to move and loses.

....

Theorem 8.11 shows that no polynomial time algorithm exists for optimal play in generalized geography unless P = PSPACE. We'd like to prove a similar theorem regarding the difficulty of computing optimal play in board games such as chess, but an obstacle arises. Only a finite number of different game positions may occur using the standard 8×8 chess board. In principle, all these positions may be placed in a table, along with the best move in each position. The table would be too large to fit inside our galaxy but, being finite, could be stored in the control of a Turing machine (or even that of a finite automaton!). Thus the machine would be able to play optimally in linear time using table lookup. Perhaps at some time in the future, methods that can quantify the complexity of finite problems will be developed, but current methods are asymptotic and hence apply only to the rate of growth of the complexity as the problem size increases—not to any fixed size. Nevertheless, we can give some evidence for the difficulty of computing optimal play for many board games by generalizing them to an $n \times n$ board. Such generalizations of chess, checkers, and GO have been shown to be PSPACE-hard or hard for even larger complexity classes, depending on the details of the generalization.

8.4

THE CLASSES L AND NL

Until now, we have considered only time and space complexity bounds that are at least linear, that is, bounds where $f(n)$ is at least n. Now we examine smaller, *sublinear* space bounds. In time complexity, sublinear bounds are insufficient for reading the entire input, so we don't consider them here. In sublinear space complexity the machine may read the entire input but it doesn't have enough space to store the input. To consider this situation meaningfully, we must modify our computational model.

We introduce a Turing machine with two tapes: a read-only input tape and a read/write work tape. On the read-only tape the input head can detect symbols but not change them. This head must remain on the portion of the tape containing the input. We provide a way for the machine to detect when the head is at the left-hand and right-hand ends of the input. The work tape may be read and written in the usual way. Only the cells scanned on the work tape contribute to the space complexity of this type of Turing machine.

Think of a read-only input tape as a CD-ROM, a device used for input on many personal computers. Often, the CD-ROM contains more data than the computer can store in its main memory. Sublinear space algorithms allow the computer to manipulate the data without storing all of it in main memory.

For space bounds that are at least linear, the two-tape TM model is equivalent to the standard one-tape model (see Exercise 8.1). For sublinear space bounds, we use only the two-tape model.

DEFINITION 8.12

L is the class of languages that are decidable in logarithmic space on a deterministic Turing machine. In other words,

$$L = SPACE(\log n).$$

NL is the class of languages that are decidable in logarithmic space on a nondeterministic Turing machine. In other words,

$$NL = NSPACE(\log n).$$

We focus on $\log n$ space instead of, say, $\sqrt{n}$ or $\log^2 n$ space, for several reasons that are similar to those for our selection of polynomial time and space bounds. Logarithmic space is just large enough to solve a number of interesting computational problems, and it has attractive mathematical properties such as robustness even when machine model and input encoding method change. Pointers into the input may be represented in logarithmic space, so one way to think about the power of log space algorithms is to consider the power of a fixed number of input pointers.

EXAMPLE 8.13

The language $A = \{0^k 1^k | k \geq 0\}$ is a member of L. In section 7.1 on page 225 we described a Turing machine that decides A by zigzagging back and forth across the input, crossing off the 0s and 1s as they are matched. That algorithm uses linear space to record which positions have been crossed off, but it can be modified to use only log space.

The log space TM for A cannot cross off the 0s and 1s that have been matched on the input tape because that tape is read-only. Instead, the machine counts the number of 0s and, separately, the number of 1s in binary on the work tape. The only space required is that used to record the two counters. In binary, each counter uses only logarithmic space, and hence the algorithm runs in $O(\log n)$ space. Therefore $A \in$ L.

EXAMPLE 8.14

Recall the language

$PATH = \{\langle G, s, t\rangle | G$ is a directed graph that has a directed path from s to $t\}$

defined in Section 7.2. Theorem 7.12 shows that $PATH$ is in P but that the algorithm given uses linear space. We don't know whether $PATH$ can be solved in logarithmic space deterministically, but we do know a nondeterministic log space algorithm for $PATH$.

The nondeterministic log space Turing machine deciding *PATH* operates by starting at node s and nondeterministically guessing the steps of a path from s to t. The machine records only the position of the current node at each step on the work tape, not the entire path (which would exceed the logarithmic space requirement). The machine nondeterministically selects the next node from among those pointed at by the current node. Then it repeats this action until it reaches node t and *accepts*, or until it has gone on for m steps and *rejects*, where m is the number of nodes in the graph. Thus *PATH* is in NL.

Our earlier claim that any $f(n)$ space bounded Turing machine also runs in time $2^{O(f(n))}$ is no longer true for very small space bounds. For example, a Turing machine that uses $O(1)$ (i.e., constant) space may run for n steps. To obtain a bound on the running time that applies for every space bound $f(n)$ we give the following definition.

DEFINITION 8.15 ···

If M is a Turing machine that has a separate read-only input tape and w is an input, a **configuration of M on w** is a setting of the state, the work tape, and the positions of the two tape heads. The input w is not a part of the configuration of M on w.

If M runs in $f(n)$ space and w is an input of length n, the number of configurations of M on w is $n2^{O(f(n))}$. To explain this result, let's say that M has c states and g tape symbols. The number of strings that can appear on the work tape is $g^{f(n)}$. The input head can be in one of n positions and the work tape head can be in one of $f(n)$ positions. Therefore the total number of configurations of M on w, which is an upper bound on the running time of M on w, is $cnf(n)g^{f(n)}$, or $n2^{O(f(n))}$.

We focus almost exclusively on space bounds $f(n)$ that are at least $\log n$. Our earlier claim that the time complexity of a machine is at most exponential in its space complexity remains true for such bounds because $n2^{O(f(n))}$ is $2^{O(f(n))}$ when $f(n) \geq \log n$.

Recall that Savitch's theorem shows that we can convert nondeterministic TMs to deterministic TMs and increase the space complexity $f(n)$ by only a squaring, provided that $f(n) \geq n$. We can extend Savitch's theorem to hold for sublinear space bounds down to $f(n) \geq \log n$. The proof is identical to the original we gave on page 279, except that we use Turing machines with a read-only input tape and instead of referring to configurations of N we refer to configurations of N on w. Storing a configuration of N on w uses $\log(n2^{O(f(n))}) = \log n + O(f(n))$ space. If $f(n) \geq \log n$, the storage used is $O(\log f(n))$ and the remainder of the proof remains the same.

8.5 ■■■■■■■■■■■■■■■■■■■■■■■■■■■■■■■■■■

NL-COMPLETENESS

As we mentioned in Example 8.14, the *PATH* problem is known to be in NL but isn't known to be in L. We believe that *PATH* doesn't belong to L but we don't know how to prove this conjecture. In fact, we don't know of any problem in NL that can be proven to be outside L. Analogous to the question of whether P = NP we have the question of whether L = NL.

As a step toward resolving the L versus NL question, we can exhibit certain languages that are NL-complete. As with complete languages for other complexity classes, the NL-complete languages are examples of languages that are, in a certain sense, the most difficult languages in NL. If L and NL are different, all NL-complete languages don't belong to L.

As with our previous definitions of completeness, we define an NL-complete language to be one which is in NL and to which any other language in NL is reducible. However, we don't use polynomial time reducibility here because, as you will see, all problems in NL are solvable in polynomial time. Therefore every two problems in P except $\emptyset$ and Σ^* are polynomial time reducible to one another (see the discussion of polynomial time reducibility in the definition of PSPACE-completeness on page 283 and Problem 7.17). Hence polynomial time reducibility is too strong to differentiate problems in NL from one another. Instead we use a new type of reducibility called log space reducibility.

DEFINITION 8.16 ···

A *log space transducer* is a Turing machine with a read-only input tape, a write-only output tape, and a read/write work tape. The work tape may contain $O(\log n)$ symbols. A log space transducer M computes a function $f: \Sigma^* \longrightarrow \Sigma^*$, where $f(w)$ is the string remaining on the output tape after M halts when it is started with w on its input tape. We call f a *log space computable function*. Language A is *log space reducible* to language B, written $A \leq_L B$, if A is mapping reducible to B using a log space computable function f.

Now we are ready to define NL-completeness.

DEFINITION 8.17 ···

A language B is *NL-complete* if

1. $B \in NL$, and
2. every A in NL is log space reducible to B.

If one language is log space reducible to another language already known to be in L, the original language is also in L, as the following theorem demonstrates.

THEOREM **8.18** ··

If $A \leq_L B$ and $B \in L$, then $A \in L$.

PROOF A tempting approach to the proof of this theorem follows the model set by Theorem 7.25, the analogous result for polynomial time reducibility. In that approach, a log space algorithm for A first maps its input w to $f(w)$, using the log space reduction f, and then applies the log space algorithm for B. However, the storage required for $f(w)$ may be too large to fit within the log space bound, so we need to modify this approach.

Instead, A's machine M_A computes individual symbols of $f(w)$ as requested by B's machine M_B. In the simulation, M_A keeps track of where M_B's input head would be on $f(w)$. Every time B moves, M_A restarts the computation of f on w from the beginning and ignores all of the output except for the desired location of $f(w)$. Doing so may require occasional recomputation of parts of $f(w)$ and so is inefficient in its time complexity. The advantage of this method is that only a single symbol of $f(w)$ need be stored at any point, in effect trading time for space.

··

COROLLARY **8.19** ··

If any NL-complete language is in L, then L = NL.

SEARCHING IN GRAPHS

THEOREM **8.20** ··

PATH is NL-complete.

··

PROOF IDEA Example 8.14 shows that *PATH* is in NL, so we only need to show that *PATH* is NL-hard. In other words, we must show that every language A in NL is log space reducible to *PATH*.

The idea behind the log space reduction from A to *PATH* is to construct a graph that represents the computation of the nondeterministic log space Turing machine for A. The reduction maps a string w to a graph whose nodes correspond to the configurations of the NTM on input w. One node points to a second node if the corresponding first configuration can yield the second configuration in a single step of the NTM. Hence the machine accepts w whenever some path from the node corresponding to the start configuration leads to the node corresponding to the accepting configuration.

PROOF We show how to give a log space reduction from any language A in NL to *PATH*. Say that NTM machine M decides A in $O(\log n)$ space. Given an input w, we construct $\langle G, s, t \rangle$ in log space, where G is a directed graph that contains a path from s to t if and only if M accepts w.

The nodes of G are the configurations of M on w. For configurations c_1 and c_2 of M on w, the pair (c_1, c_2) is an edge of G if c_2 is one of the possible next configurations of M starting from c_1. More precisely, if M's transition function indicates that c_1's state together with the tape symbols under its input and work tape heads can yield the next state and head actions to make c_1 into c_2, then (c_1, c_2) is an edge of G. The node s is the start configuration of M on w. Machine M is modified to have a unique accepting configuration, and we designate this configuration to be node t.

This mapping reduces A to $PATH$ because, whenever M accepts its input, some branch of its computation accepts, which corresponds to a path from the start configuration s to the accepting configuration t in G. Conversely, if some path exists from s to t in G, some computation branch accepts when M runs on input w, and M accepts w.

To show that the reduction operates in log space, we give a log space transducer which, on input w, outputs a description of G. This description comprises two lists: G's nodes and G's edges. Listing the nodes is easy because each node is a configuration of M on w and can be represented in $c \log n$ space for some constant c. The transducer sequentially goes through all possible strings of length $c \log n$, tests whether each is a legal configuration of M on w, and outputs those that pass the test. The transducer lists the edges similarly. Log space is sufficient for verifying that a configuration c_1 of M on w can yield configuration c_2 because the transducer only needs to examine the actual tape contents under the head locations given in c_1 to determine that M's transition function would give configuration c_2 as a result. The transducer tries all pairs (c_1, c_2) in turn to find which qualify as edges of G. Those that do are added to the output tape.

One immediate spinoff of Theorem 8.20 is the following corollary which states that NL is a subset of P.

COROLLARY 8.21 ....

NL $\subseteq$ P.

PROOF   Theorem 8.20 shows that any language in NL is log space reducible to $PATH$. Recall that a Turing machine that uses space $f(n)$ runs in time $n \, 2^{O(f(n))}$, so a reducer that runs in log space also runs in polynomial time. Therefore any language in NL is polynomial time reducible to $PATH$, which in turn is in P, by Theorem 7.12. We know that every language that is polynomial time reducible to a language in P is also in P, so the proof is complete.

8.6

NL EQUALS CONL

This section contains one of the most surprising results known concerning the relationships among complexity classes. The classes NP and coNP are generally believed to be different. At first glance, the same appears to hold for the classes NL and coNL. The fact that NL equals coNL, as we are about to prove, shows that our intuition about computation still has many gaps in it.

THEOREM **8.22** ....

NL = coNL.

....

PROOF IDEA   To show that every problem in coNL is also in NL, we show that $\overline{PATH}$ is in NL because $PATH$ is NL-complete. The NL algorithm M that we present for $\overline{PATH}$ must have an accepting computation whenever the input graph G does *not* contain a path from s to t.

First, lets tackle an easier problem. Let c be the number of nodes in G that are reachable from s. We assume that c is provided as an input to M and show how to use c to solve $\overline{PATH}$. Later we show how to compute c.

Given G, s, t, and c, the machine M operates as follows. One by one, M goes through all the nodes of G and nondeterministically guesses whether each one is reachable from s. Whenever a node u is guessed to be reachable, M verifies this fact by guessing a path from s to u. If a computation branch fails to verify the guess within m steps, it rejects. In addition, if a branch guesses that t is reachable, it rejects. Machine M counts the number of nodes that have been verified to be reachable. When a branch has gone through all of G's nodes, it checks that the number of nodes that it verified to be reachable from s equals c, the number of nodes that actually are reachable, and rejects if not. Otherwise, this branch accepts.

In other words, if M nondeterministically selects exactly c nodes reachable from s, not including t, and proves that each is reachable from s by guessing the path, M knows that the remaining nodes, including t, are *not* reachable, so it can accept.

Next, we show how to calculate c, the number of nodes reachable from s. We describe a nondeterministic log space procedure whereby at least one computation branch has the correct value for c and all other branches reject. Say that G has m nodes.

For each i from 0 to m, define A_i to be the collection of nodes of G of distance at most i from s (i.e., having a path of length at most i from s). So $A_0 = \{s\}$, each $A_i \subseteq A_{i+1}$, and A_m contains all nodes that are reachable from s. Let c_i be the number of nodes in A_i. We next describe a procedure that calculates c_{i+1} from c_i. Repeated application of this procedure obtains the desired value of $c = c_m$.

We calculate c_{i+1} from c_i, using an idea similar to the one presented earlier in this proof sketch. The algorithm goes through all the nodes of G, determines whether each is a member of A_{i+1}, and counts the members.

To determine whether a node v is in A_{i+1}, we use an inner loop to go through all the nodes of G and guess whether each node is in A_i. Each positive guess is verified by guessing the path of length at most i from s. For each node u verified to be in A_i, the algorithm tests whether (u, v) is an edge of G. If it is an edge, v is in A_{i+1}. Additionally, the number of nodes verified to be in A_i is counted. At the completion of the inner loop, if the total number of nodes verified to be in A_i is not c_i, all of A_i has not been found, so this computation branch rejects. If the count does equal c_i and v has not yet been shown to be in A_{i+1}, we can conclude that it isn't in A_{i+1}. Then we go on to the next v in the outer loop.

PROOF   Here is an algorithm for $\overline{PATH}$.

$M = $ "On input $\langle G, s, t \rangle$:

1. Let $c_0 = 0$.
2. For $i = 0$ to $m - 1$:
3.   Let $c_{i+1} = 0$.
4.   Let $d = 0$.
5.   For each node v in G:
6.   For each node u in G:
7.   Nondeterministically either perform or skip these steps:
8.   Nondeterministically follow a path of length i from s and if none of the nodes encountered are u, *reject*.
9.   Increment d.
10.   If (u, v) is a edge of G, increment c_{i+1}.
11.   If $d \neq c_i$, then *reject*.
12.   For each node u in G:
13.   Nondeterministically either perform or skip these steps:
14.   Nondeterministically follow a path of length i from s and if none of the nodes encountered are u, *reject*.
15.   If $u = t$, then *reject*.
16.   Increment d.
17.   If $d \neq c_m$, then *reject*; otherwise, *accept*."

This algorithm only needs to store c_i, d, i, j, and a pointer to the head of a path, at any given time. Hence it runs in log space.

We summarize our present knowledge of the relationships among several complexity classes as follows:

$$L \subseteq NL = coNL \subseteq P \subseteq PSPACE.$$

We don't know whether any of these containments are proper, although we prove $\mathrm{NL} \subsetneq \mathrm{PSPACE}$[4] in Corollary 9.6 of Chapter 9. Consequently, either $\mathrm{coNL} \subsetneq \mathrm{P}$ or $\mathrm{P} \subsetneq \mathrm{PSPACE}$ must hold, but we don't know which one does! Most researchers conjecture that all of these containments are proper.

EXERCISES

8.1 Show that for any function $f \colon \mathcal{N} \longrightarrow \mathcal{N}$, where $f(n) \geq n$, the space complexity class $\mathrm{SPACE}(f(n))$ is the same whether you define the class by using the single-tape TM model or the two tape read-only input TM model.

8.2 Consider the following position in the standard tic-tac-toe game.

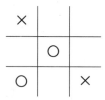

Say that it is the ✕-player's turn to move next. Describe the winning strategy for this player. (Recall that a winning strategy isn't merely the best move to make in the current position. It also includes all the responses that this player must make in order to win, however the opponent moves.)

8.3 Consider the following generalized geography game wherein the start node is the one with the arrow pointing in from nowhere. Does Player I have a winning strategy? Does Player II? Give reasons for your answers.

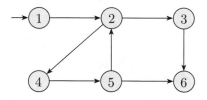

8.4 Show that PSPACE is closed under the operations union, complementation, and star.

8.5 Show that NL is closed under the operations union, intersection, and star.

8.6 Show that any PSPACE-hard language is also NP-hard.

8.7 Show that $A_{\mathsf{DFA}} \in \mathrm{L}$.

8.8 Show that A_{NFA} is NL-complete.

---

[4]We write $A \subsetneq B$ to mean that A is a proper (i.e., not equal) subset of B.

PROBLEMS

8.9 Show that, if every NP-hard language is also PSPACE-hard, then PSPACE = NP.

8.10 The Japanese game *go-moku* is played by two players, "X" and "O," on a 19×19 grid. Players take turns placing markers, and the first player to achieve 5 of his markers consecutively in a row, column, or diagonal, is the winner. Consider this game generalized to an $n \times n$ board. Let

$$GM = \{\langle P \rangle | \ P \text{ is a position in generalized go-moku,}$$
$$\text{where player "X" has a winning strategy}\}.$$

By a *position* we mean a board with markers placed on it, such as may occur in the middle of a play of the game. Show that $GM \in$ PSPACE.

8.11 Let A be the language of properly nested parentheses. For example, (()) and (()(()))() are in A, but)(is not. Show that A is in L.

8.12 Let B be the language of properly nested parentheses and brackets. For example, ([()()]()[]) is in B but ([)] is not. Show that B is in L.

8.13 Show that *TQBF* restricted to formulas where the part following the quantifiers is in conjunctive normal form is still PSPACE-complete.

8.14 Consider the following two-person version of the language *PUZZLE* that was described in Problem 7.26. Each player starts with an ordered stack of puzzle cards. They take turns placing them in order in the box and may chose which side faces up. Player I wins if, in the final stack, all hole positions are blocked, and Player II wins if some hole position remains unblocked. Show that the problem of determining which player has a winning strategy for a given starting configuration of the cards is PSPACE-complete.

8.15 The cat-and-mouse game is played by two players, "Cat" and "Mouse," on an arbitrary undirected graph. At a given point each player occupies a node of the graph. The players take turns moving to a node adjacent to the one that they currently occupy. A special node of the graph is called "Hole." Cat wins if the two players ever occupy the same node. Mouse wins if it reaches the Hole before the preceding happens. The game is a draw if the two players ever simultaneously reach positions that they previously occupied. Let

$$HAPPY\text{-}CAT = \{\langle G, c, m, h \rangle | \ G, c, m, h, \text{ are respectively a graph, and}$$
$$\text{positions of the Cat, Mouse, and Hole, such that}$$
$$\text{Cat has a winning strategy, if Cat moves first}\}.$$

Show that *HAPPY-CAT* is in P.

8.16 Let $EQ_{\mathrm{REX}} = \{\langle R, S \rangle | \ R \text{ and } S \text{ are equivalent regular expressions}\}$. Show that $EQ_{\mathrm{REX}} \in$ PSPACE.

8.17 Give an example of an NL-complete context-free language.

8.18 A *chain* is a sequence of strings $s_1, s_2, \ldots, s_k$, wherein every string differs from the preceding one in exactly one character. For example the following is a chain of English words:

head, hear, near, fear, bear, beer, deer, deed, feed, feet, fret, free

Let

$DFACHAIN = \{\langle M, s, t\rangle |\ M$ is a DFA where $L(M)$ contains a

chain of strings, starting with s, and ending with $t\}$.

Show that $DFACHAIN$ is in PSPACE.

8.19 Recall that a directed graph is ***strongly connected*** if every two nodes are connected by a directed path in each direction. Let

$STRONGLY\text{-}CONNECTED = \{\langle G\rangle |\ G$ is a strongly connected graph$\}$.

Show that $STRONGLY\text{-}CONNECTED$ is NL-complete.

8.20 An undirected graph is ***bipartite*** if its nodes may divided into two sets so that all edges go from a node in one set to a node in the other set. Show that a graph is bipartite if and only if it doesn't contain a cycle that has an odd number of nodes. Let

$BIPARTITE = \{\langle G\rangle |\ G$ is a bipartite graph$\}$.

Show that $BIPARTITE \in$ NL.

*8.21 The game of ***nim*** is played with a collection of piles of sticks. In one move a player may remove any nonzero number of sticks from a single pile. The players alternately take turns making moves. The player who removes the very last stick loses. Say that we have a game position in *NIM* with k piles containing $s_1, \ldots, s_k$ sticks. Call the position ***balanced*** if, when each of the numbers s_i is written in binary and the binary numbers are written as rows of a matrix aligned at the low order bits, each column of bits contains an even number of 1s. Prove the following two facts.

    a. Starting in an unbalanced position, a single move exists that changes the position into a balanced one.

    b. Starting in a balanced position, every single move changes the position into an unbalanced one.

Let

$NIM = \{\langle s_1, \ldots, s_k\rangle |\$ each s_i is a binary number and Player I has a winning

strategy in the *NIM* game starting at this position$\}$.

Use the preceding facts about balanced positions to show that $NIM \in$ L.

9

···

INTRACTABILITY

Certain computational problems are solvable in principle, but the solutions require so much time or space that they can't be used in practice. Such problems are called *intractable*. Intractability can take many forms, depending on the computational resources available and the type of solution desired. For example, a problem that is easy to solve most of the time, yet occasionally difficult, would be intractable only in the worst case. Or a problem may be easily solvable on a supercomputer but may require an inordinate amount of time on a personal computer. We focus on problems whose worst case complexity is so enormous that any computer that we could conceivably build would need more time than is thought to remain in the lifetime of the universe.

In Chapters 7 and 8, we introduced several problems thought to be intractable but none that are provably intractable. For example, most people believe the *SAT* problem and all other NP-complete problems are intractable, although we don't know how to prove that they are. In this chapter we give examples of problems that we can prove to be intractable.

In order to present these examples, we develop several theorems that relate the power of Turing machines to the amount of time or space available for computation. We conclude the chapter with a discussion of the possibility of proving that problems in NP are intractable and thereby solving the P versus NP question. First, we introduce the relativization technique and use it to argue that certain methods won't allow us to achieve this goal. Then, we discuss circuit complexity theory, an approach taken by researchers that has shown some promise.

9.1

HIERARCHY THEOREMS

Common sense suggests that giving a Turing machine more time or more space should increase the class of problems that it can solve. In other words, Turing machines should be able to decide more languages in time n^3 than they can in time n^2. This intuition is correct, subject to certain conditions. The **hierarchy theorems** formalize and prove this intuition. We use the term *hierarchy theorem* because each of these theorems proves that the time and space complexity classes aren't all the same—they form a hierarchy whereby the classes with larger bounds contain more languages than do the classes with smaller bounds.

We first present the hierarchy theorem for space complexity because it is slightly simpler than the one for time complexity. Before getting to the actual statement of the theorem, we need to make the following technical definition.

DEFINITION 9.1

A function $f \colon \mathcal{N} \longrightarrow \mathcal{N}$, where $f(n) \geq \log n$, is called **space constructible** if the function that maps 1^n to the binary representation of $f(n)$ is computable in space $O(f(n))$. [1]

In other words, f is space constructible if some TM M exists that runs in $O(f(n))$ space and always halts with the binary representation of $f(n)$ on its tape when started on input 1^n. Fractional functions such as $n \log n$ and $\sqrt{n}$ are rounded down to the next lower integer for the purposes of time and space constructibility.

EXAMPLE 9.2

All commonly occurring functions that are at least $\log n$ are space constructible, including the functions $\log n$, $n \log n$, and n^2.

For example, n^2 is space constructible because a machine may take its input 1^n, obtain n in binary by counting the number of 1s, and output n^2 by using any standard method for multiplying n by itself. The total space used is $O(n)$ which is certainly $O(n^2)$.

When showing that functions $f(n)$ that are $o(n)$ to be space constructible, we use a separate read only input tape, as we did when we defined sublinear space complexity in Section 8.4. For example, such a machine can compute the function which maps 1^n to the binary representation of $\log n$ as follows. It first counts the number of 1s in its input in binary using its work tape as it moves its head along the input tape. Then, with n in binary on its work tape, it can compute $\log n$ by counting the number bits in the binary representation of n.   ■

---

[1] Recall that 1^n means a string of n 1s.

The role of space constructibility in the space hierarchy theorem may be understood from the following situation. If $f(n)$ and $g(n)$ are two space bounds, where $f(n)$ is asymptotically larger than $g(n)$, we would expect a machine to be able to compute more languages in $f(n)$ space than in $g(n)$ space. However, suppose that $f(n)$ exceeds $g(n)$ by only a very small and hard to compute amount. Then, the machine may not be able to use the extra space profitably because even computing the amount of extra space may require more space than is available. In this case, a machine may not be able to compute more languages in $f(n)$ space than it can in $g(n)$ space. Stipulating that $f(n)$ is space constructible avoids this situation and allows us to prove that a machine can compute more than it would be able to in any asymptotically smaller bound, as the following theorem shows.

THEOREM   **9.3**   ···

Space Hierarchy Theorem   For any space constructible function $f : \mathcal{N} \longrightarrow \mathcal{N}$, there exists a language A that is decidable in space $O(f(n))$ but not in space $o(f(n))$.

···

PROOF IDEA   We must demonstrate a language A that has two properties. The first says that A is decidable in $O(f(n))$ space. The second says that A isn't decidable in $o(f(n))$ space.

We describe A by giving an algorithm B that decides it. Algorithm B will run in $O(f(n))$ space, thereby ensuring the first property. Furthermore, B will guarantee that A is different from any language that is decidable in $o(f(n))$ space, thereby ensuring the second property.

Do not expect to get as simple and clear a mental picture of the language A as you may have for the other languages appearing so far in this book. These other languages have been described as collections of strings satisfying specified properties. From this semantic description, we have often gone on to give an algorithm to test membership in the language. Language A is different in that it is described only by an algorithm and lacks a simpler, nonalgorithmic definition.

In order to ensure that A not be decidable in $o(f(n))$ space, we design B to implement the diagonalization method that we used to prove the unsolvability of the halting problem A_{TM} in Theorem 4.9 on page 165. If M is a machine that decides a language in $o(f(n))$ space, B guarantees that A differs from M's language in at least one place. Which place? The place corresponding to a description of M itself.

Let's look at that way B operates. Roughly speaking, B takes its input to be the description of a TM M. (If the input isn't the description of any TM, then B's action is inconsequential on this input, so we arbitrarily make B reject.) Then B runs M on the same input, namely, $\langle M \rangle$, within the space bound $f(n)$. If M halts within that much space, B accepts iff M rejects. If M doesn't halt, B just rejects. So if M runs within space $f(n)$, B has enough space to ensure that its language is different from M's. If not, B doesn't have enough space to figure out what M

does, but fortunately B has no requirement to act differently from machines that don't run in $o(f(n))$ space, so B's action on this input is inconsequential.

This description captures the essence of the proof but omits several important details. If M runs in $o(f(n))$ space, B must guarantee that its language is different from M's language. But even when M runs in $o(f(n))$ space, it may use more than $f(n)$ space for small n, when the asymptotic behavior hasn't "kicked in" yet. Possibly, B might not have enough space to run M to completion on input $\langle M \rangle$, and hence B will miss its one opportunity to avoid M's language. So, if we aren't careful, B might end up deciding the same language that M decides, and the theorem wouldn't be proved.

We can fix this problem by modifying B to give it additional opportunities to avoid M's language. Instead of running M only when B receives input $\langle M \rangle$, it runs M whenever it receives an input of the form $\langle M \rangle 10^*$, that is, an input of the form $\langle M \rangle$ followed by a 1 and some number of 0s. Then, if M really is running in $o(f(n))$ space, B will have enough space to run it to completion on input $\langle M \rangle 10^k$ for some large value of k because the asymptotic behavior must eventually kick in.

One last technical point arises. When B runs M on some string, M may get into an infinite loop while using only a finite amount of space. But B is supposed to be a decider so we must ensure that B doesn't loop while simulating M. Any machine that runs in space $o(f(n))$ uses only $2^{o(f(n))}$ time. We modify B so that it counts the number of steps used in simulating M. If this count ever exceeds $2^{f(n)}$, then B rejects.

PROOF   The following $O(f(n))$ space algorithm B decides a language A that is not decidable in $o(f(n))$ space.

$B =$ "On input w:

1. Let n be the length of w.
2. Compute $f(n)$ using space constructibility, and mark off this much tape. If later stages ever attempt to use more, *reject*.
3. If w is not of the form $\langle M \rangle 10^*$ for some TM M, *reject*.
4. Simulate M on w while counting the number of steps used in the simulation. If the count ever exceeds $2^{f(n)}$, *reject*.
5. If M accepts, *reject*. If M rejects, *accept*."

In stage 4, we need to give additional details of the simulation in order to determine the amount of space used. The simulated machine M has an arbitrary tape alphabet and B has a fixed tape alphabet, so we represent each cell of M's tape with several cells on B's tape. Therefore the simulation introduces a constant factor overhead in the space used. In other words, if M runs in $g(n)$ space then B uses $d\,g(n)$ space to simulate M, for some constant d that depends on M.

Machine B is a decider because each of its stages can run for a limited time. Let A be the language that B decides. Clearly, A is decidable in space $O(f(n))$ because B does so. Next, we show that A is not decidable in $o(f(n))$ space.

Assume to the contrary that some Turing machine M decides A in space $g(n)$, where $g(n)$ is $o(f(n))$. As mentioned earlier, B can simulate M using space $d\,g(n)$ for some constant d. Because $g(n)$ is $o(f(n))$, some constant n_0 exists, where $d\,g(n) < f(n)$ for all $n \geq n_0$. Therefore B's simulation of M will run to completion as long as the input has length n_0 or more. Consider what happens when B is run on input $\langle M \rangle 10^{n_0}$. This input is longer than n_0, so the simulation in stage 4 will complete. Therefore B will do the opposite of M on the same input. Hence M doesn't decide A, which contradicts our assumption. Therefore A is not decidable in $o(f(n))$ space.

COROLLARY **9.4**

For any two functions $f_1, f_2 \colon \mathcal{N} \longrightarrow \mathcal{N}$, where $f_1(n)$ is $o(f_2(n))$ and f_2 is space constructible, $\mathrm{SPACE}(f_1(n)) \subsetneq \mathrm{SPACE}(f_2(n)).$[2]

This corollary allows us to separate various space complexity classes from one another. For example, we can easily show that the function n^c is space constructible, for any natural number c. Hence for any two natural numbers $c_1 < c_2$ we can prove that $\mathrm{SPACE}(n^{c_1}) \subsetneq \mathrm{SPACE}(n^{c_2})$. With a bit more work we can show that n^c is space constructible for any rational number $c > 0$ and thereby extend the preceding containment to hold for any rational numbers $0 \leq c_1 < c_2$. Observing that two rational numbers c_1 and c_2 always exist between any two real numbers $\epsilon_1 < \epsilon_2$ such that $\epsilon_1 < c_1 < c_2 < \epsilon_2$ we obtain the following additional corollary demonstrating a fine hierarchy within the class PSPACE.

COROLLARY **9.5**

For any two real numbers $0 \leq \epsilon_1 < \epsilon_2$,

$$\mathrm{SPACE}(n^{\epsilon_1}) \subsetneq \mathrm{SPACE}(n^{\epsilon_2}).$$

We can also use the space hierarchy theorem to separate two space complexity classes we previously encountered.

COROLLARY **9.6**

$\mathrm{NL} \subsetneq \mathrm{PSPACE}$.

PROOF   Savitch's theorem shows that $\mathrm{NL} \subseteq \mathrm{SPACE}(\log^2 n)$, and the space hierarchy theorem shows that $\mathrm{SPACE}(\log^2 n) \subsetneq \mathrm{SPACE}(n)$. Hence the corollary follows.

---

[2]The expression $A \subsetneq B$ means that A is a proper (i.e., not equal) subset of B.

Now we establish the main objective of this chapter: proving the existence of problems that are decidable in principle but not in practice, that is, problems that are decidable but intractable. Each of the classes $\text{SPACE}(n^k)$ is contained within the class $\text{SPACE}(n^{\log n})$, which in turn is strictly contained within the class $\text{SPACE}(2^n)$. Therefore we obtain the following additional corollary separating PSPACE from EXPSPACE $= \bigcup_k \text{SPACE}(2^{n^k})$.

COROLLARY **9.7**

PSPACE $\subsetneq$ EXPSPACE.

This corollary establishes the existence of decidable problems that are intractable, in the sense that their decision procedures must use more than polynomial space. The languages themselves are somewhat artificial—interesting only for the purposes of separating complexity classes. We use these languages to prove the intractability of other, more natural, languages after we discuss the time hierarchy theorem.

DEFINITION **9.8**

A function $t \colon \mathcal{N} \longrightarrow \mathcal{N}$, where $t(n) \geq n \log n$, is called ***time constructible*** if the function that maps 1^n to the binary representation of $t(n)$ is computable in time $O(t(n))$.

In other words, t is time constructible if some TM M exists that runs in $O(t(n))$ time and always halts with the binary representation of $t(n)$ on its tape when started on input 1^n.

EXAMPLE **9.9**

All commonly occurring functions that are at least n are time constructible, including the functions n, $n \log n$, $n\sqrt{n}$, and 2^n.

For example, to show that $n\sqrt{n}$ is time constructible, we first design a TM to count the number of 1s in binary. To do so the TM moves a binary counter along the tape, incrementing it by 1 for every input position, until it reaches the end of the input. This part uses $O(n \log n)$ steps because $O(\log n)$ steps are used for each of the n input positions. Then, we compute $\lfloor n\sqrt{n} \rfloor$ in binary from the binary representation of n. Any reasonable method of doing so will work in $O(n \log n)$ time because the length of the numbers involved is $O(\log n)$.

The time hierarchy theorem is an analog for time complexity to Theorem 9.3. For technical reasons that will appear in its proof the time hierarchy theorem is slightly weaker than the one we proved for space. Whereas *any* space constructible asymptotic increase in the space bound enlarges the class of languages so decidable, for time we must further increase the time bound by a logarithmic factor in order to guarantee that we can obtain additional languages. Conceivably, a tighter time hierarchy theorem is true, but at present we don't know how to prove it. This aspect of the time hierarchy theorem arises because we measure time complexity using single-tape Turing machines. We can prove tighter time hierarchy theorems for other models of computation.

THEOREM **9.10** ....

Time Hierarchy Theorem   For any time constructible function $t\colon \mathcal{N}\longrightarrow\mathcal{N}$, there exists a language A that is decidable in time $O(t(n))$ but not in time $o(t(n)/\log t(n))$.

....

PROOF IDEA   The proof of this theorem is similar to the proof of Theorem 9.3. We construct a machine B that decides a language A in time $O(t(n))$ whereby A cannot be decided in $o(t(n)/\log t(n))$ time. Here, B takes an input w of the form $\langle M\rangle 10^*$ and simulates M on input w, making sure not to use more than $t(n)$ time. If M halts within that much time, B gives the opposite output.

The important difference in the proof concerns the cost of simulating M while, at the same time, counting the number of steps that the simulation is using. Machine B must perform this timed simulation efficiently so that B runs in $O(t(n))$ time while accomplishing the goal of avoiding all languages decidable in $o(t(n)/\log t(n))$ time. For space complexity, the simulation introduced a constant factor overhead, as we observed in the proof of Theorem 9.3. For time complexity, the simulation introduces a logarithmic factor overhead. The larger overhead for time is the reason for the appearance of the $1/\log n$ factor in the statement of this theorem. If we had a way of simulating a single-tape Turing machine by another single-tape Turing machine for a prespecified number of steps, using only a constant factor overhead in time, we would be able to strengthen this theorem by changing $o(t(n)/\log t(n))$ to $o(t(n))$. No such efficient simulation is known.

PROOF   The following $O(t(n))$ time algorithm B decides a language A that is not decidable in $o(t(n)/\log t(n))$ time.

$B =$ "On input w:
1. Let n be the length of w.
2. Compute $t(n)$ using time constructibility, and store the value $\lceil t(n)/\log t(n)\rceil$ in a binary counter. Decrement this counter before each step used to carry out stages 3, 4, and 5. If the counter ever hits 0, *reject*.
3. If w is not of the form $\langle M\rangle 10^*$ for some TM M, *reject*.
4. Simulate M on w.
5. If M accepts, then *reject*. If M rejects, then *accept*."

We examine each of the stages of this algorithm to determine the running time. Obviously, stages 1, 2 and 3 can be performed within $O(t(n))$ time.

In stage 4, every time B simulates one step of M, it takes M's current state together with the tape symbol under M's tape head and looks up M's next action in its transition function so that it can update M's tape appropriately. All three of these objects (state, tape symbol, and transition function) are stored on B's tape somewhere. If they are stored far from each other, B will need many steps to gather this information each time it simulates one of M's steps. Instead, B always keeps this information close together.

We can think of B's single tape as organized into *tracks*. One way to get two tracks is by storing one track in the odd positions and the other in the even positions. Alternatively, the two-track effect may be obtained by enlarging B's tape alphabet to include each pair of symbols, one from the top track and the second from the bottom track. We can get the effect of additional tracks similarly. Note that multiple tracks introduce only a constant factor overhead in time, provided that only a fixed number of tracks are used. Here, B has three tracks.

One of the tracks contains the information on M's tape, and a second contains its current state and a copy of M's transition function. During the simulation, B keeps the information on the second track near the current position of M's head on the first track. Every time M's head position moves, B shifts all the information on the second track to keep it near the head. Because the size of the information on the second track depends only on M and not on the length of the input to M, the shifting adds only a constant factor to the simulation time. Furthermore, because the required information is kept close together, the cost of looking up M's next action in its transition function and updating its tape is only a constant. Hence if M runs in $g(n)$ time, B can simulate it in $O(g(n))$ time.

At every step in stages 3 and 4, B must decrement the step counter originally set in stage 2. Here, B can do so without adding excessively to the simulation time by keeping the counter in binary on a third track and moving it to keep it near the present head position. This counter has a magnitude of about $t(n)/\log t(n)$, so its length is $\log(t(n)/\log t(n))$, which is $O(\log t(n))$. Hence the cost of updating and moving it at each step adds a $\log t(n)$ factor to the simulation time, thus bringing the total running time to $O(t(n))$. Therefore A is decidable in time $O(t(n))$.

To show that A is not decidable in $o(t(n)/\log t(n))$ time we use an argument similar to one used in the proof of Theorem 9.3. Assume to the contrary that TM M decides A in time $g(n)$, where $g(n)$ is $o(t(n)/\log t(n))$. Here, B can simulate M using time $d\,g(n)$ for some constant d. If the total simulation time (not counting the time to update the step counter) is at most $t(n)/\log t(n)$, the simulation will run to completion. Because $g(n)$ is $o(t(n)/\log t(n))$, some constant n_0 exists where $d\,g(n) < t(n)/\log t(n)$ for all $n \geq n_0$. Therefore B's simulation of M will run to completion as long as the input has length n_0 or more. Consider what happens when we run B on input $\langle M \rangle 10^{n_0}$. This input is longer than n_0 so the simulation in stage 4 will complete. Therefore B will do the opposite of M on the same input. Hence M doesn't decide A, which contradicts our assumption. Therefore A is not decidable in $o(t(n)/\log t(n))$ time.

Now we can establish analogs to Corollaries 9.4, 9.5, and 9.7 for time complexity.

COROLLARY   **9.11**   ....

For any two functions $t_1, t_2 \colon \mathcal{N} \longrightarrow \mathcal{N}$, where $t_1(n)$ is $o(t_2(n)/\log t_2(n))$ and t_2 is time constructible, $\mathrm{TIME}(t_1(n)) \subsetneq \mathrm{TIME}(t_2(n))$.

COROLLARY   **9.12**   ....

For any two real numbers $1 \leq \epsilon_1 < \epsilon_2$,

$$\mathrm{TIME}(n^{\epsilon_1}) \subsetneq \mathrm{TIME}(n^{\epsilon_2}).$$

COROLLARY   **9.13**   ....

P $\subsetneq$ EXPTIME.

EXPONENTIAL SPACE COMPLETENESS

We can use the preceding results to demonstrate that a specific language is actually intractable. We do so in two steps. First, the hierarchy theorems tell us that a Turing machine can decide more languages in EXPSPACE than it can in PSPACE. Then, we show that a particular language concerning generalized regular expressions is complete for EXPSPACE and hence can't be decided in polynomial time or even in polynomial space.

Before getting to their generalization, let's briefly review the way we introduced regular expressions in Definition 1.26. They are built up from the atomic expressions $\emptyset$, ε, and members of the alphabet, by using the regular operations union, concatenation, and star, denoted $\cup$, $\circ$, and *, respectively. From Problem 8.16 we know that we can test the equivalence of two regular expressions in polynomial space.

We show that, by allowing regular expressions with more operations than the usual regular operations, the complexity of analyzing the expressions may grow dramatically. Let $\uparrow$ be the ***exponentiation operation***. If R is a regular expression and k is a nonnegative integer, writing $R \uparrow k$ is equivalent to the concatenation of R with itself k times. We also write R^k as shorthand for $R \uparrow k$. In other words,

$$R^k = R \uparrow k = \overbrace{R \circ R \circ \cdots \circ R}^{k}.$$

Generalized regular expressions allow the exponentiation operation in addition to the usual regular operations. Obviously, these generalized regular expressions still generate the same class of regular languages as do the standard regular expressions. The reason is that we can eliminate the exponentiation operation by repeating the expression to which it applied.

Let

$$EQ_{\mathsf{REX\uparrow}} = \{\langle Q, R\rangle | \ Q \text{ and } R \text{ are equivalent regular}$$
$$\text{expressions with exponentiation}\}$$

To show that $EQ_{\mathsf{REX\uparrow}}$ is intractable we show that it is complete for the class EXPSPACE. Any EXPSPACE-complete problem cannot be in PSPACE, much less in P. Otherwise EXPSPACE would equal PSPACE, contradicting Corollary 9.7.

DEFINITION 9.14 ··

A language B is **EXPSPACE-complete** if

1. $B \in$ EXPSPACE, and
2. every A in EXPSPACE is polynomial time reducible to B.

THEOREM 9.15 ··

$EQ_{\mathsf{REX\uparrow}}$ is EXPSPACE-complete.

PROOF IDEA   In measuring the complexity of deciding $EQ_{\mathsf{REX\uparrow}}$ we assume that all exponents are written as binary integers. The length of an expression is the total number of symbols that it contains.

We sketch an EXPSPACE algorithm for $EQ_{\mathsf{REX\uparrow}}$. To test whether two expressions with exponentiation are equivalent, we first use repetition to eliminate exponentiation, then convert the resulting expressions to NFAs. Finally we use an NFA equivalence testing procedure similar to the one used for deciding E_{NFA} in Example 8.4.

To show that a language A in EXPSPACE is polynomial time reducible to $EQ_{\mathsf{REX\uparrow}}$, we utilize the technique of reductions via computation histories that we introduced in Section 5.1. The construction is similar to the construction given in the proof of Theorem 5.10.

Given a TM for A we design a polynomial time reduction that maps an input w to a pair of expressions, Q and R, that are equivalent exactly when M accepts w. The expressions Q and R simulate the computation of M on w. Expression Q simply generates all strings over the alphabet consisting of symbols that may appear in computation histories. Expression R generates all strings that are not rejecting computation histories. So, if the TM accepts its input, no rejecting computation histories exist, and expressions Q and R generate the same language. Recall that a rejecting computation history is the sequence of configurations that the machine enters in a rejecting computation on the input. See page 176 in Section 5.1 for a review of computation histories.

The difficulty in this proof is that the size of the expressions constructed must be polynomial in n (so that the reduction can run in polynomial time), whereas the simulated computation may have exponential length. The exponentiation operation is useful here to represent the long computation with a relatively short expression.

PROOF   First we present a nondeterministic algorithm for testing whether two NFAs are inequivalent.

N = "On input $\langle N_1, N_2 \rangle$, where N_1 and N_2 are NFAs:
1. Place a marker on each of the start states of N_1 and N_2.
2. Repeat $2^{q_1+q_2}$ times, where q_1 and q_2 are the numbers of states in N_1 and N_2.
3.   Nondeterministically select an input symbol and change the positions of the markers on the states of N_1 and N_2 to simulate reading that symbol.
4. If at any point, a marker was placed on an accept state of one of the finite automata and not on any accept state of the other finite automaton, *accept*. Otherwise, *reject*."

If automata N_1 and N_2 are equivalent, N clearly rejects because it only accepts when it determines that one machine accepts a string that the other does not accept. If the automata are not equivalent, some string is accepted by one and not by the other. Some such string must be of length at most $2^{q_1+q_2}$. Otherwise, consider using the shortest such string as the sequence of nondeterministic choices. Only $2^{q_1+q_2}$ different ways exist to place markers on the states of N_1 and N_2, so in a longer string the positions of the markers would repeat. By removing the portion of the string between the repetitions a shorter such string would be obtained. Hence algorithm N would guess this string among its nondeterministic choices and would accept. Thus N operates correctly.

Algorithm N runs in nondeterministic linear space and thus, by applying Savitch's theorem, we obtain a deterministic $O(n^2)$ space algorithm for this problem. Next we use the deterministic form of this algorithm to design the following algorithm E that decides $EQ_{\text{REX}\uparrow}$.

E = "On input $\langle R_1, R_2 \rangle$ where R_1 and R_2 are regular expressions with exponentiation:
1. Convert R_1 and R_2 to equivalent regular expressions Q_1 and Q_2 that use repetition instead of exponentiation.
2. Convert Q_1 and Q_2 to equivalent NFAs N_1 and N_2, using the conversion procedure given in the proof of Lemma 1.29.
3. Use the deterministic version of algorithm N to determine whether N_1 and N_2 are equivalent."

Algorithm E obviously is correct. To analyze its space complexity observe that using repetition to replace exponentiation may increase the length of an expression by a factor of 2^l, where l is the sum of the lengths of the exponents. Thus expressions Q_1 and Q_2 have a length of at most $n2^n$, where n is the input length. The conversion procedure of Lemma 1.29 increases the size linearly and hence

NFAs N_1 and N_2 have at most $O(n2^n)$ states. Thus with input size $O(n2^n)$, the deterministic version of algorithm N uses space $O((n2^n)^2) = O(n^2 2^{2n})$. Hence $EQ_{\mathsf{REX}\uparrow}$ is decidable in exponential space.

Next, we show that $EQ_{\mathsf{REX}\uparrow}$ is EXPSPACE-hard. Let A be a language that is decided by TM M running in space $2^{(n^k)}$ for some constant k. The reduction maps an input w to a pair of regular expressions, Q and R. Expression Q is Δ^* where, if Γ and Q are M's tape alphabet and states, $\Delta = \Gamma \cup Q \cup \{\#\}$ is the alphabet consisting of all symbols that may appear in a computation history. We construct expression R to generate all strings that aren't rejecting computation histories of M on w. Of course, M accepts w iff M on w has no rejecting computation histories. Therefore the two expressions are equivalent iff M accepts w. The construction is as follows.

A rejecting computation history for M on w is a sequence of configurations separated by $\#$ symbols. We use our standard encoding of configurations whereby a symbol corresponding to the current state is placed to the left of the current head position. We assume that all configurations have length $2^{(n^k)}$ and are padded on the right by blank symbols if they otherwise would be too short. The first configuration in a rejecting computation history is the start configuration of M on w. The last configuration is a rejecting configuration. Each configuration must follow from the preceding one according to the rules specified in the transition function.

A string may fail to be a rejecting computation in several ways. Either it fails to start properly, fails to end properly, or is incorrect somewhere in the middle. Expression R equals $R_{\text{bad-start}} \cup R_{\text{bad-window}} \cup R_{\text{bad-reject}}$, where each R_i corresponds to one of the three ways a string may fail.

We construct expression $R_{\text{bad-start}}$ to generate all strings that fail to start with the start configuration C_1 of M on w, as follows. Configuration C_1 looks like $q_0 w_1 w_2 \cdots w_n \sqcup \sqcup \cdots \sqcup \#$. We write $R_{\text{bad-start}}$ as the union of several subexpressions to handle each part of C_1:

$$R_{\text{bad-start}} = S_0 \cup S_1 \cup \cdots \cup S_n \cup S_b \cup S_{\#}.$$

Expression S_0 generates all strings that don't start with q_0. We let S_0 be the expression $\Delta_{-q_0} \Delta^*$. The notation Δ_{-q_0} is shorthand for writing the union of all symbols in Δ except q_0.

Expression S_1 generates all strings that don't contain w_1 in the second position. We let S_1 be $\Delta \Delta_{-w_1} \Delta^*$. In general, for $1 \leq i \leq n$ expression S_i is $\Delta^i \Delta_{-w_i} \Delta^*$. Thus S_1 generates all strings that contain any symbols in the first i positions, any symbol except w_i in position $i+1$ and any string of symbols following position $i+1$. Note that we have used the exponentiation operation here. Actually, at this point, exponentiation is more of a convenience than a necessity because we could have instead repeated the symbol Δ i times without excessively increasing the length of the expression. But, in the next subexpression, exponentiation is crucial to keeping the size polynomial.

Expression S_b generates all strings that fail to contain a blank symbol in some position $n + 2$ through $2^{(n^k)}$. We could introduce subexpressions S_{n+2} through

$S_{2^{(n^k)}}$ for this purpose, but then expression $R_{\text{bad-start}}$ would have exponential length. Instead we let

$$S_b = \Delta^{(n+1)} \, (\Delta \cup \varepsilon)^{(2^{(n^k)} - n)} \, \Delta_{-\sqcup} \, \Delta^*.$$

Thus S_b generates strings that contain any symbols in the first $n + 1$ positions, any symbols in the next l positions, where t can range from 0 to $2^{(n^k)} - n$, and any symbol except blank in the next position.

Finally $S_\#$ generates all strings that don't have a # symbol in position $2^{(n^k)} + 1$. Let $S_\#$ be $\Delta^{(2^{(n^k)})} \, \Delta_{-\#} \, \Delta^*$.

Now that we have completed the construction of $R_{\text{bad-start}}$, we turn to the next piece, $R_{\text{bad-reject}}$. It generates all strings that don't end properly, that is, strings that fail to contain a rejecting configuration. Any rejecting configuration contains the state q_{reject}, so we let

$$R_{\text{bad-reject}} = \Delta^*_{-q_{\text{reject}}}.$$

Thus $R_{\text{bad-reject}}$ generates all strings that don't contain q_{reject}.

Finally, we construct $R_{\text{bad-window}}$, the expression that generates all strings whereby one configuration does not properly lead to the next configuration. Recall that in the proof of the Cook–Levin theorem, we determined that one configuration legally yields another whenever every three consecutive symbols in the first configuration correctly yield the corresponding three symbols in the second configuration according to the transition function. Hence, if one configuration fails to yield another, the error will be apparent by examining the appropriate six symbols. We use this idea to construct $R_{\text{bad-window}}$:

$$R_{\text{bad-window}} = \bigcup_{\text{bad}(abc, def)} \Delta^* \, abc \, \Delta^{(2^{(n^k)} - 2)} \, def \, \Delta^*,$$

where $\text{bad}(abc, def)$ means that abc doesn't yield def according to the transition function. The union is only taken over such symbols a, b, c, d, e, and f in Δ. The following figure illustrates the placement of these symbols in a computation history.

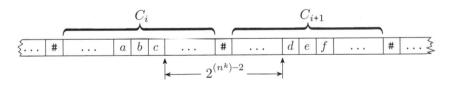

FIGURE 9.1
Corresponding places in adjacent configurations

To calculate the length of R, we need to determine the length of the exponents that appear in it. Several exponents of magnitude roughly $2^{(n^k)}$ appear, and their total length in binary is $O(n^k)$. Therefore the length of R is polynomial in n.

9.2
■ ■

RELATIVIZATION

The proof that $EQ_{\mathsf{REX}\uparrow}$ is intractable rests on the diagonalization method. Why don't we show that SAT is intractable in the same way? Possibly we could use diagonalization to show that a nondeterministic polynomial time TM can decide a language that is provably not in P. In this section we introduce the method of **relativization** to give strong evidence against the possibility of solving the P versus NP question by using a proof by diagonalization.

In the relativization method, we modify our model of computation by giving the Turing machine certain information essentially for "free." Depending on which information is actually provided, the Turing machine may be able to solve some problems more easily than before.

For example, suppose that we grant the Turing machine the ability to solve the satisfiability problem in a single step, for any size Boolean formula. Never mind how this feat is accomplished—imagine an attached "black box" that gives the machine this capability. We call the black box an **oracle** to emphasize that it doesn't necessarily correspond to any physical device. Obviously, the machine could use the oracle to solve any NP problem in polynomial time, regardless of whether P equals NP, because every NP problem is polynomial time reducible to the satisfiability problem. Such a Turing machine is said to be computing *relative to* the satisfiability problem; hence the term **relativization**.

In general, an oracle can correspond to any particular language, not just the satisfiability problem. The oracle allows the Turing machine to test membership in the language without actually having to compute the answer itself. We formalize this notion shortly. You may recall that we encountered oracles once before, in Section 6.3. There, we defined them for the purpose of classifying problems according to the degree of unsolvability. Here, we use oracles to better understand the power of the diagonalization method.

DEFINITION 9.16 ....

An **oracle** is a language A. An **oracle Turing machine** M^A is an ordinary Turing machine with an extra tape called the **oracle tape**. Whenever M writes a string on the oracle tape it is informed whether that string is a member of A, in a single computation step.

Let P^A be the class of languages decidable with a polynomial time oracle Turing machine that uses oracle A. Define NP^A similarly.

EXAMPLE 9.17 ....

As we mentioned earlier, polynomial time computation relative to the satisfiability problem contains all of NP. In other words, $\mathrm{NP} \subseteq \mathrm{P}^{SAT}$. Furthermore, coNP $\subseteq$ P^{SAT} because P^{SAT}, being a deterministic complexity class, is closed under complementation.

EXAMPLE 9.18 ....

Just as P^{SAT} contains languages that we believe are not in P, NP^{SAT} contains languages that we believe are not in NP. For example, say that two Boolean formulas ϕ and ψ over the variables $x_1, \ldots, x_l$ are *equivalent* if the formulas have the same value on any assignment to the variables. Say that a formula is *minimal* if no smaller formula is equivalent to it. Let

$$\textit{NONMIN-FORMULA} = \{\langle\phi\rangle|\ \phi \text{ is not a minimal Boolean formula}\}.$$

NONMIN-FORMULA doesn't seem to be in NP (though whether it actually belongs to NP is not known). However, *NONMIN-FORMULA* is in NP^{SAT} because a nondeterministic polynomial time oracle Turing machine with a *SAT* oracle can test whether ϕ is a member, as follows. First, the inequivalence problem for two Boolean formulas is solvable in NP, and hence the equivalence problem is in coNP, because a nondeterministic machine can guess the assignment on which the two formulas have different values. Then, the nondeterministic oracle machine for *NONMIN-FORMULA* nondeterministically guesses the smaller equivalent formula, tests whether it actually is equivalent using the *SAT* oracle, and accepts if it is.

LIMITS OF THE DIAGONALIZATION METHOD

The next theorem demonstrates oracles A and B for which P^A and NP^A are provably different and P^B and NP^B are provably equal. These two oracles are important because their existence indicates that we are unlikely to resolve the P versus NP question by using the diagonalization method.

At its core, the diagonalization method is a simulation of one Turing machine by another. The simulation is done so that the simulating machine can determine the behavior of the other machine and then behave differently. Suppose that both of these Turing machines were given identical oracles. Then, whenever the simulated machines queries the oracle, so can the simulator, and therefore the simulation can proceed as before. Consequently, any theorem proved about Turing machines by using only the diagonalization method would still hold if both machines were given the same oracle.

In particular, if we could prove that P and NP were different by diagonalizing, we could conclude that they are different relative to any oracle as well. But P^B and NP^B are equal, so that conclusion is false. Hence diagonalization isn't sufficient to separate these two classes. Similarly, no proof that relies on a simple simulation could show that the two classes are the same because that would show that they are the same relative to any oracle, but in fact P^A and NP^A are different.

THEOREM **9.19** ....

1. An oracle A exists whereby $\mathrm{P}^A \neq \mathrm{NP}^A$.
2. An oracle B exists whereby $\mathrm{P}^B = \mathrm{NP}^B$.

....

PROOF IDEA   Exhibiting oracle B is easy. Simply let B be any PSPACE-complete problem such as *TQBF*.

We exhibit oracle A by construction. We design A so that a certain language L_A in NP^A provably requires brute force search and so L_A cannot be in P^A. Hence we can conclude that $\mathrm{P}^A \neq \mathrm{NP}^A$. The construction considers every polynomial time oracle machine in turn, and ensures that each one fails to decide the language L_A.

PROOF   Let B be *TQBF*. We have the following series of containments:

$$\mathrm{NP}^{TQBF} \overset{1}{\subseteq} \mathrm{NPSPACE} \overset{2}{\subseteq} \mathrm{PSPACE} \overset{3}{\subseteq} \mathrm{P}^{TQBF}.$$

Containment 1 holds because we can convert the nondeterministic polynomial time oracle machine to a nondeterministic polynomial space machine that computes the answers to queries regarding *TQBF* instead of using the oracle. Containment 2 follows from Savitch's theorem. Containment 3 holds because *TQBF* is PSPACE-complete. Hence we conclude that $\mathrm{P}^{TQBF} = \mathrm{NP}^{TQBF}$.

Next, we show how to construct oracle A. For any oracle A, let L_A be the collection of all strings for which a string of equal length appears in A. Thus

$$L_A = \{w|\ \exists x \in A\ [\,|x| = |w|\,]\}.$$

Obviously, for any A, the language L_A is in NP^A.

To show L_A is not in P, we design A as follows. Let $M_1, M_2, \ldots$ be a list of all polynomial time oracle TMs. We may assume for simplicity that M_i runs in time n^i. The construction proceeds in stages, where stage i constructs a part of A, which ensures that M_i^A doesn't decide L_A. We construct A by declaring that certain strings are in A and others aren't in A. Each stage determines the status of only a finite number of strings. Initially, we have no information about A. We begin with stage 1.

Stage i.   So far, a finite number of strings have been declared to be in or out of A. We choose n greater than the length of any such string and large enough so that 2^n is greater than n^i, the running time of M_i. We now show how to extend our information about A so that M_i^A accepts 1^n whenever that string is not in L_A.

We run M_i on input 1^n and respond to its oracle queries as follows. If M_i queries about a string y whose status has already been determined, we respond consistently. If y's status is undetermined, we respond NO to the query and declare y to be out of A. We continue the simulation of M_i until it halts.

Now consider the situation from M_i's perspective. If it finds a string of length n in A, it should accept because it knows that 1^n is in A. If M_i determines that all strings of length n aren't in A, it should reject because it knows that 1^n is not in A. However, it doesn't have enough time to ask about all strings of length n, and we have answered NO to each of the queries it has made. Hence when M_i halts and must decide whether to accept or reject, it doesn't have enough information to be sure that its decision is correct.

Our goal is to make sure that its decision is not correct. We do so by observing its decision and then extending A so that the reverse is true. Thus, if M_i accepts 1^n, we declare all the remaining strings of length n to be out of A and so determine that 1^n is not in L_A. If M_i rejects 1^n, we find a string of length n that M_i hasn't queried and declare that string to be in A to guarantee that 1^n is in L_A. Such a string must exist because M_i runs for n^i steps, which is fewer than 2^n, the total number of strings of length n. We have achieved the goal of stage i, so it is completed. We proceed with stage $i + 1$.

After finishing all stages, we complete the construction of A by arbitrarily declaring that any string whose status remains undetermined by all stages is out of A. No polynomial time oracle machine decides L_A with oracle A, and so the theorem is proved.

In summary, the relativization method tells us that to solve the P versus NP question we must *analyze* computations, not just simulate them. In Section 9.3, we introduce one approach that may lead to such an analysis.

9.3

CIRCUIT COMPLEXITY

Computers are built from electronic devices wired together in a design called a *digital circuit*. We can also simulate theoretical models, such as Turing machines, with the theoretical counterpart to digital circuits, called **Boolean circuits**. Two purposes are served by establishing the connection between Turing machines and Boolean circuits. First, researchers believe that circuits provide a convenient computational model for attacking the P versus NP and related questions. Second, circuits provide an alternative proof of the Cook–Levin theorem that *SAT* is NP-complete. We cover both topics in this section.

A *Boolean circuit* is a collection of *gates* and *inputs* connected by *wires*. Cycles aren't permitted. Gates take three forms: AND gates, OR gates, and NOT gates, as shown schematically in the following figure.

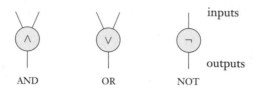

FIGURE 9.2
An AND gate, an OR gate, and a NOT gate

The wires in a Boolean circuit carry the Boolean values 0 and 1. The gates are simple processors that compute the Boolean functions AND, OR, and NOT. The AND function outputs 1 if both of its inputs are 1 and outputs 0 otherwise. The OR function outputs 0 if both of its inputs are 0 and outputs 1 otherwise. The NOT function outputs the opposite of its input; in other words, it outputs a 1 if its input is 0 and a 0 if its input is 1. The inputs are labeled $x_1, \ldots, x_n$. One of the gates is designated the *output gate*. The following figure depicts a Boolean circuit.

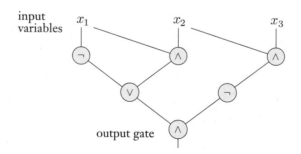

FIGURE 9.3
An example of a Boolean circuit

A Boolean circuit computes an output value from a setting of the inputs by propagating values along the wires and computing the function associated with the respective gates until the output gate is assigned a value. The following figure shows a Boolean circuit computing a value from a setting of its inputs.

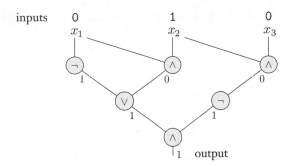

FIGURE **9.4**
An example of a Boolean circuit computing

We use functions to describe the input/output behavior of Boolean circuits. To a Boolean circuit C with n input variables, we associate a function $f_C \colon \{0,1\}^n \longrightarrow \{0,1\}$, where if C outputs b when its inputs $x_1, \ldots, x_n$ are set to $a_1, \ldots, a_n$, we write $f_C(a_1, \ldots, a_n) = b$. We say that C computes the function f_C. We sometimes consider Boolean circuits that have multiple output gates. A function with k output bits computes a function whose range is $\{0,1\}^k$.

EXAMPLE **9.21**

The n-input **_parity function_** $parity_n \colon \{0,1\}^n \longrightarrow \{0,1\}$ outputs 1 if an odd number of 1s appear in the input variables. The following circuit computes $parity_4$, the parity function on 4 variables.

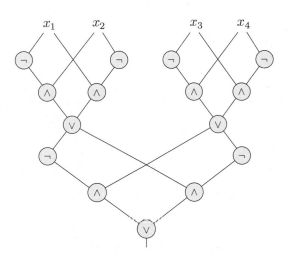

FIGURE **9.5**
A Boolean circuit that computes the parity function on four variables

We plan to use circuits to test membership in languages, suitably encoded into $\{0,1\}$. One problem that occurs is that any particular circuit can handle only inputs of some fixed length, whereas a language may contain strings of different lengths. So, instead of using a single circuit to test language membership, we use an entire *family* of circuits, one for each input length, to perform this task. We formalize this notion in the following definition.

DEFINITION **9.22** ....

A *circuit family* C is an infinite list of circuits, $(C_0, C_1, C_2, \dots)$ where C_n has n input variables. We say that C decides a language A over $\{0,1\}$ if, for every string w,

$$w \in A \quad \text{iff} \quad C_n(w) = 1,$$

where n is the length of w.

The *size* of a circuit is the number of gates that it contains. Two circuits are equivalent if they have the same input variables and output the same value on every input assignment. A circuit is *(size) minimal* if no smaller circuit is equivalent to it. The problem of minimizing circuits has obvious engineering application but is very difficult to solve in general. Even testing whether a particular circuit is minimal does not appear to be solvable in P or in NP. A circuit family for a language is minimal if every C_i on the list is a minimal circuit. The *size complexity* of a circuit family $(C_0, C_1, C_2, \dots)$ is the function $f\colon \mathcal{N} \longrightarrow \mathcal{N}$, where $f(n)$ is the size of C_n.

The *depth* of a circuit is the length (number of wires) of the longest path from an input variable to the output gate. We define *depth minimal* circuits and circuit families, and the *depth complexity* of circuit families as we did with circuit size. Circuit depth complexity will be of particular interest in Section 10.5 on parallel computation.

DEFINITION **9.23** ....

The *circuit (size) complexity* of a language is the size complexity of a minimal circuit family for that language. The *circuit depth complexity* of a language is defined similarly using depth instead of size.

EXAMPLE **9.24** ....

We can easily generalize Example 9.21 to give circuits that compute the parity function on n variables with $O(n)$ gates. One way to do so is to build a binary tree of gates that compute the **XOR** function, where the **XOR** function is the same as the 2-*parity* function, and then implement each **XOR** gate with 2 NOTs, 2 ANDs, and 1 OR, as we did in that earlier example.

Let A be the language of strings that contain an odd number of 1s. Then A has circuit complexity $O(n)$.

The circuit complexity of a language is related to its time complexity. Any language with small time complexity also has small circuit complexity, as the following theorem shows.

THEOREM **9.25** ··

Let $t: \mathcal{N} \longrightarrow \mathcal{N}$ be a function, where $t(n) \geq n$. If $A \in \text{TIME}(t(n))$, then A has circuit complexity $O(t^2(n))$.

This theorem gives an approach to proving that $\text{P} \neq \text{NP}$ whereby we attempt to show that some language in NP has more than polynomial circuit complexity.

··

PROOF IDEA   Let M be a TM that decides A in time $t(n)$. (For simplicity, we ignore the constant factor in $O(t(n))$, the actual running time of M.) For each n we construct a circuit C_n that simulates M on inputs of length n. The gates of C_n are organized in rows, one for each of the $t(n)$ steps in M's computation on an input of length n. Each row of gates represents the configuration (state, head position, and tape contents) of M at the corresponding step. Each row is wired into the previous row so that it can calculate its configuration from the previous row's configuration. We modify M so that the input is encoded into $\{0,1\}$. Moreover, when M is about to accept, it moves its head onto the leftmost tape cell and writes the $\sqcup$ symbol on that cell prior to entering the accept state. That way we can designate a gate in the final row of the circuit to be the output gate.

PROOF   Let $M = (Q, \Sigma, \Gamma, \delta, q_0, q_{\text{accept}}, q_{\text{reject}})$ decide A in time $t(n)$ and let w be an input of length n to M. Define a ***tableau*** for M on w to be a $t(n) \times t(n)$ table whose rows are configurations of M. The top row of the tableau contains the start configuration of M on w. The ith row contains the configuration at the ith step of the computation.

For convenience, we modify the representation format for configurations in this proof. Instead of the old format, described on page 128, where the state appears to the left of the symbol that the head is reading, we represent both the state and the tape symbol under the tape head by a single composite character. For example, if M is in state q and its tape contains the string 1011 with the head reading the second symbol from the left, the old format would be 1q011 and the new format would be 1$\boxed{q0}$11, where the composite character $\boxed{q0}$ represents both q, the state, and 0, the symbol under the head.

Each entry of the tableau can contain a tape symbol (member of Γ) or a combination of a state and a tape symbol (member of $Q \times \Gamma$). Call the entry at the ith row and jth column of the tableau $cell[i,j]$. The top row of the tableau is $cell[1,1], \ldots, cell[1,t(n)]$ and contains the starting configuration.

We make two assumptions about M in defining the notion of a tableau. First, as we mentioned in the proof idea, M accepts only when its head is on the leftmost tape cell and that cell contains the $\sqcup$ symbol. Second, once M does halt it stays in the same configuration for all future time steps. So, by looking at the leftmost cell in the final row of the tableau, $cell[t(n), 1]$, we can determine whether M has accepted. The following figure shows part of a tableau for M on the input 0010.

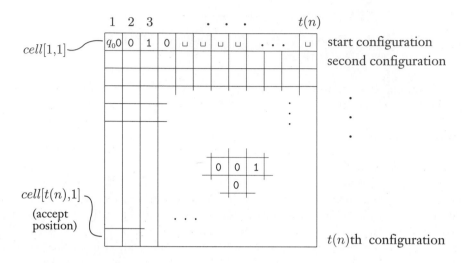

FIGURE 9.6
A tableau for M on input 0010

The content of each cell is determined by certain cells in the preceding row. If we know the values at $cell[i-1, j-1]$, $cell[i-1, j]$, and $cell[i-1, j+1]$, we can obtain the value at $cell[i, j]$ with M's transition function. For example, the following figure magnifies a portion of the tableau in Figure 9.6. The three top symbols, 0, 0, and 1, are tape symbols without states, so the middle symbol must remain a 0 in the next row, as shown.

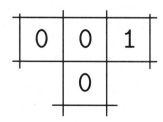

Now we can begin to construct the circuit C_n. It has several gates for each cell in the tableau. These gates compute the value at a cell from the values of the three cells that affect it.

To make the construction easier to describe, we add lights that show the output of some of the gates in the circuit. The lights are for illustrative purposes only and don't affect the operation of the circuit.

Let k be the number of elements in $\Gamma \cup (\Gamma \times Q)$. We create k lights for each cell in the tableau, one light for each member of Γ and one light for each member of $(\Gamma \times Q)$ —a total of $kt^2(n)$ lights. We call these lights $light[i, j, s]$, where $1 \le i, j \le t(n)$ and $s \in \Gamma \cup (\Gamma \times Q)$. The condition of the lights in a cell indicates the contents of that cell. If $light[i, j, s]$ is on, $cell[i, j]$ contains the symbol s. Of course, if the circuit is constructed properly, only one light would be on per cell.

Let's pick one of the lights, say, $light[i, j, s]$ in $cell[i, j]$. This light should be on if that cell contains the symbol s. We consider the three cells that can affect $cell[i, j]$ and determine which of their settings cause $cell[i, j]$ to contain s. This determination can be made by examining the transition function δ.

Suppose that, if the cells—$cell[i-1, j-1]$, $cell[i-1, j]$, and $cell[i-1, j+1]$— contain a, b, and c, respectively, $cell[i, j]$ contains s, according to δ. We wire the circuit so that, if $light[i-1, j-1, a]$, $light[i-1, j, b]$, and $light[i-1, j+1, c]$ are on, then so is $light[i, j, s]$. We do so by connecting the three lights at the $i-1$ level to an AND gate whose output is connected to $light[i, j, s]$.

In general, several different settings (a_1, b_1, c_1), (a_2, b_2, c_2), $\ldots$, (a_l, b_l, c_l) of $cell[i-1, j-1]$, $cell[i-1, j]$, and $cell[i-1, j+1]$ may cause $cell[i, j]$ to contain s. In this case we wire the circuit so that for each setting a_i, b_i, c_i the respective lights are connected with an AND gate, and all the AND gates are connected with an OR gate. This circuitry is illustrated in the following figure.

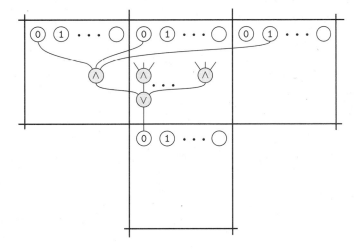

FIGURE **9.7**
Circuitry for one light

The circuitry just described is repeated for each light, with a few exceptions at the boundaries. Each cell at the left boundary of the tableau, that is, $cell[i, 1]$ for

$1 \leq i \leq t(n)$, has only two preceding cells that affect its contents. The cells at the right boundary are similar. In these cases, we modify the circuitry to simulate the behavior of M in this situation.

The cells in the first row have no predecessors and are handled in a special way. These cells contain the start configuration, and their lights are wired accordingly. Thus $light[1, 1, q_0]$ is on because the start configuration begins with the start state symbol q_0. Then $light[1, 2, 1], \ldots, light[1, n+1, 1]$ are connected to inputs $w_1, \ldots, w_n$, and $light[1, 2, 0], \ldots, light[1, n+1, 0]$ are connected by NOT gates to inputs $w_1, \ldots, w_n$ because the input string w determines these values. Additionally, $light[1, n+2, \sqcup], \ldots, light[1, t(n), \sqcup]$ are on, because the remaining cells in the first row correspond to positions on the tape that initially are blank ($\sqcup$ is the blank symbol). Finally, all other lights in the first row are off.

So far, we have constructed a circuit that simulates M through its $t(n)$th step. All that remains to be done is to assign one of the gates to be the output gate of the circuit. We know that M accepts w if it is in an accept state q_{accept} at the left-hand end of the tape at step $t(n)$. So we designate the output gate to be the one attached to $light[t(n), 1, q_{\text{accept}}]$. This completes the proof of the theorem.

....

Besides linking circuit complexity and time complexity, Theorem 9.25 yields an alternative proof of Theorem 7.22, the Cook–Levin theorem, as follows. We say that a Boolean circuit is ***satisfiable*** if some setting of the inputs causes the circuit to output 1. The ***circuit-satisfiability*** problem tests whether a circuit is satisfiable. Let

$$CIRCUIT\text{-}SAT = \{\langle C\rangle|\ C \text{ is a satisfiable Boolean circuit}\}.$$

The preceding theorem shows that Boolean circuits are capable of simulating Turing machines. We use that result to show that $CIRCUIT\text{-}SAT$ is NP-complete.

THEOREM **9.26** ....

$CIRCUIT\text{-}SAT$ is NP-complete.

PROOF   To prove this theorem, we must show that $CIRCUIT\text{-}SAT$ is in NP and that any language A in NP is reducible to $CIRCUIT\text{-}SAT$. The first is obvious. To do the second we must give a polynomial time reduction f that maps strings to circuits, where

$$f(w) = \langle C\rangle$$

implies that

$$w \in A \iff \text{Boolean circuit } C \text{ is satisfiable.}$$

Because A is in NP, it has a polynomial time verifier V whose input has the form $\langle x, c \rangle$, where c may be the certificate showing that x is in A. To construct f, we obtain the circuit simulating V using the method in Theorem 9.25. Fill in the inputs to the circuit that correspond to x with the symbols of w. The only remaining inputs to the circuit correspond to the certificate c. Call this circuit C and output it.

If C is satisfiable, a certificate exists, so w is in A. Conversely, if w is in A, a certificate exists, so C is satisfiable.

To show that this reduction runs in polynomial time, we must examine the proof of Theorem 9.25 and observe that the construction of the circuit can be done in time that is polynomial in n. The running time of the verifier is n^k for some k, so the size of the circuit constructed is $O(n^{2k})$. The structure of the circuit is quite simple (actually it is highly repetitious), so the running time of the reduction is $O(n^{2k})$.

Now we show that *3SAT* is NP-complete, completing the alternative proof of the Cook–Levin theorem.

THEOREM 9.27

3SAT is NP-complete.

PROOF IDEA   *3SAT* is obviously in NP. We show that all languages in NP reduce to *3SAT* in polynomial time. We do so by reducing *CIRCUIT-SAT* to *3SAT* in polynomial time. The reduction converts a circuit C to a formula ϕ, whereby C is satisfiable iff ϕ is satisfiable. The formula contains one variable for each variable and each gate in the circuit.

Conceptually, the formula simulates the circuit. A satisfying assignment for ϕ contains a satisfying assignment to C. It also contains the values at each of C's gates in the computation on the satisfying assignment. The formula is constructed so that its satisfying assignment has this property, by ANDing conditions for each gate to specify that the gate output correctly corresponds to the gate inputs. Finally, ϕ contains one clause stipulating that C's output is 1.

PROOF   We give a polynomial time reduction f from *CIRCUIT-SAT* to *3SAT*. Let C be a circuit containing inputs $x_1, \ldots, x_l$, and gates $g_1, \ldots, g_m$. The reduction builds from C a formula ϕ with variables $x_1, \ldots, x_l, g_1, \ldots, g_m$. Each of ϕ's variables corresponds to a wire in C. The x_i variables correspond to the input wires and the g_i variables correspond to the wires at the gate outputs. We relabel ϕ's variables as $w_1, \ldots, w_{l+m}$.

Now we describe ϕ's clauses. Each NOT gate in C with input wire w_i and output wire w_j becomes the two clauses

$$(w_i \lor w_j) \land (\overline{w_i} \lor \overline{w_j}).$$

Observe that both clauses are satisfied when an assignment is made to the variables w_i and w_j corresponding to the correct functioning of the NOT gate.

Each AND gate in C with inputs w_i and w_j and output w_k becomes the four clauses

$$(w_i \lor w_j \lor \overline{w_k}) \land (w_i \lor \overline{w_j} \lor \overline{w_k}) \land (\overline{w_i} \lor w_j \lor \overline{w_k}) \land (\overline{w_i} \lor \overline{w_j} \lor w_k),$$

and each OR gate in C with inputs w_i and w_j and output w_k becomes the four clauses

$$(w_i \lor w_j \lor \overline{w_k}) \land (w_i \lor \overline{w_j} \lor w_k) \land (\overline{w_i} \lor w_j \lor w_k) \land (\overline{w_i} \lor \overline{w_j} \lor w_k).$$

In each case all four clauses are satisfied when an assignment is made to the variables w_i, w_j, and w_k, corresponding to the correct functioning of the gate.

Additionally, add the clause (w_m) to ϕ, where w_m is C's output gate.

Some of the clauses described contain fewer than three literals. We can easily expand them to the desired size by repeating literals. Thus the preceding clause (w_m) is expanded to the equivalent clause $(w_m \lor w_m \lor w_m)$. That completes the construction.

We briefly argue that the construction works. If a satisfying assignment for C exists, we obtain a satisfying assignment for ϕ by assigning the g_i variables according to C's computation on this assignment. Conversely, if a satisfying assignment for ϕ exists, it gives an assignment for C because it describes C's entire computation where the output value is 1. The reduction can be done in polynomial time because it is simple to compute and the output size is polynomial (actually linear) in the size of the input.

EXERCISES

9.1 Prove that $\mathrm{TIME}(2^n) = \mathrm{TIME}(2^{n+1})$.

9.2 Prove that $\mathrm{TIME}(2^n) \subsetneq \mathrm{TIME}(2^{2n})$.

9.3 Prove that $\mathrm{NTIME}(n) \subsetneq \mathrm{PSPACE}$.

9.4 Show how the circuit depicted in Figure 9.5 computes on input 0110 by showing the values computed by all of the gates, as we did in Figure 9.4.

9.5 Give a circuit that computes the parity function on three input variables and show how it computes on input 011.

9.6 Prove that if $A \in \mathrm{P}$ then $\mathrm{P}^A = \mathrm{P}$.

9.7 Give regular expressions with exponentiation that generate the following languages over the alphabet $\{0,1\}$.

    a. All strings of length 500.

    b. All strings of length 500 or less.

    c. All strings of length 500 or more.

    d. All strings of length different than 500.

    e. All strings that contain exactly 500 1s.

    f. All strings that contain at least 500 1s.

    g. All strings that contain at most 500 1s.

    h. All strings of length 500 or more that contain a 0 in the 500th position.

    i. All strings that contain two 0s that have at least 500 symbols between them.

9.8 If R is a regular expression, let $R^{\{m,n\}}$ represent the expression

$$R^m \cup R^{m+1} \cup \cdots \cup R^n.$$

Show how to implement the $R^{\{m,n\}}$ operator using the ordinary exponentiation operator, but without "$\cdots$".

9.9 Show that if $\mathrm{NP} = \mathrm{P}^{SAT}$ then $\mathrm{NP} = \mathrm{coNP}$.

PROBLEMS

9.10 Show the error in the following fallacious "proof" that $\mathrm{P} \neq \mathrm{NP}$. Proof by contradiction. Assume that $\mathrm{P} = \mathrm{NP}$. Then $SAT \in \mathrm{P}$. So, for some k, $SAT \in \mathrm{TIME}(n^k)$. Because every language in NP is polynomial time reducible to SAT, $\mathrm{NP} \subseteq \mathrm{TIME}(n^k)$. Therefore $\mathrm{P} \subseteq \mathrm{TIME}(n^k)$. But, by the time hierarchy theorem, $\mathrm{TIME}(n^{k+1})$ contains a language which isn't in $\mathrm{TIME}(n^k)$, which contradicts $\mathrm{P} \subseteq \mathrm{TIME}(n^k)$. Therefore $\mathrm{P} \neq \mathrm{NP}$.

9.11 Show that the language *MAX-CLIQUE* from problem 7.30 is in NP^{SAT}.

9.12 Prove that an oracle C exists for which $\mathrm{NP}^C \neq \mathrm{coNP}^C$.

9.13 In computability theory, we made an important distinction between languages that are decidable and those that are recognizable. This problem asks you to show why these two terms are generally interchangeable in complexity theory.

When we say that a TM M decides a language A in time $t(n)$, we require that M halt on all inputs of length n within $t(n)$ steps. Say that a TM *recognizes* A in time $t(n)$ if $t(n)$ is the maximum number of steps that M uses when it accepts an input of length n, disregarding inputs which are rejected. Show that, for time constructible functions $t(n)$, the notions of decidable and recognizable are equivalent. In other words, prove that A is decided by some TM in time $O(t(n))$ if and only if A is recognized by some TM in time $O(t(n))$, assuming that $t(n)$ is time constructible.

9.14 Define the function $parity_n$ as in Example 9.21. Show that $parity_n$ can be computed with $O(n)$ size circuits.

9.15 Recall that we may consider circuits that output strings over $\{0,1\}$ by designating several output gates. Let $add_n \colon \{0,1\}^{2n} \longrightarrow \{0,1\}^{n+1}$ take the sum of two n bit binary integers and produce the $n + 1$ bit result. Show that we can compute the add_n function with $O(n)$ size circuits.

9.16 Define the function $majority_n: \{0,1\}^n \longrightarrow \{0,1\}$ as

$$majority_n(x_1, \ldots, x_n) = \begin{cases} 0 & \sum x_i < n/2 \\ 1 & \sum x_i \geq n/2 \end{cases}.$$

Thus the $majority_n$ function returns the majority vote of the inputs. Show that $majority_n$ can be computed with

    a. $O(n^2)$ size circuits.

    b. $O(n \log n)$ size circuits. (Hint: Recursively divide the number of inputs in half and use the result of Problem 9.15.)

*9.17 Define the problem $majority_n$ as in Problem 9.16. Show that it may be computed with $O(n)$ size circuits.

9.18 Consider the function $pad: \Sigma^* \times \mathcal{N} \longrightarrow \Sigma^*$ where $pad(s,l) = s \sqcup^j$ where $j = \max(0, l-n)$ and n is the length of s. Thus, $pad(s,l)$ simply adds enough blanks to the end of s so that the length of the result is l. For any language A and function $f: \mathcal{N} \longrightarrow \mathcal{N}$ define the language $pad(A, f(n))$ as

$$pad(A, f(n)) = \{pad(s, f(n)) | \text{ where } n \text{ is the length of } s\}.$$

Prove that if $A \in \mathrm{TIME}(n^2)$ then $pad(A, n^2) \in \mathrm{TIME}(n)$.

9.19 Prove that if $\mathrm{NEXPTIME} \neq \mathrm{EXPTIME}$ then $\mathrm{P} \neq \mathrm{NP}$. You may find the function pad, defined in Problem 9.18, to be helpful.

9.20 Define pad as in Problem 9.18. Prove that, for any language A and any natural number k, $A \in \mathrm{P}$ if and only if $pad(A, n^k) \in \mathrm{P}$.

9.21 Use the result of Problem 9.20 to show that $\mathrm{P} \neq \mathrm{SPACE}(n)$.

10

··

ADVANCED TOPICS IN COMPLEXITY THEORY

In this chapter we briefly sample a few additional topics in complexity theory. If you are interested in further information you should examine *The Handbook of Theoretical computer Science* [71] which presents an extensive survey.

This chapter contains sections on approximation algorithms, probabilistic algorithms, interactive proof systems, parallel computation, and cryptography. These sections are independent except that probabilistic algorithms are used in the sections on interactive proof systems and cryptography.

10.1 ■

APPROXIMATION ALGORITHMS

In certain problems called *optimization problems* we seek to find the best solution among a collection of possible solutions. For example, we may want to find a largest clique in a graph, a smallest vertex cover, or a shortest path connecting two nodes. When an optimization problem is NP-hard, as is the case with the first two of these types of problems, no polynomial time algorithm exists that finds the best solution unless P = NP.

In practice, we may not need the absolute best or *optimal* solution to a problem. A solution that is nearly optimal may be good enough and may be much easier to find. As its name implies, an ***approximation algorithm*** is designed to find such approximately optimal solutions.

For example, take the vertex cover problem that we introduced in Section 7.5. There we presented the problem as the language *VERTEX-COVER* representing a ***decision problem***—one that has a yes/no answer. In the optimization version of this problem, called *MIN-VERTEX-COVER*, we aim to produce one of the smallest vertex covers among all possible vertex covers in the input graph. The following polynomial time algorithm approximately solves this optimization problem. It produces a vertex cover that is never more than twice the size of one of the smallest vertex covers.

$A =$ "On input $\langle G \rangle$, where G is an undirected graph:

1. Repeat the following until all edges in G touch a marked edge.
2. Find an edge in G untouched by any marked edge.
3. Mark that edge.
4. Output all nodes that are endpoints of marked edges."

THEOREM **10.1** ....

A is a polynomial time algorithm that produces a vertex cover of G that is no more than twice as large as a smallest vertex cover.

PROOF A obviously runs in polynomial time. Let X be the set of nodes that it outputs. Let H be the set of edges that it marks. We know that X is a vertex cover because H contains or touches every edge in G, and hence X touches all edges in G.

To prove that X is at most twice as large as a smallest vertex cover Y we establish two facts: X is twice as large as H; and H is not larger than Y. First, every edge in H contributes two nodes to X, so X is twice as large as H. Second, Y is a vertex cover, so every edge in H is touched by some node in Y. No such node touches two edges in H because the edges in H do not touch each other. Therefore vertex cover Y is at least as large as H because Y contains a different node that touches every edge in H. Hence X is no more than twice as large as Y.

....

MIN-VERTEX-COVER is an example of a ***minimization problem*** because we aim to find the *smallest* among the collection of possible solutions. In a ***maximization problem*** we seek the *largest* solution. An approximation algorithm for a minimization problem is ***k-optimal*** if it always finds a solution that is not more than k times optimal. The preceding algorithm is 2-optimal for the vertex cover problem. For a maximization problem a k-optimal approximation algorithm always finds a solution that is at least $\frac{1}{k}$ times the size of the optimal.

The following is an approximation algorithm for a maximization problem called *MAX-CUT*. A ***cut*** in an undirected graph is a separation of the vertices V into two disjoint subsets S and T. A ***cut edge*** is an edge that goes between a node in S and a node in T. An ***uncut edge*** is an edge that is not a cut edge. The size of a cut is the number of cut edges. The *MAX-CUT* problem asks for a largest cut in the input graph G. As we showed in Problem 7.23, this problem is NP-complete. The following algorithm approximates *MAX-CUT* within a factor of 2.

B = "On input $\langle G \rangle$ where G is an undirected graph with nodes V:
1. Let $S = \emptyset$ and $T = V$.
2. If moving a single node, either from S to T or from T to S, increases the size of the cut, make that move and repeat this stage.
3. If no such node exists, output the current cut and halt."

This algorithm starts with a (presumably) bad cut and makes local improvements until no further local improvement is possible. Although this procedure won't give an optimal cut in general, we show that it does give one that is at most half the size of the optimal one.

THEOREM   10.2 ....

B is a polynomial time approximation algorithm that is 2-optimal for *MAX-CUT*.

PROOF B runs in polynomial time because every execution of stage 2 increases the size of the cut to a maximum of the total number of edges in G.

Now we show that B's cut is at least half optimal. Actually, we show something stronger: B's cut contains at least half of all edges in G. Observe that, at every node of G, the number of cut edges is at least as large as the number of uncut edges, or B would have shifted that node to the other side. We add up the numbers of cut edges at every node. That sum is twice the total number of cut edges because every cut edge is counted once for each of its two endpoints. By the the preceding observation, that sum must be at least the corresponding sum of the numbers of uncut edges at every node. Thus G has at least as many cut edges as uncut edges, and therefore the cut contains at least half of all edges.

....

10.2
PROBABILISTIC ALGORITHMS

A ***probabilistic algorithm*** is an algorithm designed to use the outcome of a random process. Typically, such an algorithm would contain an instruction to "flip a coin" and the result of that coin flip would influence the algorithm's subsequent execution and output. Certain types of problems seem to be more easily solvable by probabilistic algorithms than by deterministic algorithms.

How can making a decision by flipping a coin ever be better than actually calculating, or even estimating, the best choice in a particular situation? Sometimes, calculating the best choice may require excessive time and estimating it may introduce a bias that invalidates the result. For example, statisticians use random sampling to determine information about the individuals in a large population, such as their tastes or political preferences. Querying all the individuals might take too long, and querying a nonrandomly selected subset might tend to give erroneous results.

THE CLASS BPP

We begin our formal discussion of probabilistic computation by defining a model of a probabilistic Turing machine. Then we give a complexity class associated with efficient probabilistic computation and a few examples.

DEFINITION   **10.3**   ....

A ***probabilistic Turing machine*** M is a type of nondeterministic Turing machine where each nondeterministic step is called a ***coin-flip step*** and has two legal next moves. We assign a probability to each branch b of M's computation on input w as follows. Define the probability of branch b to be

$$\Pr[b] = 2^{-k},$$

where k be the number of coin-flip steps that occur on branch b. Define the probability that M accepts w to be

$$\Pr[M \text{ accepts } w] = \sum_{\substack{b \text{ is an} \\ \text{accepting branch}}} \Pr[b].$$

In other words, the probability that M accepts w is the probability that you would reach an accepting configuration if you simulated M on w by flipping a coin to determine which move to follow at each coin-flip step. We let

$$\Pr[M \text{ rejects } w] = 1 - \Pr[M \text{ accepts } w].$$

When a probabilistic Turing machine recognizes a language, it must accept all strings in the language and reject all strings out of the language as usual, except that now we allow the machine a small probability of error. For $0 \le \epsilon < \frac{1}{2}$ we say that ***M recognizes language A with error probability*** ϵ if

1. $w \in A$ implies $\Pr[M \text{ accepts } w] \ge 1 - \epsilon$, and
2. $w \notin A$ implies $\Pr[M \text{ rejects } w] \ge 1 - \epsilon$.

We also consider error probability bounds that depend on the input length n. For example, error probability $\epsilon = 2^{-n}$ indicates an exponentially small probability of error.

We are interested in probabilistic algorithms that run efficiently in time and/or space. We measure the time and space complexity of a probabilistic Turing machine in the same way as for a nondeterministic Turing machine, by using the worst case computation branch on each input.

DEFINITION 10.4

BPP is the class of languages that are recognized by probabilistic polynomial time Turing machines with an error probability of $\frac{1}{3}$.

We defined this class with an error probability of $\frac{1}{3}$, but any constant error probability would yield an equivalent definition as long it is strictly between 0 and $\frac{1}{2}$ by virtue of the following *amplification lemma*. It gives a simple way of making the error probability exponential small. Note that a probabilistic algorithm with an error probability of 2^{-100} is far more likely to give an erroneous result because the computer on which it runs has a hardware failure than because of an unlucky toss of its coins.

LEMMA 10.5

Let ϵ be a fixed constant strictly between 0 and $\frac{1}{2}$. Then for any polynomial $\text{poly}(n)$ a probabilistic polynomial time Turing machine M_1 that operates with error probability ϵ has an equivalent probabilistic polynomial time Turing machine M_2 that operates with an error probability of $2^{-\text{poly}(n)}$.

PROOF IDEA M_2 simulates M_1 by running it a polynomial number of times and taking the majority vote of the outcomes. The probability of error decreases exponentially with the number of runs of M_1 made.

Consider the case where $\epsilon = \frac{1}{3}$. This situation corresponds to a box that contains many red and blue balls. We know that $\frac{2}{3}$ of the balls are of one color and that the remaining $\frac{1}{3}$ are of the other color, but we don't know which color is predominant. We can test for that color by sampling several (say, 100) balls at random to determine which color comes up most frequently. Almost certainly, the predominant color in the box will be the most frequent one in the sample.

The balls correspond to branches of M_1's computation: red to accepting and blue to rejecting. M_2 samples the color by running M_1. A calculation shows that M_2 errs with exponentially small probability if it runs M_1 a polynomial number of times and outputs the result that comes up most often.

PROOF Given TM M_1 recognizing a language with an error probability of $\epsilon < \frac{1}{2}$ and a polynomial $\text{poly}(n)$, we construct the following TM M_2 that recognizes the same language with an error probability of $2^{-\text{poly}(n)}$. We describe an algorithm that implements the proof idea and a detailed[1] computation to prove that it improves the error probability as claimed. First we assign variable names to the following values. All logarithms are base 2. Fix n and let

$$t = 2^{\text{poly}(n)},$$
$$a = 1/(4\epsilon(1 - \epsilon)),$$
$$b = \max(1, 1/\log a),$$
$$c = 2\log(bt), \text{ and}$$
$$k = \lceil bc \rceil.$$

$M_2 =$ "On input w
1.   Calculate the value k, and repeat the following $2k$ times:
2.   Simulate M_2 on input w.
3.   If most runs of M_2 accept, then *accept*; otherwise *reject*."

We verify that M_2 runs in polynomial time by observing that a and b depend only on ϵ, so c and k are $O(\log t)$ and thus polynomial in n.

We show that M_2 is equivalent to M_1 but with an error probability of $2^{-\text{poly}(n)}$ by using the following calculation. Assume that $t \geq 9$ without any loss of generality. Select an input w. M_1 errs on w with some probability $\delta \leq \epsilon < \frac{1}{2}$. We show that M_2 errs on w with a probability of at most $2^{-\text{poly}(n)}$.

If M_2 errs on w, it obtains at least k erroneous results from its $2k$ runs of M_1 in w. The probability of that occurring is

$$\sum_{k \leq i \leq 2k} \Pr\big[M_2 \text{ errs exactly } i \text{ times on } 2k \text{ runs} \big]$$
$$= \sum_{k \leq i \leq 2k} \binom{2k}{i} \delta^i (1 - \delta)^{2k-i}.$$

No term of the sum is diminished if we let $i = k$ because $\delta/(1 - \delta) < 1$ when $\delta < \frac{1}{2}$, so we can place an upper bound on the sum by

$$\leq (k+1) \binom{2k}{k} \delta^k (1 - \delta)^k \ \leq \ (k+1)\, 2^{2k} \delta^k (1 - \delta)^k \ \leq \ (k+1)\, (4\delta(1 - \delta))^k.$$

In the preceding step we bounded $\binom{2k}{k}$, the number of subsets of size k out of $2k$ elements, by 2^{2k}, the number of all subsets. Next we have $\delta(1 - \delta) \leq \epsilon(1 - \epsilon)$ because $\delta \leq \epsilon < \frac{1}{2}$, so we can bound the preceding expression by

$$\leq (k+1)\, (4\epsilon(1 - \epsilon))^k.$$

---

[1]The analysis of the error probability follows immediately from a standard result in probability theory called the **Chernoff bound**. Here we give an alternative and self-contained, albeit technical, calculation that avoids any dependence on that result.

We must show that the previous expression is at most $2^{-\text{poly}(n)}$. We do so by showing that $(k+1)(1/a)^k \leq 1/t$, which is equivalent to showing that

$$a^k \geq (k+1)t.$$

We use a series of (in)equalities:

$$a^k = a^{\lceil bc \rceil} \geq a^{bc} \overset{1}{\geq} 2^c = 2^{2\log(bt)} = (bt)^2.$$

Inequality 1 derives from two cases. If $1/\log a \geq 1$, then $b = 1/\log a$ and $a^{bc} = a^{(1/\log a)c} = 2^c$. If $1/\log a < 1$, then $b = 1$ and $a > 2$ and $a^{bc} = a^c > 2^c$.

We have $b \geq 1$ and assumed that $t \geq 9$, so $bt \geq 9$. Therefore $bt > 2 + 2\log(bt)$ and thus

$$(bt)^2 > bt(2 + 2\log(bt)) = t(2b + 2b\log(bt)).$$

Hence, because $b \geq 1$,

$$a^k \geq t(2 + 2b\log(bt)) \geq t(1 + \lceil 2b\log(bt) \rceil) \geq t(1 + \lceil bc \rceil) = (k+1)t.$$

··

PRIMALITY

A **prime number** is a integer greater than 1 that is not divisible by positive integers other than 1 and itself. A nonprime number greater than 1 is called **composite**. In this section we describe a probabilistic polynomial time algorithm for testing whether a number is prime or composite.

One way to determine whether a number is prime is to try all possible integers less than that number and see whether any are divisors, also called **factors**. That algorithm has exponential time complexity because the magnitude of a number is exponential in its length. The probabilistic primality testing algorithm that we describe operates in a different manner entirely. It doesn't search for factors. Indeed, no probabilistic polynomial time algorithm for finding factors is known to exist.

Before discussing the algorithm, we need to mention some notation and facts from number theory. All numbers in this section are integers. For any number p greater than 1, let $\mathcal{Z}_p^+$ be the set $\{1, \ldots, p-1\}$ and $\mathcal{Z}_p$ be the same with the addition of 0. We think of these sets as numbers modulo p, and we may refer to their elements by other numbers that are equivalent modulo p such as -1 for $p-1$. (Two numbers are equivalent modulo p if they differ by a multiple of p.) If numbers x and y are equivalent modulo p, we write $x \equiv y \pmod{p}$. Let $x \bmod p$ be the smallest nonnegative y where $x \equiv y \pmod{p}$.

Two numbers are relatively prime if they have no common divisor other than 1. The **Chinese remainder theorem** says that a one-to-one correspondence exists between $\mathcal{Z}_{pq}$ and $\mathcal{Z}_p \times \mathcal{Z}_q$. Each number $r \in \mathcal{Z}_{pq}$ corresponds to a pair (a, b), where $a \in \mathcal{Z}_p$ and $b \in \mathcal{Z}_q$, such that

$$r \equiv a \pmod{p}, \text{ and}$$
$$r \equiv b \pmod{q}.$$

The main idea behind the algorithm stems from the following result, called *Fermat's little theorem*.

If p is prime and $a \in \mathcal{Z}_p^+$ then $a^{p-1} \equiv 1 \pmod{p}$.

For example, if $p = 7$ and $a = 2$, the theorem says that $2^{(7-1)} \bmod 7$ should be 1 because 7 is prime. The simple calculation

$$2^{(7-1)} = 2^6 = 64 \quad \text{and} \quad 64 \bmod 7 = 1$$

confirms this result. Suppose that we try $p = 6$ instead. Then

$$2^{(6-1)} = 2^5 = 32 \quad \text{and} \quad 32 \bmod 6 = 2$$

gives a different result than 1, implying by the theorem that 6 is not prime. Of course, we already knew that. However, this method demonstrates that 6 is composite without finding its factors. Problem 10.15 asks for a proof of this theorem.

Think of the preceding theorem as providing a type of "test" for primality called a *Fermat test*. When we say that p passes the Fermat test at a, we mean that $a^{p-1} \equiv 1 \pmod{p}$. The theorem states that primes pass all Fermat tests for $a \in \mathcal{Z}_p^+$. We observed that 6 fails some Fermat test, so 6 isn't prime.

Can we use these tests to give an algorithm for determining primality? Almost. Call a number *pseudoprime* if it passes all Fermat tests. With the exception of the relatively few *Carmichael numbers*, the pseudoprime numbers are identical to the prime numbers. We give a probabilistic polynomial time pseudoprimality testing algorithm and afterward one for testing primality.

A pseudoprimality algorithm that goes through all Fermat tests would require exponential time. The key to the probabilistic polynomial time algorithm is that, if a number fails at any one test, it fails at least half of all tests. (Just accept this assertion for now. Problem 10.16 asks for a proof.) The algorithm works by trying several tests chosen at random. If any fail, the number must be composite. If all pass, the number is likely to be pseudoprime. The algorithm contains a parameter k that determines the error probability.

PSEUDOPRIME = "On input p:

    1. Select $a_1, \ldots, a_k$ randomly in $\mathcal{Z}_p^+$.
    2. Compute $a_i^{p-1} \bmod p$ for each i.
    3. If all computed values are 1, *accept*; otherwise *reject*."

If p is pseudoprime, it passes all tests and the algorithm accepts with certainty. If p isn't pseudoprime, it passes at most half of all tests. In that case it passes each randomly selected test with probability at most $\frac{1}{2}$. The probability that it passes all k randomly selected tests is thus at most 2^{-k}. Hence this probabilistic algorithm recognizes the language of all pseudoprime numbers with an error probability of 2^{-k}. It operates in polynomial time because modular exponentiation is computable in polynomial time (see Problem 7.12).

To convert this pseudoprimality algorithm to a primality algorithm we give a more sophisticated test that avoids the problem with the Carmichael numbers. The underlying principle is that the number 1 has exactly two square roots, namely 1 and -1, modulo any prime p. For many composite numbers, including all the Carmichael numbers, 1 has four or more square roots. For example, ± 1 and ± 8 are the four square roots of 1, modulo 21. If a number passes the Fermat test at a, the algorithm finds one of its square roots of 1 at random and determines whether that square root is 1 or -1. If it isn't, we know that the number isn't prime.

We can obtain square roots of 1 if p passes the Fermat test at a because $a^{p-1} \bmod p = 1$ and so $a^{(p-1)/2} \bmod p$ is a square root of 1. If that value is still 1 we may repeatedly divide the exponent by two, so long as the resulting exponent remains an integer, and see whether the first number that is different from 1 is -1 or some other number. We give a formal proof of the correctness of the algorithm immediately following its description. Select $k \geq 1$ as a parameter that determines the maximum error probability to be 2^{-k}.

$PRIME$ = "On input p:

1. If p is even, *accept* if $p = 2$; otherwise *reject*.
2. Select $a_1, \ldots, a_k$ randomly in $\mathcal{Z}_p^+$.
3. For each i from 1 to k:
4.   Compute $a_i^{p-1} \bmod p$ and *reject* if different from 1.
5.   Let $p - 1 = st$ where s is odd and $t = 2^h$ is a power of 2.
6.   Compute the sequence $a_i^{s \cdot 2^0}, a_i^{s \cdot 2^1}, a_i^{s \cdot 2^2}, \ldots, a_i^{s \cdot 2^h}$ modulo p.
7.   If some element of this sequence is not 1, find the last element that is not 1 and *reject* if that element is not -1.
8. All tests have passed at this point, so *accept*."

The following two lemmas show that algorithm *PRIME* works correctly. Obviously the algorithm is correct when p is even, so we only consider the case when p is odd. Say that a_i is a *(compositeness) witness* if the algorithm rejects at either stage 4 or 7, using a_i.

LEMMA 10.7 ....

If p is an odd prime number, $\Pr[\,PRIME \text{ accepts } p\,] = 1$.

PROOF We first show that if p is prime, no witness exists and so no branch of the algorithm rejects. If a were a stage 4 witness, $(a^{p-1} \bmod p) \neq 1$ and Fermat's little theorem implies that p is composite. If a were a stage 7 witness, some b exists in $\mathcal{Z}_p^+$, where $b \not\equiv \pm 1 \pmod{p}$ and $b^2 \equiv 1 \pmod{p}$.

Therefore $b^2 - 1 \equiv 0 \pmod{p}$. Factoring $b^2 - 1$ yields

$$(b-1)(b+1) \equiv 0 \pmod{p},$$

which implies that

$$(b-1)(b+1) = cp$$

for some positive integer c. Because $b \not\equiv \pm 1 \pmod{p}$, both $b-1$ and $b+1$ are strictly between 0 and p. Therefore p is composite because a multiple of a prime number cannot be expressed as a product of numbers that are smaller than it is.

LEMMA **10.8**

If p is an odd composite number, $\Pr\left[\,PRIME \text{ accepts } p\,\right] \leq 2^{-k}$.

PROOF   We show that, if p is an odd composite number and a is selected randomly in $\mathcal{Z}_p^+$,

$$\Pr\left[\,a \text{ is a witness}\,\right] \geq \tfrac{1}{2}$$

by demonstrating that at least as many witnesses as nonwitnesses exist in $\mathcal{Z}_p^+$. We do so by finding a unique witness for each nonwitness.

In every nonwitness, the sequence computed in stage 6 is either all 1s or contains -1 at some position, followed by 1s. For example, 1 itself is a nonwitness of the first kind, and -1 is a nonwitness of the second kind because s is odd and $(-1)^{s \cdot 2^0} \equiv -1$ and $(-1)^{s \cdot 2^1} \equiv 1$. Among all nonwitnesses of the second kind, find a nonwitness for which the -1 appears in the largest position in the sequence. Let h be that witness and let j be the position of -1 in its sequence, where the sequence positions are numbered starting at 0. Hence $h^{s \cdot 2^j} \equiv -1 \pmod{p}$.

Because p is composite, we can write p as the product of q and r, two numbers that are relatively prime. The Chinese remainder theorem implies that some number c exists in $\mathcal{Z}_p$ whereby

$$t \equiv h \pmod{q} \quad \text{and}$$
$$t \equiv 1 \pmod{r}.$$

Therefore

$$t^{s \cdot 2^j} \equiv -1 \pmod{q} \quad \text{and}$$
$$t^{s \cdot 2^j} \equiv 1 \pmod{r}.$$

Hence t is a witness because $t^{s \cdot 2^j} \not\equiv \pm 1 \pmod{p}$ but $t^{s \cdot 2^{j+1}} \equiv 1 \pmod{p}$.

Next we prove that $dt \bmod p$ is a unique witness for each nonwitness d by making two observations. First, $d^{s \cdot 2^j} \equiv \pm 1 \pmod{p}$ and $d^{s \cdot 2^{j+1}} \equiv 1 \pmod{p}$ owing to the way j was chosen. Therefore $dt \bmod p$ is a witness because $(dt)^{s \cdot 2^j} \not\equiv \pm 1$ and $(dt)^{s \cdot 2^{j+1}} \equiv 1 \pmod{p}$.

Second, if d_1 and d_2 are distinct nonwitnesses, $d_1 t \bmod p \neq d_2 t \bmod p$. The reason is that $t^{s \cdot 2^{j+1}} \bmod p = 1$. Hence $t \cdot t^{s \cdot 2^{j+1} - 1} \bmod p = 1$. Therefore, if $td_1 \bmod p = td_2 \bmod p$, then

$$d_1 = t \cdot t^{s \cdot 2^{j+1} - 1} d_1 \bmod p = t \cdot t^{s \cdot 2^{j+1} - 1} d_2 \bmod p = d_2.$$

Thus the number of witnesses must be as large as the number of nonwitnesses, and the proof is complete.

The preceding algorithm and its analysis establishes the following theorem. Let *PRIMES* = $\{n \mid n$ is a prime number in binary$\}$.

THEOREM 10.9

PRIMES $\in$ BPP

Note that the probabilistic primality algorithm has ***one-sided error***. When the algorithm outputs *reject*, we know that the input must be composite. When the output is *accept*, we know only that the input probably is prime. Thus an incorrect answer can only occur when the input is a composite number. The one-sided error feature is common to many probabilistic algorithms, so the special complexity class RP is designated for it.

DEFINITION 10.10

RP is the class of languages that are recognized by probabilistic polynomial time Turing machines where inputs in the language are recognized with a probability of at least $\frac{1}{2}$ and inputs not in the language are rejected with a probability of 1.

We can make the error probability exponentially small and maintain a polynomial running time by using a probability amplification technique similar to (actually simpler than) the one we used in Lemma 10.5. Our earlier algorithm shows that *COMPOSITES* $\in$ RP.

READ-ONCE BRANCHING PROGRAMS

A ***branching program*** is a model of computation used in complexity theory and in certain practical areas such as computer-aided design. This model represents a decision process that queries the values of input variables and bases decisions about the way to proceed on the answers to those queries. We represent this decision process as a graph whose nodes correspond to the particular variable queried at that point in the process.

In this section we investigate the complexity of testing whether two branching programs are equivalent. In general, that problem is NP-complete. If we place a certain natural restriction on the class of branching programs, we can give a probabilistic polynomial time algorithm for testing equivalence. This algorithm is especially interesting for two reasons. First, no polynomial time algorithm is known for this problem, so we have another example of probabilism apparently expanding the class of languages whereby membership can be tested efficiently. Second, this algorithm introduces the technique of assigning non-Boolean values to normally Boolean variables in order to analyze the behavior of some Boolean function of those variables. That technique is used to great effect in interactive proof systems, as we show in Section 10.4.

DEFINITION **10.11** ···

A *branching program* is a directed acyclic[2] graph where all nodes are labeled by variables, except for two *output nodes* labeled 0 or 1. The nodes that are labeled by variables are called *query nodes*. Every query node has two outgoing edges, one labeled 0 and the other labeled 1. Both output nodes have no outgoing edges. One of the nodes in a branching program is designated the start node.

A branching program determines a Boolean function as follows. Take any assignment to the variables appearing on its query nodes and, beginning at the start node, follow the path determined by taking the outgoing edge from each query node according to the value assigned to the indicated variable until one of the output nodes is reached. The output is the label of that output node. The following diagram gives two examples of branching programs.

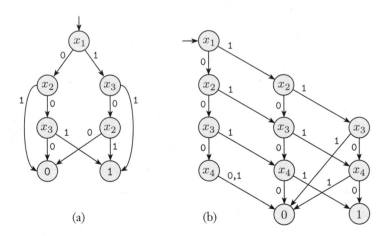

(a)   (b)

FIGURE **10.1**
Two read-once branching programs

---

[2]A directed graph is *acyclic* if it has no directed cycles.

Branching programs are related to the class L in a way that is analogous to the relationship between Boolean circuits and the class P. Problem 10.17 asks you to show that a branching program with polynomially many nodes can test membership in any language over {0,1} that is in L.

Two branching programs are equivalent if they determine equal functions. Problem 10.19 asks you to show that the problem of testing whether two branching programs are equivalent is NP-complete. Here we consider a restricted form of branching programs. A ***read-once branching program*** is one that can query each variable at most one time on every directed path from the start node to an output node. Both branching programs in Figure 10.1 have the read-once feature. Let

$EQ_{\mathrm{ROBP}} = \{\langle B_1, B_2 \rangle |\ B_1 \text{ and } B_2 \text{ are equivalent read-once branching programs}\}.$

THEOREM 10.12 ....

EQ_{ROBP} is in BPP.

....

PROOF IDEA First let's try assigning random values to the variables x_1 through x_m that appear in B_1 and B_2, and evaluate these branching programs on that setting. We accept if B_1 and B_2 agree on the assignment and reject otherwise. However, this strategy doesn't work because two inequivalent read-once branching programs may disagree only on a single assignment out of the 2^m possible Boolean assignments to the variables. The probability that we would select that assignment is exponentially small. Hence we would accept with high probability even when B_1 and B_2 are not equivalent, and that is unsatisfactory.

Instead, we modify this strategy by randomly selecting a non-Boolean assignment to the variables and evaluate B_1 and B_2 in a suitably defined manner. We can then show that, if B_1 and B_2 are not equivalent, the random evaluations will likely be unequal.

PROOF We assign polynomials over $x_1, \ldots, x_m$ to the nodes and to the edges of a read-once branching program B as follows. The constant function 1 is assigned to the start node. If a node labeled x has been assigned polynomial p, assign the polynomial xp to its outgoing 1-edge, and assign the polynomial $(1-x)p$ to its outgoing 0-edge. If the edges incoming to some node have been assigned polynomials, assign the sum of those polynomials to that node. Finally, the polynomial that has been assigned to the output node labeled 1 is also assigned to the branching program itself. Now we are ready to present the probabilistic polynomial time algorithm for EQ_{ROBP}. Let $\mathcal{F}$ be a field with at least $3m$ elements.

$D = $ "On input $\langle B_1, B_2 \rangle$ where B_1 and B_2 are read-once branching programs:

    1. Obtain the assigned polynomials p_1 and p_2.

    2. Select elements a_1 through a_m at random from $\mathcal{F}$.

    3. If $p_1(a_1, \ldots, a_m) = p_2(a_1, \ldots, a_m)$, *accept*; otherwise *reject*."

This algorithm obviously runs in polynomial time. We show that it decides EQ_{ROBP} with an error probability of at most $\frac{1}{3}$.

Let's examine the relationship between a read-once branching program B and its assigned polynomial p. Observe that for any Boolean assignment to B's variables, all polynomials assigned to its nodes evaluate to either 0 or 1. The polynomials that evaluate to 1 are those on the computation path for that assignment. Hence B and p agree when the variables take on Boolean values. Similarly, because B is read-once, we may write p as a sum of product terms $y_1 y_2 \cdots y_m$, where each y_i is x_i, $(1 - x_i)$, or 1, and where each product term corresponds to a path in B from the start node to the output node labeled 1. The case of $y_i = 1$ occurs when a path doesn't contain variable x_i.

Take each such product term of p containing a y_i that is 1 and split it into the sum of two product terms, one where $y_i = x_i$ and the other where $y_i = (1 - x_i)$. Doing so yields an equivalent polynomial because $1 = x_i + (1 - x_i)$. Continue splitting product terms until each y_i is either x_i or $(1 - x_i)$. The end result is an equivalent polynomial q that contains a product term for each assignment on which B evaluates to 1. Now we are ready to analyze the behavior of the algorithm D.

First, we show that, if B_1 and B_2 are equivalent, D always accepts. If the branching programs are equivalent, they evaluate to 1 on exactly the same assignments. Consequently, the polynomials q_1 and q_2 are equal because they contain identical product terms. Therefore p_1 and p_2 are equal on every assignment.

Second we show that, if B_1 and B_2 aren't equivalent, D rejects with a probability of at least $\frac{2}{3}$. This conclusion follows immediately from Lemma 10.14.

The preceding proof relies on the following lemmas concerning the probability of randomly finding a root of a polynomial as a function of the number of variables it has, the degrees of its variables, and the size of the underlying field.

LEMMA **10.13**

For every $d \geq 0$, a degree-d polynomial p on a single variable x either has at most d roots, or is everywhere equal to 0.

PROOF   We use induction on d.

Basis: Prove for $d = 0$. A polynomial of degree 0 is constant. If that constant is not 0, the polynomial clearly has no roots.

Induction step: Assume true for $d - 1$ and prove true for d. If p is a nonzero polynomial of degree d with a root at a, the polynomial $x - a$ divides p evenly. Then $p/(x - a)$ is a nonzero polynomial of degree $d - 1$, and it has at most $d - 1$ roots by virtue of the induction hypothesis.

LEMMA **10.14**

Let $\mathcal{F}$ be a finite field with f elements and let p be a nonzero polynomial on the variables x_1 through x_m, where each variable has degree at most d. If a_1 through a_m are selected randomly in $\mathcal{F}$, then $\Pr\left[\,p(a_1, \ldots, a_m) = 0\,\right] \leq md/f$.

PROOF   We use induction on m.

Basis: Prove for $m = 1$. By Lemma 10.13, p has at most d roots, so the probability that a_1 is one of them is at most d/f.

Induction step: Assume true for $m - 1$ and prove true for m. Let x_1 be one of p's variables. For each $i \leq d$ let p_i be the polynomial comprising the terms of p containing x_1^i, but where x_1^i has been factored out. Then

$$p = p_0 + x_1 p_1 + x_1^2 p_2 + \cdots + x_1^d p_d.$$

If $p(a_1, \ldots, a_m) = 0$, one of two cases arise. Either all p_i evaluate to 0 or some p_i doesn't evaluate to 0 and a_1 is a root of the single variable polynomial obtained by evaluating p_0 through p_d on a_2 though a_m.

To bound the probability that the first case occurs observe that one of the p_j must be nonzero because p is nonzero. Then the probability that all p_i evaluate to 0 is at most the probability that p_j evaluates to 0. By the induction hypothesis, that is at most $(m - 1)d/f$ because p_j has at most $m - 1$ variables.

To bound the probability that the second case occurs observe that if some p_i doesn't evaluate to 0, then on the assignment of a_2 through a_m, p reduces to a nonzero polynomial in the single variable x_1. The basis already shows that a_1 is a root of such a polynomial with a probability of at most d/f.

Therefore the probability that a_1 through a_m is a root of the polynomial is at most $(m - 1)d/f + d/f = md/f$.

We conclude this section with one important point concerning the use of randomness in algorithms. Our analyses of probabilistic algorithms are based on the assumption that a source of true randomness is available for their computation. True randomness may be difficult (or impossible) to obtain, so it is usually simulated with ***pseudorandom generators***, which are deterministic algorithms whose output appears random. Although the output of any deterministic procedure can never be truly random, some of these procedures generate results that have certain characteristics of randomly generated results. Algorithms that are designed to use randomness may work equally well with these pseudorandom generators, but proving that they do is generally more difficult. Indeed, sometimes probabilistic algorithms may not work well with certain pseudorandom generators. Sophisticated pseudorandom generators have been devised that produce results indistinguishable from truly random results by any test that operates in polynomial time, under the assumption that a one-way function exists. (See Section 10.6 for a discussion of one-way functions.)

10.3

ALTERNATION

Alternation is a generalization of nondeterminism that has proven to be useful in elucidating relationships among complexity classes and in classifying specific problems according to their complexity. Using alternation, we may simplify various proofs in complexity theory and exhibit a surprising connection between the time and space complexity measures.

An alternating algorithm may contain instructions to branch a process into multiple child processes, just as in a nondeterministic algorithm. The difference between the two lies in the mode of determining acceptance. A nondeterministic computation accepts if any one of the initiated processes accepts. When an alternating computation divides into multiple processes, two possibilities arise. The algorithm can designate that the current process accepts if *any* of the children accept, or it can designate that the current process accepts if *all* of the children accept.

Picture the difference between alternating and nondeterministic computation with trees that represent the branching structure of the spawned processes. Each node represents a configuration in a process. In a nondeterministic computation, each node computes the OR operation of its children. That corresponds to the usual nondeterministic acceptance mode whereby a process is accepting if any of its children are accepting. In an alternating computation, the nodes may compute the AND or OR operations as determined by the algorithm. That corresponds to the alternating acceptance mode whereby a process is accepting if all or any of its children accept.

Figure 10.2 shows nondeterministic and alternating computation trees. We label the nodes of the alternating computation tree with $\wedge$ or $\vee$ to indicate which function of their children they compute.

DEFINITION   **10.15**

An *alternating Turing machine* is a nondeterministic Turing machine with an additional feature. Its states, except for q_{accept} and q_{reject}, are divided into *universal states* and *existential states*. When we run an alternating Turing machine on an input string, we label each node of its nondeterministic computation tree with $\wedge$ or $\vee$, depending on whether the corresponding configuration contains a universal or existential state. We determine acceptance by designating a node to be accepting if it is labeled with $\wedge$ and all of its children are accepting or if it is labeled with $\vee$ and any of its children are accepting.

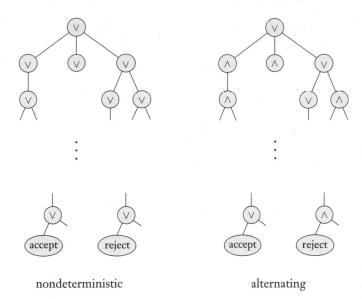

nondeterministic   alternating

FIGURE   10.2
Nondeterministic and alternating computation trees

ALTERNATING TIME AND SPACE

We define the time and space complexity of these machines as for nondeterministic Turing machines by taking the maximum time or space used by any computation branch. The alternating time and space complexity classes are defined as
follows.

$$\text{ATIME}(t(n)) = \{L | \; L \text{ is a language decided by an } O(t(n)) \text{ time}$$
$$\text{alternating Turing machine}\}.$$
$$\text{ASPACE}(f(n)) = \{L | \; L \text{ is a language decided by an } O(f(n)) \text{ space}$$
$$\text{alternating Turing machine}\}.$$

We define AP, APSPACE, and AL to be the classes of languages that are decided by alternating polynomial time, alternating polynomial space, and alternating logarithmic space Turing machines, respectively.

EXAMPLE   **10.16** ···

A *tautology* is a Boolean formula that evaluates to 1 on every assignment to its variables. Let $TAUT = \{\langle\phi\rangle|\ \phi$ is a tautology$\}$. The following alternating algorithm shows that $TAUT$ is in AP.

"On input $\langle\phi\rangle$:
1. Universally select all assignments to the variables of ϕ.
2. For a particular assignment, evaluate ϕ.
3. If ϕ evaluates to 1, *accept*; otherwise *reject*."

Stage 1 of this algorithm nondeterministically selects every assignment to ϕ's variables with universal branching. That requires all branches to accept in order for the entire computation to accept. Stages 2 and 3 deterministically check whether the assignment that was selected on a particular computation branch satisfies the formula. Hence this algorithm accepts its input if it determines that all assignments are satisfying.

Observe that $TAUT$ is a member of coNP. In fact, any problem in coNP can easily be shown to be in AP by using an algorithm similar to the preceding one.

EXAMPLE   **10.17** ···

This example features a language in AP that isn't known to be in NP or in coNP. Let ϕ and ψ be two Boolean formulas. Say that ϕ and ψ are equivalent if they evaluate to the same value on all assignments to their variables. A *minimal formula* is one that has no shorter equivalent. (The length of a formula is the number of symbols that it contains.) Let

$$MIN\text{-}FORMULA = \{\langle\phi\rangle|\ \phi \text{ is a minimal Boolean formula}\}.$$

The following algorithm shows that $MIN\text{-}FORMULA$ is in AP.

"On input ϕ:
1. Universally select all formulas ψ that are shorter than ϕ.
2. Existentially select an assignment to the variables of ϕ.
3. Evaluate both ϕ and ψ on this assignment.
4. *Accept* if the formulas evaluate to different values. *Reject* if they evaluate to the same value."

This algorithm starts with universal branching to select all shorter formulas in stage 1 and then switches to existential branching to select an assignment in stage 2. The term *alternation* stems from the ability to alternate, or switch, between universal and existential branching.

Alternation allows us to make a remarkable connection between the time and space measures of complexity. Roughly speaking, the following theorem demonstrates an equivalence between alternating time and deterministic space for polynomially related bounds, and another equivalence between alternating space and deterministic time when the time bound is exponentially more than the space bound.

For $f(n) \geq n$ we have $\mathrm{ATIME}(f(n)) \subseteq \mathrm{SPACE}(f(n)) \subseteq \mathrm{ATIME}(f^2(n))$.

For $f(n) \geq \log n$ we have $\mathrm{ASPACE}(f(n)) = \mathrm{TIME}(2^{O(f(n))})$.

Consequently, $\mathrm{AL} = \mathrm{P}$, $\mathrm{AP} = \mathrm{PSPACE}$, and $\mathrm{APSPACE} = \mathrm{EXPTIME}$. We break the proof of this theorem into the following four lemmas.

For $f(n) \geq n$ we have $\mathrm{ATIME}(f(n)) \subseteq \mathrm{SPACE}(f(n))$.

PROOF   We convert an alternating time $O(f(n))$ machine M to a deterministic space $O(f(n))$ machine S that simulates M as follows. On input w, the simulator S performs a depth first search of M's computation tree to determine which nodes in the tree are accepting. Then S accepts if it determines that the root of the tree, corresponding to M's starting configuration, is accepting.

Machine S requires space for storing the recursion stack that is used in the depth-first search. Each level of the recursion stores one configuration. The recursion depth is M's time complexity. Each configuration uses $O(f(n))$ space and M's time complexity is $O(f(n))$. Hence S uses $O(f^2(n))$ space.

We can improve the space complexity by observing that S does not need to store the entire configuration at each level of the recursion. Instead it records only the nondeterministic choice that M made to reach that configuration from its parent. Then S can recover this configuration by replaying the computation from the start and following the recorded "signposts." Making this change reduces the space usage to a constant at each level of the recursion. The total used now is thus $O(f(n))$.

For $f(n) \geq n$ we have $\mathrm{SPACE}(f(n)) \subseteq \mathrm{ATIME}(f^2(n))$.

PROOF   We start with a deterministic space $O(f(n))$ machine M and construct an alternating machine S that uses time $O(f^2(n))$ to simulate it. The approach is similar to that used in the proof of Savitch's theorem (Theorem 8.5) where we constructed a general procedure for the yieldability problem.

In the yieldability problem, we are given configurations c_1 and c_2 of M and a number t. We must test whether M can get from c_1 to c_2 within t steps. An alternating procedure for this problem first branches existentially to guess a configuration c_m midway between c_1 and c_2. Then it branches universally into two processes, one that recursively tests whether c_1 can get to c_m within $t/2$ steps and the other whether c_m can get to c_2 within $t/2$ steps.

Machine S uses this recursive alternating procedure to test whether the start configuration can reach an accepting configuration within $2^{df(n)}$ steps. Here, d is selected so that M has no more than $2^{df(n)}$ configurations within its space bound.

The maximum time used on any branch of this alternating procedure is $O(f(n))$ to write a configuration at each level of the recursion, times the depth of the recursion, which is $\log 2^{df(n)} = O(f(n))$. Hence this algorithm runs in alternating time $O(f^2(n))$.

....

LEMMA 10.21 ....

For $f(n) \geq \log n$ we have $\text{ASPACE}(f(n)) \subseteq \text{TIME}(2^{O(f(n))})$.

PROOF   We construct a deterministic time $2^{O(f(n))}$ machine S to simulate an alternating space $O(f(n))$ machine M. On input w, the simulator S constructs the following graph of the computation M on w. The nodes are the configurations of M on w that use at most $df(n)$ space, where d is the appropriate constant factor for M. Edges go from a configuration to those configurations it can yield in a single move of M. After constructing the graph, S repeatedly scans it and marks certain configurations as accepting. Initially, only the actual accepting configurations of M are marked this way. A configuration that performs universal branching is marked accepting if all of its children are so marked, and an existential configuration is marked if any of its children are marked. Machine S continues scanning and marking until no additional nodes are marked on a scan. Finally, S accepts if the start configuration of M on w is marked.

The number of configurations of M on w is $2^{O(f(n))}$ because $f(n) \geq \log n$. Therefore the size of the configuration graph is $2^{O(f(n))}$ and constructing it may be done in $2^{O(f(n))}$ time. Scanning the graph once takes roughly the same time. The total number of scans is at most the number of nodes in the graph, because each scan except for the final one marks at least one additional node. Hence the total time used is $2^{O(f(n))}$.

....

LEMMA 10.22 ....

For $f(n) \geq \log n$ we have $\text{ASPACE}(f(n)) \supseteq \text{TIME}(2^{O(f(n))})$.

PROOF   We show how to simulate a deterministic time $2^{O(f(n))}$ machine M by an alternating Turing machine S that uses space $O(f(n))$. This simulation is tricky because the space available to S is so much less than the size of M's computation. In this case S has only enough space to store pointers into a tableau for M on w, as depicted in the following figure.

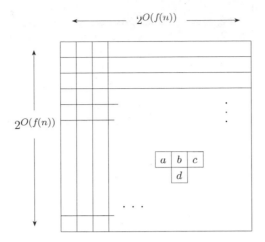

FIGURE 10.3
A tableau for M on w

We use the representation for configurations as given in the proof of Theorem 9.25 whereby a single symbol may represent both the state of the machine and the contents of the tape cell under the head. The contents of cell d in Figure 10.3 is then determined by the contents of its parents a, b, and c. (A cell on the left or right boundary has only two parents.)

Simulator S operates recursively to guess and then verify the contents of the individual cells of the tableau. To verify the contents of a cell d outside the first row, simulator S existentially guesses the contents of the parents, checks whether their contents would yield d's contents according to M's transition function, and then universally branches to verify these guesses recursively. If d were in the first row, S verifies the answer directly because it knows M's starting configuration. We assume that M moves its head to the left-hand end of the tape on acceptance, so S can determine whether M accepts w by checking the contents of the lower leftmost cell of the tableau. Hence S never needs to store more than a single pointer to a cell in the tableau, so it uses space $\log 2^{O(f(n))} = O(f(n))$.

THE POLYNOMIAL TIME HIERARCHY

Alternating machines provide a way to define a natural hierarchy of problems within the class PSPACE.

DEFINITION 10.23

Let i be an integer greater than 0. A Σ_i-*alternating Turing machine* is an alternating Turing machine that contains at most i runs of universal or existential steps, starting with existential steps. A Π_i-*alternating Turing machine* is similar except that it starts with universal steps.

Let $\Sigma_i \text{TIME}(f(n))$ be the class of languages that a Σ_i alternating Turing machine can recognize in $O(f(n))$ time. Similarly define the class $\Pi_i \text{TIME}(f(n))$ for Π_i-alternating Turing machines, and the classes $\Sigma_i \text{SPACE}(f(n))$ and $\Pi_i \text{SPACE}(f(n))$ for space bounded alternating Turing machines. We define the *polynomial time hierarchy* to be the collection of classes

$$\Sigma_i \text{P} = \bigcup_k \Sigma_i \text{TIME}(n^k) \quad \text{and}$$

$$\Pi_i \text{P} = \bigcup_k \Pi_i \text{TIME}(n^k).$$

Define $\text{PH} = \bigcup_i \Sigma_i \text{P} = \bigcup_i \Pi_i \text{P}$.

Clearly, $\text{NP} = \Sigma_1 \text{P}$ and $\text{coNP} = \Pi_1 \text{P}$. Additionally, *MIN-FORMULA* $\in$ $\Pi_2 \text{P}$.

10.4

INTERACTIVE PROOF SYSTEMS

Interactive proof systems provide a way to define a probabilistic analog of the class NP, much as probabilistic polynomial time algorithms provide a probabilistic analog to P. The development of interactive proof systems has profoundly affected complexity theory and has led to important advances in the fields of cryptography and approximation algorithms. To get a feel for this new concept, let's revisit our intuition about NP.

The languages in NP are those whose members all have short certificates of membership that can be easily checked. If you need to, go back to page 247 to review this formulation of NP. Let's rephrase this formulation by creating two entities: a Prover that finds the proofs of membership and a Verifier that checks them. Think of the Prover as if it were *convincing* the Verifier of w's membership in A. We require the Verifier to be a polynomial time bounded machine; otherwise it could figure out the answer itself. We don't impose any computational bound on the Prover because finding the proof may be time-consuming.

Take the *SAT* problem for example. A Prover can convince a polynomial time Verifier that a formula ϕ is satisfiable by supplying the satisfying assignment. Can a Prover similarly convince a computationally limited Verifier that a formula is *not* satisfiable? The complement of *SAT* is not known to be in NP so we can't rely on the certificate idea. Nonetheless the answer, surprisingly, is yes, provided we give the Prover and Verifier two additional features. First, they are permitted to engage in a *two-way* dialog. Second, the Verifier may be a *probabilistic* polynomial time machine that reaches the correct answer with a high degree of, but not absolute, certainty. Such a Prover and Verifier constitute an interactive proof system.

GRAPH NONISOMORPHISM

We illustrate the interactive proof concept through the elegant example of the graph isomorphism problem. Call graphs G and H ***isomorphic*** if the nodes of G may be reordered so that it is identical to H. Let

$$ISO = \{\langle G, H\rangle |\ G \text{ and } H \text{ are isomorphic graphs}\}.$$

Although *ISO* is obviously in NP, extensive research has so far failed to demonstrate either a polynomial time algorithm for this problem or a proof that it is NP-complete. It is one of a relatively small number of naturally occurring languages in NP that haven't been placed in either category.

Here, we consider the language that is complementary to *ISO*, namely, the language *NONISO* = $\{\langle G, H\rangle |\ G \text{ and } H \text{ are } not \text{ isomorphic graphs}\}$. *NONISO* is not known to be in NP because we don't know how to provide short certificates that graphs aren't isomorphic. Nonetheless, when two graphs aren't isomorphic, a Prover can convince a Verifier of this fact, as we will show.

Suppose that we have two graphs G_1 and G_2. If they are isomorphic, the Prover can convince the Verifier of this fact by presenting the isomorphism or reordering. But if they aren't isomorphic, how can the Prover convince the Verifier of that fact? Don't forget: the Verifier doesn't necessarily trust the Prover, so it isn't enough for the Prover to *declare* that they aren't isomorphic. The Prover must *convince* the Verifier. Consider the following short protocol.

The Verifier randomly selects either G_1 or G_2 at random and then randomly reorders its nodes to obtain a graph, H. The Verifier sends H to the Prover. The Prover must respond by declaring whether G_1 or G_2 was the source of H. That concludes the protocol.

If G_1 and G_2 were indeed nonisomorphic, the Prover could always carry out the protocol because the Prover could identify whether H came from G_1 or G_2. However, if the graphs were isomorphic, H might have come from either G_1 or G_2, so even with unlimited computational power, the Prover would have no better than a 50-50 chance of getting the correct answer. Thus if the Prover is able to answer correctly consistently (say in 100 repetitions of the protocol) the Verifier has convincing evidence that the graphs are actually nonisomorphic.

DEFINITION OF THE MODEL

To define the interactive proof system model formally, we describe the Verifier, Prover, and their interaction. You'll find it helpful to keep the graph nonisomorphism example in mind. We define the ***Verifier*** to be a function V that computes its next transmission to the Prover from the message history sent so far. The function V has three inputs:

1. **Input string.** The objective is to determine whether this string is a member of some language. In the *NONISO* example, the input string encoded the two graphs.

2. **Random input.** For convenience in making the definition, we provide the Verifier with a randomly chosen input string instead of the equivalent capability to make probabilistic moves during its computation.

3. **Partial message history.** A function has no memory of the dialog that has been sent so far, so we provide the memory externally via a string representing the exchange of messages up to the present point. We use the notation $m_1\#m_2\#\cdots\#m_i$ to represent the exchange of messages m_1 through m_i.

The Verifier's output is either the next message m_{i+1} in the sequence or *accept* or *reject*, designating the conclusion of the interaction. Thus V has the functional form $V \colon \Sigma^* \times \Sigma^* \times \Sigma^* \longrightarrow \Sigma^* \cup \{accept, reject\}$.

$V(w, r, m_1\#\cdots\#m_i) = m_{i+1}$ means that the input string is w, the random input is r, the current message history is m_1 through m_i, and the Verifier's next message to the Prover is m_{i+1}.

The ***Prover*** is a party with unlimited computational ability. We define it to be a function P with two inputs:

1. **Input string.**

2. **Partial message history.**

The Prover's output is the next message to the Verifier. Formally, P has the form $P \colon \Sigma^* \times \Sigma^* \longrightarrow \Sigma^*$.

$P(w, m_1\#\cdots\#m_i) = m_{i+1}$ means that the Prover sends m_{i+1} to the Verifier after having exchanged messages m_1 through m_i so far.

Next we define the interaction between the Prover and the Verifier. For particular strings w and r, we write $(V\leftrightarrow P)(w, r) = accept$ if a message sequence m_1 through m_k exists for some k whereby

1. for $0 \le i < k$, where i is an even number, $V(w, r, m_1\#\cdots\#m_i) = m_{i+1}$;

2. for $0 < i < k$, where i is an odd number, $P(w, m_1\#\cdots\#m_i) = m_{i+1}$; and

3. the final message m_k in the message history is *accept*.

To simplify the definition of the class IP we assume that the lengths of the Verifier's random input and each of the messages exchanged between the Verifier and the Prover are $p(n)$ for some polynomial p that depends only on the Verifier. Furthermore we assume that the total number of messages exchanged is at most $p(n)$. The following definition gives the probability that an interactive proof system accepts an input string w. For any string w of length n, we define

$$\Pr[V\leftrightarrow P \text{ accepts } w] = \Pr[(V\leftrightarrow P)(w, r) = accept],$$

where r is a randomly selected string of length $p(n)$.

DEFINITION 10.24 ···

Say that language A is in IP if some polynomial time function V and arbitrary function P exist, where for every function $\widetilde{P}$ and string w

> **1.** $w \in A$ implies $\Pr\left[V \leftrightarrow P \text{ accepts } w\right] \geq \frac{2}{3}$, and
> **2.** $w \notin A$ implies $\Pr\left[V \leftrightarrow \widetilde{P} \text{ accepts } w\right] \leq \frac{1}{3}$.

We may amplify the success probability of an interactive proof system through repetition as in Lemma 10.5 to make the error probability exponentially small. Obviously, IP contains both the classes NP and BPP. We have also shown that it contains the language *NONISO*, which is not known to be in either NP or BPP. As we will next show, IP is a surprisingly large class, equal to the class PSPACE.

IP = PSPACE

In this section we will prove one of the more remarkable theorems in complexity theory: the equality of the classes IP and PSPACE. Thus for any language in PSPACE, a Prover can convince a probabilistic polynomial time Verifier about the membership of a string in the language, even though a conventional proof of membership might be exponentially long.

THEOREM 10.25 ···

IP = PSPACE.

We break this theorem into lemmas that establish containment in each direction. The first lemma shows IP $\subseteq$ PSPACE. Though a bit technical, the proof of this lemma is a standard simulation of an interactive proof system by a polynomial space machine.

LEMMA 10.26 ··

IP $\subseteq$ PSPACE.

PROOF   Let A be a language in IP. Assume that A's Verifier V exchanges exactly $p = p(n)$ messages when the input w has length n. We construct a PSPACE machine M that simulates V. First, for any string w we define

$$\Pr\left[V \text{ accepts } w\right] \; - \; \max_{P} \Pr\left[V \leftrightarrow P \text{ accepts } w\right].$$

This value is at least $\frac{2}{3}$ if w is in A and is at most $\frac{1}{3}$ if not. We show how to calculate this value in polynomial space. Let M_j denote a message history $m_1 \# \cdots \# m_j$.

We generalize the definition of the interaction of V and P to start with an arbitrary message stream M_j. We write $(V \leftrightarrow P)(w, r, M_j) = accept$ if we can extend M_j with messages m_{j+1} through m_p so that

1. for $j \leq i < p$, where i is an even number, $V(w, r, M_i) = m_{i+1}$;
2. for $j \leq i < p$, where i is an odd number, $P(w, M_i) = m_{i+1}$; and
3. the final message m_p in the message history is *accept*.

Further generalizing our earlier definitions we define

$$\Pr\big[V \leftrightarrow P \text{ accepts } w \text{ starting at } M_j\big] \;=\; \Pr\big[(V \leftrightarrow P)(w, r, M_j) = accept\big]$$

for a random string r of length p. We then define

$$\Pr\big[V \text{ accepts } w \text{ starting at } M_j\big] \;=\; \max_{P} \Pr\big[V \leftrightarrow P \text{ accepts } w \text{ starting at } M_j\big].$$

For every $0 \leq j \leq p$ and every message stream M_j let N_{M_j} be defined inductively as follows. The base case is $j = p$ for every M_j.

$$N_{M_j} = \begin{cases} 0 & j = p \text{ and } m_p = reject \\ 1 & j = p \text{ and } m_p = accept \\ \max_{m_{j+1}} N_{M_{j+1}} & \text{odd } j < p \\ \text{wt-avg}_{m_{j+1}} N_{M_{j+1}} & \text{even } j < p \end{cases}$$

Here, $\text{wt-avg}_{m_{j+1}} N_{M_{j+1}}$ means $\sum_{m_{j+1}} \big(\Pr_r\big[V(w, r, M_j) = m_{j+1}\big] \cdot N_{M_{j+1}}\big)$, where $\Pr_r$ denotes a probability taken over a random r of length p. The expression is the average of $N_{M_{j+1}}$, weighted by the probability that the Verifier sent message m_{j+1}.

Let M_0 be the empty message stream. We make two claims about value N_{M_0}. First, an algorithm can calculate N_{M_0} in polynomial space. That algorithm recursively calculates the values N_{M_j} for every j and M_j. The depth of the recursion is p, and therefore only polynomial space is needed. Second, N_{M_0} equals $\Pr\big[V \text{ accepts } w\big]$, the value needed in order to determine whether w is in A. We prove this second claim by induction as follows.

CLAIM **10.27** ....

For every $0 \leq j \leq p$ and every M_j,

$$N_{M_j} = \Pr\big[V \text{ accepts } w \text{ starting at } M_j\big].$$

We prove this claim by induction on j, where the basis occurs at $j = p$ and the induction proceeds from p down to 0.

Basis: Prove for $j = p$. We know that m_p is either *accept* or *reject*. If m_p is *accept*, N_{M_p} is defined to be 1, and $\Pr\big[V \text{ accepts } w \text{ starting at } M_j\big] = 1$ because the message stream already indicates acceptance, so the claim is true. The case for m_p is *reject* is similar.

Induction step: Assume that the claim is true for some $j+1 \leq p$ and any message stream M_{j+1}. Prove that it is true for j and any message stream M_j. If j is even, m_{j+1} is a message from V to P. We then have the series of equalities:

$$N_{M_j} \stackrel{1}{=} \sum_{m_{j+1}} \left(\Pr_r \left[V(w, r, M_j) = m_{j+1} \right] \cdot N_{M_{j+1}} \right)$$

$$\stackrel{2}{=} \sum_{m_{j+1}} \left(\Pr_r \left[V(w, r, M_j) = m_{j+1} \right] \cdot \Pr \left[V \text{ accepts } w \text{ starting at } M_{j+1} \right] \right)$$

$$\stackrel{3}{=} \Pr \left[V \text{ accepts } w \text{ starting at } M_j \right].$$

Equality 1 is the definition of N_{M_j}. Equality 2 is based on the induction hypothesis. Equality 3 follows from the definition of $\Pr \left[V \text{ accepts } w \text{ starting at } M_j \right]$. Thus the claim holds if j is even. If j is odd, m_{j+1} is a message from P to V. We then have the series of equalities:

$$N_{M_j} \stackrel{1}{=} \max_{m_{j+1}} N_{M_{j+1}}.$$

$$\stackrel{2}{=} \max_{m_{j+1}} \Pr \left[V \text{ accepts } w \text{ starting at } M_{j+1} \right]$$

$$\stackrel{3}{=} \Pr \left[V \text{ accepts } w \text{ starting at } M_j \right]$$

Equality 1 is the definition of N_{M_j}. Equality 2 uses the induction hypothesis. We break equality 3 into two inequalities. We have $\leq$ because the Prover that maximizes the lower line could send the message m_{j+1} that maximizes the upper line. We have $\geq$ because that same Prover cannot do any better than send that same message. Sending anything other than a message that maximizes the upper line would lower the resulting value. That proves the claim for odd j and completes the proof of the theorem.

Now we prove the other direction of Theorem 10.25. The proof of this lemma introduces a novel algebraic method of analyzing computation.

LEMMA 10.28 ....

PSPACE $\subseteq$ IP.

Before getting to the proof of this lemma, we prove a weaker result that illustrates the technique. Define the ***counting problem*** for satisfiability to be the language

$\#SAT = \{ \langle \phi, k \rangle | \ \phi \text{ is a cnf-formula with exactly } k \text{ satisfying assignments} \}.$

THEOREM **10.29**

$\#SAT \in$ IP.

PROOF IDEA This proof presents a protocol whereby the Prover persuades the Verifier that k is the actual number of satisfying assignments of a given cnf-formula ϕ. Before getting to the protocol itself let's consider another protocol that has some of the flavor of the correct one but is unsatisfactory because it requires an exponential time Verifier. Say that ϕ has variables x_1 through x_m.

Let f_i be the function where for $0 \le i \le m$ and $a_1, \ldots, a_i \in \{0, 1\}$ we set $f_i(a_1, \ldots, a_i)$ equal to the number of satisfying assignments of ϕ such that each $x_j = a_j$ for $j \le i$. The constant function $f_0()$ is the number of satisfying assignments of ϕ. The function $f_m(a_1, \ldots, a_m)$ is 1 if those a_i's satisfy ϕ; otherwise it is 0. An easy identity holds for every $i < m$ and $a_1, \ldots, a_i$:

$$f_i(a_1, \ldots, a_i) = f_{i+1}(a_1, \ldots, a_i, 0) + f_{i+1}(a_1, \ldots, a_i, 1).$$

The protocol for $\#SAT$ begins with phase 0 and ends with phase $m + 1$. The input is the pair $\langle \phi, k \rangle$.

Phase 0. P sends $f_0()$ to V.
V checks that $k = f_0()$ and *rejects* if not.

Phase 1. P sends $f_1(0)$ and $f_1(1)$ to V.
V checks that $f_0() = f_1(0) + f_1(1)$ and *rejects* if not.

Phase 2. P sends $f_2(0,0)$, $f_2(0,1)$, $f_2(1,0)$, and $f_2(1,1)$ to V.
V checks that $f_1(0) = f_2(0,0) + f_2(0,1)$ and $f_1(1) = f_2(1,0) + f_2(1,1)$ and *rejects* if not.

$\vdots$

Phase m. P sends $f(a_1, \ldots, a_m)$ for each assignment to the a_i's.
V checks the 2^{m-1} equations linking f_{m-1} with f_m and *rejects* if any fail.

Phase $m+1$. V checks that the values $f(a_1, \ldots, a_m)$ for each assignment to the a_i's are correct by evaluating ϕ on that assignment. If all assignments are correct it *accepts*; otherwise it *rejects*. That complete the description of the protocol.

This protocol doesn't provide a proof that $\#SAT$ is in IP because the Verifier must spend exponential time just to read the exponentially long messages that the Prover sends. Let's examine it for correctness, anyway, because that helps us understand the next, more efficient protocol.

Intuitively, a protocol recognizes a language A if a Prover can convince the Verifier of the membership of strings in A. In other words, if a string is a member of A, some Prover can cause the Verifier to accept with high probability. If the string isn't a member of A, no Prover—not even a crooked or devious one—can cause the Verifier to accept with more than low probability. We use the symbol P to designate the Prover who correctly follows the protocol and who thereby makes V accept with high probability when the input is in A. We use the symbol

$\widetilde{P}$ to designate any Prover that interacts with the Verifier when the input isn't in A. Think of $\widetilde{P}$ as an adversary—as though $\widetilde{P}$ were attempting to make V accept when V should reject. The notation $\widetilde{P}$ is suggestive of a "crooked" Prover.

In the *#SAT* protocol we just described, the Verifier ignores its random input and operates deterministically once the Prover has been selected. Hence we don't need probabilities to show that the protocol operates correctly. We need to show that, if k were the correct number of satisfying assignments ϕ in the input $\langle \phi, k \rangle$, some Prover P would cause V to accept. This case is obviously true. If k weren't correct, every Prover $\widetilde{P}$ would cause V to reject. We argue that case as follows.

If k were not correct and $\widetilde{P}$ follows the protocol as described for P, V rejects outright in phase 0 because $f_0()$ is the number of ϕ's satisfying assignments and therefore $f_0() \neq k$. To prevent V from rejecting in phase 0, $\widetilde{P}$ must deviate from the protocol by sending an incorrect value for $f_0()$, denoted $\widetilde{f}_0()$. Intuitively, $\widetilde{f}_0()$ is a *lie* about the value of $f_0()$. As in real life, lies beget lies, and $\widetilde{P}$ will be forced to continue lying about other values of f_i in order to avoid being caught during later phases. Eventually these lies will catch up with $\widetilde{P}$ in phase $m+1$ where V checks the values of f_m directly.

More precisely, because $\widetilde{f}_0() \neq f_0()$, at least one of the values $f_1(0)$ and $f_1(1)$ that $\widetilde{P}$ sends in phase 1 must be incorrect; otherwise V rejects when it checks whether $f_0() = f_1(0) + f_1(1)$. Let's say that $f_1(0)$ was incorrect and call the value that was sent instead $\widetilde{f}_1(0)$. Continuing in this way we see that at every phase $\widetilde{P}$ must end up sending some incorrect value $\widetilde{f}_i(a_1, \ldots, a_i)$, or V would have rejected by that point. But when V checks the incorrect value $\widetilde{f}_m(a_1, \ldots, a_m)$ in phase $m+1$ it will reject anyway. Thus we have shown that if k is incorrect, V rejects no matter what $\widetilde{P}$ does. Therefore the protocol is correct.

The problem with this protocol is that the number of messages doubles with every phase. This doubling occurs because the Verifier requires the two values $f_{i+1}(\ldots, 0)$ and $f_{i+1}(\ldots, 1)$ to confirm the one value $f_i(\ldots)$. If we could find a way for the Verifier to confirm a value of f_i with only a single value of f_{i+1}, the number of messages wouldn't grow at all. We can do so by extending the functions f_i to non-Boolean inputs and confirming the single value $f_{i+1}(\ldots, z)$ for some z selected at random from a finite field.

PROOF   Let ϕ be a cnf-formula with variables x_1 through x_m. In a technique called ***arithmetization***, we associate with ϕ a polynomial $p(x_1, \ldots, x_m)$ where p mimics ϕ by simulating the Boolean $\wedge$, $\vee$, and $\neg$ operations with the arithmetic operations $+$ and $\times$ as follows. If α and β are subformulas we replace expressions

$$\begin{aligned} \alpha \wedge \beta \quad &\text{by} \quad \alpha\beta, \\ \neg\alpha \quad &\text{by} \quad 1 - \alpha, \text{ and} \\ \alpha \vee \beta \quad &\text{by} \quad \alpha * \beta = 1 - (1-\alpha)(1-\beta). \end{aligned}$$

One observation regarding p that will be important to us later is that the degree of any of its variables is not large. The operations $\alpha\beta$ and $\alpha * \beta$ each produce a polynomial whose degrees are at most the sum of the degrees of the polynomials for α and β. Thus the degree of any variable is at most n, the length of ϕ.

If p's variables are assigned Boolean values, it agrees with ϕ on that assignment. Evaluating p when the variables are assigned non-Boolean values has no obvious interpretation in ϕ. However, the proof uses such assignments anyway to analyze ϕ, much as the proof of Theorem 10.12 uses non-Boolean assignments to analyze read-once branching programs. The variables range over a finite field $\mathcal{F}$ with q elements where q is at least 2^n.

We use p to redefine the functions f_i that we defined in the proof idea section. For $0 \leq i \leq m$ and for $a_1, \ldots, a_i \in \mathcal{F}$ let

$$f_i(a_1, \ldots, a_i) = \sum_{a_{i+1}, \ldots, a_m \in \{0,1\}} p(a_1, \ldots, a_m).$$

Observe that this redefinition extends the original definition because the two agree when the a_i's take on Boolean values. Thus $f_0()$ is still the number of satisfying assignments of ϕ. Each of the functions $f_i(x_1, \ldots, x_i)$ can be expressed as a polynomial in x_1 through x_i. The degrees of each of these polynomials is at most that of p.

Next we present the protocol for *#SAT*. Initially V receives input $\langle \phi, k \rangle$ and arithmetizes ϕ to obtain polynomial p. A comment in double brackets appears at the start of the description of each phase.

Phase 0.   ⟦ P sends $f_0()$. ⟧
$P{\rightarrow}V$: P sends a prime q that is larger than 2^n and a short proof of its primality,[3] and P sends $f_0()$ to V. All further arithmetic is in the field $\mathcal{F}$ with q elements. V checks the proof that q is prime and that $k = f_0()$. V *rejects* if either fail.

Phase 1.   ⟦ P persuades V that $f_0()$ is correct if $f_1(r_1)$ is correct. ⟧
$P{\rightarrow}V$: P sends the coefficients of $f_1(z)$ as a polynomial in z.
V uses these coefficients to evaluate $f_1(0)$ and $f_1(1)$. It then checks that the degree of the polynomial is at most n and that $f_0() = f_1(0) + f_1(1)$. V *rejects* if either fail. (Remember that all calculations are done over $\mathcal{F}$.)
$V{\rightarrow}P$: V selects r_1 at random from $\mathcal{F}$ and sends it to P.

Phase 2.   ⟦ P persuades V that $f_1(r_1)$ is correct if $f_2(r_1, r_2)$ is correct. ⟧
$P{\rightarrow}V$: P sends the coefficients of $f_2(r_1, z)$ as a polynomial in z.
V uses these coefficients to evaluate $f_2(r_1, 0)$ and $f_2(r_1, 1)$. It then checks that the degree of the polynomial is at most n and that $f_1(r_1) = f_2(r_1, 0) + f_2(r_1, 1)$. V *rejects* if either fail.
$V{\rightarrow}P$: V selects r_2 at random from $\mathcal{F}$ and sends it to P.

$\vdots$

Phase i.   ⟦ P persuades V that $f_{i-1}(r_1, \ldots, r_{i-1})$ is correct if $f_i(r_1, \ldots, r_i)$ is correct. ⟧
$P{\rightarrow}V$: P sends the coefficients of $f_i(r_1, \ldots, r_{i-1}, z)$ as a polynomial in z.
V uses these coefficients to evaluate $f_i(r_1, \ldots, r_{i-1}, 0)$ and $f_i(r_1, \ldots, r_{i-1}, 1)$.

---

[3]Here we use the fact that *PRIMES* $\in$ NP. The proof we give shortly of the stronger result IP = PSPACE doesn't depend on this fact, but here it simplifies the argument.

It then checks that the degree of the polynomial is at most n and also that $f_{i-1}(r_1, \ldots, r_{i-1}) = f_i(r_1, \ldots, r_{i-1}, 0) + f_i(r_1, \ldots, r_{i-1}, 1)$. V *rejects* if either fail.

$V \to P$: V selects r_i at random from $\mathcal{F}$ and sends it to P.

$\vdots$

Phase $m+1$.   ⟦ V checks directly that $f_m(r_1, \ldots, r_m)$ is correct. ⟧
V evaluates $p(r_1, \ldots, r_m)$ to compare with the value V has for $f_m(r_1, \ldots, r_m)$. If they are equal, V *accepts*; otherwise V *rejects*. That completes the description of the protocol.

Now we show that this protocol accepts #*SAT*. First, if ϕ has k satisfying assignments, V obviously accepts with certainty if Prover P follows the protocol. Second, we show that if ϕ doesn't have k assignments, no Prover can make it accept with more than a low probability. Let $\widetilde{P}$ be any Prover.

To prevent V from rejecting outright, $\widetilde{P}$ must send an incorrect value $\widetilde{f}_0()$ for $f_0()$ in phase 0. Therefore in phase 1 one of the values that V calculates for $f_1(0)$ and $f_1(1)$ must be incorrect, and thus the coefficients that $\widetilde{P}$ sent for $f_1(z)$ as a polynomial in z must be wrong. Let $\widetilde{f}_1(z)$ be the function that these coefficients represent instead. Next comes a key step of the proof.

When V picks a random r_1 in $\mathcal{F}$, we claim that $\widetilde{f}_1(r_1)$ is unlikely to equal $f_1(r_1)$. For $n \geq 10$ we show that

$$\Pr\left[\widetilde{f}_1(r_1) = f_1(r_1)\right] < n^{-2}.$$

That bound on the probability follows from Lemma 10.13: A polynomial in a single variable of degree at most d can have no more than d roots, unless it always evaluates to 0. Therefore any two polynomials in a single variable of degree at most d can agree in at most d places, unless they agree everywhere.

Recall that the degree of the polynomial for f_1 is at most n and that V rejects if the degree of the polynomial $\widetilde{P}$ sends for $\widetilde{f}_1$ is greater than n. We have already determined that these functions don't agree everywhere, so Lemma 10.13 implies they can agree in at most n places. The size of $\mathcal{F}$ is greater than 2^n. The chance that r_1 happens to be be one of n places where the functions agree is at most $n/2^n$, which is less than n^{-2} for $n \geq 10$.

To recap what we've shown so far, if $\widetilde{f}_0()$ is wrong, $\widetilde{f}_1$'s polynomial must be wrong, and then $\widetilde{f}_1(r_1)$ would likely be wrong by virtue of the preceding claim. In the unlikely event that $\widetilde{f}_1(r_1)$ agrees with $f_1(r_1)$, $\widetilde{P}$ was "lucky" at this phase and it will be able to make V accept (even though V should reject) by following the instructions for P in the rest of the protocol.

Continuing further with the argument, if $\widetilde{f}_1(r_1)$ were wrong, at least one of the values V computes for $f_2(r_1, 0)$ and $f_2(r_1, 1)$ in phase 2 must be wrong, so the coefficients that $\widetilde{P}$ sent for $f_2(r_1, z)$ as a polynomial in z must be wrong. Let $\widetilde{f}_2(r_1, z)$ be the function these coefficients represent instead. The polynomials for $f_2(r_1, z)$ and $\widetilde{f}_2(r_1, z)$ have degree at most n, so as before the probability that they agree at a random r_2 in $\mathcal{F}$ is at most n^{-2}. Thus, when V picks r_2 at random, $\widetilde{f}_2(r_1, r_2)$ is likely to be wrong.

The general case follows in the same way to show that for each $1 \le i \le m$ if

$$\widetilde{f}_{i-1}(r_1, \dots, r_{i-1}) \ne f_{i-1}(r_1, \dots, r_{i-1}),$$

then for $n \ge 10$ and for r_i is chosen at random in $\mathcal{F}$

$$\Pr\big[\widetilde{f}_i(r_1, \dots, r_i) = f_i(r_1, \dots, r_i)\big] \le n^2.$$

Thus, by giving an incorrect value for $f_0()$, $\widetilde{P}$ is probably forced to give incorrect values for $f_1(r_1)$, $f_2(r_1, r_2)$, and so on to $f_m(r_1, \dots, r_m)$. The probability that $\widetilde{P}$ gets lucky because V selects an r_i, where $\widetilde{f}_i(r_1, \dots, r_i) = f_i(r_1, \dots, r_i)$ even though $\widetilde{f}_i$ and f_i are different in some phase, is the number of phases m times n^{-2} or at most $1/n$. If $\widetilde{P}$ never gets lucky, it eventually sends an incorrect value for $f_m(r_1, \dots, r_m)$. But V checks that value of f_m directly in phase $m+1$ and will catch any error at that point. So if k is not the number of satisfying assignments of ϕ, no Prover can make the Verifier accept with probability greater than $1/n$.

To complete the proof of the theorem, we need only show that the Verifier operates in probabilistic polynomial time, which is obvious from its description.

....

Next, we return to the proof of Lemma 10.28, that PSPACE $\subseteq$ IP. The proof similar to that of Theorem 10.29 except for an additional idea used here to lower the degrees of polynomials that occur in the protocol.

....

PROOF IDEA   Let's first try the idea we used in the preceding proof and determine where the difficulty occurs. To show that every language in PSPACE is in IP, we need only show that the PSPACE-complete language *TQBF* is in IP. Let ψ be a quantified Boolean formula of the form

$$\psi = \mathsf{Q}_1 x_1 \, \mathsf{Q}_2 x_2 \cdots \mathsf{Q}_m x_m \, [\phi],$$

where ϕ is a cnf-formula and each Q_i is $\exists$ or $\forall$. We define functions f_i as before, except that now we take the quantifiers into account. For $0 \le i \le m$ and $a_1, \dots, a_m \in \{0, 1\}$ let

$$f_i(a_1, \dots, a_i) = \begin{cases} 1 & \text{if } \mathsf{Q}_{i+1} x_{i+1} \cdots \mathsf{Q}_m x_m \, [\phi(a_1, \dots, a_i)] \text{ is true,} \\ 0 & \text{otherwise.} \end{cases}$$

where $\phi(a_1, \dots, a_i)$ is ϕ with a_1 through a_i substituted for x_1 through x_i. Thus $f_0()$ is the truth value of ψ. We then have the arithmetic identities

$$\mathsf{Q}_i = \forall: \quad f_i(a_1, \dots, a_i) = f_{i+1}(a_1, \dots, a_i, 0) \cdot f_{i+1}(a_1, \dots, a_i, 1) \quad \text{and}$$

$$\mathsf{Q}_i = \exists: \quad f_i(a_1, \dots, a_i) = f_{i+1}(a_1, \dots, a_i, 0) * f_{i+1}(a_1, \dots, a_i, 1).$$

Recall that we defined $x * y$ to be $1 - (1 - x)(1 - y)$.

A natural variation of the protocol for *#SAT* suggests itself where we extend the f_i's to a finite field and use the identities for quantifiers instead of the identities for summation. The problem with this idea is that, when arithmetized, every quantifier may double the degree of the resulting polynomial. The degrees of the polynomials might then grow exponentially large, which would require the Verifier to run for exponential time to process the exponentially many coefficients that the Prover would need to send to describe the polynomials.

To keep the degrees of the polynomials small, we introduce a reduction operation R that reduces the degrees of polynomials without changing their behavior on Boolean inputs.

PROOF   Let $\psi = Qx_1 \cdots Qx_m [\phi]$ be a quantified Boolean formula, where ϕ is a cnf-formula. To arithmetize ψ we introduce the expression

$$\psi' = Qx_1 \, Rx_1 \, Qx_2 \, Rx_1 Rx_2 \, Qx_3 \, Rx_1 Rx_2 Rx_3 \, \cdots \, Qx_m \, Rx_1 \cdots Rx_m \, [\phi].$$

Don't worry about the meaning of Rx_i for now. It is useful only for defining the functions f_i. We rewrite ψ' as

$$\psi' = S_1 y_1 \, S_2 y_2 \, \cdots \, S_k y_k \, [\phi],$$

where each $S_i \in \{\forall, \exists, R\}$ and $y_i \in \{x_1, \ldots, x_m\}$.

For each $i \le k$ we define the function f_i. We define $f_k(x_1, \ldots, x_m)$ to be the polynomial $p(x_1, \ldots, x_m)$ obtained by arithmetizing ϕ. For $i < k$ we define f_i in terms of f_{i+1}:

$$S_i = \forall: \quad f_i(\ldots) = f_{i+1}(\ldots, 0) \cdot f_{i+1}(\ldots, 1)$$
$$S_i = \exists: \quad f_i(\ldots) = f_{i+1}(\ldots, 0) * f_{i+1}(\ldots, 1)$$
$$S_i = R: \quad f_i(\ldots, a) = (1-a) f_{i+1}(\ldots, 0) + a f_{i+1}(\ldots, 1).$$

If S is $\forall$ or $\exists$, f_i has one fewer input variable than f_{i+1} does. If S is R, the two functions have the same number of input variables. Thus, function f_i will not, in general, depend on i variables. To avoid cumbersome subscripts we use "$\ldots$" in place of a_1 through a_j for the appropriate values of j. Furthermore, we reorder the inputs to the functions so that input variable y_{i+1} is the last argument.

Note that the Rx operation on polynomials doesn't change their values on Boolean inputs. Therefore $f_0()$ is still the truth value of ψ. However, note that the Rx operation produces a result that is linear in x. We added $Rx_1 \cdots Rx_i$ after $Q_i x_i$ in ψ' in order to reduce the degree of each variable to 1 prior to the squaring due to arithmetizing Q_i.

Now we are ready to describe the protocol. All arithmetic operations in this protocol are over a field $\mathcal{F}$ of size at least n^4, where n is the length of ψ. V can find a prime of this size on its own, so P doesn't need to provide one.

Phase 0. $[\![P \text{ sends } f_0().]\!]$
$P \rightarrow V$: P sends $f_0()$ to V.
V checks that $f_0() = 1$ and *rejects* if not.

$\vdots$

Phase i.   ⟦ P persuades V that $f_{i-1}(r_1 \cdots)$ is correct if $f_i(r_1 \cdots, r)$ is correct. ⟧
$P \rightarrow V$: P sends the coefficients of $f_i(r_1 \cdots, z)$ as a polynomial in z. (Here $r_1 \cdots$ denotes a setting of the variables to the previously selected random values $r_1, r_2, \ldots$)
V uses these coefficients to evaluate $f_i(r_1 \cdots, 0)$ and $f_i(r_1 \cdots, 1)$. Then it checks that the polynomial degree is at most n and that the identities hold, namely,

$$f_{i-1}(r_1 \cdots) = \begin{cases} f_i(r_1 \cdots, 0) \cdot f_i(r_1 \cdots, 1) & \mathsf{S} = \forall \\ f_i(r_1 \cdots, 0) * f_i(r_1 \cdots, 1) & \mathsf{S} = \exists \end{cases}$$

or

$$f_{i-1}(r_1 \cdots, r) = (1 - r)f_i(r_1 \cdots, 0) + rf_i(r_1 \cdots, 1) \quad \mathsf{S} = \mathsf{R}.$$

If either fails, V *rejects*.
$V \rightarrow P$: V picks a random r in $\mathcal{F}$ and sends it to P. (When $\mathsf{S} = \mathsf{R}$ this r replaces the previous r.)
Go to Phase $i + 1$, where P must persuade V that $f_i(r_1 \cdots, r)$ is correct.

$\vdots$

Phase k+1.   ⟦ V checks directly that $f_k(r_1, \ldots, r_m)$ is correct. ⟧
V evaluates $p(r_1, \ldots, r_m)$ to compare with the value V has for $f_m(r_1, \ldots, r_m)$. If they are equal, V *accepts*; otherwise V *rejects*. That completes the description of the protocol.

Proving the correctness of this protocol is similar to proving the correctness of the #*SAT* protocol. Clearly, if ψ is true, P can follow the protocol and V will accept. If ψ is false $\tilde{P}$ must lie at phase 0 by sending an incorrect value for $f_0()$. At phase i, if V has an incorrect value for $f_{i-1}(r_1 \cdots)$, one of the values $f_i(r_1 \cdots, 0)$ and $f_i(r_1 \cdots, 1)$ must be incorrect and the polynomial for f_i must be incorrect. Consequently, for a random r the probability that $\tilde{P}$ gets lucky at this phase because $f_i(r_1 \cdots, r)$ is correct is at most the polynomial degree divided by the field size or n/n^4. The protocol proceeds for $O(n^2)$ phases, so the probability that $\tilde{P}$ gets lucky at some phase is at most $1/n$. If $\tilde{P}$ is never lucky, V will reject at phase $k + 1$.

10.5

PARALLEL COMPUTATION

A ***parallel computer*** is one that can perform multiple operations simultaneously. Parallel computers may solve certain problems much faster than ***sequential computers***, which can only do a single operation at a time. In practice, the distinction between the two is slightly blurred because most real computers (including "sequential" ones) are designed to use some parallelism as they execute individual instructions. We focus here on *massive* parallelism whereby a huge number (think of millions or more) of processing elements are actively participating in a single computation.

In this section we briefly introduce the theory of parallel computation. We describe one model of a parallel computer and use it to give examples of certain problems that lend themselves well to parallelization. We also explore the possibility that parallelism may not be suitable for certain other problems.

UNIFORM BOOLEAN CIRCUITS

One of the most popular models in theoretical work on parallel algorithms is called the ***Parallel Random Access Machine*** or ***PRAM***. In the PRAM model, idealized processors with a simple instruction set patterned on actual computers interact via a shared memory. In this short section we can't describe PRAMs in detail. Instead we use an alternative model of parallel computer that we introduced for another purpose in Chapter 9: Boolean circuits.

Boolean circuits have certain advantages and disadvantages as a parallel computation model. On the positive side, the model is simple to describe, which make proofs easier. Circuits also bear an obvious resemblance to actual hardware designs and in that sense the model is realistic. On the negative side, circuits are awkward to "program" because the individual processors are so weak. Furthermore, we disallow cycles in our definition of Boolean circuits, in contrast to circuits that we can actually build.

In the Boolean circuit model of a parallel computer, we take each gate to be an individual processor, so we define the ***processor complexity*** of a Boolean circuit to be its *size*. We consider each processor to compute its function in a single time step, so we define the ***parallel time complexity*** of a Boolean circuit to be its *depth*, or the longest distance from an input variable to the output gate.

Any particular circuit has a fixed number of input variables, so we use circuit families as defined in Definition 9.22 for recognizing languages. We need to impose a technical requirement on circuit families so that they correspond to parallel computation models such as PRAMs where a single machine is capable of handling all input lengths. That requirement states that we can easily obtain all members in a circuit family. This ***uniformity*** requirement is reasonable because knowing that a small circuit exists for recognizing certain elements of a language isn't very useful if the circuit itself is hard to find. That leads us to the following definition.

DEFINITION 10.30

A family of circuits $(C_1, C_2, \dots)$ is ***uniform*** if some log space transducer T outputs $\langle C_n \rangle$ when T's input is 1^n.

Recall that Definition 9.23 defined the size and depth complexity of languages in terms of families of circuits of minimal size and depth. Here, we consider the *simultaneous* time and depth of a single circuit family in order to identify how many processors we need in order to achieve a particular parallel time complexity or vice versa. Say that a language has ***simultaneous size–depth*** circuit complexity at most $(f(n), g(n))$ if a uniform circuit family exists for that language with size complexity $f(n)$ and depth complexity $g(n)$.

EXAMPLE **10.31**

Let A be the language over $\{0,1\}$ consisting of all strings with an odd number of 1s. We can test membership in A by computing the parity function. We can implement the two input parity gate $x \oplus y$ with the standard AND, OR, and NOT operations as $(x \wedge \neg y) \vee (\neg x \wedge y)$. Let the inputs to the circuit be $x_1, \ldots, x_n$. One way to get a circuit for the parity function is to construct gates g_i whereby $g_1 = x_1$ and $g_i = x_i \oplus g_{i-1}$ for $i \leq m$. This construction uses $O(n)$ size and depth.

Example 9.24 describes another circuit for the parity function with $O(n)$ size and $O(\log n)$ depth by constructing a binary tree of $\oplus$ gates. This construction is a significant improvement because it uses exponentially less parallel time than does the preceding construction. Thus the size–depth complexity of A is $(O(n), O(\log n))$.

EXAMPLE **10.32**

Recall that we may use circuits to compute functions that output strings. Consider the ***Boolean matrix multiplication*** function. The input has $2m^2 = n$ variables representing two $m \times m$ matrices $A = \{a_{ik}\}$ and $B = \{b_{ik}\}$. The output is m^2 values representing the $m \times m$ matrix $C = \{c_{ik}\}$, where

$$c_{ik} = \bigvee_j (a_{ij} \wedge b_{jk}).$$

The circuit for this function has gates g_{ijk} that compute $a_{ij} \wedge b_{jk}$ for each i, j, and k. Additionally, for each i and k the circuit contains a binary tree of $\vee$ gates to compute $\bigvee_j g_{ijk}$. Each such tree contains $m-1$ OR gates and has $\log m$ depth. Consequently these circuits for Boolean matrix multiplication have size $O(m^3) = O(n^{3/2})$ and depth $O(\log n)$.

EXAMPLE **10.33**

If $A = \{a_{ij}\}$ is an $m \times m$ matrix we let the ***transitive closure*** of A be the matrix

$$A \vee A^2 \vee \cdots \vee A^m,$$

where A^i is the matrix product of A with itself i times and $\vee$ is the bitwise OR of the matrix elements. The transitive closure operation is closely related to the *PATH* problem and hence to the class NL. If A is the adjacency matrix of a directed graph G, A^i is the adjacency matrix of the graph with the same nodes in which an edge indicates the presence of a path of length i in G. The transitive closure of A is the adjacency matrix of the graph in which an edge indicates the presence of a path of any length in G.

We can represent the computation of A^i with a binary tree of size i and depth $\log i$ wherein a node computes the product of the two matrices below it. Each node is computed by a circuit of $O(n^{3/2})$ size and logarithmic depth. Hence the circuit computing A^n has size $O(n^{5/2})$ and depth $O(\log^2 n)$. We make circuits for each A^i which adds another factor of n to the size and an additional layer of $O(\log n)$ depth. Hence the size–depth complexity of transitive closure is $(O(n^{7/2}), O(\log^2 n))$.

THE CLASS NC

Many interesting problems have size–depth complexity $(O(n^k), O(log^k n))$ for some constant k. Such problems may be considered to be highly parallelizable with a moderate number of processors. That prompts the definition of the class NC. [4]

DEFINITION   **10.34**

For $i \geq 1$ let NC^i be the class of languages that can be recognized by a uniform[5] family of circuits with polynomial size and $O(\log^i n)$ depth. Let NC be the class of languages that are in NC^i for some i. Functions that are computed by such circuit families are called **NC^i computable** or **NC computable**.

We explore the relationship of these complexity classes with other classes of languages we have encountered. First we make a connection between Turing machine space and circuit depth. Problems that are solvable in logarithmic depth are also solvable in logarithmic space. Conversely, problems that are solvable in logarithmic space, even nondeterministically, are solvable in logarithmic squared depth.

THEOREM   **10.35**

$NC^1 \subseteq L$.

PROOF   We sketch a log space algorithm to recognize a language A in NC^1. On input w of length n, the algorithm can construct the description as needed of the nth circuit in the uniform circuit family for A. Then the algorithm can

---

[4]Steven Cook coined the name NC for "Nick's class" because Nick Pippenger was the first person to recognize its importance.

[5]Defining uniformity in terms of log space transducers is standard for NC^i when $i \geq 2$ but gives a non-standard result for NC^1 (which contains the standard class NC^1 as a subset). We give this definition anyway, because it is simpler and adequate for our purposes.

evaluate the circuit by using a depth-first search from the output gate. The only memory that is necessary to keep track of the progress of the search is to record the path to the current gate that is being explored and to record any partial results that have been obtained along that path. The circuit has logarithmic depth, hence only logarithmic space is required by the simulation.

THEOREM **10.36** ....

$NL \subseteq NC^2$.

PROOF IDEA   Compute the transitive closure of the graph of configurations of an NL-machine. Output the position corresponding to the presence of a path from the start configuration to the accept configuration.

PROOF   Let A be a language that is accepted by an NL machine M, where A has been has been encoded into $\{0,1\}$. We construct a uniform circuit family $C_0, C_1, \ldots$ for A. To get C_i we construct a graph G that is similar to the computation graph for M on an input w of length n. We do not know the input w when we construct the circuit—only its length n. The inputs to the circuit are variables w_1 through w_n, each corresponding to a position in the input.

Recall that a configuration of M on w describes the state, the contents of the work tape, and the positions of both the input and the work tape heads, but does not include w itself. Hence the collection of configurations of M on w does not actually depend on w—only on w's length n. These polynomially many configurations form the nodes of G.

The edges of G are labeled with the input variables w_i. If c_1 and c_2 are two nodes of G and c_1 indicates input head position i, we put edge (c_1, c_2) in G with label w_i (or $\overline{w_i}$) if c_1 can yield c_2 in a single step when the input head is reading a 1 (or 0), according to M's transition function. If c_1 can yield c_2 in a single step, whatever the input head is reading, we put that edge in G unlabeled.

If we set the edges of G according to a string w of length n, a path exists from the start configuration to the accepting configuration if and only if M accepts w. Hence a circuit that computes the transitive closure of G and outputs the position indicating the presence of such a path accepts all strings in A of length n. That circuit has polynomial size and $O(\log^2 n)$ depth.

A log space transducer is capable of constructing G and therefore C_n on input 1^n. See Theorem 8.20 for a more detailed description of a similar log space transducer.

The class of problems solvable in polynomial time includes all the problems solvable in NC, as the following theorem shows.

THEOREM 10.37

$NC \subseteq P$.

PROOF   A polynomial time algorithm can run the log space transducer to generate circuit C_n and simulate it on an input of length n.

P-COMPLETENESS

Now we consider the possibility that all problems in P are also in NC. Equality between these classes would be surprising because it would imply that all polynomial time solvable problems are highly parallelizable. We introduce the phenomenon of P-completeness to give theoretical evidence that some problems in P are inherently sequential.

DEFINITION 10.38

A language B is **P-*complete*** if

1. $B \in P$, and
2. every A in P is log space reducible to B.

The next theorem follows in the spirit of Theorem 8.18 and has a similar proof because NL and NC machines can compute log space reductions. We leave its proof as Exercise 10.3.

THEOREM 10.39

If $A \leq_L B$ and B is in NC then A is in NC.

We show that the problem of circuit evaluation is P-complete. For a circuit C and input setting x we write $C(x)$ to be the value of C on x. Let

$$CIRCUIT\text{-}VALUE = \{\langle C, x \rangle |\ C \text{ is a Boolean circuit and } C(x) = 1\}.$$

THEOREM 10.40

CIRCUIT-VALUE is P-complete.

PROOF   The construction given in Theorem 9.25 shows how to reduce any language A in P to *CIRCUIT-VALUE*. On input w the reduction produces a circuit that simulates the polynomial time Turing machine for A. The input to the circuit is w itself. The reduction can be carried out in log space because the circuit it produces has a simple and repetitive structure.

10.6

CRYPTOGRAPHY

The practice of encryption, using secret codes for private communication, dates back thousands of years. During Roman times, Julius Caesar encoded messages to his generals to protect against the possibility of interception. More recently, Alan Turing, the inventor of the Turing machine, led a group of British mathematicians who broke the German code used in World War II for sending instructions to U-boats patrolling the Atlantic Ocean. Governments still depend on secret codes and invest a great deal of effort in devising codes that are hard to break and in finding weaknesses in codes that others use. These days, corporations and individuals use encryption to increase the security of their information. Soon, nearly all electronic communication will be cryptographically protected.

In recent years computational complexity theory has led to a revolution in the design of secret codes. The field of cryptography, as this areas is known, now extends well beyond secret codes for private communication and addresses a broad range of issues concerning the security of information. For example, we now have the technology to digitally "sign" messages to authenticate the identity of the sender; to allow electronic elections whereby participants can vote over a network and the results can be publicly tallied without revealing any individual's vote and preventing multiple voting and other violations; and to construct new kinds of secret codes that do not require the communicators to agree in advance on the encryption and decryption algorithms.

Cryptography is an important practical application of complexity theory. Digital cellular telephones, direct satellite television broadcast, and electronic commerce over the internet, all depend on cryptographic measures to protect information. Such systems will soon play a role in most people's lives. Indeed, cryptography has stimulated much research in complexity theory and in other mathematical fields.

SECRET KEYS

Traditionally, when a sender wants to encrypt a message so that only a certain recipient could decrypt it, the sender and receiver share a *secret key*. The secret key is a piece of information that is used by the encrypting and decrypting algorithms. Maintaining the secrecy of the key is crucial to the security of the code because any person with access to the key can encrypt and decrypt messages.

A key that is too short may be discovered through a brute-force search of the entire space of possible keys. Even a somewhat longer key may be vulnerable to certain kinds of attack—we say more about that shortly. The only way to get perfect cryptographic security is with keys that are as long as the combined length of all messages sent.

A key that is as long as the combined message length is called a *one-time pad*. Essentially, every bit of a one-time pad key is used just once to encrypt a bit of the message, and then that bit of the key is discarded. The main problem with one-time pads is that they may be rather large if a significant amount of communication is anticipated. For most purposes, one-time pads are too cumbersome to be considered practical.

A cryptographic code that allows an unlimited amount of secure communication with keys of only moderate length is preferable. Interestingly, such codes can't exist in principle but paradoxically are used in practice. This type of code can't exist in principle because a key that is significantly shorter than the combined message length can be found by a brute-force search through the space of possible keys. Therefore a code that is based on such keys is breakable in principle. But therein lies the solution to the paradox. A code could provide adequate security in practice anyway because brute-force search is extremely slow when the key is moderately long, say in the range of 100 bits. Of course, if the code could be broken in some other, fast way, it is insecure and shouldn't be used. The difficulty lies in being sure that the code can't be broken quickly.

Unfortunately, we currently have no way of ensuring that a code with moderate length keys is actually secure. To guarantee that a code can't be broken quickly, we'd need a *mathematical proof* that, at the very least, finding the key can't be done quickly. However, such proofs seem beyond the capabilities of contemporary mathematics! The reason is that, once a key is discovered, verifying its correctness is easily done by inspecting the messages that have been decrypted with it. Therefore the key verification problem can be formulated so as to be in P. If we could prove that keys can't be found in polynomial time, we would achieve a major mathematical advance by proving that P is different from NP.

Because we are unable to prove mathematically that codes are unbreakable, we rely instead on circumstantial evidence. In the past, evidence for a code's quality was obtained by hiring experts who tried to break it. If they were unable to do so, confidence in its security increased. That approach has obvious deficiencies. If someone has better experts than ours, or if we can't trust our own experts, the integrity of our code may be compromised. Nonetheless, this approach was the only one available until recently and was used to support the reliability of widely used codes such as the Data Encryption Standard (DES) that was sanctioned by the U.S. National Bureau of Standards.

Complexity theory provides another way to gain evidence for a code's security. We may show that the complexity of breaking the code is linked to the complexity of some other problem for which compelling evidence of intractability is already available. Recall that we have used NP-completeness to provide evidence that certain problems are intractable. Reducing an NP-complete problem to the code breaking problem would show that the code breaking problem was itself NP-complete. However, that doesn't provide sufficient evidence of security because NP-completeness concerns worst-case complexity. A problem may be NP-complete, yet easy to solve most of the time. Codes must almost always be difficult to break, so we need to measure average-case complexity rather than worst-case complexity.

One problem that is generally believed to be difficult for the average case is the problem of integer factorization. Top mathematicians have been interested in factorization for centuries, but no one has yet discovered a fast procedure for doing so. Certain modern codes have been built around the factoring problem so that breaking the code corresponds to factoring a number. That constitutes convincing evidence for the security of these codes, because an efficient way of breaking such a code would lead to a fast factoring algorithm, which would be a remarkable development in computational number theory.

PUBLIC-KEY CRYPTOSYSTEMS

Even when cryptographic keys are moderately short, their management still presents an obstacle to their widespread use in conventional cryptography. One problem is that every pair of parties that desires private communication needs to establish a joint secret key for this purpose. Another problem is that each individual needs to keep a secret database of all keys that have been so established.

The recent development of public-key cryptography provides an elegant solution to both problems. In a conventional, or *private-key cryptosystem*, the same key is used for both encryption and decryption. Compare that with the novel *public-key cryptosystem* for which the decryption key is different from, and not easily computed from, the encryption key.

Although it is a deceptively simple idea, separating the two keys has profound consequences. Now each individual only needs to establish a single pair of keys: an encryption key, E and a decryption key, D. The individual keeps D secret but publicizes E. If another individual wants to send him a message, she looks up E in the public directory, encrypts the message with it, and sends it to him. The first individual is the only one who knows D, so only he can decrypt that message.

Certain public-key cryptosystems can also be used for *digital signatures*. If an individual applies his secret decryption algorithm to a message before sending it, anyone can check that it actually came from him by applying the public encryption algorithm. He has thus effectively "signed" that message. This application assumes that the encryption and decryption functions may be applied in either order, as is the case with the RSA cryptosystem.

ONE-WAY FUNCTIONS

Now we briefly investigate some of the theoretical underpinnings of the modern theory of cryptography, called one-way functions and trapdoor functions. One of the advantages of using complexity theory as a foundation for cryptography is that it helps to clarify the assumptions being made when we argue about security. By assuming the existence of a one-way function we may construct secure private-key cryptosystems. Assuming the existence of trapdoor functions allows us to construct public-key cryptosystems. Both assumptions have additional theoretical and practical consequences. We define these types of functions after some preliminaries.

A function $f: \Sigma^* \longrightarrow \Sigma^*$ is *length-preserving* if the lengths of w and $f(w)$ are equal for every w. A length-preserving function is a *permutation* if it never maps two strings to the same place, that is, if $f(x) \neq f(y)$ whenever $x \neq y$.

Recall the definition of probabilistic Turing machine given in Section 10.2. Say that a probabilistic Turing machine M computes a ***probabilistic function*** $M: \Sigma^* \longrightarrow \Sigma^*$ where, if w is an input and x is an output, we assign

$$\Pr[M(w) = x]$$

to be the probability that M halts in an accept state with x on its tape when it is started on input w. Note that M may sometimes fail to accept on input w, so

$$\sum_{x \in \Sigma^*} \Pr[M(w) = x] \leq 1.$$

Next we get to the definition of a one-way function. Roughly speaking, a function is one-way if it is easy to compute but nearly always hard to invert. In the following definition, f denotes the easily computed one-way function and M denotes the probabilistic polynomial time algorithm that we may think of as trying to invert f. We define one-way permutations first because that case is somewhat simpler.

DEFINITION   **10.41**

A ***one-way permutation*** is a length-preserving permutation f with the following two properties.

1. It is computable in polynomial time.
2. For every probabilistic polynomial time Turing machine M, every k, and sufficiently large n, if we pick a random w of length n and run M on input w,

$$\Pr_{M,w}[M(f(w)) = w] \leq n^{-k}.$$

Here, $\Pr_{M,w}$ means that the probability is taken over the random choices made by M and the random selection of w.

A ***one-way function*** is a length-preserving function f with the following two properties.

1. It is computable in polynomial time.
2. For every probabilistic polynomial time Turing machine M, every k, and sufficiently large n, if we pick a random w of length n and run M on input w,

$$\Pr[M(f(w)) = y \text{ where } f(y) = f(w)] \leq n^{-k}.$$

For one-way permutations, any probabilistic polynomial time algorithm has only a small probability of inverting f; that is, it is unlikely to compute w from $f(w)$. For one-way functions, any probabilistic polynomial time algorithm is unlikely to be able to find any y that maps to $f(w)$.

EXAMPLE   **10.42**   ....

The multiplication function *mult* is a candidate for a one-way function. We let $\Sigma = \{0,1\}$ and for any $w \in \Sigma^*$ let $mult(w)$ be the string representing the product of the first and second halves of w. Formally,

$$mult(w) = w_1 \cdot w_2,$$

where $w = w_1 w_2$ such that $|w_1| = |w_2|$, or $|w_1| = |w_2| + 1$ if $|w|$ is odd. The strings w_1 and w_2 are treated as binary numbers. We pad $mult(w)$ with leading 0s so that it has the same length as w. Despite a great deal of research into the integer factorization problem, no probabilistic polynomial time algorithm is known that can invert $mult$, even on a polynomial fraction of inputs.   ■

If we assume the existence of a one-way function, we may construct a private-key cryptosystem that is provably secure. That construction is too complicated to present here. Instead, we illustrate how to implement a different cryptographic application using a one-way function.

One simple application of a one-way function is a provably secure password system. In a typical password system, a user must enter a password to gain access to some resource. The system keeps a database of users' passwords in an encrypted form. The passwords are encrypted to protect them if the database is left unprotected either by accident or design. Password databases are often left unprotected so that various application programs can read them and check passwords. When a user enters a password, the system checks it for validity by encrypting it to determine whether it matches the version stored in the database. Obviously, an encryption scheme that is difficult to invert is desirable because it makes the unencrypted password difficult to obtain from the encrypted form. A one-way function is a natural choice for a password encryption function.

TRAPDOOR FUNCTIONS

We don't know whether the existence of a one-way function alone is enough to allow the construction of a public-key cryptosystem. To get such a construction we use a related object called a ***trapdoor function***, which can be efficiently inverted in the presence of special information.

First, we need to discuss the notion of a function that indexes a family of functions. If we have a family of functions $\{f_i\}$ for i in Σ^*, we can represent them by the single function $f \colon \Sigma^* \times \Sigma^* \longrightarrow \Sigma^*$, where $f(i, w) = f_i(w)$ for any i and w. We call f an indexing function. Say that f is length-preserving if each of the indexed functions f_i is length preserving.

DEFINITION   **10.43**   ....

A ***trapdoor function*** is a length-preserving indexing function $f \colon \Sigma^* \times \Sigma^* \longrightarrow \Sigma^*$ with an auxiliary probabilistic polynomial time TM G and an auxiliary function $h \colon \Sigma^* \times \Sigma^* \longrightarrow \Sigma^*$. The trio f, G, and h satisfy the following three conditions.

1. Functions f and h are computable in polynomial time.
2. For every probabilistic polynomial time TM E and every k and sufficiently large n, if we take a random output $\langle i, t \rangle$ of G on 1^n and a random $w \in \Sigma^n$ then

$$\Pr\left[E(i, f_i(w)) = y, \text{ where } f_i(y) = f_i(w) \right] \leq n^{-k}.$$

3. For every n, every w of length n, and every output $\langle i, t \rangle$ of G that occurs with nonzero probability for some input to G

$$h(t, f_i(w)) = y, \text{ where } f_i(y) = f_i(w).$$

The probabilistic TM G generates an index i of a function in the index family while simultaneously generating a value t that allows f_i to be inverted quickly. Condition 2 says that f_i is hard to invert in the absence of t. Condition 3 says that f_i is easy to invert when t is known. Function h is the inverting function.

EXAMPLE **10.44**

Here, we describe the trapdoor function that underlies the well-known RSA cryptosystem. We give its associated trio f, G, and h. The generator machine G operates as follows. It selects two numbers of roughly equal size at random and tests them for primality by using a probabilistic polynomial time primality testing algorithm. If they aren't prime, it repeats the selection until it succeeds or until it reaches a prespecified timeout limit and reports failure. After finding p and q, it computes $N = pq$ and the value $\phi(N) = (p-1)(q-1)$. It selects a random number e between 1 and N. It checks whether that number is relatively prime to $\phi(N)$. If not, the algorithm selects another number and repeats the check. Finally, the algorithm computes the multiplicative inverse d of e modulo $\phi(N)$. Doing so is possible because the set of numbers in $\{1, \ldots, \phi(N)\}$ that are relatively prime to $\phi(N)$ form a group under the operation of multiplication modulo $\phi(N)$. Finally G outputs $((N, e), d)$. The index to the function f consists of the two numbers N and e. Let

$$f_{N,e}(w) = w^e \bmod N.$$

The inverting function h is

$$h(d, x) = x^d \bmod N.$$

Function h properly inverts because $h(d, f_{N,e}(w)) = w^{ed} \bmod N = w$.

We can use a trapdoor function such as the RSA trapdoor function, to construct a public-key cryptosystem as follows. The public key is the index i generated by the probabilistic machine G. The secret key is the corresponding value t. The encryption algorithm breaks the message m into blocks of size at most $\log N$. For each block w the sender computes f_i. The resulting sequence of strings is the encrypted message. The receiver uses the function h to obtain the original message from its encryption.

EXERCISES

10.1 Show that a circuit family with depth $O(\log n)$ is also a polynomial size circuit family.

10.2 Show that 12 is not pseudoprime because it fails some Fermat test.

10.3 Prove that if $A \leq_L B$ and B is in NC then A is in NC.

10.4 Show that the parity function with n inputs can be computed by a branching program that has $O(n)$ nodes.

10.5 Show that the majority function with n inputs can be computed by a branching program that has $O(n^2)$ nodes.

10.6 Show that any function with n inputs can be computed by a branching program that has $O(2^n)$ nodes.

10.7 Show that BPP $\subseteq$ PSPACE.

PROBLEMS

10.8 Let A be a regular language over $\{0,1\}$. Show that A has size–depth complexity $(O(n), O(\log n))$.

*10.9 A *Boolean formula* is a Boolean circuit wherein every gate has only one output wire. The same input variable may appear in multiple places of a Boolean formula. Prove that a language has a polynomial size family of formulas iff it is in NC^1. Ignore uniformity considerations.

*10.10 A *k-head pushdown automaton* (k-PDA) is a deterministic pushdown automaton with k read-only, two-way input heads and a read/write stack. Define the class $PDA_k = \{A| \ A$ is recognized by a k-PDA$\}$. Show that $P = \bigcup_k PDA_k$. (Hint: Recall that P equals alternating log space.)

10.11 Let B be a probabilistic polynomial time Turing machine and let C be a language where, for some fixed $0 < \epsilon_1 < \epsilon_2 < 1$,

    a. $w \notin C$ implies $\Pr[M \text{ accepts } w] \leq \epsilon_1$, and
    b. $w \in C$ implies $\Pr[M \text{ accepts } w] \geq \epsilon_2$.

Show that $C \in$ BPP. (Hint: Use the result of Lemma 10.5.)

10.12 Show that, if P $=$ NP, then P $=$ PH.

10.13 Show that, if PH $=$ PSPACE, then the polynomial time hierarchy has only finitely many distinct levels.

10.14 Recall that NP^{SAT} is the class of languages that are recognized by nondeterministic polynomial time Turing machines with an oracle for the satisfiability problem. Show that $NP^{SAT} = \Sigma_2 P$.

10.15 Prove Fermat's little theorem, which is given in Theorem 10.6. (Hint: Consider the sequence $a^1, a^2, \ldots$. What must happen, and how?)

10.16 Prove that, for any integer $p > 1$, if p fails the Fermat test for some number in $\mathcal{Z}_p$, then p fails for at least half of all numbers in $\mathcal{Z}_p$.

10.17 Prove that, if A is a language in L, a family of family programs $B_1, B_2, \ldots$ exists wherein each B_n accepts exactly the strings in A of length n and is bounded in size by a polynomial in n.

10.18 Prove that, if A is a regular language, a family of family programs $B_1, B_2, \ldots$ exists wherein each B_n accepts exactly the strings in A of length n and is bounded in size by a constant times n.

10.19 Show that the problem of testing whether two branching programs compute the same function is solvable in polynomial time if and only if $P = NP$.

SELECTED BIBLIOGRAPHY

1. ADLEMAN, L. Two theorems on random polynomial time. In *Proceedings of the Nineteenth IEEE Symposium on Foundations of Computer Science* (1978), pp. 75–83.

2. ADLEMAN, L. M., AND HUANG, M. A. Recognizing primes in random polynomial time. In *Proceedings of the Nineteenth Annual ACM Symposium on the Theory of Computing* (1987), pp. 462–469.

3. ADLEMAN, L. M., POMERANCE, C., AND RUMELY, R. S. On distinguishing prime numbers from composite numbers. *Annals of Mathematics* *117* (1983), 173–206.

4. AHO, A. V., HOPCROFT, J. E., AND ULLMAN, J. D. *Data Structures and Algorithms*. Addison-Wesley, 1982.

5. AHO, A. V., SETHI, R., AND ULLMAN, J. D. *Compilers: Principles, Techniques, Tools*. Addison-Wesley, 1986.

6. AKL, S. G. *The Design and Analysis of Parallel Algorithms*. Prentice-Hall International, 1989.

7. ALON, N., ERDÖS, P., AND SPENCER, J. H. *The Probabilistic Method*. John Wiley & Sons, 1992.

8. ANGLUIN, D., AND VALIANT, L. G. Fast probabilistic algorithms for Hamiltonian circuits and matchings. *Journal of Computer and System Sciences* *18* (1979), 155–193.

9. ARORA, S., LUND, C., MOTWANI, R., SUDAN, M., AND SZEGEDY, M. Proof verification and hardness of approximation problems. In *Proceedings of the Thirty-third IEEE Symposium on Foundations of Computer Science* (1992), pp. 14–23.

10. BAASE, S. *Computer Algorithms: Introduction to Design and Analysis*. Addison-Wesley, 1978.

11. BABAI, L. E-mail and the unexpected power of interaction. In *Proceedings of the Fifth Annual Conference on Structure in Complexity Theory* (1990), pp. 30–44.

12. BACH, E., AND SHALLIT, J. *Algorithmic Number Theory, Vol. 1.* MIT Press, 1996.

13. BALCÁZAR, J. L., DÍAZ, J., AND GABARRÓ, J. *Structural Complexity I, II.* EATCS Monographs on Theoretical Computer Science. Springer Verlag, 1988 (I) and 1990 (II).

14. BEAME, P. W., COOK, S. A., AND HOOVER, H. J. Log depth circuits for division and related problems. *SIAM Journal on Computing 15*, 4 (1986), 994–1003.

15. BLUM, M., CHANDRA, A., AND WEGMAN, M. Equivalence of free boolean graphs can be decided probabilistically in polynomial time. *Information Processing Letters 10* (1980), 80–82.

16. BRASSARD, G., AND BRATLEY, P. *Algorithmics: Theory and Practice.* Prentice-Hall, 1988.

17. CARMICHAEL, R. D. On composite numbers p which satisfy the Fermat congruence $a^{p-1} \equiv p$. *American Mathematical Monthly 19* (1912), 22–27.

18. CHOMSKY, N. Three models for the description of language. *IRE Trans. on Information Theory 2* (1956), 113–124.

19. COBHAM, A. The intrinsic computational difficulty of functions. In *Proceedings of the International Congress for Logic, Methodology, and Philosophy of Science*, Y. Bar-Hillel, Ed. North-Holland, 1964, pp. 24–30.

20. COOK, S. A. The complexity of theorem-proving procedures. In *Proceedings of the Third Annual ACM Symposium on the Theory of Computing* (1971), pp. 151–158.

21. CORMEN, T., LEISERSON, C., AND RIVEST, R. *Introduction to Algorithms.* MIT Press, 1989.

22. EDMONDS, J. Paths, trees, and flowers. *Canadian Journal of Mathematics 17* (1965), 9–467.

23. ENDERTON, H. B. *A Mathematical Introduction to Logic.* Academic Press, 1972.

24. EVEN, S. *Graph Algorithms.* Pitman, 1979.

25. FELLER, W. *An Introduction to Probability Theory and Its Applications, Vol. 1.* John Wiley & Sons, 1970.

26. FEYNMAN, R. P., HEY, A. J. G., AND ALLEN, R. W. *Feynman lectures on computation.* Addison-Wesley, 1996.

27. GAREY, M. R., AND JOHNSON, D. S. *Computers and Intractability—A Guide to the Theory of NP-completeness.* W. H. Freeman, 1979.

28. GILL, J. T. Computational complexity of probabilistic Turing machines. *SIAM Journal on Computing 6*, 4 (1977), 675–695.

29. GÖDEL, K. On formally undecidable propositions in *Principia Mathematica* and related systems I. In *The Undecidable*, M. Davis, Ed. Raven Press, 1965, pp. 4–38.

30. GOEMANS, M. X., AND WILLIAMSON, D. P. .878-approximation algorithms for MAX CUT and MAX 2SAT. In *Proceedings of the Twenty-sixth Annual ACM Symposium on the Theory of Computing* (1994), pp. 422–431.

31. GOLDWASSER, S., AND MICALI, S. Probabilistic encryption. *Journal of Computer and System Sciences* (1984), 270–229.

32. GOLDWASSER, S., MICALI, S., AND RACKOFF, C. The knowledge complexity of interactive proof-systems. *SIAM Journal on Computing* (1989), 186–208.

33. GREENLAW, R., HOOVER, H. J., AND RUZZO, W. L. *Limits to Parallel Computation: P-completeness Theory.* Oxford University Press, 1995.

34. HARARY, F. *Graph Theory*, 2d ed. Addison-Wesley, 1971.

35. HARTMANIS, J., AND STEARNS, R. E. On the computational complexity of algorithms. *Transactions of the American Mathematical Society 117* (1965), 285–306.

36. HILBERT, D. Mathematical problems. Lecture delivered before the International Congress of Mathematicians at Paris in 1900. In *Mathematical Developments Arising from Hilbert Problems*, vol. 28. American Mathematical Society, 1976, pp. 1–34.

37. HOFSTADTER, D. R. *Goedel, Escher, Bach: An Eternal Golden Braid.* Basic Books, 1979.

38. HOPCROFT, J. E., AND ULLMAN, J. D. *Introduction to Automata Theory, Languages and Computation.* Addison-Wesley, 1979.

39. JOHNSON, D. S. The NP-completeness column: Interactive proof systems for fun and profit. *Journal of Algorithms 9*, 3 (1988), 426–444.

40. KARP, R. M. Reducibility among combinatorial problems. In *Complexity of Computer Computations* (1972), R. E. Miller and J. W. Thatcher, Eds., Plenum Press, pp. 85–103.

41. KARP, R. M., AND LIPTON, R. J. Turing machines that take advice. *EN-SEIGN: L'Enseignement Mathematique Revue Internationale 28* (1982).

42. LAWLER, E. L. *Combinatorial Optimization: Networks and Matroids.* Holt, Rinehart and Winston, 1991.

43. LAWLER, E. L., LENSTRA, J. K., RINOOY KAN, A. H. G., AND SHMOYS, D. B. *The Traveling Salesman Problem.* John Wiley & Sons, 1985.

44. LEIGHTON, F. T. *Introduction to Parallel Algorithms and Architectures: Array, Trees, Hypercubes.* Morgan Kaufmann, 1991.

45. LEVIN, L. Universal search problems (in russian). *Problemy Peredachi Informatsii 9*, 3 (1973), 115–116.

46. LEWIS, H., AND PAPADIMITRIOU, C. *Elements of the Theory of Computation.* Prentice-Hall, 1981.

47. LI, M., AND VITANYI, P. *Introduction to Kolmogorov Complexity and its Applications.* Springer-Verlag, 1993.

48. LICHTENSTEIN, D., AND SIPSER, M. GO is PSPACE hard. *Journal of the ACM* (1980), 393–401.

49. LUBY, M. *Pseudorandomness and Cryptographic Applications*. Princeton University Press, 1996.

50. LUND, C., FORTNOW, L., KARLOFF, H., AND NISAN, N. Algebraic methods for interactive proof systems. *Journal of the ACM 39*, 4 (1992), 859–868.

51. MILLER, G. L. Riemann's hypothesis and tests for primality. *Journal of Computer and System Sciences 13* (1976), 300–317.

52. NIVEN, I., AND ZUCKERMAN, H. S. *An Introduction to the Theory of Numbers*, 4th ed. John Wiley & Sons, 1980.

53. PAPADIMITRIOU, C. H. *Computational Complexity*. Addison-Wesley, 1994.

54. PAPADIMITRIOU, C. H., AND STEIGLITZ, K. *Combinatorial Optimization (Algorithms and Complexity)*. Prentice-Hall, 1982.

55. PAPADIMITRIOU, C. H., AND YANNAKAKIS, M. Optimization, approximation, and complexity classes. *Journal of Computer and System Sciences 43*, 3 (1991), 425–440.

56. POMERANCE, C. On the distribution of pseudoprimes. *Mathematics of Computation 37*, 156 (1981), 587–593.

57. PRATT, V. R. Every prime has a succinct certificate. *SIAM Journal on Computing 4*, 3 (1975), 214–220.

58. RABIN, M. O. Probabilistic algorithms. In *Algorithms and Complexity: New Directions and Recent Results*, J. F. Traub, Ed. Academic Press, 1976, pp. 21–39.

59. RIVEST, R. L., SHAMIR, A., AND ADLEMAN, L. A method for obtaining digital signatures and public key cryptosytems. *Communications of the ACM 21*, 2 (1978), 120–126.

60. ROCHE, E., AND SCHABES, Y. *Finite-State Language Processing*. MIT Press, 1997.

61. SCHAEFER, T. J. On the complexity of some two-person perfect-information games. *Journal of Computer and System Sciences 16*, 2 (1978), 185–225.

62. SEDGEWICK, R. *Algorithms*, 2d ed. Addison-Wesley, 1989.

63. SHAMIR, A. IP = PSPACE. *Journal of the ACM 39*, 4 (1992).

64. SHEN, A. IP = PSPACE: Simplified proof. *Journal of the ACM 39*, 4 (1992), 878–880.

65. SIPSER, M. Lower bounds on the size of sweeping automata. *Journal of Computer and System Sciences 21*, 2 (1980), 195–202.

66. SIPSER, M. The history and status of the P versus NP question. In *Proceedings of the Twenty-fourth Annual ACM Symposium on the Theory of Computing* (1992), pp. 603–618.

67. STINSON, D. R. *Cryptography: Theory and Practice*. CRC Press, 1995.

68. TARJAN, R. E. *Data structures and network algorithms*, vol. 44 of *CBMS-NSF Reg. Conf. Ser. Appl. Math.* SIAM, 1983.

69. TURING, A. M. On computable numbers, with an application to the Entscheidungsproblem. In *Proceedings, London Mathematical Society*, (1936), pp. 230–265.

70. ULLMAN, J. D., AHO, A. V., AND HOPCROFT, J. E. *The Design and Analysis of Computer Algorithms*. Addison-Wesley, 1974.

71. VAN LEEUWEN, J., Ed. *Handbook of Theoretical Computer Science A: Algorithms and Complexity*. Elsevier, 1990.

INDEX

Symbols

$\mathcal{N}$ (natural numbers), 4, 206
$\emptyset$ (empty set), 4
$\in$ (element), 3
$\notin$ (not element), 3
$\subseteq$ (subset), 3
$\subsetneq$ (proper subset), 4, 309
$\cup$ (union operation), 4, 44
$\cap$ (intersection operation), 4
$\times$ (Cartesian or cross product), 6
ε (empty string), 13
$w^{\mathcal{R}}$ (reverse of w), 14
$\neg$ (negation operation), 14
$\wedge$ (conjunction operation), 14
$\vee$ (disjunction operation), 14
$\oplus$ (exclusive OR operation), 15
$\rightarrow$ (implication operation), 15
$\leftrightarrow$ (equality operation), 15
$\Leftarrow$ (reverse implication), 18
$\Rightarrow$ (implication), 18
$\Longleftrightarrow$ (logical equivalence), 18
$\circ$ (concatenation operation), 44
* (star operation), 44
$\mathcal{P}(Q)$ (power set), 53
Σ (alphabet), 53
Σ_{ε} ($\Sigma \cup \{\varepsilon\}$), 53
$\leq_{m}$ (mapping reduction), 191
$\leq_{T}$ (Turing reduction), 212
$\leq_{L}$ (log space reduction), 297
$\leq_{P}$ (polynomial time reduction), 250
$d(x)$ (minimal description), 215
$\mathrm{Th}(\mathcal{M})$ (theory of model), 206
$K(x)$ (descriptive complexity), 215
$\forall$ (universal quantifier), 284
$\exists$ (existential quantifier), 284
$\uparrow$ (exponentiation), 313
$O(f(n))$ (big-O notation), 226–228
$o(f(n))$ (small-o notation), 228

Accept state, 34, 35
Acceptance problem
    for CFG, 156
    for DFA, 152
    for LBA, 177
    for NFA, 153
    for TM, 159
Accepting computation history, 176
Accepting configuration, 129
Accepts a language, meaning of, 36
A_{CFG}, 156
Acyclic graph, 344
A_{DFA}, 152
Adjacency matrix, 237
Adleman, Leonard M., 381, 384
Aho, Alfred V., 381, 385
Akl, Selim G., 381
A_{LBA}, 177
Algorithm
    complexity analysis, 226–231
    decidability and undecidability,
        151–168
    defined, 142–144
    describing, 144–147
    Euclidean, 239
    polynomial time, 234–241
    running time, 226
ALL_{CFG}, 181
Allen, Robin W., 382
Alon, Noga, 381
Alphabet, defined, 13
Alternating Turing machine, 348
Alternation, 348–354
Ambiguity, 97–98
Ambiguous grammar, 97, 196
Amplification lemma, 337
AND operation, 14
A_{NFA}, 153

387